The critics are tall

"Extraordinary detail, itineraries organized by theme, and a unique up-to-the-minute black book of what's hot provides readers with the ultimate guide." **—Forbes.com**

"Opening chapters set the spirited tone ... a host of food-focused entries accommodate all tastes." ***—Travel + Leisure***

"Focus[es] their information to attract vacationers who don't want cookie-cutter itineraries." ***—Wall Street Journal***

"Well-written, cleverly organized ... remarkably comprehensive." ***—Passport Magazine***

"The most enjoyable feature may be the various three-day itineraries ... I don't know that I'd want a manicure and a martini at the Beauty Bar around 10 p.m. on a Friday night, but I'm delighted to know it's possible." ***—New York Times***

"Perfect for the business person or jet-setter who's in town for a few days and has little time to research a visit. But area residents can pluck a few gems from its pages, too."***—Sacramento Bee***

"Numerous three-day itineraries to mix and match to your heart's delight."***—Chicago Tribune***

"Your one-stop guide to shopping, nightlife, restaurants, hotels and other attractions in the city."***—DC Style Magazine***

But it's your opinion that counts.

Let us know what you think at pulseguides.com

Pulse Guides' **Night+Day Sydney (and Melbourne)** is an independent guide. We do not accept payment of any kind from events or establishments for inclusion in this book. We welcome your views on our selections. Please email us: **feedback@pulseguides.com**.

The information contained in this book was checked as rigorously as possible before going to press. The publisher accepts no responsibility for any changes that may have occurred since, or for any other variance of fact from that recorded here in good faith.

Distributed worldwide by Publishers Group West.
First Edition. Printed in the United States. 30% postconsumer content.

ISBN-10: 1-934724-00-9; ISBN-13: 978-1-934724-00-2

Credits

Executive Editor	Alan S. Davis
Senior Editor	Christina Henry de Tessan
Editor	Anita Chabria
Contributing Editor	Derek Peck
Author	Marc Llewellyn
Contributors	Emily Dunn, Michael Harden, Clara Iaccarino, Freya Lombardo
Copy Editors	Gail Nelson-Bonebrake, Elizabeth Stroud
Maps	Chris Gillis, Mapping Specialists
Production	Samia Afra, Jo Farrell, Samantha Glorioso, Tess Herrmann

Photo Credits: (Front cover, left to right) *martini*, Les Byerley; *couple dining*, Tony Yeates, courtesy of Tourism NSW; *Sydney Bridge*, Istockphoto; (Back cover, left to right) *Gallery of New South Wales (NSW)* courtesy of Tourism NSW; *Forty One Restaurant*, Robert Billington; *Lady Lux Lounge*, courtesy of Lady Lux; *Jet Boating*, Oz Jet Boating Sydney Harbour; (Inside cover, top to bottom) *Establishment Hotel*, Merivale Group; *Marque*, Rendezvous Hotels; *Langham Hotel Melbourne,* Leonardo Media. (p.6) *Alan Davis*, Mary Lou Dauray. (p.13) *Jørn Utzon*, Pierre Philippe Marcou.

Special Sales

For information about bulk purchases of Pulse Guides (ten copies or more), email us at bookorders@pulseguides.com. Special bulk rates are available for charities, corporations, institutions, and online and mail-order catalogs, and our books can be customized to suit your company's needs.

NIGHT+DAY
the Cool Cities series from **PULSE**GUIDES 

P.O. Box 590780, San Francisco, CA 94159
pulseguides.com

Pulse Guides is an imprint of ASDavis Media Group, Inc.

NIGHT+DAY SYDNEY

(AND MELBOURNE)

By Marc Llewellyn

PULSE GUIDES

About the Author and the Contributors

Marc Llewellyn is an award-winning professional travel writer and guide-book author based in Sydney. He writes for most newspaper travel sections and travel magazines in Australia. Marc is also the author of *Riders to the Midnight Sun*, about an epic 2,500-mile journey by bicycle from the Black Sea in the Ukraine to Arctic Russia. His second travelogue is based on a year spent working as a prawn fisherman on a tiny island off Sicily. He is currently the President of the Australian Society of Travel Writers.

Emily Dunn is a journalist at the *Sydney Morning Herald* and has previously written for the *Australian* and community newspapers across the city. A devotee of all things edible, Emily acquired a taste for fine dining while moonlighting as a pizza waitress in her college years, where she learned to juggle four dinner plates and a Parmesan grinder. Now, Emily likes nothing more than frocking up and sampling the Sydney restaurant scene from the other side of the table, but she still can't resist a good crust.

Michael Harden is a freelance writer who worked in restaurants for 15 years to support his writing habit. Writing is now supporting his restaurant habit, and he reviews restaurants and writes food and travel-related articles for a number of Melbourne-based newspapers, contributes to national magazines, and has authored and co-authored four food- and wine-related books. He assumes there is still a novel in there somewhere.

Clara Iaccarino is a features journalist at the *Sun-Herald,* where she regularly contributes to the travel, arts, lifestyle, and current affairs sections. Her work has also appeared in *FILMINK*, the *Brag*, the *Sunday Age*, the *Sydney Morning Herald,* and *Revolver*. A journalist by day and a theater, music, and festival producer by night, Clara is passionate about Sydney's vibrant arts scene and is the executive producer of MAKEbeLIVE Productions. Leaving no stone unturned, no thirst unquenched, she is a Sydney nightlife connoisseur.

Freya Lombardo is a features writer who contributes to a number of leading architecture, design, and style magazines. She has produced two series for ABC TV on animation, music videos, and digital media. Before moving to Sydney, she was deeply ensconced in Melbourne's cultural circuit and its vibrant bar and restaurant scene.

The Night+Day Difference

The Pulse of the City

Our job is to point you to all of the city's peak experiences: amazing museums, unique spas, and spectacular views. But the complete *urbanista* experience is more than just impressions—it is grownup fun, the kind that thrives by night as well as by day. Urban fun is a hip nightclub or a trendy restaurant. It is people-watching and people-meeting. Lonely planet? We don't think so. **Night+Day** celebrates our lively planet.

The Right Place. The Right Time. It Matters.

A **Night+Day** city must have exemplary restaurants, a vibrant nightlife scene, and enough attractions to keep a visitor busy for six days without having to do the same thing twice. In selecting restaurants, food is important, but so is the scene. Our hotels, most of which are 4- and 5-star properties, are rated for the quality of the concierge staff (can they get you into a hot restaurant?) as well as the rooms. You won't find kids with fake IDs at our nightlife choices. And the attractions must be truly worthy of your time. But experienced travelers know that timing is almost everything. Going to a restaurant at 7pm can be a very different experience (and probably less fun) than it is at 9pm; a champagne boat cruise might be ordinary in the morning but spectacular at sunset. We believe providing the reader with this level of detail makes the difference between a good experience and a great one.

The Bottom Line

Your time is precious. Our guides must be easy to use and dead-on accurate. That is why our executive editor, editors, and writers (locals who are in touch with what is great—and what is not) spend hundreds of hours researching, writing, and debating selections for each guide. The results are presented in four unique ways: the *99 Best* with our top three choices in 33 categories that highlight what is great about the city; the *Experience* chapters, in which our selections are organized by distinct themes or personalities (*Classic* and *Hot & Cool Sydney*, and *Melbourne*); a *Perfect Plan* (3 Nights and Days) for each theme, showing how to get the most out of the city in a short period of time; and the *Sydney* and *Melbourne Black Books*, listing all the hotels, restaurants, nightlife, and attractions, with key details, contact information, and page references.

Our bottom line is this: If you find our guide easy to use and enjoyable to read, and with our help you have an extraordinary time, we have succeeded. We review and value all feedback from our readers, so please contact us at **feedback@pulseguides.com**.

At Federation Square

From the Publisher

My brief retirement more than ten years ago came to an end when I set out on a journey to find the 100 most fun places to be in the world at the right time. The challenge of unearthing the world's greatest events—from the Opera Ball in Vienna to the Calgary Stampede—led me to write a guidebook. In fact, it was two guidebooks, *The Fun Also Rises North America* and *The Fun Also Rises International*, named after Ernest Hemingway's *The Sun Also Rises*, which helped popularize what has become perhaps the most thrilling party on earth (Pamplona's Fiesta de San Fermín, also known as the Running of the Bulls).

Two of my stops along the road to discovering the world's greatest events were Melbourne (the Melbourne Cup) and Sydney (the Gay and Lesbian Mardi Gras). These festivals transform their host cities, so it wasn't until I revisited them in 2005 that I had a chance to experience ordinary life. Our author and contributors will show you that cool Sydney and majestic Melbourne are anything but ordinary—their combined spirit of fun will captivate the traveler.

As I pursued my research and traveled the world, I became aware of a gaping hole in the travel guide industry. Not a single guide adequately served my needs. I found budget, gourmet, upscale, historic, and more, but none provided the kinds of details I needed to hit the ground running and make the most of my limited time. I wanted a selective list of options provided by reliable local sources with valuable insider tips. I decided to fill the hole myself, and Pulse Guides was born. **Night+Day**, the first series from Pulse Guides, presents the best that a city has to offer, in a totally new format that allows you to find the places that are right for you quickly and easily. The goal is to provide the best content available in the travel business—and based on the first reviews, we are off to a fine start. We hope you'll agree.

Pulse Guides abides by one guiding principle: Never settle for the ordinary. I hope that our new approach allows you to experience the very best these cities have to offer.

Wishing you extraordinary times,

Alan S. Davis, Publisher and Executive Editor
Pulse Guides

P.S. To contact me, or for updated information on all of our **Night+Day** guides, please visit our website at **pulseguides.com**.

TOC

Arafura Sea
Gulf of Carpentaria
Coral Sea
Cape York
Bamaga
Weipa
Cape York Pen.
Jabiru
Katherine
Numbulwar
Kowanyama
GREAT BARRIER REEF
GREAT DIVIDING RANGE
Cairns
Normanton
Townsville
NORTHERN TERRITORY
Tennant Creek
Mount Isa
Mackay
QUEENSLAND
Rockhampton
Longreach
Gladstone
Alice Springs
SIMPSON DESERT
Uluru (Ayers Rock)
Bundaberg
Hervey Bay
AUSTRALIA
Brisbane
Toowoomba
Gold Coast
Lake Eyre
SOUTH AUSTRALIA
Lake Frome
Lake Torrens
Lake Gardiner
Macintyre
Lismore
Darling
Broken Hill
NEW SOUTH WALES
Tamworth
Coffs Harbour
Dubbo
Taree
Port Augusta
Whyalla
Port Pirie
Orange
Newcastle
Bathurst
SYDNEY
Mildura
Griffith
Port Lincoln
Spencer Gulf
Adelaide
Wollongong
Murray Bridge
Swan Hill
Murray
Wagga Wagga
Canberra
Kangaroo Island
Horsham
Bendigo
Albury
Mt. Kosciuszko
VICTORIA
Ballarat
MELBOURNE
Mount Gambier
Geelong
Cranbourne
Warrnambool
Bass Strait
Tasman Sea
N
Smithton
Miles
400
Devonport
Launceston
TASMANIA
Kilometers
800
Hobart

Introduction to Sydney

Spread out alongside one of the most picturesque harbors in the world, and defined by those famous icons, the Sydney Harbour Bridge and the Sydney Opera House, the Emerald City is a sexy, vibrant place that lives for the outdoors. With dozens of white-sand beaches strung out along the glittering coastline—and many more within its harbor—Sydney is a sun-seeker's paradise. There's something for everyone here, ranging from historic precincts and ferry rides to a sparkling nightlife scene and action attractions geared for an adrenaline kick.

Sydney: What It Was

The area's history begins long before Europeans sailed into Sydney Harbour. From time immemorial, the Cadigal tribe fished the azure and green waters of the bay using lines made from the inner bark of trees, hooks carved from shells, and multi-pronged spears tipped with bone. They traveled across the waterway in bark canoes, collecting oysters, mussels, and cockles, and they supplemented their diet with vegetables, grubs, birds, possums, wombats, and kangaroos. But everything was doomed to change when Captain James Cook appeared on the scene in 1770.

After charting the coastline and claiming the land for king and country, Cook landed in Botany Bay, close to where Sydney Airport is now. He named the land New South Wales, probably as a favor to Thomas Pennant, a Welsh patriot and a close friend of the ship's botanist, Joseph Banks. Traveling north, he passed the entrance to a cove, which seemed likely to offer safe anchorage. He called it Port Jackson, after the secretary of the admiralty, George Jackson. Today we know it as Sydney Harbour.

Following the Declaration of Independence in the United States in 1776, the British authorities no longer had a place to dump their convicts. They needed somewhere new, and New South Wales seemed the best option. In May 1787, the First Fleet, captained by Arthur Phillip, set out in a bid to form a penal settlement in Botany Bay. Onboard were 1,480 people, including 759 convicts. The fleet arrived in January 1788, but Phillip decreed that the soil around Botany Bay was too poor to sustain the group's needs.

While the fleet was still anchored in the bay, two ships appeared flying the French colors. Panicked by the thought that the French might beat them to it, the British lifted anchor and sailed for Port Jackson, where they unfurled a British flag at the entrance. Phillip recorded that when they

THE URBIE AWARD: Jørn Utzon

The most distinctive architectural feature in Australia is undoubtedly the Sydney Opera House, and since its creation, it has changed the way the world views this city. The building, with its famous curving, white-sailed roof, was the result of a design competition in the 1950s, aimed at giving Sydney a centerpiece for the performing arts. No one realized just how iconic it would eventually become.

The renowned Danish architect, **Jørn Utzon**, is the creator behind this landmark, and a man credited with changing the way Australians think about architecture and design. He has said that he likes "to be on the edge of the possible." When he first put forward his plan for a building modeled after a ship at full sail, the judges loved it. However, there was one problem: It was beyond the capabilities of engineering at the time. By 1961, Utzon had solved the problem of how to build the most distinguishing feature—the "sails"—and construction began. But it was far from smooth sailing. Utzon fought with the government of New South Wales about everything from payment to interior design. The building was eventually completed in 1973, but the interior had strayed so far from Utzon's vision that he vowed never to return to Australia to see his finished project.

Then, in 1999 Utzon was re-engaged as the Opera House's architect, charged with re-designing the interiors in line with his original plans. Utzon produced a bold proposal for the building exterior too. He urged that the Western foyers be opened up onto a new colonnade. This would extend and enliven public areas, and develop closer links between the building and the harbor. It would also extend his imprint on this city far into the future.

Night+Day's Sydney Urbie

Night+Day cities are chosen because they have a vibrant nightlife scene, standard-setting and innovative restaurants, cutting-edge hotels, and enough attractions to keep one busy for six days without doing the same thing twice. In short, they are fun. They represent the quintessential *urbanista* experience. This wouldn't exist but for the creativity and talents of many people and organizations. In honor of all who have played a role in making Sydney one of the world's coolest cities, Pulse Guides is pleased to give special recognition, and our Urbie Award, to an individual whose contribution is exemplary.

"got into Port Jackson early in the afternoon" he "had the satisfaction of finding the finest Harbour in the world."

The new settlers set up camp where the Rocks are today, and called the inlet Sydney Cove, after Lord Sydney, the British Secretary of State for the Colonies. Early life in the fledgling colony was tough, with failed harvests, threats of starvation, and an uneasy truce with the Aborigines, which quickly erupted into shootings and spearings.

Within 18 months of the arrival of the First Fleet, smallpox, introduced by the Europeans, swept through the local Aboriginal population. Just three members of the Cadigal tribe survived.

Key Dates

1770 Captain James Cook lands at Botany Bay.

1787 First convicts leave Britain for Sydney.

1788 Captain Arthur Phillip raises British flag at Port Jackson (Sydney Harbour).

1810 Governor Macquarie begins extensive building projects.

1840 Last convicts arrive in Sydney.

1932 Sydney Harbour Bridge completed.

1942 Japanese midget submarines torpedo a ferry in Sydney Harbour.

1973 Sydney Opera House finished.

1975 The Rocks saved by union work bans refusing to demolish them.

1988 Bicentennial celebrations see re-enactment of First Fleet in Sydney Harbour.

2000 Sydney Olympics held.

More convicts followed, and soldiers and settlers, too. In 1810, Lachlan Macquarie was appointed governor of New South Wales. He took over from William Bligh (of *Mutiny on the Bounty* fame), whose controversial governorship ended with the Rum Rebellion. This, the only successful armed takeover of government in Australia's recorded history, came about when Bligh attempted to normalize trading conditions by prohibiting the use of spirits as payment for commodities. It was a threat to the power base of the rum merchants and their soldier backers.

Once Macquarie had restored discipline, he set out on an ambitious building program that would see the tiny settlement expand into the bones of a city. When gold was discovered in NSW in 1851, and then in Victoria some six months later, immigrants flooded into Sydney in search of their fortunes.

The city expanded. The area called the Rocks turned into a slum, and the streets were ruled at night by rats, cut-throats, and press gangs. Then, in January 1900, the bubonic plague hit. Spreading from the waterfront, the rats carried the plague throughout the city. Within eight months, 303 cases

Soon, Sydney was a multicultural city aspiring to hold the 2000 Olympics. And with the Games, the city came of age. There was a new sense of pride and a worldwide wave of interest in the Land Down Under and its largest city—glorious, sun-kissed Sydney.

were reported and 103 people were dead. Buildings classified as slums, especially in the Rocks, were pulled down, and more than 44,000 rats were officially killed in the cleansing operations.

Many more buildings were bulldozed to make way for the Sydney Harbour Bridge, which was opened in March 1932, not by the NSW premier, Jack Lang, who was about to cut the ribbon, but by a Dublin-born antique dealer who had worked his way on horseback into the official party. With a slash of his cavalry sword, Francis de Groot declared the bridge open: "in the name of the decent and respectable people of New South Wales."

The Rocks were in the spotlight again in the 1960s, when plans were revealed to raze much of the historic area and replace the workers' houses and narrow lanes with a sea of high-rise towers. The National Trust was asked to nominate historic buildings it considered worthy of preservation. It advised that only Cadman's Cottage, built in 1816, had any significant heritage appeal. Even then, it said, it should be dismantled and re-erected somewhere else, out of the way. The final development scheme was exhibited in 1971, and it sparked bitter protests from the local community. It was left to the Builders Labourers Federation, and their leader Jack Mundey, to refuse to work and slap so-called "Green Bans" on the development proposals. The pressure paid off, and in 1975 the Rocks were finally saved.

People had woken up to their inheritance. But they were beginning to realize that the winds of change were whistling over their heads, too. For generations, Sydney had largely been the domain of Europeans, with a few Aboriginals cast out on the outskirts. Italians and Greeks were settling down in the thousands, and had been since the end of the Second World War. But, thanks to the White Australia Policy, which had resulted from discontent about Chinese prospectors in the 1850s Gold Rush, there was barely an Asian in sight. When the policy was officially abandoned in 1974, Asian immigration boomed.

Soon, Sydney was a multicultural city aspiring to hold the 2000 Olympics. And with the Games, the city came of age. There was a new sense of pride and a worldwide wave of interest in the Land Down Under and its largest city—glorious, sun-kissed Sydney.

Sydney: What It Is

Today's Sydney is a thrilling harbor and beach destination, with a population of more than 4 million. You'll find almost anything you want in Sydney, whether you are seeking cocktail bars with terrific views, world-class restaurants, and pulsating clubs, or just the chance to laze on the golden sand among the beautiful bodies on Bondi Beach. If you are seeking greenery, then go watch the fruit bats clamber around the rainforest in the Royal Botanic Gardens or take a ferry trip across the harbor and look out for cockatoos in the Sydney Harbour National Park.

You'll find almost anything you want in Sydney, whether you are seeking cocktail bars with terrific views, world-class restaurants, and pulsating clubs, or just the chance to laze on the golden sand among the beautiful bodies on Bondi Beach.

As well as sporting a relaxed, carefree nature, Sydney is a party town. So, whether it's a rave during the famous Sydney Gay and Lesbian Mardi Gras, or a fun-filled fiesta on an ordinary night, Sydney will keep you entertained until the sun comes up. Need an added zip during your stay? Then try fishtailing past the Opera House on a jet boat, or diving with sharks, or climbing the arch of the Sydney Harbour Bridge, or inching your way above the city streets on a see-through walkway hundreds of feet above the ground.

People often liken Sydney to San Francisco because of its bayside location, In spirit, though, it's much closer to Los Angeles, with its cool crowd, thriving beach scene, and partying ways. But by far the best way to get a feel for Sydneysiders' own distinct brand of hospitality is to come see the place for yourself.

Welcome to fabulous Sydney...

THE 99 BEST of SYDNEY AND MELBOURNE

When you're on vacation, you don't want a city with all its little flaws and inconveniences, you want the perfect city. You want the hottest, hippest, most fantastic places to be, and you want them now. We've taken the guesswork out of finding these cities' treasures, and present to you 99 of the best ways to enjoy Sydney and Melbourne, divided among 33 categories from food to fun. The first twenty-two categories cover Sydney's top restaurants, nightlife, and attractions, with the remaining eleven reserved for the top spots in Melbourne.

Always-Hot Restaurants

#1–3: Few restaurants have what it takes to transcend the fads and create enduring appeal. These hot spots are perennial favorites, drawing sophisticated crowds year after year with fabulous food, stunning decor, and flawless service.

Guillaume at Bennelong (G)

Sydney Opera House, Circular Quay, 02 9241 1999 • Classic

The Draw: The Sydney Opera House has one of Sydney's best restaurants, a gracious glassy affair with stunning views of the Harbour Bridge.

The Scene: Oh, indeed, what a view! You can feel the excitement of the brushed-up tourists and theater-goers as they realize that they're dining in one of the modern wonders of the world. But what's on the plate is almost as stunning—French classics prepared with the freshest ingredients, all served in white-tablecloth style. *Mon-Wed and Sat 8-10:30pm, Thu-Fri noon-3pm and 8-10:30pm.* $$$$ B ≡

Hot Tip: Start with tapas and a glass of champagne at the bar. When you sit down, don't miss out on the basil-infused tuna, the signature first-course dish.

Quay (G)

Upper Level, Overseas Passenger Term., The Rocks, 02 9251 5600 • Classic

The Draw: Glittering harbor views of green-and-yellow ferries, the Sydney Opera House right in front of you, and world-class contemporary creations on your plate—no wonder Quay is a must for savvy travelers and locals alike.

The Scene: This fashionable, contemporary spot, with lots of windows and gorgeous water views, invites its sophisticated clientele to relax and linger over a few bottles of good wine. *Sat-Mon 6-10pm, Tue-Fri noon-2:30pm and 6-10pm.* $$$$ ≡

Hot Tip: You can't book a particular table, but a bit of sweet-talking and you can put in a request for a table in the lower or upper tower. These have the best views of the Opera House—as long as there isn't a cruise ship docked in front.

Rockpool (G)

107 George St., The Rocks, 02 9252 1888 • Classic

The Draw: The philosophy behind Modern Australian cuisine, as it is still often called, refers to using the freshest and best local ingredients and adding the flavors of Asia. No place does this better than Rockpool, where creatures of the sea wait in tanks to be dressed in mushroom soy.

The Scene: Famous Aussie chef and television personality Neil Perry might not always make an appearance on the floor, but he brings food-savvy locals, celebrities, and international experimenters to this superbly sleek eatery with a deceptively casual street-front location. *Tue-Sat 6-11pm.* $$$$ ≡

Hot Tip: Ask for a downstairs table for the most buzz.

Art Spaces

#4–6: Combine Sydney's liberal, hip cultural attitude with the complex and rich history of the country's indigenous populations, and you'll find a varied and vastly rewarding art experience.

Art Gallery of New South Wales (NSW)

Art Gallery Rd., CBD, 02 9225 1744 • Classic

The Draw: The best all-round art gallery in Sydney shows off an impressive collection of local painting, Aboriginal works, European masters, and Asian offerings.

The Scene: Don't expect a fusty place—some of the exhibitions, including those showcasing photography, can be really avant-garde. Families, culture hounds, and those looking for a mind-spark wander the light and spacious galleries. Apparently it's quite a pick-up joint, too. *Daily 10am-5pm, Wed until 9pm.* $

Hot Tip: Stop for lunch at the Art Gallery Restaurant. It's like a little treasure trove hidden by works of art, and it looks out at the wharves and water.

Gavala Aboriginal Art Gallery

Shop 131, Harbourside Centre, Darling Harbour, 02 9212 7232 • Classic

The Draw: Sydney's premier Aboriginal art gallery and retail shop shows off beautiful dot paintings produced by some of the country's best artists.

The Scene: It's a real clutter inside and a real tourist mecca too, so don't be surprised if you have to fight your way through the racks of boomerangs to the emu eggs. Pick up a boomerang, a didgeridoo, or some masks and handiwork. *Daily 10am-9pm.*

Hot Tip: Ask the owners about Sydney and its Aboriginal connections and they'll be glad to spell it all out for you—they are both knowledgeable and friendly.

Museum of Contemporary Art

140 George St., The Rocks, 02 9245 2400 • Hot & Cool

The Draw: Set in an imposing building in Circular Quay, the MCA, as it's known, reveals a collection of the weirdest and wackiest aspects of modern-day art.

The Scene: To the majority of Aussies, someone balancing a can of Victoria Bitter on their belly best expresses modern art, so don't expect to meet up with too many locals. But Australia does have a complex and exciting contemporary art history, and this heavily interactive spot is a fun place to gain some insight into the local psyche. *Daily 10am-5pm.* $

Hot Tip: The gift shop here is worth a stop for great handmade postcards to send home.

Bars with a View

#7–9: You can sit on the beach at Bondi and think yourself blessed with one of the world's most beautiful views, but to really get a feel for the magnificence of Sydney, you need a bit of perspective. Find yourself a high elevation and a cool drink, and you'll come to truly appreciate the Emerald City.

Orbit Bar

Level 47, 264 George St., CBD, 02 9247 9777 • Classic

The Draw: Beautiful views across the harbor and to the Sydney Opera House make this a stellar spot.

The Scene: Pre-dinner drinkers join partying 30-somethings with a thirst for cocktails to celebrate special occasions and survival of the workday by lounging in retro-inspired vinyl swivel chairs. Bright red carpet and an edgy vibe round out the chic-casual appeal. Tourists don't outnumber locals. *Daily 5pm-late.*

Hot Tip: The oyster shots are delicious and complement any cocktail.

Opera Bar

Sydney Opera House, Lower Concourse, Circular Quay, 02 9247 1666 • Classic

The Draw: Nestled beneath the Sydney Opera House, Opera Bar has magnificent views of the Harbor Bridge and Luna Park, enhanced by a funky jazz soundtrack and sleek design.

The Scene: Always bustling from noon until late, Opera Bar operates in shifts: photo-snapping tourists by day are followed by after-work suits, then pre-theater champagne darlings, and finally post-show actor debriefings late at night. Inside, the vibe is somewhat formal compared to outside, where it's pure relaxation and revelry. *Mon-Thu noon-midnight, Fri-Sat noon-1am, Sun noon-midnight.*

Hot Tip: The best tables are outside beneath the umbrellas where there's shade in the summer and heaters for winter evenings.

360 Bar and Dining Room*

Sydney Tower, Gallery Level, 100 Market St., CBD, 02 8223 3800 • Classic

The Draw: The highest bar in Sydney, and one of the city's highest vantage points in general, 360 provides uninterrupted views with plush surroundings, funky bar staff, and excellent martinis.

The Scene: With a blend of locals and tourists admiring the vistas, 360 is popular with after-work thrill-seeking suits who want a drink with a difference—it's all sophistication here, with leather banquettes and white linens. *Sun-Thu 11:30am-1am, Fri-Sat 11:30am-1:30am.*

Hot Tip: To secure the best lounge at either end of the bar, arrive before 7pm and stay for sunset.

Beachside Romance

#10–12: Australia's waters are of the deepest turquoise. The sandy beaches are powder-soft and nearly pure white. Add windswept cliffs with dramatic walking paths and quaint neighborhoods filled with charming spots for a meal or a drink, and you'll certainly be in the mood for romance.

Bathers' Pavilion Restaurant

4 The Esplanade, Balmoral Beach, 02 9969 5050 • Classic

The Draw: Water views and sumptuous food are complemented by a romantic post-dinner stroll along the promenade.

The Scene: This is a fancy dining place, where wealthy locals and boating types come to enjoy the romance of eating top-notch cuisine close to the sea. *Daily noon-2:30pm and 6:30-10pm.* $$$$

Hot Tip: The adjoining cafe is open for coffee, afternoon tea, or light meals—and is far more casual if you're not dressed your best. French doors open onto the beach, and the interior features an eclectic mix of artwork.

Doyles on the Beach

11 Marine Parade, Watsons Bay, 02 9337 2007 • Classic

The Draw: On a warm sunny day, there is no better place to sit and watch the world go by, which is why Sydneysiders always bring their out-of-town friends here for a drink.

The Scene: A bottle of wine, a lobster lunch, and a stroll to the cliffs to work it off is what Sydney's made for. Almost everyone here is on vacation, so the atmosphere is very relaxed and the wine flows in copious quantities. *Daily noon-3:30pm and 6-9:30pm.* $$$

Hot Tip: There's a nudist beach a short walk away, so if you don't mind getting an all-over tan, then take the plunge after lunch.

Icebergs Dining Room & Bar*

1 Notts Ave., Bondi Beach, 02 9365 9000 • Hot & Cool

The Draw: Come here for some of the most glorious ocean views you will ever see.

The Scene: The panorama stretches across the Pacific and along Bondi Beach, Sydney's most famous stretch of sand. The seafood menu complements the outlook, with the fish so fresh that their tails are practically still in the sea. Bondi is relaxed—so don't dress up. Everyone who is anyone wants a table outside in summer, though, so book well ahead. *Tue-Sun noon-3pm and 6:30-10pm.* $$$

Hot Tip: You can have a pre-dinner drink on the terrace, but the best spot for swinging with the views is in one of the hanging wicker seat baskets inside (get here as close to 6pm as possible for these, as they're in high demand).

Beer Gardens

#13–15: The ultimate Aussie experience involves drinking beer on a sun-drenched summer's day in a beer garden. To be outside—toasting the sun's rays, drinking schooners, and grinning with your mates—is to be Down Under.

Doyles Palace Hotel*

10 Marine Parade, Watsons Bay, 02 9337 4299 • Classic

The Draw: At the water's edge, this is Sydney at its best. The harbor sparkles before you and the fish 'n' chips are sublime.

The Scene: Everyone loves this beer garden, from moms and dads to tourists, backpackers, Eastern Suburbs locals in their leather moccasins and designer sunglasses, and football jocks. Hundreds of tables sprawl across two levels, with seafood platters complementing vino or ale choices. *Daily 10am-10pm.* ≡

Hot Tip: Bypass the other bars at the Doyles and head straight to the beer garden to grab a waterside table if you can.

The Oaks Hotel*

118 Military Rd., Neutral Bay, 02 9953 5515 • Classic

The Draw: The cook-your-own barbecue, shady oak tree, mussels, Belgian beer, and country charm make the Oaks a family favorite.

The Scene: Conservative North Shore folk, athletic types, blokey blokes, and their girlfriends flood the Oaks, a casual, anything-goes spot on weekends and after rugby matches. *Daily 10am-1am.* ≡

Hot Tip: The beer garden is the best spot, but if you've got a group, reserve a function room upstairs at no cost, where you can play pool, jive to the jukebox, and lounge on the couches.

Slip Inn*

111 Sussex St., CBD, 02 8295 9911 • Hot & Cool

The Draw: Intimate enough not to be a sprawling mega-pub, the Slip Inn's courtyard is fairy-lit by night, cool and shady by day.

The Scene: An oasis in the Central Business District (CBD), the Slip Inn provides a sunshine burst for nearby suits on lunch break, and the greenery makes it a refreshing change from the gray cityscape. It's always popular for after-work or pre-clubbing on balmy evenings when the trendy set descends. *Mon-Thu noon-midnight, Fri noon-4am, Sat 4:30pm-4am, Sun 2-10pm.* ≡

Hot Tip: If you feel like partying by day, come on a Sunday when the beer garden buzzes with go-hard clubbers, bopping to uplifting house and breaks until 10pm.

Cocktail Lounges

#16–18: Sydney bartenders know their stuff: The competition for best cocktail list is fierce, as bartenders muddle, stir, and shake their way through innovative menus, adding spices, seasonal fruits, and exotic twists from lychee to rose.

Firefly*

17 Hickson Rd., Dawes Point, 02 9241 2031 • Classic

The Draw: Sydney's only true wine bar, this local favorite offers a fabulous selection of Australian wines and excellent tapas to accompany them in an elegant setting.

The Scene: Far from the tourist traps crowding Circular Quay, Firefly is in a league of its own. Hushed and sophisticated, with waterside views, Firefly redefines intimacy, with barely enough tables to seat 40. Well-heeled, cultured, and aware of Sydney's secrets, the crowd is stylish but low-key. *Mon-Sat noon-10:30pm.*

Hot Tip: Reserve a table for pre-show drinks, allowing at least an hour to soak up the atmosphere and sample the delicious tapas before the curtain goes up, usually around 8pm, at both the nearby Sydney and Wharf Theaters.

Hemmesphere

Establishment Hotel, Level 4, 252 George St., CBD, 02 9240 3040 • Hot & Cool

The Draw: Everything about Hemmesphere caters to premium tastes: the spirits in the cocktails, the Dom Perignon, the cigars, plush lounges, ottomans, and attentive staff.

The Scene: Hip pre-drinking clubbers and gray-haired gents puffing on cigars make for an eclectic mix of indulgents—what they all share in common is a love of the good life, which is found in abundance at this sleek spot atop one of the city's chicest hotels. *Tue-Fri 6pm-late, Sat 7pm-late.*

Hot Tip: Reservations are essential Thursday to Saturday and the best lounge in the house is table 32 for non-smokers or table 42 for smokers.

The Loft

3 Lime St., King Street Wharf, 02 9299 4770 • Hot & Cool

The Draw: With a sublime cocktail menu, a sexy decor, sweeping water views, and a cool crowd, the Loft has perfected the recipe for a sophisticated good time.

The Scene: Plush lounges, a Moroccan boudoir ambience, and harbor breezes combine with house tunes, creating a relaxed lounge room where sipping cocktails from all over the globe is encouraged. Romantics canoodle, partiers groove on the dance floor, and a laid-back waterside atmosphere prevails well into the night. *Mon-Thu 4pm-midnight, Fri-Sun noon-2am.*

Hot Tip: Arrive before 6pm to secure a balcony spot and be front row for the sunset over the water.

Cool Museums

#19–21: From Aboriginal heritage and the first European settlers, to ships of the line and modern-day technology, Sydney's museums incorporate some of the best elements of Australia's cultural timeline.

Australian National Maritime Museum

2 Murray St., CBD, 02 9298 3777 • Classic

The Draw: Harbor cities have a fascination with the sea. Sydney is no different, and this museum gives you a porthole-peek into its maritime history.

The Scene: Ay, me hearties, there are kids aplenty here. In addition to viewing indoor displays of maps, art, and maritime technology, you can clamber around on several floating vessels. Though there's no climbing of the rigging, the confined cabin spaces and submarine gangways are heaving with one-legged visitors with parrots on their shoulders. *Daily 9:30am-5pm.* $

Hot Tip: Budding captains can charter a yacht or have an introductory sailing lesson with Sydney by Sail (02 9280 1110, sydneybysail.com), which operates from an adjoining wharf.

Hyde Park Barracks Museum

Queens Square, Macquarie St., Hyde Park, 02 8239 2311 • Classic

The Draw: This museum reeks with atmosphere, from the swinging hammocks to the displays on the rations and routines of convicted felons.

The Scene: Being transported to Australia for kicking a policeman up the backside or stealing a bolt of cloth meant a stint in leg irons in the hold of a rat-infested convict ship. Once on land, you might have ended up in these convict barracks doing your best to avoid a flogging. *Daily 9:30am-5pm.* $

Hot Tip: Wander down historic Macquarie Street and visit some of Sydney's oldest buildings, including St. James' Church and the site of the old Sydney Hospital.

Powerhouse Museum

500 Harris St., Ultimo, 02 9217 0111 • Hot & Cool

The Draw: The Powerhouse Museum is an interactive mind-meld of touch-screen computers, audio phones, science experiments, virtual-reality 3-D theaters, movies, and displays.

The Scene: On weekdays, school kids run amok, and the squeals of battle can deflect your attention from a mock autopsy room or the traveling collection of Kylie Minogue's stage costumes—so come on a weekend if you can. *Daily 10am-5pm.* $

Hot Tip: Take the monorail from Town Hall to the Powerhouse Museum, and for lunch try some sushi and hang out with the pelicans at the nearby Sydney Fishmarkets.

Fine Dining

#22–24: The Italians may have the Slow Food movement, and the French still enjoy their nouvelle cuisine, but the culinary concept of note in the Land Down Under is "Modern Australian"—which puts an emphasis on fresh ingredients and creatively blends European and Asian influences.

Bilson's

Radisson Plaza Hotel, 27 O'Connell St., CBD, 02 8214 0496 • Classic

The Draw: Foodies from as far away as Paris flock to taste French food prepared by one of Australia's iconic chefs, Tony Bilson—an unabashed Francophile.

The Scene: Bilson's refined, classical dishes will send you to gastronomic heaven. Located in the foyer of the Radisson Plaza Hotel, Bilson's seduces guests into staying put rather than wandering the streets. Political bigwigs, in-town stars, and social butterflies flutter over the menu with gleeful abandon. *Mon-Fri noon-2:30pm and 6-10pm, Sat 6-10pm.* $$$$

Hot Tip: The degustation menu with paired wines really is so special we have to nudge you—it's a life-enhancing experience you shouldn't miss. But be warned: Bilson's is an all-night affair, as service is slow-paced.

Marque (G)

355 Crown St., Surry Hills, 02 9332 2255 • Classic

The Draw: Mark Best was named Chef of the Year by the influential *Sydney Morning Herald*'s *Good Food Guide*, and the restaurant gained a near-perfect score for its food, service, and ambience.

The Scene: An elegant aubergine room sets the scene as patrons enjoy carefully crafted French cuisine with touches of the unexpected. Dedicated staff dressed in starched white and a terrific sommelier work the floor, catering to the needs of a sophisticated, foodie crowd. *Mon-Sat 6:30-10:30pm.* $$$$

Hot Tip: Tables here are close together and the room can get loud—making it more of a spot for fun than for romance or privacy.

Tetsuya's (G)

529 Kent St., Haymarket, 02 9267 2900 • Classic

The Draw: Master chef Tetsuya Wakuda fuses French and Japanese influences into a crescendo of flavors at Sydney's most prestigious restaurant. This is considered the top foodie spot in Sydney.

The Scene: A ten-course meal served in Japanese-style rooms by one of the planet's most creative chefs doesn't come cheap. Expect the cream of society and others out celebrating the most special of occasions. *Tue-Fri 6-10:30pm and Sat noon-2pm and 6-10:30pm.* $$$$

Hot Tip: Book two months ahead for a Friday or Saturday night and three weeks in advance for a weekday evening.

Gay Scenes

#25–27: Sydney is said to have the second-largest gay and lesbian community in the world after San Francisco. Gay bars and clubs are concentrated along Oxford Street, and whether you are cruising the scene or taking in the atmosphere, there's no lack of options.

Arq

16 Flinders St., Taylor Square, 02 9380 8700 • Hot & Cool

The Draw: This after-hours venue for boys who like boys is split into separate spaces. Upstairs is for cocktails while downstairs is for solid gyrating.

The Scene: This is the place to dress up in your sequins, or full drag if that's the way you like it, to shake, shimmy, imbibe, and maybe even score. A few stray ladies come here with their best gay buddies, too. *Thu-Sun 9pm-9am.* C≡

Hot Tip: Saturday is the biggest party night, when almost everyone stays up until after dawn.

The Colombian Hotel

117-123 Oxford St., Darlinghurst, 02 9360 2151 • Hot & Cool

The Draw: This enormous heritage building sparkles with a high-energy clientele that likes to put its polished bodies on display.

The Scene: A lively vibe and casual surroundings appeal to everyone from older queens to barely legals, with a light scattering of women getting high on a lack of attention. Downstairs is a gay bar, while upstairs it's strictly dancing and romancing. *Sun-Thu 10am-4am, Fri-Sat 9am-6am.* C≡

Hot Tip: Explore the darkened corners for an intimate "chat."

Midnight Shift

85 Oxford St., Darling Harbour, 02 9360 4319 • Classic

The Draw: This Oxford Street institution offers a bar and a club split into three areas, including Shift, where Sydney's hottest DJs work beneath the laser beams.

The Scene: Night and day, the Midnight Shift is abuzz with cruising. While mostly enjoyed by men on the prowl, not all may be what it seems. Young straight backpackers reckon it's a great place to pick up women. *Bar: Mon-Fri noon-late, Sat-Sun 2pm-late; club: Fri-Sun 10am-late.* C=

Hot Tip: Saturday nights feature Dancing Queen, an all-dancing, all-singing tribute to Kylie Minogue.

Harbor Experiences

#28–30: Sydney Harbour is the focal point of Sydney life—the jewel in the city's crown. It's crisscrossed by ferry boats, lined with prime waterside homes, and rimmed by a national park to boot.

Ferry to Manly

Circular Quay, Wharf 2, CBD, 131 500 • Classic

The Draw: The state-owned ferries that ply the bay offer gorgeous views and a chance to experience one of the world's best commutes.

The Scene: Commuters take them to work during rush hour, and tourists take them anytime they want, but either way, when the ferry passes beside the entrance to the harbor and the big waves roll in after a storm, they all buck the bronco. *Daily 8:30am-5pm, followed by fast jet cat service until 11:45pm.* $

Hot Tip: Take the ferry at dusk when the city office towers glow orange and cast an array of colors across the harbor.

Jet Boating on Sydney Harbour

20A Waterview St., Putney, 02 9808 3700 • Hot & Cool

The Draw: Pull some fishtails, spins, and power-break stops on a high-performance V8 jet boat on Sydney Harbour. It's a guaranteed adrenaline rush with views to match.

The Scene: Wrapped in spray jackets and water-spotted sunglasses, tourists scream and carry on as they zip across the water at breakneck speed. There's the Opera House! No, it's gone. And that island rushing towards us? Yikes! *Daily 11am-sunset.* $$$

Hot Tip: Sit in the middle if you want to stay drier than the suckers on the outside.

Walking the Harbour Bridge

Bridge Stairs, Cumberland St., The Rocks, 02 247 7777

The Draw: Why just look at it when you can walk across the harbor without getting your feet wet? One of Sydney's iconic attractions is a working roadway, railway crossing, and pedestrian bridge.

The Scene: OK, so it gets a bit polluted with all the exhaust fumes, but that doesn't stop fitness freaks from jogging across it on their lunch break, or riding their bicycles from one end to the other. For tourists, it provides a view of the city and bay that's hard to forget.

Hot Tip: At the city end of the bridge you'll find the Pylon Lookout in one of the sandstone towers. Inside there are bridge-related displays, and 200 steps up you get bird's-eye views of the harbor.

Historic Drinking Holes

#31–33: The old sandstone pubs of the Rocks were once quarrelsome places haunted by emancipated convicts, whalers, press gangs, and drunken sailors. These days they act as atmospheric colonial refuges, where tall tales and good beer dominate.

The Australian Heritage Hotel*

100 Cumberland St., The Rocks, 02 9247 2229 • Classic

The Draw: This hugely popular heritage icon built in 1916 has plenty of historic flair and benefits from a great location close to the main drag.

The Scene: Inside it's warm and cozy and has a real 1920s feel, while seating out on the sidewalk means you can enjoy the fresh air, too. Beer is served in British pint glasses. Office workers flood in on Friday evenings to order some of Sydney's best pub pizzas. Lunchtime can be crowded too, often with tourists relaxing after climbing the arches of the Harbour Bridge. *Mon-Sat 11am-midnight, Sun 11am-10pm.* ≡

Hot Tip: You have to order and pay for your pizza at the bar. The best toppings are the tandoori chicken and roast duck.

Hero of Waterloo*

81 Lower Fort St., The Rocks, 02 9252 4553 • Classic

The Draw: With its exposed sandstone walls, fireplace, and old wooden floorboards, the 1850s Hero of Waterloo takes you back to the days of early settlement.

The Scene: You had to be wary back in the early days. Press gangs would spike a man's drink at this pub, and he'd be hauled into the cellar, where a tunnel led down to the sea. He'd wake up on a ship and be required to work as a sailor. Historic drinking places attract characters, and it's no different here. It's the place to get talking to a local with a few yarns to tell. *Mon-Sat 10am-11pm, Sun 10am-10pm.* ≡

Hot Tip: Head to the pub on a Sunday and enjoy lunchtime jazz by old-timers in the swing.

The Lord Nelson Brewery Hotel*

19 Kent St., The Rocks, 02 9251 4044 • Classic

The Draw: Wooden floors and exposed walls mark this as another 1850s gem—but the real highlight is the beer list, which features six varieties brewed on-site.

The Scene: The pub can be packed in the evenings with pub crawlers and office workers, but lunchtime is much more relaxed, with deals being done over a few pints and a pie. *Mon-Sat 11am-11pm, Sun noon-10pm.* ≡

Hot Tip: The malty Three Sheets in-house brew is a favorite and has won many awards. Don't miss the house specialty, a meat pie on a bed of mashed potatoes with mushy peas on top. (It's much better than it sounds.)

Historic Sydney

#34–36: Before Europeans arrived in 1788, the area that became known as Sydney was made up of forest, swamp, and beaches. Hastily erected wood and bark huts gave way to convict-built structures made from bricks and local sandstone, and before long the colony was a thriving outpost of the British Empire.

Kings Cross

Kings Cross • Hot & Cool

The Draw: If you have a fascination for the seamier side of life, then head down to "The Cross," an energetic cluster of strip clubs, adult shops, and popular restaurants and bars.

The Scene: Once popular with American G.I.s, who flocked here during World War II and Vietnam, it's now frequented by everyone from prostitutes and druggies to celebrities and artists rambling among the bars, restaurants, and shops.

Hot Tip: Don't mind the doorman if he asks for an exorbitant entry fee to see a nude stage show—you can bargain him down to less than $10.

Mrs. Macquaries Chair

Royal Botanic Gardens • Classic

The Draw: This historic seating spot in the Royal Botanic Gardens was carved out of a rock ledge for a governor's wife, who visited the area to take in the harbor panorama.

The Scene: The view of the Opera House and the Harbour Bridge are unbeatable, and you can even see the tiny island of Fort Denison (nicknamed Pinchgut), with its 19th-century prison. Just ignore the busloads of tourists, including Japanese visitors on their annual week holiday, who rush to the foreshore with cameras in hand. A few quick clicks of the shutter and they're gone.

Hot Tip: If you're up before dawn, this is a great place to take in the sunrise.

The Rocks

The Rocks • Classic

The Draw: The site of Sydney's original European convict and port community, the Rocks is a cluttered area of simple houses, lanes, pubs, boutiques, and hotels. Its history is colored by shanghaied sailors and cutthroat gangs.

The Scene: By day it's a place for tourists, who come here to squander some money on art and fashion. But when the sun goes down, the area heaves with local revelers making the most of the old sandstone drinking dens.

Hot Tip: You can pick your way through the Rocks on a pub crawl tour (the Rocks Pub Tour, 02 9240 8788), or more sedately on a hearse-drawn ghost tour (Destiny Tours, 02 9943 0167).

Hot Club Scenes

#37–39: The Harbor City knows how to party, and Sydney's best clubs attract the young, hip, and beautiful. While many nightclubs are constantly changing hands and reinventing themselves, these hot spots have a loyal following and are here for the long haul.

Dragonfly

1 Earl St., Potts Point, 02 9356 2666 • Hot & Cool

The Draw: The sophisticated option for the late-night reveler, Dragonfly provides suave surroundings in which to sip cocktails and check out the talent on the dance floor.

The Scene: Tucked away in a Kings Cross alley, sexy Dragonfly lures fashion-conscious boys and well-manicured girls who preen and pout their way past the velvet rope. *Wed, Fri-Sun 9pm-5am.* C≡

Hot Tip: The crowd is younger on Wednesdays; visit on a Saturday for prime-time fun with the cool crowd.

Lady Lux

2 Roslyn St., Potts Point, 02 9361 5000 • Hot & Cool

The Draw: Intimate, funky, and always throbbing with the latest sounds from party electro to funk, Lady Lux is for innovators and shakers and marks a move away from cavernous mega-clubs.

The Scene: In the heart of the red light district, Lady Lux and her regulars ooze cool, sometimes laced with a little too much attitude. A party spirit permeates, though, and there's no stopping the boogie. *Thu-Sun 10pm-late.* C≡

Hot Tip: Dress to impress and be assertive with the door staff. If you want to get in, you've got to earn it.

Tank

Establishment Hotel, 3 Bridge Ln., CBD, 02 8295 9966 • Hot & Cool

The Draw: This exclusive club draws the city's elite hipsters for drinking, dancing, and lounging.

The Scene: From clubbers in the latest "it" jeans and sneakers to urban sophisticates, Tank draws a crowd from all echelons of Sydney nightlife, with one thing in common—a deep love of house music. Genuinely respected in dance music circles for top-quality house beats, Tank also provides exclusive "booth" options in its loungey back room for those who just want to soak up the atmosphere. *Fri-Sat 10pm-6am.* C≡

Hot Tip: Arrive before 11pm when your chances of easy entry are much better.

Late-Night Bites

#40–42: It's 4am; you've exhausted the must-see bars and clubs and are dying for a bite. Whatever you're craving, Sydney delivers, from an Australian national dish—the meat pie—to an early breakfast of fresh lobster, or the friendliest burger joint in town.

Dean's Café

1/5 Kellett St., Kings Cross, 02 9368 0953 • Hot & Cool

The Draw: With kitsch furniture and a surfboard on the ceiling, Dean's is a melting pot of late-night diners in the center of the Red Light district.

The Scene: Pull up a mismatched chair at one of the tables and put some songs on the jukebox. If you're alone, it won't be long before someone strikes up a conversation. *Mon-Thu 7pm-3am, Fri-Sun 7pm-6am.* $

Hot Tip: For a sweet nightcap, order the chocolate milkshake, the best in the southern hemisphere.

Golden Century

393-399 Sussex St., Haymarket, 02 9212 3901 • Classic

The Draw: This vast, bustling Chinatown favorite is a fun place to refuel after a big night of clubbing.

The Scene: It's all hustle and bustle, with flying waiters and a crush of Chinese diners and casual outsiders. In the early hours of the morning, it's a favorite with Chinese chefs who've finished their shifts and are yearning for a bowl of congee, and clubbers looking for sustenance. *Daily noon-4am.* $$

Hot Tip: Try the famed abalone—the king of all shellfish—scooped from local waters.

Harry's Cafe de Wheels

Cowper Road Wharf, Woolloomooloo, 02 9357 3074 • Hot & Cool

The Draw: Down-market Australian cuisine in an uptown harborside locale, a "tiger" pie from the Harrys caravan makes it well worth your while to break the carb-free diet.

The Scene: From sailors returning to base, to suits fresh from a late night at the stock exchange, and the flashy post-party crowd, diners at Harry's are an eclectic bunch with one thing in common—they eat their pies standing up or sitting on the curb. Harry's is little more than an outdoor stand—but a local legend nonetheless. *Mon-Thu 7:30am-2am, Fri 7:30am-4am, Sat 9am-4am, Sun 9am-1:30am.* $

Hot Tip: Skip the hotdogs and order a "tiger" pie with peas and gravy—you'll thank us later.

Late-Night Hangouts

#43–45: When you're dead set to keep rolling on a bender, the last port of call doesn't happen until well into the dawn. It's always a pleasure to find like-minded debauched souls sipping and babbling in the early morning light.

The Bourbon

24 Darlinghurst Rd., Kings Cross, 02 9358 1144 • Classic

The Draw: This Kings Cross spot offers pulsating music in the upstairs nightclub, lights and action at the ground-level bar, good service, and cheap steaks.

The Scene: It's a jovial mix of drunken north-shore boys chatting with the bouncers outside, pretty girls, and tie-less suits, and 40-somethings on the make, all enjoying easy cocktails and conversations. *Daily 10am-6am.*

Hot Tip: Don't be put off by the line outside, especially earlier in the evening. It's just the bouncers making a point.

Judgement Bar

180 Oxford St., Darlinghurst, 02 9360 4831 • Hot & Cool

The Draw: High above Taylor Square, the Judgie, as it's known locally, is the place for shooter nightcaps, ridiculous barfly banter, and late-night snogs.

The Scene: Actors, musicians, cross-eyed gig pigs, and mischievous hooligans make weekend nights feel like a chaotic house party overrun by funky dressers and bad pickup lines at this local favorite. *Nightly 6pm-late.*

Hot Tip: This is a place where stars come to be incognito—if you see a famous face, leave them to their drinking or toast them without being sycophantic.

Q Bar

34-44 Oxford St., Darlinghurst, 02 9360 1375 • Hot & Cool

The Draw: Open seven days a week and going strong until late, centrally located Q Bar is the place to go if you want the night to never end.

The Scene: A mishmash of drugged-up dance-floor heathens, 20-something hotties, and well-groomed Easties with a devilish thirst and a mission to party hard gather here to frolic freely in the darkened warehouse-like space where daylight is the enemy. *Nightly 9pm-late.*

Hot Tip: Play it cool with the bouncers, and your time will come—the line here can be long, but it does move.

Best Live Music Venues

#46–48: It's not all Kylie Minogue and Midnight Oil. Pub rock, New Wave, jazz, blues, reggae, and funk—Sydney's diverse cultural mix ensures there's a vibrant blend of music on offer. The pub scene unearths local legends-to-be, and the more upmarket clubs make foreigners feel welcome.

The Annandale Hotel

17 Parramatta Rd., Annandale, 02 9550 1078 • Hot & Cool

The Draw: With its black-and-white band photos on the wall, well-worn couches, and sticky scuffed floor, the well-worn, well-loved Annandale is committed to serving up the city's best live music to a loyal crowd.

The Scene: Stovepipe jeans and asymmetrical haircuts are the norm. Rowdy moshing and loud conversations cut above the music, and beer swilling is encouraged. It's a serious musical and beer appreciation society. *Mon-Sat 11am-midnight, Sun noon-10pm.* C≡

Hot Tip: Unless you're game enough to brave the crush of punters at the foot of the stage, the best view in the house is beside the sound and lighting booth.

The Basement Club*

29 Reiby Pl., Circular Quay, 02 9251 2797 • Classic

The Draw: From Dizzy Gillespie to Roy Ayers and Prince, jazz greats and modern heroes have cemented the reputation of this timber-paneled underground club as a music lover's mecca.

The Scene: Expect anything from under-20s jiving to funk bands to the 50-plus punters swaying to blues classics. The Basement prides itself on musical diversity and bringing you close to the music, literally. *Mon-Fri noon-late, Sat-Sun 7pm-late.* C≡

Hot Tip: For the best seats in the house, reserve a table for dinner and show right beneath the stage.

Spectrum

34 Oxford St., Darlinghurst, 02 9360 1375 • Hot & Cool

The Draw: It's got an underground, grungey vibe dominated by New Wave and a promise of unearthing the next big thing in Oz rock.

The Scene: Edgy post-punk, post-rock fashionistas with an ear for new sounds twirl beneath the multiple mirror balls in this hip dive, and you're face to face with Sydney's hottest rockers. *Tue-Sun 8pm-late.* C≡

Hot Tip: For most gigs, tickets are only available at the door, so be sure to head down close to opening hour to secure a spot in the intimate venue.

Only-in-Sydney Experiences

#49–51: You don't come to Sydney to do the same old things you do at home. While its beaches, harbor, and restaurant and nightlife scenes are high on anyone's itinerary, there are a few only-here things you just can't miss.

BridgeClimb Sydney

5 Cumberland St., The Rocks, 02 8274 7777 • Hot & Cool

The Draw: Weave through catwalks, climb up ladders, and walk across the upper arch of the Sydney Harbour Bridge for jaw-dropping 360-degree views of the harbor and city. Don't eat breakfast first if you're the queasy type.

The Scene: Families, daredevils, nervous tourists, and corpulent executives staring down their fear of heights all dress up in special suits and get strapped to the iron work. *Hours vary by season.* $$$$

Hot Tip: Aim for an early or late "twilight climb" to watch the lights of the city go on—or go for a night climb to add even more adrenaline to the experience.

Sydney Opera House

Bennelong Point, Circular Quay, 02 9250 7111 • Classic

The Draw: The Sydney Opera House is Australia's number one attraction, and if you don't like opera, try some ballet, a symphony, a play—or just a tour.

The Scene: While you won't see anyone in a tux or a ball gown, you should dress up in your finest casual evening wear on your night out with the local social set. During the day, just show up in normal tourist togs for a tour of this icon. *One-hour guided tours take place daily from 9am-5pm.* $$

Hot Tip: The best deal at the Opera House is the Performance Package, but you'll need to do your research in advance. You get a one-hour tour, dinner at Guillaume at Bennelong or Aria Restaurant, and entry to a show of your choice. Book through the Opera House website (sydneyoperahouse.com.au).

Sydney Tower Skywalk

100 Market St., CBD, 02 9333 9222 • Hot & Cool

The Draw: This high-altitude adrenaline rush will get your heart pumping!

The Scene: It looks like a skewered marshmallow from street level, but walking around the outside edge at the top of Sydney Tower is not for softies. Step out of a door onto a see-through floor and inch your way along a walkway some 853 feet (260 m), above the ground. *Daily walks at: 9:30 and 11:30am, 2:30, 4:30, and 6:30pm night walk (Sat only).* $$$$

Hot Tip: Inside Sydney Tower you'll find OzTrek, a virtual adventure ride around Australia. It features a 180-degree cinema screen, 3-D holograms, and motion seating. And as with the bridge, doing this at night adds an extra thrill.

Restaurants with Views

#52–54: In the Emerald City, real estate is a religion, and views—of the city, the harbor, and the beach—are worth their weight in gold. Restaurants, accordingly, squabble over the best waterfront locations to satisfy vista-hungry diners.

Catalina

1 Sunderland Ave., Rose Bay, 02 9371 0555 • Hot & Cool

The Draw: From its position right on the water's edge, Catalina's boasts stunning views across seaplanes and sailboats to the mansions beyond.

The Scene: A sunny day, a bottle of wine, and a plate of seafood, and you'll feel like you're floating in heaven here. Beautiful couples and the landed gentry sit back and indulge in the sparkling scenery and the sparkling wine. *Mon-Sat noon-late, Sun noon-5pm.* $$$

Hot Tip: The best seats are outside with the pelicans—but be sure to ask for one when you make your reservation.

Forty One Restaurant (G)

Level 42, The Chifley Tower, 2 Chifley Sq., CBD, 02 9221 2500 • Classic

The Draw: The views of the Royal Botanical Gardens and Sydney Harbour complement elegant accoutrements and Deitmar Sawyer's sumptuous French cuisine with Asian touches.

The Scene: The elevator whisks you up 42 floors to this plush top-flight restaurant. A top-ranking chef draws in local gourmands, but the eye-popping view is a huge draw for tourists, too. Whichever category they fall into, the crowd is well dressed and sophisticated. *Mon, Sat 6-10pm, Tue-Fri noon-2:30pm and 6-10pm.* $$$$

Hot Tip: Request a window table and enjoy cocktails and oysters in the lounge beforehand—it's a great place to watch the sunset.

Swell*

Shop 3, 465 Bronte Rd., Bronte, 02 9386 5001 • Hot & Cool

The Draw: The beautiful, bohemian-chic people dine with a beautiful ocean backdrop—who could want more?

The Scene: This simple cafe draws in Bronte hipsters at every meal. Just across the street from a sweeping white-sand beach, Swell is the local gathering spot for the young and fabulous who call Bronte home (Heath Ledger among them). Whether you're here for a Sunday brunch or an evening cocktail followed by dinner, you'll find a trendy, convivial crowd. *Daily 7:30am-late.* $$

Hot Tip: Swell has live music on Wednesday nights in winter—and dress for the weather. Evenings here can be cool.

Swank Lunch Spots

#55–57: Friday has become the biggest power lunch day on the Sydney scene—but while it may be professionals in suits enjoying the meal, it's far from a stuffy business affair. Friday lunchers often take the entire afternoon off, drinking and socializing until the office is safely closed.

Danks Street Depot

1/2 Danks St., Waterloo, 02 9698 2201 • Hot & Cool

The Draw: This edgy cafe-gallery in an up-and-coming part of town is a favorite with bohemians and foodies who dart in for a quick bite to eat before heading off into the cut and thrust.

The Scene: This was once considered an iffy part of town, but now Danks' open windows face out onto a trendy strip of designer stores. Inside, long timber tables are ideal for brushing shoulders with an interesting stranger, so the noise level can accelerate with newfound acquaintances—all sipping wine and munching on chic entrées such as rabbit pasta. *Tue-Fri 7:30am-4pm and 6-10pm, Sat 8am-midnight.* $$

Hot Tip: The attached store is a great spot to pick up a to-go bite.

Est.

The Establishment Hotel, Level 1, 252 George St., CBD, 02 9240 3010 • Hot & Cool

The Draw: Enjoy top-rate nosh at the swankiest lunchtime location in town. Est. is where the Friday lunchers go to show each other they have made it.

The Scene: Without a rowdy receptionist in sight, the diners at Est. are nonchalant in a way that only comes with the knowledge that you have the company card and are not afraid to use it—which is good, considering the prices here. Dress to impress and order the best bottle of champagne on the menu. *Mon-Fri noon-3pm and 6-10pm, Sat 6-10pm.* $$$

Hot Tip: For maximum exposure, stop off at the ground-floor Establishment bar for a pre-lunch aperitif.

Flying Fish

Pier 21, 19-21 Pirrama Rd., Pyrmont, 02 9518 6677 • Hot & Cool

The Draw: Sri Lankan–inspired seafood is accompanied by stunning city and harbor views from this former wharf.

The Scene: TV executives and social butterflies, including ladies doing lunch and couples yearning for a romantic setting, flutter into Flying Fish. Its heritage appeal and panoramic windows tempt your eye away from the gourmet seafood offerings on your plate. *Tue-Fri noon-2:30pm and 6:30-10:30pm, Sat 6:30-10:30pm, Sun noon-2:30pm.* $$$

Hot Tip: The best item on the menu is the mud crab in coriander and chili.

Thai Restaurants

#58–60: A vacation to Thailand is a rite of passage for young Australians and, if the number of Thai restaurants is any indication, Sydneysiders' cravings for basil, chili, and lime lingers long after they return home. Check your spice inhibitions at the door.

Longrain*

85 Commonwealth St., Surry Hills, 02 9280 2888 • Hot & Cool

The Draw: Bronzed fashionistas and a DJ spinning fresh tunes every night in this bar-restaurant make for a buzzing scene.

The Scene: Longrain doesn't take dinner bookings, but waiting is easy when you are sprawled on a couch in the bar, caiprioska in hand, alongside Sydney's hippest set. When you do get a seat, Sydney's love affair with the communal table is at its best. *Mon-Fri noon-2:30pm and 6-11pm, Sat 6-11pm.* $$

Hot Tip: You can take the sounds and flavors of Longrain home on a CD or in a sauce jar—they make great gifts. Also, it's all communal tables, so if you're looking for a private tête-à-tête with your date, this is probably not the place.

Sailors Thai Restaurant and Canteen

106 George St., The Rocks, 02 9251 2466 • Classic

The Draw: A basement landmark in The Rocks, Sailors Thai re-creates the spiciness of Siam in crisp, unadorned surroundings downstairs, and a lively cafe upstairs.

The Scene: Suits and tourists fill a sleek and stylish room hidden down a flight of stone stairs and done up in spring colors. Concentrate on the first-course signature dish—a finger food of smoked trout, pomelo, peanuts, chili, lime and a palm-sugar dressing, all served on betel leaves. *Mon-Fri noon-2:30pm and 6-10pm, Sat 6-10pm.* $$$

Hot Tip: For a great traveler's experience, eat at the communal table in the casual first-floor canteen, or ask for the only window table in the more formal lower space.

Spice I Am

90 Wentworth Ave., Surry Hills, 02 9280 0928 • Hot & Cool

The Draw: This is the most authentic Thai food this side of Phuket, set in a simple neighborhood space—OK, it's a neighborhood dive.

The Scene: Don't be put off by the hole-in-the-wall exterior; the kitchen contains a veritable treasure trove of taste sensations guaranteed to transport you far away from the makeshift tables on the sidewalk. *Tue-Sun 11am-4pm and 6-10pm.* $

Hot Tip: For the real deal, ask for your dishes to be prepared with fiery chilies. You can always put out the fire with a creamy coconut drink.

Trendy Hangouts

#61–63: Sydneysiders are a social lot. Give them a few cocktails and a good group of mates, and they'll make a night of it, and maybe even a morning after. But it's not all pubs, rugby, and Victoria Bitters—Aussies have a stylish set that loves to play, too, and they have lots of trendy spots to do it in.

Hugo's Lounge

Level 1, 33 Bayswater Rd., Kings Cross, 02 9357 4411 • Hot & Cool

The Draw: Attracting the chicest, sharpest, most well-heeled posse Sydney has to offer, Hugo's is pretentious, but as fun as it is showy.

The Scene: Bleached blondes, tight-shirted 30-something blokes, and their older mentors are always scanning the ladies, unless they're grinding their booty to lure a lover or pegging someone to the bar for a body shot. *Wed-Sat 6pm-3am, Sun 8pm-3am.* C≡

Hot Tip: If you're hungry, Hugo's Bar Pizza downstairs serves terrific thin and crispy Italian-style pizzas. Delicioso!

Victoria Room*

Level 1, 235 Victoria St., Darlinghurst, 02 9357 4488 • Classic

The Draw: Tranquility, chaise lounges, and colonial charm make the Victoria Room an oasis above churning Darlinghurst.

The Scene: Sophisticated, well-mannered sippers reclining on dimpled leather lounges with a definite 30-plus presence make this a mellow favorite. Stylish signature cocktails complement the dim, eclectic, and moody surroundings—think old Victorian furniture and shabby chic details. *Tue-Thu 6pm-midnight, Fri-Sat 6pm-2am, Sun 2pm-midnight.* ≡

Hot Tip: The place is renowned for its sugar cane–infused cocktails.

Zeta Bar

The Hilton Hotel, Level 4, 488 George St., CBD, 02 9265 6070 • Hot & Cool

The Draw: Its roomy terrace sets you face to face with Sydney's Central Business District skyline, in particular the lit-up copper dome of the Queen Victoria Building.

The Scene: Nothing like you'd expect from a hotel bar, Zeta throbs with the latest house and electro tunes, with frocked-up girls flitting past and impeccably groomed boys on their tail. International highfliers mix with Sydney socialites. *Mon-Wed 5pm-late, Thu-Fri 3pm-late, Sat 4pm-late.* ≡

Hot Tip: Take special care with your look as the bouncers can be ruthless—heels for the girls, funky open-shirted suits for the boys.

Walks

#64–66: There's no better way to appreciate the beauty and diversity of this city than on foot. Whether it's a coastal walk to marvel at the turquoise blue of the ocean, or an adventure with some very large bats, a stroll through Sydney will make some of your most memorable moments.

Bondi to Bronte

Bondi Beach • Classic

The Draw: The winding cliff-top track between Bondi and Bronte takes in three beaches and offers entrancing ocean views.

The Scene: Expect sun-kissed bodies, bronzed lifeguards, and glorious surf breaking on golden sand, not to mention locals walking their dogs, joggers and bicyclists, sarongs and bikinis, and kids flying their kites in the ocean breeze. The Bondi to Bronte walk is a must-do coastal stroll. Stop off at little Tamarama, nicknamed "Glamorama," where tops for women are optional.

Hot Tip: Just ask your cab driver to drop you at Bondi, then walk to the north end of the beach where you will see the trail winding by Icebergs—a great place for a drink.

Circular Quay to the Domain

Circular Quay • Classic

The Draw: Take in some of Sydney's iconic attractions on this meander past the Museum of Contemporary Art, the ferry terminals, and the Sydney Opera House, before cutting through the Royal Botanic Gardens to the Art Gallery of New South Wales.

The Scene: Down at Circular Quay the water glitters, the buskers try to engage a crowd, and the beautiful people saunter alongside the baseball-cap and camera brigade. From then on it's grass and rainforest until you reach the classical columns of Sydney's premier art space.

Hot Tip: Head to the central rainforest in the Botanic Gardens and look up. Above your head, you'll see hundreds of giant fruit bats.

Watsons Bay to The Gap

Watsons Bay • Classic

The Draw: This beautiful walk takes in Camp Cove (the spot where the First Fleet landed in Sydney Harbour), and the giant cliffs and roaring swell of the Gap.

The Scene: Bring your shorts and a relaxed attitude to Watsons Bay, home to Sydney's best beer garden. Discover seagulls pacing along the water's edge, boats puttering up to the jetty to take on a catch of fish, and nudists baring all beyond the gum trees.

Hot Tip: Continue past the lighthouse and through the eucalyptus on a bush track that reveals unusual views of the Opera House.

After-Hours Scenes

#67–69: There's late and then there's *way* late. For those who are no strangers to the latter, 3am is the perfect time to kiss the goodie-two-shoes types goodnight and lead those who linger astray. Choose haunts where the disco balls and DJ sets keep spinning through dawn, or clubs rich with well-worn style.

Melbourne Supper Club*

161 Spring St., City Center, 03 9654 6300

The Draw: An award-winning wine list and a gentlemen's club atmosphere make Supper Club a cut above. There's no better place for late-night lingering over fine wine and conversation. And on the food front, there's a selection of luscious snacks to sate that after-drinks hunger.

The Scene: The Supper Club attracts elegantly dressed culture lovers who've seen a show at the Princess Theatre next door, as well as a fair share of parliamentary magnates and the well-heeled who enjoy fine wine and sharp service. *Mon-Thu 5pm-4am, Fri-Sun 7pm-5am.* C ≡

Hot Tip: Try to nab a seat under the massive arch window that will give you a prized view of the illuminated St. Patrick's Cathedral.

Pony Club

68 Little Collins St., 03 9662 1026

The Draw: Giddy up! This little Pony rocks until 7am, which means you can horse around all night. Downstairs, the red walls are lined with pony portraits and hunt scenes. Upstairs, the band room has a lineup of loud acts amped to the max.

The Scene: The post-punk, post-rock, past-caring crowd congregates here for the dirty-fun vibe. The bar staff are laid-back and chatty. It's a long way from sophisticated but that's the whole point. *Tue-Thu 6pm-late, Fri-Sun 5pm-7am.* ≡

Hot Tip: Safeguard your valuables and belongings at Pony while you're frolicking (as you should). There is a seamy side, and no coat check, so jackets and umbrellas have a habit of walking.

Revolver Upstairs

Level 1, 229 Chapel St., Prahran, 03 9521 5985

The Draw: It's a cultural cauldron that bubbles all weekend and until late-late on weeknights. It's the only place worth the lineup at 6am.

The Scene: Anyone who is allergic to chichi designer life gravitates to Revolver, where red-hot DJs spark up the crowd and keep them dancing until dawn. *Mon-Thu noon-3am, Fri noon-Sat noon, Sat 5pm-Sun noon, Sun 5pm-6am.* ≡

Hot Tip: After everything else closes on a Saturday, Revolver thumps on. The Sunday morning sets are legendary.

Always-Hot Restaurants

#70–72: Hot in Melbourne usually means hidden, so you may have to search to find where the cool crowd is hanging. Down dingy alleys, behind unmarked doors, up old flights of stairs, the city's hot spots love their mystique. You'll be rewarded with good food, interesting wine, and the smug feeling of living like a local.

Comme*
7 Alfred Pl., City Center, 03 9631 4000

The Draw: An iconic restaurant location has been given a stunning makeover, smartly mixing ornate period features with smooth modern lines to create a hot spot that attracts the chic and the beautiful like bees to honey.

The Scene: Smartly dressed young professionals eye each other across the central marble-topped bar before moving to Comme Kitchen, a cozy room under the central staircase where they can keep flirting over a Spanish- and French-inspired menu. *Mon-Fri noon-2:30pm and 6-10pm, Sat 6-10pm.* $ ≡

Hot Tip: On Fridays, the upstairs Grand Room with its spectacular Murano glass chandeliers morphs into Melbourne's most stylish public bar.

Longrain*
44 Little Bourke St., City Center, 03 9671 3151

The Draw: One of Sydney's hottest restaurants, Longrain has now set up shop in Melbourne, bringing along its sparkling signature Thai flavors to a city mostly lacking in such joys.

The Scene: Word is out and there is a battle for a seat at Longrain's three communal tables. Food-savvy urbanites, well-heeled trend followers, and grateful Thai food fanatics rub shoulders in the cocktail bar while waiting for their number to come up. *Mon-Fri noon-2:30pm and 6-11pm, Sat 6-11pm.* $$ ▯≡

Hot Tip: The bar at Longrain has a menu of very fine bar snacks and brilliant, original cocktails—a fine alternative to joining the line for a table.

The Panama*
Level 3, 231 Smith St., Fitzroy, 03 9417 7663

The Draw: Located up several flights of rickety stairs from the grungy street below is a spacious loft bar and restaurant with fabulous views through floor-to-ceiling arched windows. It serves up hearty French bistro food and bohemian atmosphere in spades.

The Scene: The Panama attracts a crowd of hip inner-city types drawn to the hidden location, the quirky DJs, and the rare opportunity to drink and eat with a view. *Wed-Sat 6:30pm-late.* $$ ≡

Hot Tip: Ask for a table near a window for that god-like feeling of being above the hoi polloi.

Brunches

#73–75: Melbourne is a breakfast-lover's paradise, with some of the swankiest joints in town joining countless cafes in the eggs-fruit-and-pastry parade. Many places serve breakfast all day, and good coffee is something of a local badge of honor.

The Botanical*

169 Domain Rd., South Yarra, 03 9820 7888

The Draw: Beautiful breakfasts, chic company, and a buzzing location make this a morning favorite.

The Scene: Easy-on-the-eye modern surroundings are the backdrop to a menu that allows you to make a pig of yourself (wood-fired breakfasts include everything from beans and eggs to black pudding) or pick delicately at flaky house-made pastries while sipping a fresh juice. This is people-watching at its best, with a trendy 20- and 30-something clientele meeting, lounging, and reading well into the afternoon. *Mon-Fri 7-11:30am, noon-3pm, and 6-11pm, Sat-Sun 8-11:30am, 12:30-3pm, and 6-11pm.* $$ B =

Hot Tip: After breakfast head across the road to the Botanical Gardens for a stroll through some of Melbourne's natural beauty—don't miss the lily pond.

European*

161 Spring St., City Center, 03 9654 0811

The Draw: European's smart food (consider the corn cakes) and even smarter service make this an ideal place to ease into the day.

The Scene: A favorite with politicians, the European also attracts a stream of business folk lining up for take-out coffee. A little later, more casually dressed freelance types and city dwellers arrive to soak up the classically Melbourne vibe, choosing the dark, faux-antique wood and marble interior or perching at tree-shaded outside tables. *Sun-Thu 7:30am-11pm, Fri-Sat 7:30am-midnight.* $$ =

Hot Tip: The coffee here is the best in town.

Pearl

631-633 Church St., Richmond, 03 9421 4599

The Draw: The weekend-only brunch at this stylish, light-filled restaurant is the prettiest, most innovative, and tastiest in town.

The Scene: Just across the river from genteel South Yarra and on the fabulous furniture strip of Church Street, Pearl attracts designer couples browsing for designer couches and families soaking up the sun on the outdoor terrace, as well as food fanatics drawn by the weekend brunch's mighty reputation. *Daily 9am-3pm and 6-11pm.* $$ B =

Hot Tip: The coddled egg toasty topped with Yarra Valley salmon caviar is arguably the best breakfast dish in Melbourne.

Culture

#76–78: Melbourne is the culture capital of Australia. It's a city that prides itself on its sophistication, and almost every month boasts an internationally significant festival in art, sport, theater, dance, music, film, and any combination thereof.

Australian Centre for Contemporary Art (ACCA)

111 Sturt St., Southbank, 03 9697 9999

The Draw: Fittingly, the building itself makes reference to its function. It is a monumental sculpture in which to show art, simultaneously recalling the work of Richard Serra and the Australian landmark Uluru (or Ayers Rock).

The Scene: ACCA seems to sit in windswept isolation despite its proximity to the NGV International and the city center. You often have the galleries to yourself, but rest assured that opening nights are thronged with Melbourne's contemporary art intelligentsia. *Tue-Fri 10am-5pm, Sat-Sun 11am-6pm, Mondays by appointment.*

Hot Tip: On weekends at 3pm, artists and curators hold discussions in the galleries with patrons—just ask at the information counter.

Federation Square

Corner of Flinders and Swanston Sts.

The Draw: Federation Square is fulfilling its mission to become the cultural epicenter of Melbourne, with the Australian Centre for the Moving Image (ACMI, acmi.net.au), the Ian Potter Centre NGV Australia (ngv.vic.gov.au), and the National Design Centre (nationaldesigncentre.com) all in one spot.

The Scene: With its abundant attractions, cafe culture, and large paved plaza with outdoor screen, Federation Square is loved by locals and visitors alike.

Hot Tip: ACMI's Screen Gallery is downstairs and is not particularly well signed. As a result many people miss out on its extensive program of screen-based arts.

National Gallery of Victoria International (NGV)

180 St. Kilda Rd., 03 8620 2222

The Draw: Roy Ground's modernist landmark has been recently renovated by Italian architect Mario Bellini so that the interiors can better display the museum's ample collections of international art. You'll find contemporary art and 20th-century moderns as well as works stretching back to classical times, plus decorative arts, works on paper, and an impressive array of fashion and textiles.

The Scene: The NGV is broadening its appeal beyond classic gallery-goers with innovative programs such as Contemporary Photomedia and young members initiatives under the banner of Artbeat. *Wed-Mon 10am-5pm.*

Hot Tip: The water wall behind the archway entry is a beloved feature of the gallery's original design. Generations of children have run their hands along it.

Fine Dining

#79–81: Eating out in a food-obsessed city has many advantages, the best being a competitive jostling for position at the top. This desire to excel means that diners seeking to indulge in a sumptuous evening have a dazzling array of options to choose from.

Circa

The Prince, 2 Acland St., St. Kilda, 03 9536 1122

The Draw: Seriously good modern European food, an awesome wine list, and a stylishly romantic room with some of the best service in town is why Circa still packs them in after more than ten years.

The Scene: With its wafting black-and-pink curtains, white leather couches, and flattering lighting, Circa draws a fashionable, food-savvy crowd looking to make dinner an event. Pop downstairs for a nightcap at Mink or catch a band in the Prince Bandroom. *Daily 7am-11am, noon-3pm (except Sat) and 6:30-10:30pm.* $$$

Hot Tip: Leave room for dessert—one of Australia's most inspired dessert chefs, Philippa Sibley, is in charge of the sweet stuff here.

Taxi Dining Room

Transport Hotel, Level 1, 2 Swanston St., City Center, 03 9654 8808

The Draw: Perfectly balancing Japanese classics and modern east-meets-west fusion dishes with fabulous views through soaring glass-and-steel-mesh walls, Taxi is smart, elegantly casual, and very hip.

The Scene: Taxi's sleek but comfortable dining room attracts a mixed bag of sneaker-clad hipsters and besuited business types out to impress. After dinner, head downstairs to raucous multi-beered Transport Public Bar or upstairs to Transit for loungey DJ action and classic cocktails. *Daily noon-3pm and 6-10:30pm.* $$$ B

Hot Tip: Ask for a table in the main dining area for the best views and a brilliant 1960s airport lounge aesthetic.

Vue de Monde

430 Little Collins St., CBD, 03 9691 3888

The Draw: This stark, stylish gastro-temple has a degustation-only menu at night that showcases some of the best cooking in town. It's modern French food at its coolest and most innovative.

The Scene: Combining rough wooden floors and whitewashed walls, Vue de Monde creates a chic warehouse feel for the well-heeled crowd that flocks in night and day. *Tue-Fri noon-2:30pm and 6:30-10pm, Sat 6:30-10pm.* $$$$ B

Hot Tip: The set menu at lunch (two or three courses with a glass of wine) is an incredible value, and the always-packed room offers a glimpse of Melbourne's richest movers and shakers doing it on the cheap.

Hot Club Scenes

#82–84: Melbourne's night cats like to dance by the light of the moon. Thanks to mix-mastered DJ sets, high-voltage energy, and luxe interiors, these clubs can push thoughts of tomorrow to the farthest reaches of your mind.

Boutique

134 Greville St., Prahran, 03 9525 2322

The Draw: Boutique is an opulent club replete with chandeliers, grand floral arrangements, velvet curtains, and plush nooks for getting cozy.

The Scene: Thursday's "White Rabbit" is designed to get young clubbers feeling frisky. "Flash" Fridays is a decadent '80s-inspired night that brings boys out to doe-eye the glamour girls in tiny skirts and heels. The emphasis is on chic and exclusive everything, so expect to pay top dollar for cocktails. *Thu-Sat 9pm-4am.*

Hot Tip: Boutique boasts about its "extremely discerning door policy," so subscribe to its mailing list (boutique.net.au) and get the inside scoop.

The Esplanade Hotel

11 Upper Esplanade, St. Kilda, 03 9534 0211

The Draw: Tired of the latest minimalist trendy hot spot? Then the Espy is just the place. This long-standing night spot has been serving up local and international musical acts, comedians, and general good times to a youthful crowd since the 1930s.

The Scene: This versatile space includes a front bar, a stage, and a pool room, giving the spirited crowds lots of space and options for festive mingling. *Sun-Thu noon-1am, Fri-Sat noon-3am.*

Hot Tip: The Espy crawls with backpackers, so if you want to avoid them, choose gigs with the highest ticket prices.

The Prince Bandroom

The Prince, 29 Fitzroy St., St. Kilda, 03 9536 1168

The Draw: Gigs, gigs, and more gigs of only the highest caliber! Then late on Saturdays, a string of DJs hits the decks, turning the band room into St. Kilda's hottest club night, called One Love.

The Scene: Rockers and ravers co-exist at the Prince. When there's an act playing, the fans match the music. On club nights, you'll find travelers intermingled with the style brigade and the alt-hip as they groove to lush pop-tronica. *Pub and lounge bars daily noon-1am; Band Room select weeknights 8pm-1am, weekends 8pm-3am, Sat 9pm-6am.*

Hot Tip: If you're there for a gig, grab a spot at the top corner of the RL Bar and hobnob with the musicians and their entourages.

Outdoor Drinking Spots

#85–87: Bonhomie flows as freely as beer on warm summer afternoons in Melbourne's best outdoor spots. You'll find friendly crowds and a lawn-party atmosphere, and of course, no end of fun.

Belgian Beer Café Bluestone*

557 St. Kilda Rd., South Yarra, 03 9529 2899

The Draw: This beer garden hums all spring and summer long. It's also the only place in town where you can find Belgian beers, including Hoegaarden, Stella Artois, Leffe Blonde, and Leffe Brune, on tap.

The Scene: Live jazz, Latin, blues and soul tunes spill across the lawns where the polo shirt–and-shorts brigade enjoy pints of the finest Belgian beers and barbecued bratwurst loaded with sauerkraut and all the trimmings. On weeknights, St. Kilda Road's advertising execs and young professionals meet after work for a pint or few, while warm weekends draw casual crowds from further afield. *Mon-Fri 8am-1am, Sat 11am-1am, Sun 11am-11pm.* ≡

Hot Tip: Sunday afternoons are a highlight here, with live jazz.

Transport

Federation Sq., Princes Bridge on Swanston St., City Center, 03 9654 8808

The Draw: It's an urban take on the classic beer garden.

The Scene: Here, the "garden" is a hardscape of paving and zinc-clad walls with benches and cable-spool stools. Choose the riverside or the plaza side and enjoy the passing parade, or settle in on Sunday afternoons for live bands. A mixed set of creatives, suits, and urbanites samples the range of 100 brews and endless spirits on offer. *Mon-Thu noon-1am, Fri-Sun noon-3am.* ≡

Hot Tip: If you meet someone fun and you're hankering for a chat where you don't have to shout, try heading upstairs to Taxi Dining Room for a fine dining experience, or up to Transit Lounge for cocktails or a nightcap.

The Vineyard

71a Acland St., St. Kilda, 03 9534 1942

The Draw: A prime spot by Luna Park makes the Vineyard a draw for locals and visitors alike.

The Scene: Retro-hip kids don't have a curfew or a schedule, so you'll find the Vineyard happening any day or night of the week. What starts as a quiet beer and a snack in the sunshine can easily become a full evening once you settle in for the people-watching. The music veers from upbeat tunes to thumping sets. Triple it on Thursday nights and weekends when travelers and tourists come to soak up St. Kilda's bohemian charms. *Daily 9am-3am.* ≡

Hot Tip: Make sure you're wearing shades by day. The bigger and cooler they are, the better they'll be for all the boy-gazing and babe-watching you'll be doing.

Summer View Bars

#88–90: Where bolt-hole bars made their mark in the '90s, a new breed of bar is setting the scene. They are characterized by rooftop locations boasting broad terraces and expansive views. These new bars survey Melbourne's sparkling skyline and give you the perfect place to celebrate the high life in good weather.

The Corner Hotel Rooftop Bar

57 Swan St., Richmond, 03 9427 7300

The Draw: Here's the spot for cool ales on long summer nights. Upstairs, you can catch some fresh air between sets by the great local and international acts who rock the band room below.

The Scene: With all the hot acts that jam the band room calendar, the Corner and its rooftop are home to music lovers of all varieties. *Mon-Sat noon-3am, Sun noon-1am.* ≡

Hot Tip: The White Stripes coined the riff to their hit single *Seven Nation Army* at the Corner.

Madame Brussels

Level 3, 59 Bourke St., City Center, 03 9662 2775

The Draw: The high life! Madame Brussels flaunts plenty of graceful allure with her promise of freshly shucked oysters to sup with the finest champagnes.

The Scene: Decked-out scene-setters and anyone with a lust for the eccentric will take to Madame Brussels' charms. Enjoy it all in the terrace's white wrought-iron garden setting. *Mon-Sat 4-11pm, Sun noon-11pm.* –

Hot Tip: Be sure to visit the Grotto inside, an intriguing space with an eclectic decor and a fine lineup of rums.

Transit Lounge Garden

Federation Sq., Princes Bridge on Swanston St., City Center, 03 9654 8808

The Draw: Head straight to the deck for one of the best views down the Yarra. On the terrace, the geometrically succinct timber-lined pods are scaled for easy socializing and relaxing.

The Scene: With an interior replete with modern leather Chesterfield-like lounges, lamplight, and club atmosphere, Transit attracts sophisticated drinkers who prefer life to be lived "far from the madding crowd." *Nightly 6pm-4am.* ≡

Hot Tip: Sunset and the twilight hours are definitely prime time at Transit.

Tapas

#91–93: A tapas explosion in the '90s crashed and burned within a couple of years, but from the ashes of that Spanish flirtation sprung a new breed of tapas joint—more about authenticity than fad. Comprehensive lists of chalky dry sherry, skillfully assembled snacks, and bar-centric decor make the local tapas experience distinctly Melbarcelona.

Bar Lourinha

37 Little Collins St., City Center, 03 9663 7890

The Draw: This newcomer is the city's hottest ticket for small plates.

The Scene: The long, narrow, noisy room is always packed with a friendly, fashion-conscious, food-savvy crowd checking out the dishes and each other equally. A lengthy list of small courses that run the gamut from liver to lentils offers some of the most vibrant Spanish and Portuguese flavors in town. *Mon-Wed noon-11pm, Thu-Fri noon-1am, Sat 4pm-1am.* $$

Hot Tip: Special dinners that highlight seasonal produce (suckling pig, capretto) are held upstairs once a month. Reservations are essential.

Canary Club*

6 Melbourne Pl., City Center, 03 9663 1983

The Draw: Tucked at the end of a lane, Canary Club is a sexy double-storied lounge-bar that takes its cues from the tapas bars of Barcelona.

The Scene: Early evening sees a tie-loosening young crowd winding down over tapas and beer, but as night closes in, stylish barflies descend, drawn to the leather daybeds and lounges upstairs and the laid-back DJ-spun tunes. Delicious montaditos, tapas, and pinchos are matched with a formidable list of sherry, cocktails, wine, and beer. *Mon-Tue 4pm-1am, Wed-Sat 4pm-3am.* $$

Hot Tip: The decadent churros (sugared donuts with chocolate dipping sauce) are best shared with someone gorgeous on one of the upstairs beds.

MoVida*

1 Hosier Ln., City Center, 03 9663 3038

The Draw: Always packed to the rafters, MoVida's dimly lit terra-cotta-and-wood good looks are matched by smart and sexy service and a brilliant list of Spanish beer, wine, and tapas that begs you to order just one more.

The Scene: Arty city types, business people, and young(ish) scenesters have adopted MoVida as a home away from home and give this self-proclaimed "bar de tapas y vino" its undeniable buzz. *Sun-Mon noon-10pm, Tue-Sat noon-10:30pm.* $$

Hot Tip: A seat at the bar will give you the best authentic tapas experience—but you'll have to book well ahead.

Walks

#94–96: Melbourne is the capital of Australia's own Garden State, but that's where its kinship with Trenton, New Jersey, ends. This waterfront town is all about lush gardens, serene bays, and historic buildings. You might pass a strip club or two (the town is famous for its "table dancers"), but keep walking—there's a sight worth seeing just around the corner.

Beachfront: St. Kilda to Port Melbourne along Beaconsfield Parade

Start at Fitzroy St., St. Kilda, and follow Beaconsfield Parade

The Draw: A stroll along the palm-lined foreshore that stretches from Fitzroy Street, St. Kilda, to Station Pier, Port Melbourne, is a good 2.5 miles (4km). There are plenty of beachfront cafes and pubs along the way if you need a thirst-quencher.

The Scene: In the mornings and evenings, the strip is a favorite for fleet-footed locals keeping fit. On warm nights, it has an air of Lovers' Lane, and on weekends families, dogs, cyclists, and bladers all make way for one another.

Hot Tip: Hire rollerblades to make the journey faster. Two companies are close by: Albert Park Inline Skates (179 Victoria Ave., 03 9645 9099), or Ready To Roll (185 Victoria Ave., Albert Park, 03 9682 3933).

Riverfront: from Southbank along the Yarra

Start at Princes Bridge, Southbank; follow the river trails along Alexandra Avenue

The Draw: Walking along the Yarra, you'll see the city skyline, the boat sheds, major sporting arenas, and the fringes of Melbourne's lush parklands, including Birrarung Marr on the northern side, and Kings Domain and the Royal Botanical Gardens on the southern side.

The Scene: With barbecues, lawns, gardens, cycling tracks, and rowers, there's always plenty of river life to enjoy as you wander.

Hot Tip: Intrepid souls might like to continue roaming along the river all the way to Studley Park and the Boulevard in Kew, which boasts some iconic modernist homes from the 1950s and '60s.

The 'Tan: The Botanical Gardens Fitness Track

Start at Princes Bridge on the Arts Centre side, follow the Yarra trail, join the 'Tan at Alexandra Parade, and follow the track to the right turn up Anderson Street

The Draw: This 2.3-mile (3.7km) trail skirts Melbourne's famous Royal Botanical Gardens, Kings Domain park, and the Yarra River.

The Scene: The 'Tan track is well worn by everyone from football stars and marathon runners to joggers and power walkers. Join them for a fast-paced stroll that'll take 20 to 30 minutes or a sprint that could see you lap it in 12 minutes.

Hot Tip: If you're just out for a stroll, meander through the paths in the Botanical Gardens rather than around them. You'll find rainforests, succulent gardens, mature European trees, manicured flower beds, and gazebos.

Winter Bolt-hole Bars

#97–99: Bolt-hole bars are unique to Melbourne. The name refers to tiny, hidden drinking-hole gems tucked down unseemly alleys and lanes—some don't even bother with a sign, and are so obscure that you're certain no one but rats and muggers could possibly be down this dark, creepy street. All the better for those who love a little nocturnal hide-and-seek. They're especially inviting and popular during the damp and dark winter months (June and July).

Double Happiness and New Gold Mountain

21 Liverpool Ln. off Bourke St., City Center, 03 9650 4488

The Draw: A seriously obscure vibe and Asian accents make this a favorite local hangout for the young and restless.

The Scene: Given its bento-box size, deep-lane location, and lack of overt signage (unless you can read the Chinese characters), Double Happiness is a favorite haunt of the in-the-know crowd. An emphasis on fresh Asian herbs and spice-infused spirits makes for a seriously inventive cocktail list. Upstairs, New Gold Mountain (the name given to Melbourne by the Chinese during the gold rushes of the 1850s) is a recent addition that's quickly become an old favorite. *Mon-Wed 5pm-1am, Thu 5pm-3am, Fri 4:30pm-3am, Sat 6pm-3am, Sun 6pm-1am.* ≡

Hot Tip: Martinis come in lychee, aloe, and espresso varieties, and the Ho Ho La, Mr. Fu, and Imperial Running Dog are refreshingly unique.

Gin Palace

Russell Pl. off Little Collins St., City Center, 03 9654 0533

The Draw: Baroque elegance, rich textures, and low lighting make Gin Palace the first choice of luxe-lovers.

The Scene: Gin Palace has a strong pull for the suit set any night of the week, but they rarely have the staying power of the chic late-nighters who settle into plump cushions for hours of conversation, seduction, or both. *Nightly 4pm-3am.* ≡

Hot Tip: It doesn't have much in the way of food, but the toasted chicken sandwiches are a good nibble if you're in need.

Meyers Place

20 Meyers Pl., off Bourke St., City Center, 03 9650 8609

The Draw: This was the first of the unsigned bolt-holes that made Melbourne's night hours more vibrant in the '90s.

The Scene: It still attracts the design set—even if they have to shuffle through a forest of suits on Friday nights, with a relaxed vibe courtesy of easygoing staff and a cozy interior that mixes post-industrial concrete with recycled timbers. *Mon 5pm-2am, Tue-Thu 5pm-3am, Fri 4pm-4am, Sat 5pm-4am, Sun 5pm-1am.* ≡

Hot Tip: It's most buzzing after work on Thursday and Friday nights.

PRIME TIME SYDNEY AND MELBOURNE

Everything in life is timing—with a dash of serendipity thrown in. Would you want to arrive in Pamplona, Spain, the day *after* the Running of the Bulls? Not if you have a choice and you relish being a part of life's peak experiences. With our month-by-month calendar of events, there's no excuse to miss out on any of Sydney and Melbourne's greatest moments. From the classic to the quirky, the sophisticated to the outrageous, you'll find all you need to know about the cities' best events right here.

Prime Time Basics

Eating and Drinking

In both Sydney and Melbourne, breakfast kicks off from around 7am, with lunch at noon, and dinner around 8pm, though some restaurants near theater venues will offer a pre-theater dinner starting at around 6pm. Brunch, between 10am and noon, is becoming more popular in city center eateries. Many companies are more casual on Fridays and encourage people to dress down in the office, and a growing phenomenon is for executives to stay out eating and drinking throughout Friday afternoons. Late-night eateries exist, though restaurant kitchens usually close at around 9:30pm or 10pm. Many restaurants allow you to bring your own wine, in Australia referred to as BYO. Often they will charge you a corkage fee for the privilege, usually around A$4 per bottle, though more expensive restaurants might charge this per person, or even more.

Weather and Tourism: Sydney

June-Aug: Sydney enjoys a temperate climate, which means warm summers and cool winters. Typically, winter lasts from June to August. June to July is the cold time, when Aborigines would traditionally journey to the coast where food was more abundant. August is cold and windy. In mid-winter, it gets cold enough to wear a sweater and light jacket but, then again, many days are warm and sunny, with brilliant clear blue skies.

Sept-Oct: Sydney's six-season Aboriginal calendar is based on the flowering of various native plants. Traditionally, the first season spans September and October, when the temperature rises.

Sydney Seasonal Changes

Month	Fahrenheit High	Fahrenheit Low	Celsius High	Celsius Low	Hotel Rates
Jan	78	66	26	19	H
Feb	78	66	26	19	H
Mar	76	64	25	18	H
Apr	72	59	22	15	H
May	67	53	19	12	L
June	62	49	16	9	L
July	61	46	16	8	L
Aug	64	48	18	9	L
Sept	68	52	20	11	S
Oct	72	56	22	14	S
Nov	75	60	24	15	S
Dec	77	64	25	18	S

H-High Season; S-Shoulder; L-Low

Nov-Feb: Summer lasts from December to the end of February, but November is when the weather starts turning hot. Rain can still happen in this season as well. By the time January rolls around, it's officially summer, and it can be hot—very hot—with temperatures getting up to 100 degrees Fahrenheit on occasion, and sometimes higher. Summers are often very humid too. In the daytime you might be doing the "Aussie Wave"—flicking your hand across your face to get rid of the flies, and in the evenings you may encounter mosquitoes (though thankfully they are mostly disease-free). Summer also brings occasional thunderstorms.

Mar-May: March to May is the time of wet, cooling temperatures, a signal to bring out the jacket to keep warm. But in 1788, when English settlers first arrived in Sydney, they naturally imposed the four European seasons on their new home without any real knowledge of local weather patterns. The local Aboriginal people, however, had been living according to an annual six-season calendar. For longer-range weather forecasting they used an 11- to 12-year cycle and even an 8,000- to 10,000-year cycle—so you never know exactly what weather to expect.

Weather and Tourism: Melbourne

June-July: June and July are the coldest months. As in Sydney, this is considered the heart of winter, when winds and rains are at their fiercest. Make sure to pack for inclement weather.

Aug-Oct: October is the wettest month in Melbourne, though August and September can see rains. The temperatures are starting to warm, but as in all springs, weather can be unpredictable. But it's a glorious season in Melbourne, and many say that October is one of the best months to visit.

Nov-Feb: It's summer down under, and Melbourne is in full swing at this time of year. The weather is warm—

Melbourne Seasonal Changes

Month	Fahrenheit High	Fahrenheit Low	Celsius High	Celsius Low	Hotel Rates
Jan	79	57	26	14	H
Feb	79	59	26	15	H
Mar	75	55	24	13	H
Apr	68	52	20	11	H
May	62	48	17	9	L
June	57	44	14	7	L
July	55	43	13	6	L
Aug	59	44	15	7	L
Sept	62	46	17	8	S
Oct	68	48	20	9	S
Nov	71	52	22	11	S
Dec	75	55	24	13	S

H-High Season; S-Shoulder; L-Low

OK, hot at times—and the locals are out in droves enjoying the beer gardens and beaches. Evenings can still be cool, so bring a sweater. January and February are the hottest, but some respite is provided by the cooling sea breezes off Port Phillip Bay. Hotels around Bondi Beach and Manly in Sydney tend to charge more in summer months, though elsewhere rates remain stable year-round.

Mar-May: Melbourne is also classified as a temperate climate. In general though, it has mild autumns. The end of March is also considered a great time to visit weather-wise, and the crowds aren't as great as in summer.

National Holidays

New Year's Day	January 1
Australia Day	January 26
Good Friday	First Friday after full moon that follows March 28
Easter Monday	First Monday after Good Friday
Labor Day (Melbourne)	Mid-March
Anzac Day	April 25
Queen's Birthday	Second Monday in June
Labor Day (Sydney)	First Monday in October
Melbourne Cup Day (Melbourne)	First Tuesday in November
Christmas Day	December 25
Boxing Day	December 26

Listings in blue are major celebrations but not official holidays.

The Best Events Calendar

January	February	March
• Sydney Festival • Australian Open Tennis Championship		• Gay and Lesbian Mardi Gras*
April	**May**	**June**
• Royal Easter Show • Australian Formula One Grand Prix • Melbourne International Comedy Festival		• Sydney Film Festival • Biennale of Sydney (next 2008)
July	**August**	**September**
• Melbourne International Film Festival		• Festival of the Winds • Melbourne Fringe Festival
October	**November**	**December**
• Manly Jazz Festival • Melbourne International Arts Festival*	• Melbourne Cup Carnival* • Sculpture by the Sea	• Carols in the Domain • Sydney to Hobart Yacht Race* • New Year's Eve Fireworks*

*Events followed by a blue asterisk * are Night+Day's Top Five Events. Events in blue are located in Melbourne.*

The Best Events

January

Sydney Festival

Various venues throughout Sydney, including the Domain parklands, 02 8248 6500, sydneyfestival.org.au

The Lowdown: Australia's biggest cultural event is a celebration of summer. It attracts international and national artists in the fields of theater, music, dance, and visual arts. Highlights include the free Symphony in the Domain and Jazz in the Domain, each attended by up to 100,000 people armed with picnic baskets, blankets, food, and champagne. Other free events take place in Darling Harbour and around the Opera House forecourt.

When and How Much: *From first weekend in January, for three weeks.* Various prices, with some free events.

Australian Open Tennis Championship

Melbourne Park, Melbourne, 03 9914 4400, australianopen.com.au

The Lowdown: Watch the drama unfold as the world's best tennis players battle it out for the first Grand Slam title of the year. The Australian Open attracts over 550,000 spectators over two weeks, making it the highest attended annual sporting event in Australia. Tickets can be hard to get, especially for the finals in the Rod Laver Arena.

When and How Much: *Second two weeks in January.* Tickets range in price from A$40 for an early match to A$159 for a final.

March

Gay and Lesbian Mardi Gras*

Oxford Street, Sydney. Party: Moore Park Entertainment Precinct (formally Fox Studios), 02 9568 8600, mardigras.org.au

The Lowdown: The party to end all others is a glittering, feathered, body-pumping affair with carnival floats, sequined dancing groups, and dykes on bikes. Nearly half a million spectators of all gender identifications and ages stand on milk crates to marvel at the evening's procession; a lucky few attend the Mardi Gras Party afterwards. Book a place at the special viewing area for the best outlook.

When and How Much: *Generally the first Saturday in March.* Free. Special viewing area A$20. Party A$160.

*Events followed by a blue asterisk * are Night+Day's Top Five Events. Events in blue are located in Melbourne.*

April

Royal Easter Show

Sydney Showground, Sydney Olympic Park, 02 9704 1111, eastershow.com.au.

The Lowdown: You can get to know a lot about a country by its pigs, sheep, and cows, and other assorted farm animals. There's far more on offer at this premier agricultural event than just animals, though. For starters, you get to mix with all sorts of Aussies. There's also a world-class rodeo, plus dance, live music, and street performances. It's an iconic Sydney event that all locals go to sometime in their lives. Expect the place to be packed with children.

When and How Much: *First Friday in April for two weeks.* Entry A$31.

Australian Formula One Grand Prix

Albert Park, Melbourne, 61 132 849 (Ticketek), grandprix.com.au

The Lowdown: Four days of high-speed motor racing in converted parklands lead up to the checkered-flag finale. As well as Formula One, expect V8 Supercars and Formula 3 races. On the Friday before the big event there's the Grand Prix Ball, which has previously been attended by Prince Albert of Monaco, Naomi Campbell, Megan Gale, Bo Derek, and of course F1 star Michael Schumacher.

When and How Much: *First Sunday in April, plus three days prior.* Tickets: A$39-A$99. Four-day ticket A$175. Grand Prix Ball around A$735.

Melbourne International Comedy Festival

Various venues, 03 9417 7711, comedyfestival.com.au

The Lowdown: The joke's on Melbourne at this side-splitting festival, which ranks alongside Montreal's Just for Laughs Festival. The Comedy Festival Gala takes place on opening night and features a sensational lineup of comedians, all of whom appear in individual shows later. From then on, more than 200 individual shows kick off across the city. In the Annual Great Debate square-off comedians rant on about a topic of minimum relevance and maximum hilarity, while the Big Laugh Out offers free outdoor gags for the masses.

When and How Much: *Mid-April to the first week in May.* Tickets from A$10-A$60.

June

Sydney Film Festival

Various venues, 02 9318 0999, sydneyfilmfestival.org

The Lowdown: Sydney might not have the same reputation for movie appeal as Cannes, but this flicker-fest attracts some brilliant feature films, documentaries, shorts, and animation. The festival rolls out in theaters and movie theaters across central Sydney, and everyone with a bohemian bent turns up for the revelry.

When and How Much: *Second and third week in June.* Tickets from A$10, and multi-tickets available.

Biennale of Sydney

16 venues, 02 9368 1411, biennaleofsydney.com.au

The Lowdown: Every two years, Sydney comes up with a daring extravaganza of modern art. Artists from more than 40 countries are showcased in various city galleries and outdoor spaces. Expect to see plenty of people taking lobsters for walks.

When and How Much: *Second week in June to end of August, even years only.* Most events free.

July

Melbourne International Film Festival

Various venues, 03 9417 2011, melbournefilmfestival.com.au

The Lowdown: As the temperature drops, a large section of the Melbourne population looks forward to a couple of weeks huddled in darkness checking out the latest in silver screen magic. The festival shows the cream of the Cannes Film Festival entries, including the Palme d'Or winner, as well as hundreds of other movies from around the world.

When and How Much: *Third week in July through second week in August.* From A$10.

September

Festival of the Winds

Bondi Beach, waverley.nsw.gov.au

The Lowdown: Traditional kites as well as dragons, manta rays, lobsters, and flowers take to the skies on the cliffs between Bondi and Bronte. Bondi Beach is colorful too, with spinning bowls, wind socks, and banners. There are even skydivers, as well as acrobats, clowns, minstrels, and dance and music from all over the world. Follow the crowds of families, couples, and tourists.

When and How Much: *Second Sunday in September.* Free.

Melbourne Fringe Festival

120 venues, 03 8412 8788, melbournefringe.com.au

The Lowdown: Yes, there are people walking around on stilts, but with some 3,000 artists and around 230 events taking place almost everywhere you look, this is a festival for people with short attention spans. Expect street comedy, amazing design, cabaret, dancing, circus, and vocal art among other things.

When and How Much: *Last week in September to second week in October.* Most events are free.

October

Manly Jazz Festival

Manly Corso, 02 9976 1430, manlyweb.com.au

The Lowdown: Jazz fans from across the nation converge on Manly for Australia's largest community-based jazz festival. It features over 60 free performances on five outdoor stages from noon until sundown, with pubs and clubs taking over after dark. Bring your trumpet and play solo on the beach.

When and How Much: *First weekend in October.* Daytime events free.

Melbourne International Arts Festival*

Various venues, 03 9662 4242, melbournefestival.com.au

The Lowdown: The Melbourne International Arts Festival presents unique international and Australian dance, theater, music, opera, and visual arts. There's urban contemporary art, dance from Africa, theater from Europe, music from South America, and artistic offerings from some of the best local talent. It's a major Melbourne event and it's heavily advertised and attended by a wide cross-section of the city, so expect tickets for the best shows to be sold out well in advance. The best bet is to book ahead via the internet.

When and How Much: *For 17 days, starting in mid-October.* Free to A$40.

November

Melbourne Cup Carnival*

Flemington Racecourse, Melbourne, 1 300 727 575, vrc.net.au

The Lowdown: When a mare called Makybe Diva won the Melbourne Cup in 2005 for the third year in a row, she cemented her place as a national legend. During four days of races, the Flemington track ups the stakes with the "race that stops a nation." All over Australia, production lines grind to a halt and office workers gather in front of the television. In Melbourne, it's even an official holiday. If you're at the Melbourne Cup, you'll witness Australia at its most glamorous. Ladies don giant hats, parties are copious—from the parking lot to the VIP tents—and the entire town seems to turn out to celebrate. In fact, in 2005, 383,784 people came for the carnival, bringing along more than 46,000 hats. This is a serious fashion event, so make sure you bring your most stylish outfits, men included. If you can't make it to the track, the next best spot is the live viewing station at Federation Square, where you'll find throngs of viewers enjoying cocktails and the company.

When and How Much: *First Tuesday in November and three days after.* Tickets range from A$50 to A$200. Lawn seats cost more.

Sculpture by the Sea

Bondi to Tamarama Coastal Walk, 02 8399 0233, sculpturebythesea.com

The Lowdown: Dozens of intriguing sculptures adorn the beaches and cliffs for this intriguing display, and people from all over the city head to Bondi to see the latest in outdoor art. Even those who aren't die-hard art fans will enjoy the view here—in addition to the unique sites of the festival, the coastal walk itself is one of the highlights of any visit to Sydney, with its breathtaking views over the water.

When and How Much: *First Thursday to third Sunday in November.* Free.

December

Carols in the Domain

The Domain Gardens, Sydney, 02 9429 0611, carolsinthedomain.com

The Lowdown: Bring that picnic basket and a blanket, and grab some brandy sauce for your Christmas pudding. The grasslands in front of the Art Gallery of New South Wales twinkle with close to 100,000 candles as big names in Australian and international music woo the crowd with Christmas carols. Obviously, the earlier you get there, the better the view. Some people camp out the night before.

When and How Much: *Saturday, mid-December.* Free.

Sydney to Hobart Yacht Race*

Sydney Harbour, rolexsydneyhobart.com

The Lowdown: Hundreds of thousands of spectators line the cliffs and harbor foreshore, and thousands more take to the water in a flotilla of boats, to cheer on the start of Australia's premier ocean yacht race. For 630 nautical miles, yachts of various sizes tackle the notoriously rough water on their way to the capital of Tasmania. The best place to watch the yachts head out is Middle Head in Mosman.

When and How Much: *Boxing Day.* Free.

New Year's Eve Fireworks (Sydney)*

Sydney Harbour, cityofsydney.nsw.gov.au/nye

The Lowdown: Get to the Rocks or Circular Quay early, or sit beside the Harbour Bridge at Milsons Point and watch the spectacle—these areas have restricted access, and once they fill up, late comers are turned away. Another great option is to cross the bridge and view the celebration from Blues Point or Bradfield Park. Wherever you choose, be aware that checkpoints are set up to search bags—no glass or alcohol is allowed, but there are plenty of places to buy it. Sydney is one of the best places in the world to ring in the New Year. The Harbour Bridge gushes like a waterfall, the sky explodes above you, water barges fizz and crackle, and the Opera House glitters under the light. There are "family fireworks" at 9pm, but the real show kicks off at midnight. If you want something even more spectacular, book a cruise on the harbor—just check around the ferry station (well in advance) to see what your options are. Some tickets are even available for boats that participate in the Harbour of Lights parade that takes place earlier in the evening.

When and How Much: *New Year's Eve.* Free.

EXPERIENCE SYDNEY

Every city has a thousand faces. Which one you see depends on your angle. We've crafted two in-depth itineraries for Sydney to help you discover what makes it Australia's coolest city. Packed with hot restaurants, smart clubs, and fashionable fun, *Hot & Cool Sydney* (p.62)—planned for Thursday to Saturday (Thursdays being often the best nights for partying with locals)—and *Classic Sydney* (p.104)—Friday to Sunday—will help you find the best ways to experience the city. Whichever one—or ones—you choose, it will keep you buzzing for three perfect, high-energy days and nights. Sleep is purely optional—just the way Aussies like it.

Hot & Cool Sydney

There's a certain attitude intrinsic to Sydney that combines hot and cool effortlessly—in a way no other city in the world quite does. It's high-energy yet low-key beach culture coupled with sleek cosmopolitan flair. The two ebb and flow and mix and match throughout this harbor-front city, creating clubs, restaurants, shops, and hotels that are at once chic and friendly. While you're certain to find enough fun and culture to fill your nights and days, one thing you won't find in Sydney is pretension. Everyone is welcome here, even if you don't have the right Choos. Of course, having the right pair of perfect pumps can be great fun, but your flip-flops will do just fine, too.

Note: Venues in bold are described in detail in the listings that follow the itinerary. Venues followed by an asterisk (*) are recommended as both a restaurant and a destination bar.

Hot & Cool Sydney: The Perfect Plan (3 Nights and Days)

Perfect Plan Highlights

Thursday

Afternoon	**Jet boat tour, Seaplane tour, Harley tour**
Pre-dinner	**Hemmesphere**
Dinner	**Sushi e, Mint*, Spice I Am**
Nighttime	**Hugo's, Candy's**
Late-Night	**Lady Lux, Dragonfly**

Friday

Morning	**BridgeClimb, Sydney Tower, Msm. Contemp. Art**
Lunch	**Wildfire, Cru*, Yoshii**
Afternoon	**Swim, spa, Luna Park**
Pre-dinner	**Industrie Bar*, Aqua**
Dinner	**Longrain*, Lucio's, Local***
Nighttime	**Ruby Rabbit**
Late-Night	**Tank**

Saturday

Morning	**Glass Brasserie, Bondi, Paddington Market**
Lunch	**Swell*, Ravesi's***
Afternoon	**Bondi Beach, diving with sharks**
Pre-dinner	**Zeta Bar, Icebergs***
Dinner	**Young Alfred, Flying Fish, Café Sydney**
Nighttime	**The Loft, Cargo*, Slip Inn***
Late-Night	**Home**

Morning After

Brunch	**Kam Fook**

Hotel: **Establishment Hotel**

3pm The heart of Sydney is its bay, so don't mess around—get right to it. Try a fast-paced **jet boating** tour of **Sydney Harbour**. Expect plenty of exhilarating fishtails and tight corner turns, and close-up twirls alongside the **Opera House**. You could also get a sea-gull's view of the city with a **Sydney by Seaplane** adventure, which whisks you up above the glorious sites and puts you down with a splash. For a different take on the Emerald City, jump on the back of a Harley Davidson and zoom around the streets with **Blue Thunder Bike Tours**. A 1.5-hour ride shows off the city center and its surrounding suburbs, and even Bondi, Tamarama, and Bronte beaches.

6pm Upstairs at the Establishment Hotel's seriously seductive **Hemmesphere**, you'll find a fashionable crowd unwinding in a stylish space.

8pm Dinner If the Establishment complex is weaving its spell over you, then stay put, and slip onto a timber stool at **Sushi e**, the intimate spot beloved by a discerning and ultra-hip crowd. Alternatively, check out **Mint*** for a contemporary mix of Asian and

HOT & COOL

European dishes. Fancy some fabulous Thai food in a humble setting instead? Well, just hop in a cab for a ten-minute ride to **Spice I Am**, set below a grungy inner-city pub.

11pm Tonight you're on a first-name basis with the locals. Take a cab to Kings Cross and join the well-heeled posse at **Hugo's Lounge**. Just as cool is **Candy's Apartment**.

1am The place to dance the night away is in the intimate boudoir of **Lady Lux**, slap-bang in the middle of Sydney's red-light district. And "The Cross," as locals call King's Cross, is where you'll find **Dragonfly's** funky house.

3am **Harry's Cafe de Wheels** is an end-of-night tradition for Sydneysiders. Grab your spot in line for a meat pie.

Friday

9am Breakfast The Establishment Hotel's Garden Bar isn't just for drinking—try some eggs under its glass atrium, a space that incorporates historic brick walls from the original fire-damaged building and lots of giant columns and black bamboo.

10am Start your morning at the **Museum of Contemporary Art**, where you'll find works by some of Australia's most creative minds. If you want to get your day off to a more adventurous start, get strapped into a harness and climb right to the top of the Sydney Harbour Bridge with **BridgeClimb Sydney**. The other daredevil option is to head for **Sydney Tower Skywalk** to circumnavigate the top of the building outside on a glass-floored walkway. The views are stupendous.

1pm Lunch Swing around the water's edge to the Overseas Passenger Terminal at Circular Quay and walk into **Wildfire**. Here you can stare at the Sydney Opera House while indulging in the hot and smoky fare coming out of Sydney's most comprehensive bank of wood-fired ovens, rotisseries, and Brazilian-inspired churrasco grill. Or go for French colonial food at **Cru***, on level three of the same building. If you crave a sushi feast, then opt for **Yoshii**, one of the city's best Japanese eateries.

3pm From Circular Quay, take a water taxi across the harbor to the Milsons Point wharf and try to beat one of the 86 world records set at the outdoor swimming hole at **North Sydney Olympic Swimming Pool**. The views of the Harbour Bridge and across to the Sydney Opera House are impressive. Right next door is **Luna Park**—you can't miss the giant smiling clown face looking out across the water to Circular Quay. There are plenty of fun rides here, including a Ferris wheel to take you up high. But if the morning has left you in need of restoration, now's your chance to get hot rocks on your chakra lines at the Hilton's **LivingWell Premier Health Club**.

6:30pm You could stay on the far side of the bay for cocktails and dinner—and more fabulous Opera House and Harbour Bridge views—at **Aqua Dining**. Otherwise head back to the city for champagne cocktails in the after-work crush at the trendy **Industrie Bar***.

8:30pm Dinner If you haven't had Thai yet, take your chances with the wait and head by cab to the über-chic **Longrain*** for some communal dining. The best spot for Italian is **Lucio's**, in Paddington. You'll find **Local*** around here too, where you can enjoy high-quality bistro food with oysters and cocktails to start.

10:30pm A stroll down the Paddington and Oxford Street strip takes you into the gay heart of Sydney. If that's your scene, make some time for the bar and club mix of the **Colombian Hotel**. A less camp alternative is **Ruby Rabbit**, which exudes European cool and paisley wallpaper. Meanwhile, **Middle Bar**, above Taylor Square, is a good starting point for a big night on the town.

1am You could stay on at Ruby Rabbit, but for heavy house music, head back to the Establishment and slither into **Tank**. If you're staying at the hotel, you're sure to get in.

9am Breakfast Walk up to the **Glass Brasserie** at the Hilton Hotel for some healthy eating and wheat-grass shakes. This elegant room is the centerpiece of the newly renovated hotel and has close-up city views through glass windows.

10am Today is all about the leisurely life. If the ocean is luring you like a siren's song, have a cab drop you at Bondi Beach. Wander to the north end and onto the ocean walk, which will take you on a breathtaking stroll to nearby Bronte Beach. The 1.5-mile (2.5km) trail offers panoramic ocean views from a cliffside path. Stop off along the way for a dip in the sea at tiny Tamarama Beach. If the beach doesn't appeal, head to Paddington, where you can explore the Paddington Market—a hip Saturday-only event. Grab a cup of coffee from one of the many cafes that line the nearby shopping street, then check out trendy stores including the Diva's Closet and Scanlon Theodore.

1pm Lunch At Bronte, **Swell** is where the locals like to grab an outdoor seat and enjoy a delicious meal. You could also hang with the beach bohemians at **Ravesi's*** on Bondi.

2:30pm Throw a towel down on the sand and soak in Sydney's most famous—and most glorious—beach scene at Bondi. If you're feeling adventurous, you could even take a surfing lesson with **Let's Go Surfing**. Or cab it back to Circular Quay and jump on a fast jet cat to Manly for a late-afternoon session of diving with the sharks. No, not off the beach—but in a giant tank at **Oceanworld**, complete with enormous, mostly harmless, gray nurse sharks and huge cavernous-mouthed rays. The last dive of the afternoon starts at 4:30pm on Saturdays and runs for around 2.5 hours.

5:30pm Too early for a cocktail? Not on the patio at **Icebergs***, where you can watch Bondi's day scene slowly fade with the sun, or lie in one of the hammocks in the bar. The large glass windows here stare right along the length of the beach, making it a Sydney icon for wave watching. If you get back to the city in time for a cocktail before dinner, then the spot of choice to join socialites and international highfliers is **Zeta Bar**, at the Hilton Hotel.

8pm Dinner For something light, go for a pizza at **Young Alfred**, an institution in this city. Or head to **Café Sydney** for steak, seafood, or chicken with awesome Harbour Bridge views and a great cocktail list. Or zip across to Darling Harbour for a dinner of mud crab with coriander and chilies at **Flying Fish**.

11pm If you finish with dinner a little early, you can enjoy the laid-back waterside atmosphere at **The Loft** in Darling Harbor until midnight. Another option is the **Cargo Bar***, which has a lively drinking scene and late-night club. You can also go for a beer and a dance at the nearby **Slip Inn***.

1am Head for **Home**—it's the nightclub of choice for late night, with four levels of hot dance music until sunrise.

The Morning After

Grab a cab for the ride out to **Kam Fook**, where you'll find the best dim sum the city has to offer.

Hot & Cool Sydney: The Key Neighborhoods

Bondi Famous for its surfing, lifeguards, and sun-kissed bodies, Bondi basks in its sexy reputation.

Bronte This is an eastern-suburbs beach with nice cafes that lies only a cliff-top walk away from Bondi.

Darling Harbour Sydney's waterside playground offers cool restaurants and bars overlooking the cruise boats in the bay.

Kings Cross It's seedy in parts, but also home to some high-class restaurants and plenty of nightclubs.

Manly An across-the-bay suburb with glorious beaches and a laid-back vibe.

Milsons Point Just across the harbor from the Sydney Opera House, this little suburb is famed for its swimming pool with bridge views and the smiling clown face above a theme park.

Oxford Street and Paddington The center of Sydney's large gay community is a vibrant place strung with fashionable boutiques and restaurants with a backdrop of historic terraced houses.

The Rocks This is Sydney's oldest and most historic neighborhood.

Woolloomooloo Trendy hotels and restaurants now line historic wharves that once were the center for much of Sydney's commerce.

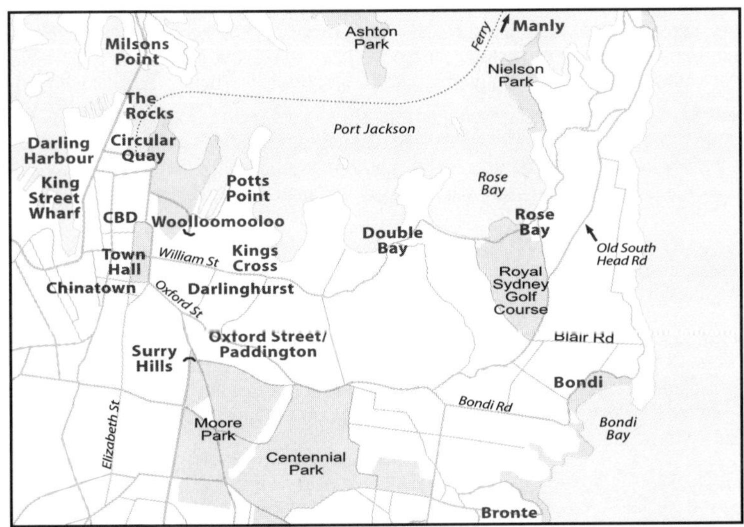

Hot & Cool Sydney: The Shopping Blocks

Bondi Beach

Life's a beach on Bondi, and bare flesh is the order of the day. Try these less-is-more clothing stores before hitting the waves.

Bikini Island The shop stocks all the major Australian surf brands including the too-hot Tigerlily, designed by Bondi local fashion babe Jodhi Meares. 38 Campbell Parade, 02 9300 9446

Purl Harbour Quirky knitwear. Shop from the shelves or order a made-to-measure knitted garment, from socks to ponchos—they will even whip up knitted homewares. Unit 4, 16 Hall St. (entry via Jacques Ave.), 02 9365 1521

Six Ounce Boardstore Retro surfboards fashioned in the style of those early riders who surfed for love rather than money, man. Pick of the rack are the Morning of the Earth boards from Byron Bay shapers Crystal Cylinders—solid boards with artwork worthy of a wall hanging. Shop 2, 144-148 Glenayr Ave., 02 9300 8339

Tuchuzy Boutique L.A.-style beachwear and streetwear for hot guys and gals, favorite picks include Hallican Boodie retro bikinis, evening dresses matched with flip-flops and Sass and Bide jeans—as seen on *Sex and the City*'s Carrie Bradshaw. Visiting luminaries include Clare Danes, Lara Flynn Boyle, and Vin Diesel. 90 Gould St., 02 9365 5371

Inner West

Hire a driver for the day and head west to the grungy edge of the city, home to writers and aspiring rock bands. You won't make the tour on foot, but if the bling of Sydney's east is getting you down, the suburbs of Glebe and Newtown are an urban refreshment.

Deus Ex Machina This motorcycle concept-store is as much a gallery as a place to shop. It's set in a huge converted warehouse, where rebels without a cause can drool over vintage motorcycles, jackets, and books, or fill up their tank with a drink at the in-store bar. 98-104 Parramatta Rd., Camperdown, 02 9557 6866

Gleebooks When a visiting author is in town, you will likely find him or her at Gleebooks. The shop is a favorite of academics and bibliophiles and the first place to get hot-to-handle publications. 49 Glebe Point Rd., 02 9660 2333

Pretty Dog Find it at Pretty Dog and you know you're ahead of the game. The store stocks men's and women's clothing by up-and-coming Australian and New Zealand designers. Pretty Dog had Tsubi in its first season. Other cult brands include Nicola Finetti, Lover, Karen Walker, and Claude Maus. 1a Brown St., Newtown, 02 9519 7839

Paddington

Sydney's shopping mecca. While the main drag of Oxford Street plays host to the big names, head down the back streets for the boutique gems.Here's a sample of the best, but you'll stumble across many more.

Collette Dinnigan Dinnigan was the first Australian to show in the Paris ready-to-wear collections, and her dreamy dresses and lingerie are top picks for local and visiting celebrities. 33 William St., 02 9360 6691

The Corner Shop The little sister of the Belinda boutiques, the Corner Shop is the place for the latest denim imports, mixed with vintage gems and customized finds, plus the hottest new Aussie designers. 43 William St., 02 9380 9828

The Diva's Closet Hollywood glamour on the other side of the world. When a girl needs a piece that she knows no one else will be wearing, she heads to the Diva, Regina Evans, for a vintage fix. *By appointment only.* 32 William St., 02 9361-6659 / 0408 964 67

Easton Pearson Boho queens flock to the gypsy-inspired designs of Easton Pearson, so expect lots of luxury fabric in ethnic patterns. The place to find women's wear for the glamorous hippie inside us all. 18 Elizabeth St., 02 9331 4433

Scanlan & Theodore Sure, it's a Melbourne label, but Sydney women claim Scanlan & Theodore as their own. Need an emergency outfit? This is your one-stop shop. 122 Oxford St., 02 9380 9388

Tim Olsen Gallery Represents more than 25 of Australia's hottest artists. Pick up a gorgeous work for your home, or as an investment. Or just browse for the pleasure of it. 76 Paddington St., 02 9360 9854

Surry Hills

The edgy end of town, home to artists, actors, and other creative types who spurn the word "fashion," Surry Hills is to Sydney what Soho is to New York, and the locals can spot a tourist a mile away. Here's where to shop to blend in.

Spence and Lyda Ultra-modern furniture and homewares in this urban warehouse space. Favorite picks include rugs and glassware from colorful Italian label Missoni. 15 Foster St., 02 9212 6747

Wheels and Doll Baby Adored by Deborah Harry, this is no place for conservative dressers. Wheels and Doll Baby mixes biker chic with 1950s glamour for a rockabilly look, sold around the world under the catchphrase of "clothes to catch a millionaire." 259 Crown St., 02 9361 6244

Zoo Emporium Zoo stocks a great range of Studio 54–era clothing and accessories for the history-conscious fashionista. 332 Crown St., 02 9380 5990

Hot & Cool Sydney: The Hotels

The Blacket • CBD • Trendy (42 rms)

This boutique hotel is right in the heart of Sydney's central business District, which makes it a top spot if you want nightclub and restaurant action right on your doorstep. By the look of the building's 1850s neoclassical architecture, you might be fooled into thinking this is a classical sort of place—but you'd be seriously misguided. Instead, it offers a contemporary and minimalist approach, with a restricted palette of creams, whites, dark browns, blacks, and charcoal gray. The heritage aspect hasn't been forgotten, though, and the majesty of the original grand staircase is reflected in the sumptuousness of some of the New York–style Loft Suites, which have the added silkiness of rich velvet drapes, claw-foot baths, and time-polished wooden floorboards. They look out over the hustle and bustle of downtown George Street. Spacious deluxe rooms come in either a standard hotel version, a studio version (with a separate living area), or a two-bedroom version. Standard rooms on the 7th floor have a small balcony overlooking King Street. The restaurant Minc is known for its intimate booths and its good lamb and seafood. $$$ 70 King St. (George St.), 02 9279 3030, theblacket.com

Blue, Woolloomooloo Bay • Woolloomooloo • Trendy (100 rms)

The Finger Wharf, built in 1914, was once the arrival point for many thousands of migrants. Today it's an ultra-modern complex featuring apartments, waterfront restaurants, and the ultra-trendy Blue. Formerly the W Hotel, Blue was bought in 2006 by the Indian Hotels Company Limited, which operates 73 luxury hotels in India and across the globe, including the Taj group in India. The wharf juts out into the water opposite a private marina, and many of the best rooms overlook the boats and the city skyline beyond. The best of the lot are the split-level loft rooms on the 5th floor. These make good use of the heritage structure of the wharf, have wonderful views and good light, and have a living area below a separate bedroom. The large, narrow foyer area leads onto the atmospheric Water Bar, lit a glorious deep blue at night, where guests—a stylish set in town for both business and pleasure—can stretch out on banquettes or lie back on the vast ottomans to soak in the casual and sophisticated ambience. A cafe and plush modernist seating areas make up the rest. The whole lot resembles the inside of a high-design whale, with its ancient ribs on display. A well-manicured spa offers body treatments, which is especially welcome after the 15-minute walk across Hyde Park from the city. $$$ The Wharf at Woolloomooloo (Cowper Wharf Rd.), 02 9331 9000, tajhotels.com

Establishment Hotel • CBD • Trendy (33 rms)

Slinky dresses, designer patterned shirts, and a cool air of sophistication ensure the clientele fit in well with the intimate refined modernity of Sydney's trendiest hotel. The Establishment Hotel occupies the back end of a historic ironmongery and general store, and is part of a huge and very glamorous entertainment complex, which includes the Moroccan-inspired Hemmesphere lounge (see p.91), Tank nightclub (see p.96), two of the city's most fashionable bars, and Est. and Sushi e restaurants (see p.77 and 84). This exciting combination was conceived by the youthful Sydney identity Justin Hemmes, who has carved his chic, clean-cut style out of the bones of this 1893 building. The hotel's back alleyway entrance, its shadowy, moody corridors, and its small windows that look out onto brick walls give it the intimate feel of an urban sanctuary. Rooms are themed "dark" and "light." The dark rooms make good use of the original exposed ceiling beams and wide wooden floorboards tinted a tea-tannin brown. Black-and-white bedding, and a black marble bathroom complement the look. Light rooms have white marble bathrooms and camel-and beige-colored carpets. The color schemes ride across both room categories—the Establishment rooms and the junior rooms. Establishment rooms have a separate living area with minimal but modish furniture. Guests eat breakfast downstairs in the palm-filled Garden Bar. $$$ 5 Bridge Ln. (Pitt St.), 02 9240 3100, merivale.com.au

The Kirketon Hotel • Darlinghurst • Trendy (40 rms)

One of the country's top hotels for ambience and design, the Kirketon is an oasis of style and glamour set in the heart of Sydney's most vibrant cafe strip. The hotel attracts plenty of fashion shoots, and the clientele includes film, TV, and design-industry types. The best rooms are the executive rooms, which have lipstick-red carpets, king-size beds with fine linen, a good-size bathtub, and mohair throws. They are simple but elegant, with a contemporary urban feel—but this is a mid-price boutique hotel, so expect trendy over true quality or luxuriousness. Many rooms are on the small side. $$ 229 Darlinghurst Rd. (Liverpool St.), 02 9332 2011 / 1 800 332 920, kirketon.com.au

Medusa Hotel • Kings Cross • Trendy (18 rms)

The Medusa is one of those discreet hotels that won't drop the names of the supermodels and celebrities that have stayed there, but rest assured that plenty of them have favored the privacy and inner-city chic that the Medusa prides itself on. Boutique in substance and cool in style, Medusa pays homage to bold theatrics in its color and furnishings, from canary-yellow chaise lounges and cream ladybug spotted bedspreads with large brown circles, to cutting-edge cubical bathrooms. It's a perfect meld of Old World Victorian charm updated with modern whimsy. The better grand rooms are in a historic part of the building, where the ceilings are high and room dimensions are huge. All have outlooks of either the passing parade of bohemians and inner-city types on Darlinghurst Road, or a beautiful inner courtyard and a shallow reflection pool. The ground-floor rooms are best if you are seeking quiet. You can sit around here with a drink from the honesty bar at reception. There's no restaurant, but you can order delivery from some great restaurants, including Oh Calcutta, just up the road. $$$ 267 Darlinghurst Rd. (Liverpool St.), 02 9331 1000, medusa.com.au

Park Hyatt Sydney • The Rocks • Timeless (158 rms)

For a real celebration, treat yourself to the best waterside hotel in Sydney—if you can get in, that is. Some that did include Elton John, the Rolling Stones, Bette Midler, and Liz Hurley. With nearly year-round 100 percent occupancy, the Park Hyatt is the kind of place that makes you wish you'd either booked many months earlier—or spent the time becoming famous. The hotel is a gorgeous sandstone structure situated right on the harbor—on the foreshore walk that leads from the Rocks to Circular Quay in one direction and underneath the Sydney Harbour Bridge in the other. There are 36 suites, but if you want something a bit less ostentatious, go for an opera view room. Here, you can lie in bed,

HOT & COOL

open the curtains with your remote control, and look directly at the white sails gleaming in the morning sunlight. These rooms also have a balcony. Visit the Little Kitchen for high tea, the Club Bar for cognacs, whiskeys, and a Cuban cigar, or the Harbour Bar for some of the city's best martinis. $$$$ 7 Hickson Rd. (Albion St.), 02 9241 1234, sydney.park.hyatt.com

The Sebel Pier One Sydney • The Rocks • Trendy (160 rms)
You can't get any closer to the harbor than this over-water hotel set on a historic wharf. Situated right under the Sydney Harbour Bridge and with exceptional close-up views of the ferries and boats plying Walsh Bay, the Sebel Pier One is a cocktail of heritage and modern lifestyle that caters to luxury business travelers and sophisticated tourists. It makes good use of restored roof beams and polished floorboards and combines them with lots of glass—the lobby even has a glass floor, and if you look hard enough you might see a few fish swimming by. The rooms sparkle with the views, with the superior water queen and the king harbour rooms ahead of the rest. All feature crisp white bedspreads and passing yachts, which ensures an enchanting nautical feel. The restaurant here has close-up water views through huge windows. A private mooring point allows you to arrive and depart by water taxi if you wish. $$$$ 11 Hickson Rd. (George St.), 02 8298 9999 / 1 800 780 485, sebelpierone.com.au

Swiss Grand Resort & Spa • Bondi Beach • Trendy (203 rms)
Bondi Beach! How cool is that? With rooms overlooking the tanned bodies, the golden sand, and the roaring surf, the Swiss Grand occupies one of the most sought-after locations in the world. This imposing white edifice hides a grand lobby and rooms so good they're all called suites—but because of its size and location, the clientele here is very mixed, with everything from wedding parties to vacationing families with kids in tow. The rooms you should opt for are the executive view suites, which have a king-size bed, a large living and dining area, a spa, and a spacious balcony overlooking the ocean. All rooms in the hotel are located on the 3rd, 4th, and 5th floors—and so all have good views—but you should put in a request for one on the 5th. It's not guaranteed that you'll get it, but the hotel will at least try. There's a good outdoor pool here and the Samsara Day Spa, which offers a revitalizing traditional Balinese massage. If you can take your eyes off the beach, you can watch the chef barbecue your steak to perfection at the outdoor Deck BBQ and Bar. $$$ Campbell Parade (Beach Rd.), 02 9365 5666 / 1 800 655 252, swissgrand.com.au

Hot & Cool Sydney: The Restaurants

The Annandale Hotel* • Annandale • Pub Grub

This Sydney icon is known for its great live music scene and crowded bar, but the food is not bad either. *See Sydney Hot & Cool Nightlife, p.87, for details.* $ ≡ 17 Parramatta Rd. (Nelson St.), 02 9550 1078, annandalehotel.com.au

Aqua Dining • Milsons Point • Modern Australian

A short ferry or water taxi ride from Circular Quay, Aqua Dining offers a stadium-style view of the Sydney Harbour Bridge framing the Opera House—the prized Sydney icons are rarely visible together from one spot. Below lies the splashing fun of Olympic Pool and Sydney Harbour, with its teeming activity visible from every table and the long deck outside. Fine food is matched by an extensive wine list, with wines by the glass and half bottles ideal for those office lunchtime escapees. For an overview, order the Aqua Tasting Plate—a mini-degustation of five perfectly formed dishes, easily shared as an entrée. The main course list at lunch and dinner strongly showcase regional produce, and may include calamari from the Hawkesbury, Yamba prawns, or WA lamb. But pace yourself so you can manage one of chef Jeff Turnbull's superb desserts. *Daily noon-2:30pm and 6:30-10pm.* $$$ ≡ North Sydney Olympic Pool (Cnr Paul and Northcliff Sts.), 02 9964 9998, aquadining.com.au

Bar Europa* • CBD • Continental

This hidden gem draws after-work crowds for cocktails and a nibble. *See Hot & Cool Nightlife, p.87, for details.* $$ ≡ Basement, 88 Elizabeth St. (King St.), 02 9232 3377

The Bayswater Brasserie • Kings Cross • Modern Australian

With bay windows that open onto the street, the restaurant at this classy pub provides one of the best vantage points to watch the colorful characters of the Cross. If you are more into being seen than people-watching, take a seat at the oyster bar or strut your way to the back bar for award-winning cocktails in the Hanging Gardens of Babylon–style courtyard. But if you are serious about food and wine, then make a reservation for a window seat and sample the best of both worlds with a fun-loving, casually sophisticated clientele. Oysters are a form of currency in Sydney food circles and the oyster bar at Bayswater has its share of riches—with wines to match. Taste oysters from Victoria or Tasmania or get lucky with a dozen from Coffin Bay on the NSW south coast, the current oysters de rigueur. When you have eaten your fill, move on to some classic Australian seafood pairings such as pork belly with seared scallops. *Mon-Thu, Sat 6pm-late, Fri noon-3pm and 6pm-late, Sun 5-10pm.* $$$ ≡ 32 Bayswater Rd. (Ward Ave), 02 9357 2177, bayswaterbrasserie.com.au

Becasse • CBD • French

Formerly a humble Surry Hills bistro dishing up exquisite plates of French classics, Becasse has caught the nouveau Parisian wave sweeping Sydney. The new, and much larger, site at the slick end of the city also signals a swing back to opulence. After more than a decade of stainless steel and polished timber in

Sydney restaurants, Becasse delights with a yard-wide chandelier and plush surfaces. Run by a husband-and-wife team, Justin is in the kitchen while Georgia works the floor. The service is smooth and knowledgeable, and the food harkens back to North's British ancestry and French training, such as the infamous confit of pig's head. The degustation menu with matching wines is nirvana for foodies. Others would be wise to order three courses, as the meals are exquisite but on the small side. The quince tart is a good dessert option. *Tue-Fri noon-2pm and 6-9:30pm, Sat 6-9:30pm.* $$$ ▭ 204 Clarence St. (Druitt St.), 02 9283 3440, becasse.com.au

Bentley Restaurant and Bar* • Surry Hills • Tapas

As any Melbournite will tell you, Sydney does not do the restaurant-bar combination as well as the Southern capital. Traditionally Sydney bars just do drinks, perhaps with some paltry bar snacks, and restaurants just do food, with wine. The Bentley, a converted pub, is the latest in a line of venues that are breaking the mold. Possibly the coolest restaurant-bar this side of the equator, the restaurant is divided down the middle by a banquette with drinkers sampling from the spirit-laden bar on one side and diners sitting on 1950s chairs at retro plywood tables, on the other. The rose-tinted lighting adds to the sense of fun. The food is also adventurous, pairing an extensive wine list (that can be sampled at the bar as well) with tapas-style meals, from sardines on toast to the unusual popcorn chicken and a banana milkshake served with a chocolate straw. The crowd, like the food, is anything but boring, a mix of foodie types and glamorous Surry Hills locals. If you like your food to entertain, this is the place to be. *Tue-Sat noon-2:30pm and 6-10:30pm.* $$ ▭ 320 Crown St. (Campbell St.), 02 9332 2344, thebentley.com.au

Bill's • Darlinghurst • Continental

Expatriate Sydneysiders will confess to "Bill's dreams," subconscious cravings for the creamy scrambled eggs and smooth ricotta hotcakes at this iconic breakfast bar. The modern atmosphere is complemented by chirpy service, befitting a cafe that's made breakfast the main meal of the day. But lunchtime doesn't disappoint. Chicken club sandwiches are devoured by well-sculpted men while their tanned female companions feast on carbohydrate-free delights such as steak salad (an updated version of the popular steak sandwich). On the weekends the line for tables snakes all the way up to Darlinghurst Road. Waits at Bill's 2, a Surry Hills outpost, are usually just as lengthy. The Surry Hills campus offers an almost identical menu, including such never-to-be-replaced dishes as coconut bread. *Mon-Sat 7:30am-3pm and 6-10pm, Sun 8:30am-3pm. Bill's 2: Daily 7am-10pm.* $ ▭ 433 Liverpool St. (Victoria Ave.), 02 9360 9631; Surry Hills: 359 Crown St., 02 9360 4762, bills.com.au

Billy Kwong • Surry Hills • Chinese

As darkness falls on Crown Street, eager diners with the latest hairstyles and imported denim gather at this hip modern Chinese restaurant that prides itself on organic produce. Hungry locals in the know arrive early to secure a table rather than risk the waiting list. Billy Kwong is also situated a stone's throw from laid-back drinking holes the Dolphin and the Clock, so a wait is not necessarily a bad thing. Once inside, the room resembles a Chinese teahouse. The open kitchen provides a theater for dramatic cooking techniques as woks are thrown from one stove to another. Don't leave without trying the signature crisp-skinned duck in blood orange sauce. *Mon-Thu 6-10pm, Fri-Sat 6-11pm, Sun 6-10pm* $$ 3/355 Crown St. (Albion St.), 02 9332 3300

Bird Cow Fish • Surry Hills • Modern Australian

Part of a recent explosion of relaxed bistros in the trendy Surry Hills district, Bird Cow Fish is the kind of comfortable restaurant you wish would set up shop on your street. Sure, on a Friday and Saturday night it can be tricky to get a table (the restaurant doesn't take reservations) but there is no shortage of nearby pubs and bars to keep you occupied while you wait. With ceiling-to-floor glass windows, the restaurant is not the most intimate venue. During the day, the L-shaped spot is a bustling cheese shop with a small espresso bar. At night, the dark timber tables and padded Thonet chairs in the bistro are home to bustling, noisy groups of casual diners. The food comes in generous servings of simple yet satisfying fare: salt cod fritters, chicken confit, and the signature beef cheek pie are the perfect comfort food for the world-weary traveler. *Mon-Sat 8am-10pm, Sun 8am-5pm.* $$$ Shops 4 and 5, 500 Crown St. (Rainford St.), 02 9380 4090, birdcowfish.com.au

Bistro Moncur • Woollahra • French

It is easy to see why this eastern suburbs stalwart was a favorite venue for Keanu Reeves while on location for *The Matrix*. A polished dining room adorned with a wall-length mural and food that says restaurant favorites rather than bistro fare combine with shiny timber surfaces that echo the murmurs and laughter from adjoining tables. The menu changes every few months, but it's the French classics such as marinated salmon and French onion soup that keep the mid-week regulars, well-groomed locals, and retail princesses coming back for more. Moncur doesn't take reservations, so mid-week is the best time to drop in. But if you do have to wait, a spare half hour is the perfect excuse to loiter in the adjoining bar at the Woollahra Hotel. *Tue-Sat noon-3pm and 6-10:30pm, Sun noon-3pm and 6-9pm.* $$$ The Woollahra Hotel, 116 Queen St. (Moncur St.), 02 9363 2519, bistromoncur.com.au

Bistrode • Surry Hills • British/French

A new kid on the block in Surry Hills, Bistrode serves up the kind of homestyle meals diners don't have time to prepare themselves. French combines with British staples such as bangers and mash on a menu that changes weekly, accompanied by a small but carefully chosen wine list. The room is a renovated butcher's shop, with an olive-tiled bar and the original window front and exterior, helping make it feel like part of the local wallpaper. Designers and workers from neighboring art galleries stop by for a low-key dinner of corned beef while other tables are taken up by casually dressed couples for a mid-week dinner where the ingredients need no explanation. Service is friendly and efficient, and the overall mood is relaxed intimacy. *Tue-Thu, Sat 6-10pm, Fri noon-3pm and 6 10pm.* $$ 478 Bourke St. (Devonshire St.), 02 9380 7333

Blue Orange* • Bondi Beach • Fusion

Relaxed cafe by day, groovy restaurant by night, Blue Orange morphs between the two faces of Bondi. It's a favorite of expat Parisians, who gather over European-quality coffee before heading down Hall Street for a day at the beach. Grab a book at the bookstore across the way, or pass the time people-watching from the lounge-style tables. At night, the lights go down in the timber-walled room and an occasional DJ spins global tunes for chiseled surfer boys and blond girls with bare shoulders and a beach glow. The food is eclectic; try starting with the za'atar-dusted Lebanese bread and yogurt dip to accompany that first cocktail. *Tue 6:30pm-late, Wed-Sat 7am-5pm and 6:30pm-late, Sun 7am-5pm.* $ ≡ 49 Hall St. (Campbell St.), 02 9300 9885

Café Sydney • Circular Quay • Continental

Possibly the chicest way to unwind on a Sunday afternoon, Café Sydney, with its raised dining room and weekend jazz sessions is the ultimate harborside dining destination. Generous servings of eye fillet with mash is the popular choice for mid-week lunchers from neighboring law firms. As the sun sets, the suits are replaced by the young and beautiful and the tables are set for romance. For maximum ambience, come Sunday afternoon, when there's live jazz. Catch the lift up to the top of the historic Customs House Building, and stop off in the bar for a cocktail before stepping up into the dining room to share a platter of Sydney seafood. Ask for a veranda table to secure the best views of the Opera House and the bridge. *Mon-Fri noon-11pm, Sat 5-11pm, Sun noon-4pm.* $$$ ≡ Level 5, Customs House, 31 Alfred St. (Loftus St.), 02 9251 8683, cafesydney.com

Cargo Bar* • King Street Wharf • Pub Grub

This rowdy spot on the wharves has some of the best pizza around. *See Sydney Hot & Cool Nightlife, p.88, for details.* $$ ≡ 52-60 The Promenade (Erskine St.), 02 9262 1777, cargobar.com.au

Catalina • Rose Bay • French

Best Restaurants with Views In one of the most idyllic waterside locations at the established end of town, Catalina provides a pelican's view of the harbor and the mansions of neighboring Point Piper. The restaurant is tucked away from busy New South Head Road by the grassy expanse of Lyne Park. The curved room and balcony are positioned to make the most of the sparkling view, and the all-white interior makes you feel as though the restaurant is floating alongside the sailing boats and seaplanes anchored in the bay. At other tables, young and beautiful couples dine on snapper with Paris mash, stepping out onto the balcony for cigarettes and private conversation in full view of the restaurant, which is exactly how they like it. *Mon-Sat noon-late, Sun noon-5pm.* $$$ ≡ 1 Sunderland Ave. (New South Head Rd.), 02 9371 0555, catalinarosebay.com.au

Cru* • Circular Quay • French

Recently revamped, Cru is the fine dining option at the tri-level Cruise Bar and lounge. While suits gather for Friday night after-work drinks at the swinging bar and lounge below, level three is fast returning to the premier cuisine made famous by former chef Warren Turnbull. With sous-chef Ed Halmagyi now running the kitchen, the restaurant has also been given a warmer, more intimate makeover with plush furnishings and sheer curtains. The food has also returned to French colonial flavors—stuffed lamb, duck leg with sweetbreads, or oysters served with a variety of dressings and washed down with vintage champagne are the order of the night. One thing has remained the same—the restaurant still boasts some of the best views in the Emerald City, with wraparound panoramas across the harbor to the Sydney Opera House. Drop in for a drink at the balcony bar before your meal. *Mon-Fri noon-3pm and 6pm-late, Sat 6pm-late.* $$$ ≡ Level 3, Overseas Passenger Terminal (Circular Quay West), 02 9251 1188

Danks Street Depot • Waterloo • Modern Australian

Best Swank Lunch Spots Try to avoid this edgy cafe-gallery on Sunday mornings, when parking can be tricky during services at the neighboring Pentecostal church. But the other six mornings of the week, this is the place to rub shoulders with artists and off-duty restaurateurs over bowls of latte and fruit toast, or lunch on foodie favorites such as rabbit pasta and a glass of boutique pinot noir. This was once considered the seedy end of town, but designer furniture outlets and providores now surround the open-windowed restaurant. By night, the restaurateurs return to their own digs and the Surry Hills set descends for wine at the bar or to pick up tasty provisions to whip up at home. *Tue-Fri 7:30am-4pm and 6-10pm, Sat 8am-midnight.* $$ 1/2 Danks St. (Young St.), 02 9698 2201, danksstreetdepot.com.au

Dean's Café • Kings Cross • Cafe

Best Late-Night Bites For a late bite with a dash of kitsch, head to Deans. With comfy couches and a '60s juke box, it's a step back in time for post-nightclub revelers. If you go on your own, it won't be long before you're joined on the couch or at one of the stainless-steel tables by a post-party crowd eager for a chat. On weekends, Deans is filled with all sorts of midnight snackers, who arrive after getting down on the dance floor of one of the neighboring nightclubs to feast on cheeseburgers, fries, and shakes. Actors from the nearby theaters make an after-work pit stop for a beer or a hot chocolate with extra marshmallows. Drop by for a drink or a meal and it won't be long before you feel like part of it all. *Mon-Thu 7pm-3am, Fri-Sun 7pm-6am.* $ 1/5 Kellett St. (Bayswater Rd.), 02 9368 0953

Est. • CBD • Modern Australian

Best Swank Lunch Spots The stable of restaurants, bars, and hangouts at the iconic Establishment Hotel comprises the hottest places to be seen and heard in Sydney. Top pick for a luxury dinner is the high-end restaurant Est., which blends fine dining with the suavest surrounds in the southern hemisphere. Step inside the sandstone heritage building and take the lift to level one, where you are greeted by creamy white walls, plush carpet, and smooth decor with an Art Deco touch. The wine list encompasses Australian classics and imported boutique labels. Like the music? It's created especially for the restaurant by resident DJs. One of the founding fathers of Mod Oz cuisine, Peter Doyle, runs the stoves, where he turns out signature dishes such as pork belly with grilled scallops, garnering rave reviews from Sydney food writers. Book for dinner and order the tasting menu for the full treatment. Follow up the meal with a visit to the bars and clubs on the neighboring floors, each seemingly more luxurious than the next. *Mon-Fri noon-3pm and 6-10pm, Sat 6-10pm.* $$$$ The Establishment Hotel, Level 1, 252 George St. (Bridge St.), 02 9240 3010, merivale.com.au

Flying Fish • Pyrmont • Seafood

Best Swank Lunch Spots Mud crabs in coriander and chili, snapper curry, and crisp barramundi are just some of the dishes on offer at this renovated wharf restaurant. Sri Lankan–inspired seafood is accompanied by stunning city and harbor views. A galaxy of lights suspended from the ceiling competes with the starry night sky. The split-level restaurant boasts both maritime heritage status and modern glamour. Soft lighting and old hardwood floors act as a reminder that the wharf, once a port of call for thirsty sailors, is now part of a new suburb of apartment towers, television studios, and high-end eateries. Sip a cocktail at the bar before you dine or, if you're feeling casual, pick up take-out at the spin-off Flying Fish and Chips at the Jones Bay Road end of the wharf, and taste the same flavors, albeit served in grease-proof paper. *Tue-Fri noon-2:30pm and 6:30-10:30pm, Sat 6:30-10:30pm, Sun noon-2:30pm.* $$$ ≡ Pier 21, 19-21 Pirrama Rd. (Harris St.), Jones Bay Wharf, 02 9518 6677, flyingfish.com.au

Glass Brasserie • CBD • French

Celebrity chef Luke Mangan has cleared his schedule of Sydney restaurants to stay hands-on in his venture at the Hilton. Warm colors temper the strict angles of New York interior designer Tony Chi's modern lines, which mix long table-and-chair combos for group gatherings with plush booths for more intimate affairs. A 43-foot (13-meter) glass wall provides a stunning cityscape view of the lights of the Queen Victoria Building, and the outdoor bar is the perfect place to soak up a starry Sydney night over a wine recommended by the resident master of wine. The food is high-class hotel fare with classical French brasserie dishes. Choose from the crustacean bar or patisserie, order à la carte dishes of poussin or viande, or go for degustation. Service is sharp and cool, so book in advance. *Mon-Fri 6-10am, noon-3pm, and 6pm-late, Sat-Sun 6-11am and 6pm-late.* $$$ ≡ Park Hyatt, Level 2, 488 George St. (Park St.), 02 9265 6068, glassbrasserie.com.au

Grand National • Paddington • Pub Grub

This is one of the new breed of Sydney pubs that has turned the traditional bangers and mash washed down with beer combo on its head. The laid-back atmosphere is still there. Perch at the front bar for a chat with the publican or venture to the restaurant at the back that serves English and French bistro classics accompanied by an extensive wine list. The open kitchen welcomes you into the room and there is a back bar with wine and cocktails if an aperitif is in order. The food is comforting stuff: leek and Parmesan tart and roast duck followed by a pannacotta makes the Grand National the place to relax after a hard day hitting the Paddington fashion strip. Wear your new heels or shirt after a Saturday afternoon shopping session to mix with well-attired locals. *Tue-Thu 6-10:30pm, Fri-Sat noon-3pm and 6-10:30pm, Sun 6-9pm.* $$ ≡ 161 Underwood St. (Elizabeth St.), 02 9363 3096

Harry's Cafe de Wheels • Woolloomooloo • Australian

Best Late-Night Bites It's the best meal you will eat standing up, unless you fancy a seat in the gutter looking up at the stars. Harry's Cafe de Wheels is both a simple pie van and a Sydney institution, as much of a tourist attraction as the Opera House. If you are going to sample the Aussie meat pie with gravy, then make sure it's at Harry's, where it comes topped with mashed potatoes and peas. The roadside caravan, decorated with old film posters, has had plenty of practice, dishing up the famous pie combination since 1938 when it was a beacon to sailors docking at the Woolloomooloo Wharf. Now it serves as a lighthouse for late-night landlubbers who turn up from neighboring bars, pubs, and posh hotels for chili hotdogs and pastries. But the real draw is the pies: Harry's serves up to 5,000 of them a day, to a mishmash of diners from business types to taxi drivers, from girls dressed up for a night out to Australia's own Russell "Rusty" Crowe, who lives in the Woolloomooloo Finger Wharf behind the van. The pies are pure comfort food, bought for a bargain price and eaten with a million dollar harbor view. *Mon-Thu 7:30am-2am, Fri 7:30am-4am, Sat 9am-4am, Sun 9am-1:30am.* Cash only. $ ≡ Cowper Road Wharf (Dowling St.), 02 9357 3074, harryscafedewheels.com.au

Icebergs Dining Room and Bar* • Bondi Beach • Modern Australian/Seafood

Best Beachside Romance A cool restaurant for the cool crowd. The Icebergs' club is steeped in history—named after the famed swimmers who brave icy winter weather to swim laps in the ocean pool below—and Icebergs the restaurant is to-the-minute hip. Since opening in December 2002, it has been a lighthouse for trendy young things with money to burn and bronzed bodies to show off. Feast your eyes on the awe-inspiring view of Bondi Beach through the ceiling-to-floor windows and breathe the salt air from the glass-encased balcony. Inside, lounge in the icy-blue bar-booths with a cocktail in hand or take a box or bench seat in the modern dining room. If you are willing to brave the weather for the best seat in the house, then ask for a balcony table. At night, the ceiling is lit by circular chandeliers, mirroring the lights shining along Bondi Beach. The food focus is on Australian seafood with a Mediterranean twist—stingray with white asparagus, wild scallops with a green chili and radish salad—and there is also a bar menu. Order as little or as much as you want, just be sure to make your reservation early, as Icebergs Dining Room fills up faster than an ocean pool. *Tue-Sun noon-3pm and 6:30-10pm.* $$$ 1 Notts Ave. (Campbell Parade), 02 9365 9000, idrb.com

Il Baretto • Surry Hills • Italian

An Italian alternative to the fast-paced Asian eateries that litter Sydney suburbs, Il Baretto gives the Thais a run for their money when it comes to frenetic dining. On a tree-lined street, the frantic pace of the open kitchen spills out onto the street from behind the bi-fold doors. Il Baretto is always cranking, whether it's serving up a breakfast fry-up for post–Friday night party-goers, a lunchtime panini, or pizza and pasta staples for evening diners. What to wear at Il Baretto depends on where you're going or where you've been. Diners arrive dressed in velvet and pearls after a night at the theater, or come in jeans and T-shirt before heading out for live music. It doesn't take reservations or credit cards, and you have to BYO vino—the pub across the road has a good selection—but Il Baretto is still a great choice for a happening night on the town—and a tasty meal. *Mon 6-10pm, Tue-Sat 8am-3pm and 6-10pm.* $ 496 Bourke St. (Cleveland St.), 02 9361 6163

Industrie Bar* • CBD • French

A hip French-inspired haunt for after-work professionals, Industrie Bar also boasts a menu that caters to the moneyed. *See Sydney Hot & Cool Nightlife, p.92, for details.* $$$ 107 Pitt St. (Hunter St.), 02 9221 8001, industriebar.com.au

Jimmy Liks* • Potts Point • Asian

Set back on leafy Victoria Street, Jimmy Liks may share the high-end Potts Point zip code, but it still has the Kings Cross edge. It's famous for its mixed drinks and cocktail-food pairings, so don't bother with wine at this pan-Asian restaurant, not when the cocktail menu is so delicious. Split into two by a dividing wall, the restaurant is a gathering point for the young and the well dressed, who use Jimmy's as a pit stop during a night on the town. This is where to eat if you want to find the hottest after-party venue. If you haven't made a reservation, take a seat at the long, warmly lit bar to the right of the dining area and order a saketini—vodka and sake mixed with pickled ginger. Then share Thai and Vietnamese dishes at the long communal tables, one of the best ways to eavesdrop and find out where to head next. *Nightly 6-11pm.* $$ 188 Victoria St. (Darlinghurst St.), 02 8354 1400, jimmyliks.com

HOT & COOL

Kam Fook • Bondi Junction/Chatswood • Chinese

When you wake up after a long flight and all you can think of is chicken feet and pork buns, Kam Fook is just the jet-lag medicine you need. Endless trolleys of Chinese yum cha, smack bang in the middle of one of Sydney's newest shopping precincts, help recharge your batteries. Relax in comfy chairs with a breakfast of sang choi bau and Peking duck before hitting the stores for that last-minute buy. Yum cha is a right of passage for Sydneysiders, and many will confess to a Sunday morning addiction to the spicy, sweet, and salty feast of foods that would never be contemplated for a mid-week breakfast. If you wake up too late for breakfast, Kam Fook is open for dinner too—a more subdued à la carte affair. *Daily 10am-3pm and 5:30-10:30pm.* $$ ≡ 600 Westfield Shopping Centre, Bondi Junction and Chatswood Rd. (Andison St.), 02 9386 9889, kamfook.com.au

Kobe Jones • King St. Wharf • Japanese

Craving sushi but not prepared to hover over a train waiting for the California rolls to arrive? Kobe Jones is the place to find the Japanese fusion cuisine popular in Los Angeles but a little slow to catch on in Sydney. With a balcony overlooking Darling Harbour and soft high-backed chairs creating a sense of intimacy inside, the restaurant has mastered the Sydney fusion of casual and chic. At lunch, Kobe Jones is full with the work brigade, and in the evenings, the long tables make it a convenient choice for groups. Order an Asahi beer while you wait for entrées of soft crab nori rolls before progressing to crispy-skinned chicken in honey and soy. Go as part of a group and be treated to the Kobe Jones banquet, a progression of dishes sure to challenge any Japanese gastronome. *Mon-Sat noon-2pm and 6pm-late, Sun 6pm-late.* $$ ▯≡ 29 Lime St. (Erskine St.), 02 9299 5290, kobejones.com.au

La Sala* • Surry Hills • Italian

This warehouse-style Italian eatery can feel more like a nightclub than a restaurant on a buzzing weekend night. Spend the pre-dinner hour in the tiny loft bar where bronzed men and girls in the latest fashion compete for attention as they sip Campari cocktails. Then take the stairs down to the banquette-lined dining room for simple antipasti platters including cured meats, whitebait, and vitello tomato, followed by pasta such as scallop risotto. The food is simple but good—don't miss the signature dish of baby snapper cooked in "crazy water," a fisherman's broth of tomato and saffron. During the week, La Sala is the favored lunchtime haunt of flashy advertising and media types. But book early if you want to visit on the weekend, when the 30-something crowd steps out of their suits and into their party wear. *Tue-Wed and Sat 6pm-late, Thu-Fri noon-3pm and 6pm-late.* $$ ≡ Ground floor, 23 Foster St. (Campbell St.), 02 9281 3352, lasala.com.au

Local* • Paddington • Modern Australian

This is one of the new age of Sydney dining places where barflies are tempted to stay for a meal of high-quality bistro food when the cocktails start to work their magic. The young and hip change into jeans and heels and gather after work at the bar for a glass of champagne and a plate of oysters, or choose from a range of cocktails. If the mood suits, they take a seat in the leafy courtyard and peruse a menu that swings from spicy paella to duck confit. Low lighting and casual bench seats with cushions only serve to make the beautiful people even more so, and the familiar service will make you wish you were a local too. *Mon-Thu 6-10:30pm, Fri noon-3:30pm and 6-10pm, Sat-Sun 9am-3:30pm and 6-10pm.* $$ ≡ 211 Glenmore Rd. (Broughton St.), 02 9332 1577, localwinebarandrestaurant.com.au

Longrain* • Surry Hills • Thai

Best Thai Restaurants The über-chic converted warehouse space that houses the groovy lounge and restaurant Longrain is also home to some of Sydney's best Thai food. In the hub of Sydney's artistic community, Longrain is a gathering place for the bold and the beautiful swingers of inner Sydney. Longrain does not take dinner reservations, so if you arrive after 7pm you will probably have to chill in the bar while waiting for a table, albeit on comfy banquettes and ottoman lounges. There's also a resident DJ spinning smooth sounds to help wash down the even smoother caprioskas whipped up by the bartenders. A menu of bar snacks is on hand, including the famous betel leaf topped with smoked trout. When you do get a seat, Sydney's communal table scene is great fun. Dishes, including fish chosen fresh from the tank, are designed to be shared. For a special event, book the private dining room behind the slatted wooden blinds. *Mon-Fri noon-2:30pm and 6-11pm, Sat 6-11pm.* $$ 85 Commonwealth St. (Hunt St.), 02 9280 2888, longrain.com.au

Lotus* • Potts Point • Continental

One of Sydney's most beloved cocktail spots—from after work to after hours—also offers good Continental fare. *See Sydney Hot & Cool Nightlife, p.93, for details.* $$ 22 Challis Ave. (McClay St.), 02 9326 9000

Lucio's • Paddington • Italian

Art and Italian food are a match made in heaven at this Italian eatery, situated in the heart of the Paddington gallery scene. Lucio's is one of those retro restaurants that is so old it's cool again. Serving classic Italian food to the famous faces of Sydney's political and media scene for more than 20 years, Lucio's is also one of the best places to view the work of some of Australia's best-known artists. The restaurant, with terra-cotta floors and simple furnishings, has an extensive collection of contemporary paintings from artists such as John Olsen and Tim Storrier, many of whom are regulars. Don't be surprised if you see the chef, Lucio Galletto, greeting diners like old friends—they probably are. The menu is the tried and true Italian formula; ricotta-filled zucchini flowers for primi piatti and marinated quail for secondi piatti. A must for art lovers who enjoy a dash of inspiration with their spaghetti. *Mon-Sat 12:30-3pm and 6:30-11pm.* $$$ 47 Windsor St. (Elizabeth St.), 02 9380 5996, lucios.com.au

Mint* • CBD • Fusion

The sandstone arcades of the Intercontinental blend into the sleek modern ambience at Mint, the hotel's in-house lounge and restaurant. The restaurant has a street entrance on Bridge Street, but for extra glamour, venture inside the hotel's sliding glass doors. A cotton-candy lamp lights the steps and there is a full-length mirror where you can check your outfit before you walk in. A glass partition separates the dedicated dining area from the informal drink-and-dine area in the long, narrow restaurant. Take a seat on a black leather ottoman and choose a wine from the specialized glass cabinet before moving on to the menu, which mixes contemporary Asian and European dishes, designed to share. Or take a seat under a sun-drenched window on a warm afternoon and sample from the cocktail menu. In the evening, the bar spills onto the sandstone terrace where well-dressed travelers mingle with the locals. The vibe is low-key and high class. *Mon-Fri noon-3pm and 6-10:30pm, Sat 6-10:30pm.* $$$ 62 Bridge St. (Phillip St.), 02 9240 1210, mintbaranddining.com.au

The Old Fitzroy Hotel* • Woolloomooloo • Pub Grub

Decent pub grub to go with your beer can be found at this old favorite. *See Sydney Hot & Cool Nightlife, p.94, for details.* $ ≡ 129 Dowling St. (Cathedral St.), 02 9356 3848, oldfitzroy.com.au

Otto • Woolloomooloo • Italian

The perennial favorite of bejeweled ladies who lunch, Otto is as much a place to be seen as a restaurant. Downstairs from the Sydney apartment of Russell Crowe on the Woolloomooloo marina, the paparazzi are never far from the waterside tables where Cristal champagne glistens in the afternoon sun, sipped by the rich and famous. Choose to have lunch at Otto and keep the rest of the afternoon appointment-free to sample casual southern Italian fare, drink wine, and people-watch. Ask for an outdoor table and get the best vantage point. In the evening, retreat to the polished interior and bar for a romantic rendezvous and make a splash by arriving by water taxi. The food alone is enough to make you swoon—stuffed zucchini flowers, oysters, and salads of vine-ripened tomatoes and buffalo mozzarella. *Mon-Sat noon-3pm and 6pm-late, Sun noon-3pm and 6-8:30pm.* $$$ ≡ Area 8, 6 Cowper Wharf Rd. (Bourke St.), 02 9368 7488, otto.net.au

Le Petit Creme • Darlinghurst • French

A gastronome haven for weekend breakfast, Le Petit Creme champions rustic French fare and wouldn't dare to be anything less than authentic. Don't bother asking for skim or soy milk; coffee is served with full cream or straight up espresso style, usually by a waiter with a thick accent and a good dose of French pride. The cramped wooden tables in the ramshackle building, decorated with sensuous art, are an antidote to the soulless modern decor of many Sydney cafes. Arrive early for breakfast and avoid being squashed at the back of the restaurant by asking for a street table—it's worth the wait to watch the sights and sounds of edgy Darlinghurst pass you by. Funky regulars return for the eggs Benedict with ham or smoked salmon, while those with a sweet tooth will love the generous servings of French toast. If the Francophile art inspires you, then duck next door, at the back of the neighboring garage, where French artist and colorful Sydney identity Bruno Dutot keeps a studio and makeshift gallery. *Daily 6:30am-3pm.* $ ≡ 118 Darlinghurst Rd. (Liverpool St), 02 9361 4738

Phamish • Darlinghurst • Vietnamese

There is no such thing as a quiet night at this bustling red-and-white Vietnamese take-out joint. On any given spring Saturday evening, it's filled with post-races party crowds. Mid-week, it's chockablock with suits dropping in for a meal of crispy prawn and duck pancakes before heading home. This is strictly BYO territory, although you may want to bring more than one bottle to sip from as you wait for a table. If this feels uncouth, staff will oblige with a glass and a spare red-and-white plastic stool. It's more than a little chaotic but always a lot of fun, so come armed with patience and you'll be rewarded with fresh flavors at bargain prices. The menu is a series of red magnets above the kitchen that are pulled off when a popular dish sells out. Prepay and order your food hawker-style from the kitchen and it will arrive piping hot when you're seated. *Tue-Sun 6-9:30pm.* $ ≡ 354 Liverpool St. (Boundry St.), 02 9357 2688

Pony • The Rocks • Modern Australian

Wander down the cobblestone laneway and into the former warehouse now known as the Rocks Centre to visit this new dining hot spot. The decor is a groovy blend of old and new—exposed timber beams and wide planked timber floorboards, goatskin lamp shades, and cowhide front on the open kitchen hint that a night at Pony is not going to be tame. Inside there are more intimate set tables, but in the warmer months, the outdoor bar and 40-foot (12-meter) communal table are the places where savvy city workers kick up their heels over cocktails and shared food plates. The open kitchen and grill adds to the restaurant's drama, best observed on a Friday night. Dishes ranges from snacks such as crispy whitebait and wood-fired chipolatas to more substantial meals such as Parmesan-crumbed lamb cutlets or the hearty beef rib, served with spinach, mushrooms, and red wine sauce. *Mon-Fri noon-late, Sat 5pm-late, Sun 8:30am-late.* $$ B ▯ ≡ The Rocks Centre (Argyle St.), 02 9252 7797, ponydining.com

Ravesi's* • Bondi Beach • Continental

Set on a corner beside a string of surf shops, Ravesi's is all glass windows and barstools, with cocktails downstairs and fine and casual dining upstairs. The best place to sit is out on the balcony overlooking the beach, where you can watch the streetlife saunter by. The salads, such as one composed of smoked chicken, avocado, chili, mango, and peanuts, are some of the best in town. There are also seafood and meat dishes, and lots of vegetarian options. Weekend breakfast is best accompanied with an excellent Bloody Mary, particularly if you're recovering from a big night out. *Mon-Fri noon-3pm and 6-10pm, Sat 9am-4pm and 6-10pm, Sun 9am-1pm.* $$ ≡ Campbell Parade (Hall St.), 02 9365 4422, ravesis.com.au

Raw Bar • Bondi Beach • Sushi

Sushi with ocean views. There isn't a whole lot of cooking going on at Raw Bar, a favorite of beachside locals. What the eatery does do is serve up generous plates of sushi and sashimi in a hip beachside location. It would be difficult to miss, with the huge block-letter awning serving as a beacon to even the most focally challenged. Take a seat at the stainless-steel tables, either on the footpath or inside, and soak up the sea breeze with a Sapporo, or something more serious like a Japanese slipper. Order a bento box for the best of both worlds. *Daily noon-9:30pm.* $$ ≡ 135 Ramsgate St. (Warners Ave.), 02 9365 7200

Sean's Panorama • Bondi Beach • British/French

There are few dining experiences more pleasurable than watching the sun set on the breakers from behind the cozy glass windows at Sean's Panorama. Of course you don't have to sit inside—this is Bondi, and alfresco is a given. In typical Sean's style, the smallest details are taken care of: welcoming wicker chairs, the best bread basket in Sydney, and even a blanket if the weather is nippy. The menu is, like the restaurant, small and perfect, scrawled on a blackboard above the kitchen with as many carefully chosen wines as there are dishes. Roast chicken and parsnip is a nod to signature old-fashioned tastes. Whimsical touches such as oyster shells holding salt and pepper and sea-urchin lamps make it a perennial favorite. *Sat noon-2:30, Wed-Sun 6-9:30pm.* $$$ ≡ 270 Campbell Parade (Ramsgate Ave.), 02 9365 4924, seanspanorama.com.au

Slip Inn* • CBD • Thai

This is Sydney's Cinderella spot—where now-princess Mary met Danish Prince Frederick. Locals flock here to try their own luck over drinks and dinner. *See Sydney Hot & Cool Nightlife, p.96, for details.* $$ ≡ 111 Sussex St. (King St.), 02 8295 9911, merivale.com.au

Spice I Am • Surry Hills • Thai

Best Thai Restaurants Spice I Am was voted Best Thai by the *Sydney Morning Herald*, and the humble downtown setting, on the ground floor of a grungy hotel, belies the amazing food on offer. Brightly colored plastic chairs sit under a purple neon sign beckoning lovers of authentic Thai food. Even on a weeknight, a line of impatient diners waiting for a table—dressed up to go out in stilettos and sport jackets or dressed down in low-slung jeans—snakes along Elizabeth Street. When you make it to the head of the line, waiters greet you with a warm smile, and despite the chaos of the open kitchen and the comings and goings, the meal runs smoothly in a slap-happy way. Spice I Am is a champion of the great Australian tradition of BYO, so pick up a light red or sweet white from a pub or bottle shop on the way. On the menu, look for meals followed by an (S) denoting signature dishes, and if you like your Asian food with bite, ask for the order to be written in Thai. *Tue-Sun 11am-4pm and 6-10pm.* $ ≡ 90 Wentworth Ave. (Elizabeth St.), 02 9280 0928, spiceiam.com

Stir Crazy • Kirribilli • Thai

This groovy Thai venue feels more like a party or club than somewhere to sit down for a sobering meal. It doesn't take credit cards or reservations, but it is one of the coolest little eateries in one of Sydney's most picturesque suburbs, and so it's worth the effort to visit. Bring your own alcoholic beverages and prepare to sit shoulder to shoulder in this tiny, noisy restaurant. Not recommended for an intimate dinner, Stir Crazy is more rowdy than romantic—pop and dance music blasts from the speakers, creating an upbeat vibe that draws funky young things from across the "northside." Even Eastern suburbanites have been tempted to make the trek across the bridge for the pad Thai and chicken fried rice served on banana leaves. *Daily noon-10:30pm.* $ ≡ Shop 5, 1 Broughton St. (Fitzroy St), 02 9922 6620, stircrazy.com.au

Sugaroom* • Pyrmont • Australian

Sweet is the perfect word to describe this restaurant-cum-bar that overlooks the industrial end of the harbor. Television executives and advertising creatives from nearby studios flock to tables for upmarket steak and fries or pan-fried barramundi on pea mash. In the evenings, locals walking home from their city offices congregate at the bar for cocktails, which often extends into dinner. If not, there is a tasty array of bar food to accompany the sugary bar concoctions. The restaurant was once the site of a sugar refinery (hence the name), so if you do decide to take a table it would be a shame to pass on dessert. Banana crepes with chocolate sorbet are, as they say in Australian slang, "sweet as." *Mon 6pm-late, Tue-Sat noon-3pm and 6pm-late, Sun noon-3pm.* $$ ≡ Shop 2, 1 Harris St. (Elizabeth St.), 02 9571 5055, sugaroom.com.au

Sushi e • CBD • Sushi

This is sushi with a view of the action. The in-house sushi bar at the Establishment is on the same floor as Hemmesphere, the place-to-be club. Pale wood stools line up against a white marble bar. Behind the bar is where the action takes place, with three chefs slicing and dicing fillets of tuna, salmon, and snapper and pairing them with deftly placed garnishes for some of the most beautifully presented sushi in town. It's the hippest live cooking show, and the food tastes better with entertainment value added. Of course, if you get bored watching the fish you can always cast your eye around the fishbowl of a restaurant and check out other posers at the bar. The slick guys and hot girls are as entertaining as the food. *Tue-Thu noon-3pm and 6-10:30pm, Fri noon-3pm and 6:30-10:30pm, Sat 7-10:30pm.* $$$ ≡ Establishment Hotel, Level 4, 252 George St. (Bridge St.), 02 9240 3041, merivale.com.au

Swell* • Bronte • Cafe

Best Restaurants with Views When the lights, camera, action of Bondi begins to overwhelm you, sister beach Bronte is the perfect retreat. Without a pub, bar, or nightclub in sight, Bronte is favored by locals and the occasional traveler who ventures down from the famous Bondi-Bronte coastal walk. Swell fulfills the functions of restaurant, bar, and cafe—open seven days a week from early morning till late. At breakfast, hungry surfers with sandy feet pop in for a famous "brekkie wrap," coffee, and a fresh fruit frappe. At lunch, chairs quickly fill with ladies who pick at salads and mezze plates. At dinner, couples huddle on the plush lounge seats inside, noshing the Swell tasting plate over a bottle of New Zealand sauvignon blanc, while at other tables groups in silk chiffon dresses and flip-flops gather for sunset cocktails. Rated as one of the best places to meet celebrities at breakfast, Swell is also a stone's throw across the park from Heath Ledger's Bronte pad. *Daily 7:30am-late.* $$ ≡ Shop 3, 465 Bronte Rd. (Nelson St.), 02 9386 5001, swellrestaurant.com.au

Wildfire • The Rocks • Brazilian

When the Sydney fashion shows are on, Wildfire is the place where models congregate after a long day on the catwalk. The huge room has banquet tables overlooking Circular Quay, with huge chandeliers and a marble oyster bar. A great venue for a party or a group, Wildfire is a place to kick up your heels in decadent surroundings. U.S.-based chef Mark Miller has created a menu that appeals to people who want to eat a little or a lot. There's an iced crustacean bar, a wall of local and imported wines, and an open-flame grill where chefs broil yard-long skewers of churrasco, Brazilian marinated meat. For a serious carnivore experience, order the all-you-can-eat churrasco, or if you're feeling tame, there is also a pizza menu. *Mon-Thu noon-2:30pm and 6-11pm, Fri-Sat noon-2:30pm and 6pm-midnight, Sun-Thu 6-11pm.* $$$ ≡ Ground Level, Overseas Passenger Terminal (Argyle St.), 02 8273 1222, wildfiresydney.com

Yoshii • The Rocks • Sushi

Master Japanese sushi chef and restaurant co-owner Yoshii Ryuichi wields his sashimi sword with style at this bamboo encased dining room. Since opening in 2001, Yoshii has been recognized by foodies, food writers, and the Sydney style set as the best sushi in Sydney. Behind the blinds, the restaurant offers smooth polished surfaces, long low tables, curved chairs, and warm, low lighting. Sit at the sushi bar to catch the action or take a seat in the elegant dining room, which holds a modest 42 guests. Diners whisper in hushed, reverent tones as perfectly presented degustation items are brought to the tables by waiters who appear to glide across the floor. Choose from four carefully established degustation menus, including the decadent Moët and Hennessy Yoshii course. Dishes range from the exotic, such as sea urchin, to classics, such as ocean trout. All are exquisite, and the serving portions leave little room for anything else. Most nights Yoshii himself is behind the sushi counter giving diners a chance to see him work his magic. *Mon 6-9:30pm; Tue-Fri noon-3pm and 6-9:30pm, Sat 6-9:30pm.* $$$$ ▭ 115 Harrington St. (Essex St.), 02 9247 2566, yoshii.com.au

Young Alfred • Circular Quay • Italian

The owners of iconic Paddington pizzeria, Arthur's, relocated to these shiny new digs at the business end of town in late 2005. The regulars are already flowing in, hungry for buffalo mozzarella on a tomato crust and other favorites. At lunch, the outdoor tables are filled with suits snacking on pizza, pasta, and salad, while at dinner romance blossoms under the wallpaper, over a plate of carpaccio and a bottle of rosé. After 9pm the tempo rises as the post-party crowds flock in from the neighboring art galleries and boutiques, nibbling on meals that are created to be shared and sampled. Feeling game? Order the "surprise" pizza. Whatever arrives at the table is sure to be made with spirit and soul. *Mon-Fri 7am-midnight; Sat-Sun 10am-midnight.* $ ≡ Ground Floor Customs House, 31 Alfred St. (Young St.), 02 9251 5192, youngalfred.com.au

Hot & Cool Sydney: The Nightlife

The Annandale Hotel* • Annandale • Live Music

Best Live Music Venues The Annandale is the bastion of Sydney pub rock. A watering hole with the motto "F— this, I'm going to the Annandale" deserves every rock accolade it gets. Anyone with a passion for live music knows the Annandale. Closing its doors to live music in 1998, the 'dale returned two years later under the watchful eye of the Rule brothers, who have returned the pub to its promise of "celebrating live music." The walls bear witness to the history of rock with band photos from Aussie legends You Am I to Gerling, Magic Dirt, and the Vines, while the scuffed carpet and ripped couches provide a lived-in feel. The back deck houses yummy noodle house Wok 'n' Roll. Posers need not apply, the 'dale is for gig pigs and true music lovers. *Mon-Sat 11am-midnight, Sun noon-10pm.* C≡ 17 Parramatta Rd. (Nelson St.), 02 9550 1078, annandalehotel.com.au

Arq • Taylor Square • Gay Club

Best Gay Scenes The darling of the Sydney gay scene, Arq is the after-hours venue for boys who like boys and the girls who hang out with them. Getting your polished toenail in the door can be difficult if you're female or a straight male. If you are of the heterosexual persuasion and you really want to visit, your best bet is to go with someone who's gay—or pretend that you are. Once inside, the dance floor goes off with all sorts of colorful costumes and characters. If you want to try your hand at dressing in drag for one night, then make sure you try it at Arq. The space has two levels: the upper mezzanine is a warmly lit cocktail and chill-out area; but if you want to meet people, your best bet is to stay downstairs where the dance floor is a light and sound show featuring the Mardi Gras prima donnas and drag queens. *Thu-Sun 9pm-9am.* C≡ 16 Flinders St. (Taylor St.), 02 9380 8700, arqsydney.com.au

Bambini Wine Room • CBD • Wine Bar

Old school. The words might as well be painted onto the walls of this elegant little haunt, which features old-style bistro chairs and a chandelier worth its weight in Old World glamour. With Parisian sensibilities, Bambini Wine Room is a small, intimate room that is often packed to the rafters. There are leather banquettes, ornate wall lamps and tapas-style snacks scribbled on gilt-framed mirrors. It's dimly lit, and for an unassuming wine bar, old baby face Bambini is friendly, sophisticated, and charming all at once. A six-page list of wines, champers, and aperitifs adds to the pleasure. Bambini knows what it is and sticks to the blueprint: It doesn't try too hard. If only there wasn't a constant queue. *Mon-Fri noon-midnight, Sat 5:30-11pm.* ≡ 185-187 Elizabeth St. (Park St.), 02 9283 7098, bambinitrust.com.au

Bar Europa* • CBD • Lounge

Everyone tries to pretend Bar Europa is their own little secret. One of the Central Business District's most comfortable and chic underground bars, Bar Europa is true to its name and does feel European. It can be relied upon after work for a sophisticated atmosphere, tasty bar food, and a good-looking crowd, mainly funky suits and magazine or PR gals. Drinkers step down off Elizabeth Street into intimate lighting, chilled beats, and a choice of two main bars. In the front bar the mood is romantic, but in back it's more social and boisterous. The London wine bar look of the low-lit interior and illuminated drinks display, and the attitude-free staff and crowd, make for a relaxed watering hole. The management has achieved the near-impossible: a friendly haven among the suit-saturated Central Business District mating markets that's lively enough for a good night out and cool enough for the image-conscious. *Tue-Sat noon-late.* ≡ Basement, 88 Elizabeth St. (King St.), 02 9232 3377, bareuropa.com.au

Bentley Restaurant and Bar* • Surry Hills • Restaurant/Bar

One of Sydney's few true restaurant/bar combos, this sleek space meets all your night-out needs with a cool lounge and decadent dinners. *See Sydney Hot & Cool Restaurants, p.74, for details.* ≡ 320 Crown St. (Campbell St.), 02 9332 2344

Blue Orange* • Bondi Beach • Restaurant/Bar

This relaxed Bondi favorite is a day and night hangout for casual cafe meals and drinks. *See Sydney Hot & Cool Restaurants, p.75, for details.* ≡ 49 Hall St. (Campbell St.), 02 9300 9885

Candy's Apartment • Kings Cross • Nightclub

Music aficionados swear by the bohemian Candy's Apartment for its relaxed vibe and dedication to high-quality sound. Sure, it's dark and the low ceiling can induce occasional bouts of claustrophobia, but there is plenty of room to move. The two-room space showcases new and established acts, and popular themed nights include Friday Night Hip Hop and Wednesday's UK-themed Mojo. The back room, with its chandelier and piano, looks like somewhere Jim Morrison would have hung out. The staff and doormen are relaxed and friendly, and the crowd consists of edgy artistic types ready to party 'til the sun comes up. *Tue-Sun 8pm-late.* C≡ 22 Bayswater Rd. (Ward Ave.), 02 9380 5600

Cargo Bar* • King Street Wharf • Bar/Nightclub

It's difficult not to associate Cargo with Olympic Games debauchery. Exploding into the Sydney bar scene in 2000, Cargo opened at 6pm on the night of the opening ceremony with little fanfare, and by 8pm the hordes were lining out the door. The place to celebrate sporting victories, boogie, and be silly, Cargo put the King Street Wharf redevelopment on the map and was the first real triumph for renowned pub kings Fraser Short and John Duncan. A waterside entertainment area brimming with restaurants and bars, King Street Wharf is a great spot for visitors craving harbor views and a lively drinking scene. Cargo has a well-earned reputation as a pick-up hot spot, and mischief-makers of all ages flood through the doors on weekends. The gourmet pizzas are popular for boozy lunches, and the upstairs lounge is often roped off for the chicest crew as well as for members and private functions. The music moves with the times, and electro bleeps and breakbeat fuse with house and neo-jazz, with big-name locals such as James Taylor often hitting the decks. A sunset tipple in the top lounge is a must. *Daily 11:30am-late.* ≡ 52-60 The Promenade (Erskine St.), 02 9262 1777, cargobar.com.au

The Colombian Hotel • Darlinghurst • Gay Bar/Nightclub

Best Gay Scenes The Colombian makes you smile. With high-energy beats pumping from both floors, it's a gay bar where heteros have just as much fun as the polished gay boys strutting their moves on the dance floor. Located in a huge heritage building on the corner of Crown and Oxford Street, the Colombian never slows down. Whether it's a group of older queens sipping beers by the folded-back windows, or barely 20-year-old boys in polo shirts and tight jeans lounging on the banquettes, there's always a lively vibe. Upstairs the clubbers pulse beneath a sparkling ruby chandelier, the bar staff bust out their own moves, and straight girls enjoy the affable attention, hooting and hollering as the bass resonates. Tastefully appointed with wooden lattice over mirrored walls, spacious bars, and darkened corners between floors for more intimate exchanges, the Colombian makes everyone feel welcome. And if you're a man on the hunt, there are plenty of gorgeous specimens on offer. *Sun-Thu 10am-4am, Fri-Sat 9am-6am.* ≡ 117-123 Oxford St. (Crown St.), 02 9360 2151

Cru* • Circular Quay • Restaurant/Lounge

This Circular Quay hot spot draws after-work crowds to the downstairs lounges, while upstairs is dedicated to fine dining with an Opera House view. *See Sydney Hot & Cool Restaurants, p.76, for details.* ≡ Level 3, Overseas Passenger Terminal (Circular Quay West), 02 9251 1188

Darlo Bar • Darlinghurst • Bar

The Darlo is a vinyl-inspired haven where the coolest cats from Sydney's trendy inner-city zip codes (Darlinghurst, Surry Hills, Potts Point) come to sip. Frequented by actors, film-industry types, and fashionistas from the surrounding boutiques, the Darlo oozes trendiness minus the pretension of some of her more upmarket neighbors. Dimly lit by colored lampshades and steel-pronged light fixtures, there are clusters of mismatched retro couches, table settings, and even stools around a vinyl padded '70s bar. The windows fold back in the warmer months, and while there is no outdoor seating, the passing parade is as sexy as the mod squad reclining on ottomans or smoking by the pool table, hiding under their rock 'n' roll locks. Prime people-watching hour is after 6pm on weeknights as the motley crew strolls home from work. As retro-inspired as the furniture, Darlo regulars keep coming back for the relaxed atmosphere, the comfy couches, and the daily specials. It's a great starting point for a big night in the Cross or a post-theater nightcap—you can order in pizza, Thai, or burgers and the grungy staff will serve up the take-out on a plate. *Mon-Sat 10am-midnight, Sun noon-midnight.* ≡ 306 Liverpool St. (Darlinghurst Rd.), 02 9331 3672

Dolphin Bar Hotel • Surry Hills • Bar

This recently renovated Surry Hills bar is drenched in aqua tiles with metal dolphins swimming along the main wall into the pool room. Through the open-plan bar and upstairs to the beer garden terrace, the Dolphin Hotel reveals its best asset—its spot overlooking Crown Street below. The aqua tiles covering the tables and skirting the walls provide a Greek isle feel, and the cane armchairs, hanging basket chairs, exposed brickwork, and fireplaces induce a country-living ambience. There's a Mediterranean flair in the open air, with countless nooks and crannies, lounges, tables, high-backed stools, and couches inside. Favored by the young and well-preened Surry barflies—fashionable, urban 20-somethings—the Dolphin has an exquisite Mediterranean fusion menu and, with chilled beats in the background, it's on cruise control. As spacious as it is, you still feel like you're in the lounge room of any Surry terrace with the attic window overhead. With the lights down low, it's an island paradise far removed from the inner city. *Mon-Sat 10am-midnight, Sun 11am-11pm.* ≡ Crown Hotel, 412 Crown St. (Fitzroy St.), 02 9331 4800

Dragonfly • Potts Point • Nightclub

Best Hot Club Scenes Dragonfly is positioned for maximum backstage-pass appeal, and that's just how the hipsters like it. It's tucked away in an alley in Sydney's red-light district, with such salacious neighbors as an adult bookshop and a strip joint; take a right off Victoria Street for the hideaway entry with its not-so-hideaway neon sign. Dress to impress to make it past the bouncers and through the two sets of glass doors into the cave-like club. The stone-walled interior is designed around a central island bar of etched marble, while the back wall features a long couch for swinging singles and leather dinner-style booths for more exclusive groups. There is a segregated cocktail bar with a lounge for those who just want to chill, but almost nobody comes to Dragonfly for a quiet drink. The music moves from R&B on school nights to funky house on the weekends, and the coiffured crowd is there to move. Boys are underdressed in designer jeans and girls are clothed following the "less-is-more" philosophy of tiny cocktail dresses, shiny hair, and perfect pouts. Although Wednesday is strictly an under-30 zone, Saturday brings a more sophisticated crowd. Inside the bar, good-looking staff are having a party of their own, but if you can grab their attention long enough, ask for a shot. They'll come through with the goods. *Wed and Fri-Sun 9pm-5am.* C≡ 1 Earl St. (Victoria St.), 02 9356 2666

Fringe Bar • Paddington • Comedy Club/Nightclub

Reminiscent of the old comedy cellars in New York's Greenwich Village, the Unicorn Hotel's Fringe Bar has settled into its new identity as a comedy club–cum-nightclub favored by Sydney's hip early adopters. In the late '90s, Monday comedy nights brimmed with cool university students and the Fringe was renowned for its sexy barmen. The past few years saw a dismal refurbishment fail, and now pub barons Fraser Short and John Duncan have injected the Fringe with their magic touch, reviving the old landmark and adding to their stable. Exposed brick, theater lights, black speakers, checkered floors, heavy velvet curtains with tassles, and a row of chandeliers above the main bar create a theatrical atmosphere, while the black-and-white photos of rock 'n' rollers and retro funksters inject the coolio factor. Monday is comedy night when stand-ups strut their stuff, poking fun at the immaculately presented Eastern Suburbs crowd. The headline act is always good, and it's worth reserving a table for dinner, drinks, and the show by phoning ahead. The back room takes a whacky turn with a giant bison head above the fireplace. *Mon-Wed noon-midnight, Thu-Sat noon-3am, Sun noon-midnight.* C≡ Unicorn Hotel, 106 Oxford St. (Hopewell St.), 02 9360 5443, thefringe.com

Gazebo Wine Garden • Elizabeth Bay • Wine Bar

With a wine list that includes "slurpables," "unpronounceables," and "pink bits," Gazebo Wine Garden is every bit your friendly neighborhood wine bar. It's disarmingly cheeky in parts: There's a fox standing on the roof wearing a boxing helmet, green grass growing behind the bar, and you can grab a fistful of chalk to add to the graffiti on the toilet doors. But it's nothing short of sophisticated, clearly targeting the well-padded pockets of Elizabeth Bay and Potts Point, furnished with studded leather chairs and wrought iron outdoor settings in a courtyard overlooking the Kings Cross fountain (and police station above the hedges). The wine list can be overwhelming, but there's an approachable sommelier to demystify it all. Take the time to be adventurous, because there are startling drops from Spain to the Barossa Valley. *Mon-Thu 3pm-midnight, Fri-Sun noon-midnight.* ≡ Shop 1 / 2 Elizabeth Bay Rd. (Greenknowe Ave.), 02 9357 5333, gazebowinegarden.com.au

Hemmesphere • CBD • Lounge

Best Cocktail Lounges Named after Merivale's hotel baron Justin Hemmes, Hemmesphere is a plush lounge dedicated to the finer things in life, from cigars to $4,700 limited edition bottles of Dom Perignon. Hemmes has his own record label, Jam Recordings, and started Good Vibrations, an annual dance party for the funky set. Comprised of pillowed lounges with exotic fabrics, ottomans, cane armchairs, and twisted copper chandeliers, Hemmesphere invites you to sink into the luxurious surroundings and enjoy the attentive service of glam Argentinian bar manager Carolina Jensen and her team of black-clad girls and guys. There's a Latin jazz band on Friday nights and DJs every evening, playing a mix of lounge tunes with a dash of old grooves, classic rock, and house. Reservations are essential Thursday to Saturday nights with a strict smart-casual dress code. Hemmesphere attracts everyone from pre-drinking clubbers to older gentlemen puffing on a cigar. Table 32, bordering the Sushi e restaurant, is the pick of the non-smoking spots, while table 42 is best for the smokers. *Tue-Fri 6pm-late, Sat 7pm-late.* ≡ Establishment Hotel, Level 4, 252 George St. (Pitt St.), 02 9240 3040, merivale.com.au

Home • Cockle Bay Wharf • Nightclub

Home is a beacon of dance music in the Darling Harbour tourist precinct. From the futuristic multi-level main dance room, a padded cell known as "the silver room," and a spacious chill-out room, the only posers you will find at Home are those practicing their experimental dance moves. On the ground floor attached to the main club is Homebar, a low-key cafe and bar. Home also houses the legendary club night Sublime. Sublime was Sydney's original "it" club on Pitt Street. It moved house to Friday nights at Home, where it's the place for clubbing bunnies to go when the work week is done, featuring four levels of music including trance, drum and base, house, and hip-hop. Saturdays see the departure of the party-hearty crowd when a smoother group moves in for funky house until the wee hours. *Fri-Sat 11pm-sunrise. Homebar: Daily noon-late.* C≡ The Promenade (Cockle Bay Wharf), 02 9266 0600, homesydney.com

Hugo's Lounge • Kings Cross • Lounge

Best Trendy Hangouts At Hugo's, the air is thick with pretension as fashionistas pout and preen. The posers, bronzed bimbos, and buff himbos size each other up, scanning the room for famous faces or influential types, as the sexy DJs spin house pop tunes. Hugo's is guaranteed to be jumping every weekend, with Sunday nights a particular favorite as Sydney's chichi up-and-comers groove to Sneaky Sound System. The balcony is always full as Sydney's beautiful people smoke their evenings away, sipping cocktails and scouting for potential lovers. While the 30-somethings reign, it's not uncommon to find a blend of ages, with silver foxes chatting up the scantily clad ladies. Prince Harry reserved Hugo's for a party when he last visited, and it's always popular with models and actor types. The bouncers are less than friendly, but as long as ladies dress sexily, and boys bring a girl or two, getting in won't be a problem. *Wed-Sat 6pm-3am, Sun 8pm-3am.* C≡ Level 1, 33 Bayswater Rd. (Ward Ave.), 02 9357 4411, hugos.com.au

HOT & COOL

Icebergs Dining Room and Bar* • Bondi Beach • Restaurant/Lounge

This seaside dining institution also boasts a great oceanfront bar perfect for watching the sunset. *See Sydney Hot & Cool Restaurants, p.79, for details.* ≡ 1 Notts Ave. (Campbell Parade), 02 9365 9000, idrb.com

Industrie Bar* • CBD • Restaurant/Bar

Enhancing the French ambience, the staff greets you at the door in their pin-striped shirts with a smile and a "bonjour." The exposed interior wall creates an urban roughness, which is offset by white table-cloths, gilded mirrors, and silvery drapes. Old World court jesters grin at the fashionable suits from behind glass, and the after-work crush between 5pm and 9pm sees Sydney's top end of town enjoying champagne cocktails and shimmying to lounge tunes on the upper level—with a balcony overlooking the ground floor. There's also an outdoor terrace facing Pitt Street. The new Emerald Room at the rear has its very own menu, plush emerald banquettes, scarlet chandeliers, and serves only Bollinger (the sponsor) champagne. There's a particular focus on older gentlemen with money to burn. Also open for breakfast, Industrie serves excellent coffee, and the French fries with aioli are delectable. *Mon-Wed 7:30am-midnight, Thu-Fri 7:30am-2am, Sat 6pm-3am.* ≡ 107 Pitt St. (Hunter St.), 02 9221 8001, industriebar.com.au

Jimmy Liks* • Potts Point • Restaurant/Bar

This hipster hangout is a favorite for a mid-evening snack at the bar, or delicious Asian food at the communal tables. *See Sydney Hot & Cool Restaurants, p.79, for details.* ≡ 188 Victoria St. (Darlinghurst St.), 02 8354 1400, jimmyliks.com

Judgement Bar • Darlinghurst • Bar

Best Late-Night Hangouts Judgement Bar is the place where weekends go to die. A graveyard of hazy memories, drunken jukebox sing-alongs, stolen kisses, and impassioned debates, the Judgie is the last port of call for tequila slammer nightcaps. The bar is above the Courthouse Hotel, on the corner of Taylor Square, and is quite possibly Sydney's seediest 24-hour pub, always teeming with undesirables and late-night hipsters. Revered in Sydney pub folklore as the last bastion for those bent on a bender, the Judgement Bar goes in and out of favor with the city's actors and rock 'n' rollers, but either way it's the bar they love to hate, so no matter how hard they resist, they'll always be back. When it's really thumping, in the early hours of Sunday morning, the Judgie is like the best warehouse party you ever crashed. But it's also responsible for some of the city's worst hangovers. Strap on your drinking boots and bring your sunglasses to fight the dawn light. *Nightly 6pm-late.* ≡ 189 Oxford St. (Flinders St.), 02 9360 4831, courthousehotel.com.au

La Sala* • Surry Hills • Restaurant/Bar

The loft bar at this Italian eatery is packed with buff boys and their girl toys, enjoying cocktails and a night out. *See Sydney Hot & Cool Restaurants, p.80, for details.* ≡ Ground floor, 23 Foster St. (Campbell St.), 02 9281 3352, lasala.com.au

Lady Lux • Potts Point • Nightclub

Best Hot Club Scenes Everybody in Lady Lux is sexy, and if they're not, at least they think they are. Cute 20-something girls and image-conscious boys pout and flirt by the DJ booth as the old-school remixed tunes throb. Those there to boogie rather than prance carve up the dance floor, weaving between the ferns or writhing about on the daybed lounges. An intimate club on Roslyn Street, a stone's throw from where the shady pot dealers linger, Lady Lux reignited Sydney's club scene with a return to intimacy and sophistication, moving away from the cavernous mega-clubs. It's overflowing with coolios, and the pretension is palpable, but Lady Lux also attracts funsters willing to leave their attitude at the door and swivel and spin on the polished floorboards beneath the disco ball. Dress funkily and ooze confidence at the door, as the door trolls can often be prickly, especially when resident "party-electro" DJ duo People's Republic hits the decks (Thursday to Sunday) and the club overflows. With everything from Prince to house, rare groove, and electro thumping, the party atmosphere means nobody has an excuse not to dance and enjoy themselves. *Thu-Sun 10pm-late.* C≡ 2 Roslyn St. (Barncleuth Ln.), 02 9361 5000, ladylux.com.au

Local* • Paddington • Restaurant/Bar

Paddington locals—the young and hip—unwind after work at this sleek bar, then move to the garden courtyard for Modern Australian dinners in a relaxed atmosphere. *See Sydney Hot & Cool Restaurants, p.80, for details.* ≡ 211 Glenmore Rd. (Broughton St.), 02 9332 1577, localwinebarandrestaurant.com.au

The Loft • King Street Wharf • Ultra Lounge

Best Cocktail Lounges With dripping amber chandeliers and a Moroccan boudoir ambience, the Loft is one of Sydney's premier cocktail lounges. It's too easy to sink back into the pillows on the leather couches, watching the sun set over Darling Harbour as you sip a cocktail from the Middle East, the Americas, or the Mediterranean. Chief mixologist Garth Foster heads a team of buff shakers and friendly waitresses, and the Loft's Sunday sessions are renowned for attracting die-hards keeping the weekend alive as well as mid-20s chillers. Sitting on the end of King Street Wharf, the Loft enjoys gorgeous sweeping vistas. The soundtrack moves from lounge to electro with ease, matching the crowd's enthusiasm. The crowd is cool, but conservative at this bastion of good times. It's highly recommended for romantic interludes, whether locking eyes with your lover over the soft flame of an oil lantern or canoodling in one of the many hidden couch settings with someone new. *Mon-Thu 4pm-midnight, Fri-Sun noon-2am.* ≡ 3 Lime St. (Erskine St.), 02 9299 4770, theloftsydney.com

Longrain* • Surry Hills • Restaurant/Lounge

Sydney's sleekest Thai hot spot doesn't take reservations, meaning the lounge is always packed with scenesters waiting their turn for a coveted table. *See Sydney Hot & Cool Restaurants, p.81, for details.* ≡ 85 Commonwealth St. (Hunt St.), 02 9280 2888, longrain.com.au

Lotus* • Potts Point • Restaurant/Bar

For such a tiny cave nestled at the back of the popular Potts Point restaurant, Lotus's cocktail bar garners a great deal of attention. It's won awards from numerous sources for numerous reasons, from being gourmet travelers' favorite bar, to bartender of the year and best cocktail list—Lotus can hardly find room to store the trophies. One of the jewels in Merivale's multi-million-dollar hotelier crown, Lotus is an intimate gem. Palm fronds, silver wallpaper, and mirrored walls create the illusion of a larger space. Impeccably groomed Eastern suburbanites struggle to hear one another over the buzz of conversation and lounge tunes, while the bartenders work up a sweat beneath a modern glass chandelier and ask each patron what mood they're in, matching a martini or tall, tropical fruit blend to suit. The pre- and post-dinner rush each night is full, but reserve a sidewalk table in the restaurant and come in before 7pm to secure a corner in the darkened bar. Frequented by Potts Point's upwardly mobile gay crowd, young professionals, and funky 50-somethings, Lotus has a vibrant, casual atmosphere with a cramped but cozy appeal. *Tue-Sat 6pm-1am.* ≡ 22 Challis Ave. (McClay St.), 02 9326 9000

Melt • Kings Cross • Restaurant/Nightclub

An art space, live music venue, restaurant, nightclub, and bar, Melt is for the effortlessly cool. The motto emblazoned on the matchboxes says it all: "slave to the rhythm not the system." Enter off Kellett Street between a couple of "gentlemen's" clubs, climb the stairs past the hanging art, and stroll past the bistro tables into the heart of the red-and-black retro lounge bar. There's exposed brick with a spectacular mural creating a raw, urban feel and a stage at the end of the room where jazz quartets play or DJs spin. Melt is best when you have it all to yourself, but when you're sharing a leather lounge with Sydney's arts-inspired coolios you're in good company, too. Preferring to quietly sneak onto the Sydney bar scene when it opened at the end of 2005, Melt was quickly discovered by the in-the-know. While the owners are still working on the exact weekly musical menu, live bands are a focus, and you'll find everything from funk to jazz and hip-hop. *Wed-Sun 8pm-late.* C≡ 12 Kellett St. (King St.), 02 9380 6060, meltbar.com.au

Middle Bar • Darlinghurst • Bar

High above Taylor Square, Middle Bar's balcony deck is the place to watch the action. Clubbers file past the gay boys and queens below, while disheveled drunks and misfits stumble about and fresh-faced 20-something barflies skip upstairs to Middle Bar. Atop the seedy Kinselas Hotel, where actors shoot the breeze and the inner city's shady characters pump dollars into the poker machines, Middle Bar is a house music–filled space with a marble-topped bar and side tables. It's also a day club on Sunday mornings from 5am until the revelers disperse. Middle Bar was once a dark box where underage teens gyrated and cocaine reigned. While it's not quite as hip as it once was, the location means Middle Bar will always be grooving. On Saturday nights it's a great starting point for a night out. Beyond the long bar and balcony is a quieter back room, with ergonomic stools and carpet to keep the throbbing bass lines at bay. *Thu 7pm-late, Fri 6pm-4am, Sat 6pm-late, Sun 5am-day, 7pm-late.* ≡ 383 Bourke St. (Campbell St.), 02 9331 6200, kinselas.com.au

Mint* • CBD • Restaurant/Lounge

The Inter-Continental's drinking and dining spot draws chic crowds looking for a bit of sophistication. *See Sydney Hot & Cool Restaurants, p.81, for details.* ≡ 62 Bridge St. (Phillip St.), 02 9240 1210, mintbaranddining.com.au

The Old Fitzroy Hotel* • Woolloomooloo • Pub/Theater

Ramshackle and bohemian, the Old Fitz is the jewel of Sydney's fringe theater scene and a place where you're guaranteed to find engaging conversationalists and pub philosophers. The Fitz combines the joy of theater with cheap beer and sensational laksas. Nestled in the back streets of Kings Cross, it's popular with travelers who venture from the red light district's main drag, actors who often grace the intimate stage, and Sydney's arts posse. But there's also a lively swarm of locals of mixed ages, who come to catch a show or simply have a beer by the fire or on the sidewalk outside. The beers are pulled by attractive actors supplementing their wages, and the Chinese kitchen pumps out satay chicken, spring rolls, and burgers. There's an open terrace in the back, and a bar upstairs with pool tables, cushioned banquettes, and beer barrels for tables. The front bar is always bursting with interesting faces, a prime spot for single mingles. *Mon-Fri 10:30am-midnight, Sat 11:30am-midnight, Sun 3-10pm.* ≡ 129 Dowling St. (Cathedral St.), 02 9356 3848, oldfitzroy.com.au

Q Bar • Darlinghurst • Nightclub

Best Late-Night Hangouts The door is always open at the Q, seven nights a week and 363 days a year. Sydney's perennial party venue caters to every type of clubber, and celebrities from Eddie Vedder to Ice-T have haunted Q bar at one time or another. From first-timers fresh out of school to older folk who still love to dance until 3am, you get all sorts at Q. Accordingly, the bouncers are some of the scariest-looking doormen in Sydney, but play it cool, and you'll have no problem getting past the rope. Enter up the rickety stairs and straight onto the main dance floor. This club provides something for everybody. At the back is the dedicated "games room" featuring pinball and pool tables, while on the right is a photo booth to document your own Q night. Photos from the booth adorn the paint-peeled walls, celebrating past revels under the Q label. *Nightly 9pm-late.* C≡ 34-44 Oxford St. (Pelican St.), 02 9360 1375, qbar.com.au

Ravesi's* • Bondi Bondi • Restaurant/Bar

Smack bang in the middle of Campbell Parade, Bondi Beach's main street, Ravesi's is a magnet for the beautiful people. Sunday nights are by far the best, and Sydney's social set hits the club in droves, dancing in the upstairs VIP bar to old-school funk, electro, and '80s mash-ups, or heading for the padded stools along the folded back windows in the main bar downstairs. *See Sydney Hot & Cool Restaurants, p.83, for details.* ≡ 118 Campbell Parade (Hall St.), 02 9365 4422, ravesis.com.au

Ruby Rabbit • Darlinghurst • Bar/Nightclub

Unlike most joints named after fluffy animals, Ruby Rabbit is anything but a sleazy strip joint. Bursting onto the Sydney bar scene with club aficionados Paul Schell and Phil Cawood at the helm, Ruby Rabbit has hosted after-parties for the Foo Fighters, film premiere soirees, and music industry parties. As the former editor of cheeky street mag *Large*, Schell has an overriding sense of fun, and with the assistance of designer Mark Lieb (of Phamish in Darlinghurst fame), his Ruby Rabbit design integrates elements of 1970s psychedelia with a custom-made finish and an eclectic entertainment policy to match. It's a unique retreat, with turquoise paisley wallpaper and white couches up front, a picket-fenced indoor "garden" bar with faux vines towards the rear, and a second floor with an abandoned grand piano, multiple globes suspended from the ceiling, and battered couches on a raised stage near the DJ, who generally blends electro with rock. There's a pervading sense of underground European cool. Weekend nights see glam 20-somethings lining up down Oxford Street, while weeknights attract the hardest partiers, teetering into their late 30s. *Wed-Sat 9pm-late.* C≡ 231 Oxford St. (Riley St.), 02 9326 0044,rubyrabbit.com.au

Slip Inn* • CBD • Restaurant/Nightclub

Best Beer Gardens Keen to emulate the success of Princess Mary's pick-up of a charming prince, single ladies know the Danish royal's fairy tale began when she met Prince Frederick at the Slip Inn. A bar of many guises, the Slip Inn houses the Chinese Laundry underground nightclub, a spectacular beer garden lit up with fairy lights and lanterns by night, a delicious Thai restaurant, a dugout bar, a gaming room, and a streetfront pub-style bar with cushioned cube stools and booths. One of seven Merivale venues (another being the much-celebrated Establishment Hotel), the Slip Inn caters to hip clubbers. The highlights are below street level and the nightclub has been known to feature international DJs playing everything from house to breaks to hip-hop and electro on Fridays and Saturdays. On Sundays, the garden bar erupts with dance DJs as university students and naughty 30-somethings boogie from noon until dark. By day, Slip Inn attracts a regular clientele of journalists (from the nearby Fairfax building), sexy suits, and Thai food fans who keep coming back for the speedy service and tantalizing flavors. *Mon-Thu noon-midnight, Fri noon-4am, Sat 4:30pm-4am, Sun 2-10pm.* ≡ 111 Sussex St. (King St.), 02 8295 9911, merivale.com.au

Spectrum • Darlinghurst • Nightclub

Best Live Music Venues Although the entrance is upstairs from the lower end of Oxford Street, Spectrum is all about the underground. The boys with their tight black stovepipes and reverse mullets lurk in the shadows, while girls in vintage dresses twirl beneath the multiple mirror balls. This is the shore where the rock 'n' roll new wave has crashed. The "spectrum" of colors starts from the bottom of the stairwell, bright reds, blues, greens, and yellows wrapping around the walls of the venue up to a chandelier. For lovers of New York's clubs of grittiness and grunge, Spectrum will feel like home. This bar does shabby chic with flair, and the bands that have packed punters into the intimate space are Australia's "next big thing" exports. Tuesday nights are reserved for unsigned bands, and a variety of acts hit the tiny stage throughout the week. It's often overcrowded and hot, but you're up close and personal with some of the most hypnotic rockers. Rock 'n' roll DJs hit the decks after the live bands, with tunes from the White Stripes to Jackson 5, glam rock to indie. Dimly lit for debauchery, Spectrum is a hothouse of cool. *Tue-Sun 8pm-late.* C≡ 34 Oxford St. (Liverpool St.), 02 9360 1375, pashpresents.com

Sugaroom* • Pyrmont • Restaurant/Bar

Overlooking the industrial end of the harbor, Sugaroom draws after-work crowds who stay for dinner. *See Sydney Hot & Cool Restaurants, p.84, for details.* ≡ Shop 2, 1 Harris St. (Elizabeth St.), 02 9571 5055, sugaroom.com.au

Swell* • Bronte Beach • Cafe

This beachfront cafe is a popular and perfect spot for just about anything from a glass of wine to a decadent breakfast. *See Sydney Hot & Cool Restaurants, p.85, for details.* ≡ Shop 3, 465 Bronte Rd. (Nelson St.), 02 9386 5001, swellrestaurant.com.au

Tank • CBD • Nightclub

Best Hot Club Scenes Five years is a long time in clubbing years, but Tank refuses to give it up. The underground arm of the suave Establishment Hotel has a strict "we only play house" policy that keeps the loyal flock of trendy urbanites coming back for more. If a big name in dance music is in town, it's likely it will be playing at Tank. If dancing is your mission, wear jeans and sneakers but make sure they are the latest models. With three bars over two levels, the best spots are strictly underground—you only head upstairs to visit the bathroom or cloakroom. Downstairs, the glowing bar of the main dance floor is offset by the original exposed beams of the historic building; to the left is the private lounge, lined on one side with private booths. Best bet for a lavish night out? Find a celebrity friend with an exclusive Tank Black membership. Privileges include priority booth bookings, reserved with a bottle of spirits, cocktail service, and access to the Parlour, the best of five exclusive lounge areas, featuring secret entry and exit points. *Fri-Sat 10pm-6am.* C≡ Establishment Hotel, 3 Bridge Ln. (George St.), 02 8295 9966, tankclub.com.au

Tonic • King's Cross • Ultra Lounge/Nightclub

A night out at Tonic is like a party in your living room complete with your own DJ, a friendly cocktail-shaking bartender, and comfy couches. Not only is the bar as intimate as a living room, it's actually set in a converted terrace house, so the homey furnishings make the space feel that much more familiar. There's a Persian rug on the dance floor, Frida Kahlo–esque paintings on the wall, and an array of indoor plants. There are often live bands wedged between the velvet-curtained windows and candlelit tables; otherwise there's a DJ spinning funky ambient tracks. With a capacity of 100, it's never too crowded, and the house-party feel keeps the crowd chatty and approachable. The doorman is friendly and everyone's welcome, but the small space means legal capacity is reached quickly, so be patient when lining up because it's one out, one in. Early in the week Tonic is great for a quiet drink, but weekends are reserved for dance-floor mayhem and booty shaking with strangers. Up the steep staircase you'll find other couch settings, all in the name of lounging, chatting, and romancing. *Wed-Sun 8pm-late.* C≡ 62-64 Kellett St. (Ward Ave.), 02 8354 1544, toniclounge.com.au

Zeta Bar • CBD • Bar/Nightclub

Best Trendy Hangouts Sipping a cocktail on the Zeta Bar terrace, face to face with the resplendent copper dome of the Queen Victoria Building, and surrounded by jet-setters and Sydney suits, you've know you've made it. Led by famed mixologist Mikey Enright, the staff know how to shake (or stir), and they do so with grace. Be sure to sample the specials. Although you wouldn't expect the Hilton to be a hot spot, Enright draws Sydney's sexy set and has brought in the House Solution crew (of Tank nightclub fame) to ensure that Saturday nights feature supreme house DJs and chic clubbers. Navigating the door can, on occasion, be tricky, so arriving before 9pm dressed to impress is recommended. Once you're settled into a cushioned room (available by phoning ahead and making a reservation) or a prime spot on the terrace overlooking the Central Business District rooftops, you'll soon forget the obstacle course. The soundtrack is chilled with house favorites, the lighting is moody, and the views from the veranda are a testament that Sydney's skyline is as spectacular as its harbor. *Mon-Wed 5pm-late, Thu-Fri 3pm-late, Sat 4pm-late.* ≡ The Hilton Hotel, Level 4, 488 George St. (Park St.), 02 9265 6070, zetabar.com.au

Hot & Cool Sydney: The Attractions

Andrew (Boy) Charlton Swimming Pool • The Domain • Sport

This historic outdoor pool is set on the shores of Woolloomooloo Bay, near the Royal Botanic Gardens, and has glorious views of the harbor. The site was once a popular swimming spot for local Aborigines before the arrival of Europeans. It was also the venue for the sporting triumphs of Australian swimming legend Andrew (Boy) Charlton, who set three world records here in 1924. It's also believed to be the birthplace of the Australian Crawl, or freestyle swimming stroke. The fastest of the swimming strokes, it was perfected by Arthur Cavill and his younger brother Dick, who evolved the stroke from the style of a young Soloman Islander, Alick Wickham, who visited Sydney in the 1890s. There is also a cafe on site with lovely views, and an adjoining yoga studio that's open to the public. *Daily 6am-7pm* (spring and summer). $ 1C Mrs. Macquaries Rd. (Cahill Expressway), 02 9358 6686, cityofsydney.nsw.gov.au

Aviation Tours Australia • Sydney Airport • Tour

Daredevil types will love the adrenaline rush of dashing across Bondi and Bronte beaches and over the harbor in a helicopter with the doors pulled off! There's nothing between you and the sea, and when the pilot starts doing aerial maneuvers your heart might jump out of your mouth. Gentler, but still exciting, helicopter trips zip above the harbor icons, while longer ones take off along Sydney's coastline or head inland as far as the Blue Mountains. A special trip is at twilight, in the glow of the setting sun. You fly over Coogee, Bondi, and Manly beaches before hovering over the magnificent North and South Headlands—the gateway to Sydney Harbour. *Hours vary.* $$$$ Sydney Airport, 02 9317 3402, sydneyhelitours.com.au

The Belinda Stores • CBD • Shop

Sydney style doyenne Belinda Seper founded her first store, stocking local and international treasures, in 1992 in Double Bay, and the branches just keep on growing. She now has eight, including a Melbourne outpost. But Belinda is no chainstore wannabe. Each store is an individual; the Menswear is just for guys, stocking top-shelf brands such as Yohji Yamamoto; the Corner Shop stocks edgier streetwear and one-offs—it is one of the only places you'll find those price-on-application dresses by Australian designer Michelle Jank; the city store caters to urban sophisticates—think Marni and Balenciaga; the Double Bay store stocks more whimsical pieces by Stella McCartney; and the shoe stores take care of footwear with brands such as Chloe and Marc Jacobs. *Mon-Sat 10am-6pm.* Double Bay: 8 Transvaal Ave., 02 9328 6288; Belinda Shoe Store, 14 Transvaal Ave., 02 9327 8199; Paddington: Belinda Menswear, 29 William St., 02 9380 8873; 39 William St., 02 9380 8728; The Corner Shop, 43 William St., 02 9380 9828; St. Martin Place: Shop 7, The MLC Building, 19 Martin Pl., 02 9233 0781; belinda.com.au

Blue Thunder • CBD • Tour

Get your motor running—with a tour of Sydney on the back of a Harley. The tours last as little as an hour to all day. They leave from Manly, Bondi, or the Rocks. Among the best runs is a two-hour ride from Manly to Bondi beach, and a fabulous four-hour cruise out into the country to follow the beautiful Hawkesbury River. Other tours go off to Watsons Bay, where you can stop for a drink, and along the Northern Beaches as far as beautiful Palm Beach. You can hire a Heritage Softtail, a Road King, or a Dyna Wide Glyde for a self-drive too. *Hours vary.* $$$$ 1 800 800 184 in Australia / mobile 0408 618 982, bluethunder.com.au

Bondi to Bronte Coast Walk • Bronte • Walk

The 2.1-mile (3.4km) walk from Bronte to Bondi beaches is one of the most scenic in Sydney. There are commanding views of the ocean from the clifftops, where people wander along in bikinis and shorts, and joggers and power walkers trot past at pace. Bronte Beach is a crescent of sand wedged in a valley and backed by a bowl of grass and a string of cafes. The first surf club in Australia was formed here in 1903. But swimmers beware—there are rip tides at either end, and often a third one in the center. Toward Bondi is little Tamarama Beach, affectionately known as Glamorama, for its bathing beauties. Bus 380, from Circular Quay via Bondi Junction

BridgeClimb Sydney • The Rocks • Sport

Best Only-in-Sydney Experiences The Harbour Bridge is the widest long-span bridge in the world, and carries eight car lanes, two train lines, a foot path and a bike path. It's 3,769 feet (1,149 meters) long, and the top of the arch is 439 feet (134 meters) above sea level. It was opened in March 1932, five years before the Golden Gate Bridge in San Francisco. Climbing the arches is a real thrill. You get dressed up in special suits and are clamped onto a rail to stop you from falling off. Climb leaders then guide groups of 12 along catwalks, up ladders, and over the arch to the bridge's summit, where you can enjoy 360-degree views of one of the world's finest harbors. Sunset and sunrise tours are especially thrilling, and there's also a climb of the bridge's interior called the Discovery Climb. The Pylon Lookout, in the southeastern stone pylon, has impressive views and a small bridge-related museum if the actual climb is too daunting. *Hours vary by season, call for reservations.* $$$$ 5 Cumberland St. (George St.), 02 8274 7777, bridgeclimb.com

Collette Dinnigan • Paddington • Shop

The first Australian to show in the Paris ready-to-wear collections in 1995, Collette Dinnigan is Australia's most fashionable export. Sure, she was born in New Zealand, but as with most successes from across the Tasman, Sydneysiders have embraced her as one of their own. Her dreamboat dresses and lingerie—made from the finest European lace, silk, and satin, or embellished with handsewn beadwork—bring out the bedroom goddess. Carried in Barneys, Dinnigan also has a boutique in London's Chelsea district, and her designs are red-carpet favorites with celebrities such as Naomi Watts and Halle Berry. *Mon-Sat 10am-6pm, Sun noon-5pm.* 33 William St. (Underwood St.), 02 9360 6691, collettedinnigan.com.au

Deus Ex Machina • Camperdown • Shop/Gallery

Rebels without a cause will find it hard to drag themselves away from this vintage bike trader and gallery. Set up by a group of motorcycle enthusiasts to promote the cycle culture of the 1940s, '50s and '60s, Deus sells classic bikes—such as Yamaha TW220s and "choppers"—as well as clothing of a bygone era. The store also features artwork from Australia and Japan, books, helmets, and paraphernalia—and there's a bar. *Mon-Fri 10am-6pm, Sat 10am-4pm.* 98-104 Parramatta Rd. (King Edward St.), 02 9557 6866, deus.com.au

The Diva's Closet • Paddington • Shop

A favorite with celebs including Cate Blanchett and Beyoncé Knowles, the Diva's Closet is a red-carpet shopping destination. Buyer and clothing collector Regina Evans provides a personalized shopping service in a boudoir-style loft space filled with the highest-quality vintage clothing and accessories. American designers such as Norell mingle with European counterparts Pucci and Dior. *By appointment only.* 32 William St. (Underwood St.), 02 9361 6659 / 0408 96467

Gleebooks • Glebe • Shop

You won't find any Borders-style coffee lounges at this iconic Sydney bookstore, a favorite haunt of artists, academics, and those who just love a good read—and you can be sure Dan Brown won't be featured, either. What you will find is a trove of international and Australian publications from fiction to DIY. Gleebooks is the bookstore that plays host to visiting writers—events that sell out fast. Explore Australian writers such as David Malouf, Peter Carey, and Kate Grenville. *Daily 9am-9pm.* 49 Glebe Point Rd. (Derby Pl.), 02 9660 2333, gleebooks.com.au

Jet Boating on Sydney Harbour • Darling Harbour/Circular Quay • Activity

Best Harbor Experiences Sydney Harbour is filled with green-and-yellow ferries and is awash with cruise boats and yachts, but the most exciting way to experience one of the world's most famous waterways is to add some speed, some sideways slides, a few fishtails, and a few "Powerbrake Stops." Three companies run jet boat adventures on the harbor, and you get a lot of grunt from their giant engines as they zip along beside the Sydney Opera House and Fort Denison and under the Sydney Harbour Bridge. *Daily 11am-sunset.* Sydney Jet: Cockle Bay Wharf, Darling Harbour, 02 9938 2000, sydneyjet.com; Harbour Jet: Convention Centre Jetty, Darling Harbour, 02 9698 2110, harbourjet.com; Oz Jet: Eastern Pontoon, Circular Quay, 02 9808 3700, ozjetboating.com

Lets Go Surfing • North Bondi Beach • Sport

Bondi Beach is known for three things—the glamorous bodies on the sand, the hunky lifeguards, and surfing. You can hire boards, or complete a surfing course at Bondi with Lets Go Surfing. The popular small-group beginner course teaches you how to safely get out and up onto your first wave. You start off in broken waves—the white foam created after the waves run their course. The company also offers private lessons, as well as intermediate and advanced courses. You'll be happy to know that a shark net is laid off the beach. 128 Ramsgate Ave. (Campbell Parade), 02 9365 1800, letsgosurfing.com.au

LivingWell Premier Health Club • CBD • Spa

The Hilton Sydney re-opened in 2005 after an extensive renovation, included the largest hotel-based health club in Australia. This veritable temple to well-being takes up a whole hotel floor. The spa's signature treatment is its Stone Therapy, which uses hot volcanic stones on your body's chakras, or energy points. The green coffee wrap is invigorating, and the caviar-and-pearl-extract anti-aging facial is positively revivifying. After a hard day traipsing the streets, you can opt for a de-stress foot massage, or if you've just stepped off the plane, then the Rejuvenating Jetlag Treatment, using hydrating gels and revitalizing oils, might be just the ticket. *Mon-Fri 5am-9:30pm, Sat-Sun 7am-8pm.* $$$$ Hilton Sydney, 3/255 Pitt St. (Market St.), 02 9273 8800, livingwell.com.au

Luna Park • Milsons Point • Theme Park

That huge smiley face across the harbor from Circular Quay is Luna Park (there's another one in St. Kilda, Melbourne). It first opened in 1935, built mainly by workers who had just completed the Sydney Harbour Bridge. The first famous face was rather stern, and over the years it's been made more friendly with cosmetic surgery. A big attraction is the Ferris wheel, which offers sweeping bay and city views. Here too is a flying saucer, a pirate ship that spins you 360 degrees, a carousel, dodge 'em cars, and Australia's only authentic 1930s fun house. *Mon-Thu 11am-6pm, Fri 11am-11pm, Sat 10am-11pm, Sun 10am-6pm.* $$ 1 Olympic Dr. (Alfred St.), 02 9033 7676, lunaparksydney.com

Museum of Contemporary Art • The Rocks • Art Museum

Best Art Spaces Located in an impressive 1952 sandstone building set back from Circular Quay across a span of grass terraces, the Museum of Contemporary Art (MCA) is Australia's best modern art museum. As well as hosting traveling exhibitions and new work by local artists—memorable exhibits have been a full-size, blow-up red automobile, and a collection of plastic knickknacks found washed up on local beaches—it also houses permanent collections. The largest of these is the J W Power Collection, an eclectic collection of works by Australian and international artists from the late 1960s. It comprises kinetic work from the '60s and '70s, performance pieces, pop art, and minimalist works from a range of artists, including Christo and Andy Warhol. The museum also exhibits Aboriginal bark paintings and other artworks made from fiber, seeds, shells, and feathers. *Daily 10am-5pm.* $ 140 George St. (Circular Quay), 02 9245 2400, mca.com.au

Museum of Sydney • Circular Quay • Cultural Museum

This fascinating interactive museum close to Circular Quay pieces together the history of colonization and Aboriginal life. The museum is built on the foundations of the first Government House, constructed in 1878 by Governor Arthur Phillip. It was the home, offices, and seat of authority for nine governors of NSW until it was demolished in 1846. In 1983, archaeologists unearthed the footings of this building, which are now on display. The museum uses objects, pictures, stories, and digital media to unlock the world of colonial and contemporary Australia. In the entrance courtyard is Edge of Trees, a public art space made of didgeridoo-type poles that "talk." *Daily 9:30am-5pm.* $ 37 Philip St. (Bridge St.), 02 9251 5988, hht.net.au

Oceanworld • Manly • Sport

If you don't think diving into a giant fish tank with sharks that are twice as long as your body is crazy, then why not attempt it before their official feeding time? At Oceanworld Manly, you can brush up on your scuba skills, or learn from scratch, and jump into an enormous tank with very inquisitive gray nurse sharks. Luckily, their preferred dinner is fish. During the 30-minute dive you'll also get close to giant stingrays and moray eels. It's not for the fainthearted. *Daily 9am-5pm.* $$ West Esplanade (Ferry Terminal), 02 8251 7878, sharkdive.oceanworld.com.au

Powerhouse Museum • Ultimo • Cultural Museum

Best Cool Museums In 1878, Sydney held Australia's first international exhibition of invention and industry. The Garden Palace was constructed in the Royal Botanic Gardens to host the show. It was so popular that the government bought many of the exhibits and set up the Technological, Industrial, and Sanitary Museum.

But before it could open to the public, a spectacular fire burned it down. These days, the renamed museum is located in a former power station, built in 1902 to provide electricity for the city's tram system. *Daily 10am-5pm.* $ 500 Harris St. (Macarthur St.), 02 9217 0111, phm.gov.au

Purl Harbour • Bondi Beach • Shop

A favorite with local fashion types, John Macarthur of Purl Harbour is Sydney's best-loved knitwear specialist. He's been operating out of his tiny Bondi shop since 1987, when he was discovered by *Vogue* magazine, and his chunky hand-knitted line includes everything from sweaters and socks to bikinis and singlets. He even claims to have tried knitting a wedding dress. Macarthur knits to order. Whatever you desire, he can create it out of wool. His designs are original and a bit hippie but the needlework would impress any craft-conscious grandmother. *Mon-Fri 9:30am-5:30pm, Sat 10am-5pm.* Unit 4, 16 Hall St. (entry via Jacques Ave.), 02 9365 1521

Scanlan & Theodore • Paddington • Shop

The cult brand Scanlan & Theodore has saved the day for many a frantic fashionista, coming to the rescue with the perfect outfit at the eleventh hour. For the more style savvy, however, a visit to Scanlan—as it is called for short—is booked into their weekly to-do list, much like a manicure. Scanlan purchases have an uncanny way of mixing and matching—even with an old piece from five seasons ago, it just works. If you make one fashion pit stop on your Sydney sojourn, make it here. *Mon-Wed 10am-6pm, Thu 10am-8pm, Fri 10am-6pm, Sat 10am-5:30pm, Sun noon-5pm.* 122 Oxford St. (Palmer St.), 02 9380 9388, scanlantheodore.com.au

Six Ounce Boardstore • Bondi Beach • Shop

Hippie Bondi surfers are as passionate about the origin of their boards as they are about the waves. Six Ounce sources short and long boards from "boutique" shapers—who love to surf as much as their customers—such as Morning of the Earth, Bear, and local brand McCoy. It also sells retro T-shirts and surf movies, like Albert Falzon's classic *Morning of the Earth. Tue-Fri 11am-6pm, Sat 10am-5pm, Sun 11am-4pm.* Shop 2, 144-148 Glenayr Ave. (Roscoe St.), 02 9300 8339, sixounceboardstore.com.au

The Spa at Four Seasons • CBD • Spa

This very pleasant spa in the Four Seasons Hotel, on the edge of the Rocks, offers the usual facials for men and women, a range of waxing, manicures, and pedicures, plus an enticing selection of massages and body therapies. How about a body scrub with lime and ginger salt, or a strawberry herbal back cleanse? A body wrap in coconut and frangipani flowers offers a bit of Tahitian magic, or you could be cocooned in a comforting foil wrap, while you have a soothing face and scalp massage. *Mon-Fri 7am-9:30pm, Sat-Sun 7am-8:30pm.* $$$$ 199 George St. (Essex St.), 02 9238 0000, fourseasons.com/sydney

Sydney by Seaplane • Rose Bay • Tour

For a pelican's-eye view of Sydney, you can't do better than take to the air in a seaplane. Two companies operate planes that take off and land on the harbor at Rose Bay, a ferry trip or short drive from the city. Flights last from 15 minutes to an hour, and you can circle over the Sydney Harbour Bridge, fly across Bondi Beach, or take a flit into the countryside. A fabulous option is a fly and dine package, which includes a seafood lunch at a waterside restaurant. These include Berowra Waters, set in bushland on the beautiful Hawkesbury River, and Jonah's, a world-class eatery a short hop from the exclusive northern suburb of Palm Beach. *Hours vary.* $$$$ Sydney by Seaplane: 02 9974 1455, sydneybyseaplane.com; Sydney Harbour Seaplanes: 02 9388 1978, seaplanes.com.au

Sydney Olympic Park • Homebush Bay • Park/Site

The site of the Sydney 2000 Olympic Games is a purpose-built sports complex surrounded by parklands, bike paths, mangrove forests, and wetlands. You can tour the Olympic stadium—once called Stadium Australia, and now called the Telstra Stadium—and also the Aquatic Centre. The Aquatic Centre Tour includes a spa and a swim. The best way to get around is by bicycle, which you can hire at the complex. Some 22 miles (35km) of cycleways take you around the site, past the Olympic Cauldron and stadiums, and out into Bicentennial Park, to see the wildfowl in the wetlands. 1 Showground Rd. (Olympic Park City Rail Station), 02 9714 7888, sydneyolympicpark.com.au

Sydney Tower Skywalk • CBD • Sport

Best Only-in-Sydney Experiences This high-altitude adventure walk takes you right around the top of Sydney Tower, in the center of the city. It's a real buzz, but definitely not suitable if you are scared of heights! First, you get dressed in special suits—to stop things from dropping out of your pockets and killing people on the streets below—then you get harnessed to safety rails by a sliding cable, and are led out onto a metal gantry some 853 feet (260 meters) above the sidewalk. Worse still, there are lots of see-through panels on the floor, so you feel like there's nothing supporting you. Scary. The whole experience lasts around one and a half hours. *Daily walks at 9:30am and 11:30am, 2:30pm, 4:30pm, and 6:30pm night walk (Sat only).* $$$$ Centrepoint Podium Level, Sydney Tower, 100 Market St. (Pitt St.), 02 9333 9222, skywalk.com.au

Tim Olsen Gallery • Paddington • Art Gallery

Run by one of Sydney's leading art families—Tim's sister Louise Olsen is part of the Dinosaur Designs team and father John Olsen is regarded as Australia's most esteemed living painter—the Tim Olsen Gallery has the right pedigree to handle contemporary art. In addition to representing established artists, including John Olsen, the gallery also hosts exhibitions by up-and-comers—carefully chosen by Olsen. *Tue-Fri 11am-6pm, Sat 11am-5pm.* 76 Paddington St. (Elizabeth St.), 02 9360 9854, timolsengallery.com

Classic Sydney

Standing in the Rocks looking out into Sydney Harbour, you can imagine what it felt like for the first colonists—OK, convicts—to lay eyes on this pristine island. It would be hard not to make comparisons to a paradise, especially after months on a boat. Like all good settlers, these early invaders quickly built bars, taverns, hotels, and even a prison or two, just for old times' sake. Then they went on with a Wild West flair to carve out a European feel in this foreign spot. A few centuries later, this classic side of Sydney is alive and well in the Botanical Gardens, stately old estates, and of course, the rambling byways of the Rocks, Sydney's oldest neighborhood. So do like the Aussies of yesterday (and frankly, those of today) and take a seat, grab a brew, and watch the afternoon slip carelessly away into night, and back to day again.

Note: Venues in bold are described in detail in the listings that follow the itinerary. Venues followed by an asterisk (*) are recommended as both a restaurant and a destination bar.

Classic Sydney: The Perfect Plan (3 Nights and Days)

Perfect Plan Highlights

Friday	
Morning	**Circular Quay, the Rocks, Opera House, Royal Botanic Gardens**
Lunch	**Art Gallery Restaurant**
Afternoon	**Art Gallery of NSW, Hyde Park Barracks, Sydney Aqu., Maritime Msm., Powerhouse Msm.**
Pre-dinner	**Bungalow 8*, Blu Horizons**
Dinner	**Quay, Bilson's, Forty One**
Nighttime	**The Golden Sheaf*, Paddington, Basement***
Late-Night	**Golden Century**
Saturday	
Morning	**Taronga Zoo, Strand Arc.**
Lunch	**Bathers' Pavilion, Sailors Thai, Imperial**
Afternoon	**Manly Beach, St. Mary's**
Pre-dinner	**Manly Wharf Hotel*, Opera Bar**
Dinner	**Guillaume at Bennelong, Tetsuya's, Fish at Rocks**
Nighttime	**Lord Nelson Brewery**
Late-Night	**Fortune of War, Victoria Rm.***
Sunday	
Morning	**Rocks Market, Spa**
Lunch	**Doyle's*, Kables**
Afternoon	**Sydney Tower, Bridge**
Pre-dinner	**360 Bar, Orbit Bar**
Dinner	**Rockpool, Summit, Marque**
Nighttime	**Arthouse**
Late-Night	**The Bourbon**

Hotel: **Shangri-La Hotel**

Friday

9am This morning is about walking through some of the Emerald City's shining gems. Slap on your sunglasses and slop on some sunscreen and stroll down to Circular Quay (pronounced "key"), where you can tuck in to some breakfast at one of the outdoor cafes and watch the ferries and the passing crowds.

10am Continue waterside until you reach the Park Hyatt, then turn left and discover the historical district of the Rocks—this is Sydney's oldest neighborhood and a charming, winding area of shops, sights, and pubs. Stop in for a quick tour of **Susannah Place Museum**, a charming "museum" made up of an old row house and its furnishings.

11am Nip back down to the waterfront and across to the **Sydney Opera House** for an hour-long tour. Or behind the Opera House is an entrance to the **Royal Botanic Gardens** and a pathway that leads you past a colony of fruit bats and out onto Art Gallery Road. Take some time to soak in the lush surrounds, speckled with lakes, statues, and greenery.

CLASSIC

1pm Lunch: After all that walking you deserve a delicious lunch. For a light contemporary meal and a commanding outlook across the water and wharfs of picturesque Woolloomooloo Bay, make your way to the **Art Gallery Restaurant**.

2:30pm Check out the collections of the **Art Gallery of New South Wales**, or stroll across the Domain parklands and through the walkway between the Sydney Hospital buildings to Macquarie Street. Rub the nose of the brass pig in front of the hospital for luck. Then turn left and pop into **Hyde Park Barracks Museum** for a fascinating perspective on convict life.

4pm Grab a cab to Darling Harbor and choose from a trio of attractions—the amazing **Sydney Aquarium**, the **Maritime Museum**, and the **Powerhouse Museum** (see Hot & Cool Attractions).

6pm Grab a seat and work your way through the wine and spirit menu at **Bungalow 8***. You could also refresh yourself with the glorious views from **Blu Horizons Bar** back at the Shangri-La Hotel.

8pm Dinner For some angelic seafood or pork belly while overlooking the illuminated Opera House, you can't miss **Quay.** Otherwise indulge in slinky fettuccini or foie gras at **Bilson's**, a Francophile favorite. Also a big-bang gourmet choice is **Forty One**, a contemporary 42nd-floor eatery that's verging on heaven.

10:30pm Jump into a cab and head out to Double Bay to join the well-heeled stylish folk at **the Golden Sheaf Hotel*** for DJs and a beer-garden scene, or party to funky jazz tunes along with some of Sydney's hottest pub enthusiasts at the **Paddington Inn**. For live music, perhaps soul or jazz, head to **The Basement*** at Circular Quay.

1am Need to refuel? Hop in a cab to the **Golden Century**, a Chinese favorite that stays open until 4am, and try some shark fin soup or fresh abalone.

Saturday

9am The breakfast buffet at the Shangri-La is one of the best in Sydney, with all the regular fare and a good selection of Asian treats too.

10am Take a water taxi or a regular ferry to **Taronga Zoo**, where you can meander past everything from gorillas and chimps to kangaroos and echidnas. Or head out for some shopping in the city's elegant arcades: the **Strand Arcade** and **Queen Victoria Building**, both filled with great local boutiques.

1pm Lunch **Bathers' Pavilion Restaurant** at Balmoral Beach near the zoo is a charming place for a seafood lunch, but book ahead as weekends attract the social set. Or back in the city, opt for some spice at **Sailors Thai**, or perhaps mouth-watering salt-and-pepper mud crab, or kangaroo Shanghai style at **Imperial Peking**.

3pm Hop on the ferry to Manly, which passes close to the Heads, which the First Fleet sailed through in 1788. It's a rocky ride on a rough day, but the half-hour trip gives you a wonderful taste of the harbor. Then laze around on Manly Beach or stroll to little Shelly Beach, to your right as you look at the ocean waves. From here it's a brief clamber up a rough track to dramatic cliffs over-looking yet more beaches. Aim to travel back to the city by jet cat at dusk to see the city lights gleaming like a colorful oil slick on the harbor. If the beach doesn't beckon, stay in town and take in some more histori-cal sites with a visit to **St. Mary's Cathedral** and a walk through Hyde Park.

6pm Have a relaxing beer at the **Manly Wharf Hotel***. Alterna-tively, back in the city, tidy yourself up and take in the lit-up Sydney Harbour Bridge from the more sophisticated **Opera Bar** in the Opera House, where you'll find a lively local scene every night.

7:30pm Dinner Stay at the Opera House for a grand meal with a superb harbor outlook at **Guillaume at Bennelong**. Otherwise, indulge yourself with the Japanese-French fusion food at **Tetsuya's**—just make sure you've booked a month in advance. Or walk up the hill through the convict-hewn Argyle Cut to **Fish at the Rocks** for a casual and delicious dose of fish and chips.

9:30pm One of the best historic pubs in the Rocks, the **Lord Nelson Brewery Hotel**, closes at 11pm, so don't linger too long over dinner.

11pm **The Fortune of War Hotel** is a good place to continue the fun.

1am Jump in a cab to the down-at-the-heels Kings Cross neighbor-hood and join the throng cruis-ing the late-night bars and seedy strip clubs. Drop into the **Victoria Room*** for a martini.

9am French accents, fabulous cof-fee, and the best croissants this side of Paris are the hallmarks of the **Renaissance Café Patisserie**, the perfect courtyard breakfast spot to begin another packed day.

10am Ease yourself into they day ahead with a stroll through the Rocks Market followed by a lime and ginger body scrub, or a relaxing massage at the Spa at Four Seasons (see Hot & Cool Attractions). Or head off by ferry to **Watsons Bay** and take a pleasant walk around the area where the First Fleet anchored.

1pm Lunch Grab a table at **Kables**, the restaurant in the Four Seasons, for a refined meal. In Watsons Bay, you have multiple options—and all are owned and operated by the Doyle family, who have been serving up seafood since 1885. On a sunny day, try to snag a table outside at the iconic restaurant **Doyle's on the Beach**.

3pm After returning to Circular Quay, take a walk back up through the Rocks to the start of the Sydney Harbour Bridge. A little way along you'll come to the Pylon Lookout, which features brilliant harbor views and a small museum. From here, walk right across the bridge—the traffic is not nearly as bad on the weekend and the exhaust fumes are far less noxious. Take a train back to Town Hall Station. Or cap off your daylight activities by taking the elevator to the top of Sydney Tower, which offers views spanning the entire city as far as the Blue Mountains. Your ticket to the top includes OzTrek, the largest simulated ride in the southern hemisphere.

6pm Stay for a cocktail or more at the **360 Bar and Dining Room**, or freshen up at your hotel and wander around the corner for a cocktail at the **Orbit Bar**. If it's summer, check local listings to see what the outdoor movie screen near the Botanical Gardens is playing—it's got an onsite bar and a view to die for.

8pm Dinner A longtime local favorite, the always-lively **Rockpool** is the perfect choice for a final night on the town. Or, for dinner with a view, make your way to **Summit**. Another popular alternative is **Marque** for an elegant dinner.

10pm The city center crowd congregates in a few ripe places on Saturday evenings, including the **Arthouse Hotel** on Pitt Street, where modern furnishings complement the magnificent 19th-century plasterwork and high ceilings. Upstairs you'll find the Attic a cozy former chess club, now transformed into a stylish and intimate drinking den.

1am Drink and dance with until the early hours at a perennially popular Sydney landmark, **The Bourbon**, a swift cab ride away at Kings Cross.

Classic Sydney: The Key Neighborhoods

Chinatown This colorful quarter is known for its busy yum cha restaurants, crispy duck, and Asian food stores.

Circular Quay The gateway for Sydney's ferries, it's also the site of the Sydney Opera House and several top-class restaurants and hotels.

Darling Harbour This hip tourist mecca features major attractions, such as the Sydney Aquarium and the Australian Maritime Museum.

Kings Cross and Darlinghurst Sydney's red-light area runs into nearby Darlinghurst with cafe culture and a string of eateries.

Manly Reached by ferry or the faster jet cat from Circular Quay, this beachside suburb boasts a lengthy stretch of golden sand and access to part of the Sydney Harbour National Park.

The Rocks A compact historic center packed with colonial sandstone buildings, pubs, tourist stores, and alleyways.

Town Hall The beating heart of the city's shopping precinct is home to major department stores, historic shopping malls like the Queen Victoria Building, and the Strand Arcade.

CLASSIC

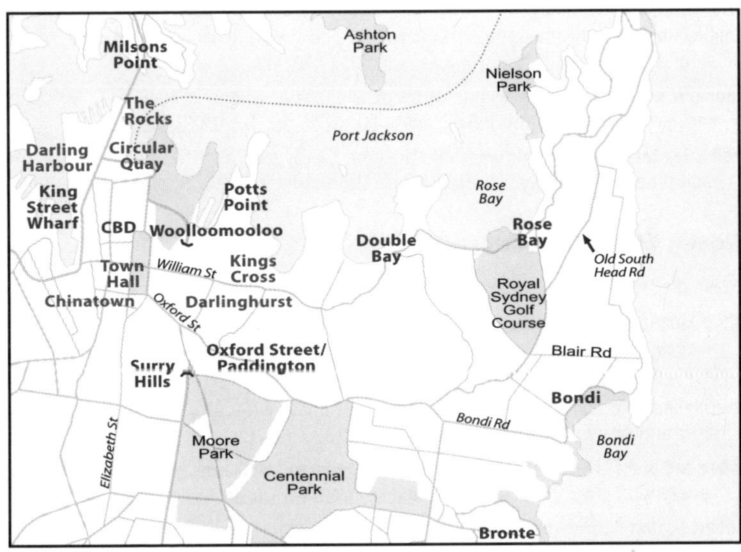

Classic Sydney: The Shopping Blocks

Central Business District (CBD)

If you want international fashion houses, head to Castlereagh Street. To sample Australian designers that you won't find at home, don't miss the Strand Arcade.

Dinosaur Designs Chunky resin jewelry and housewares with a Stone Age charm. Level 1, The Strand Arcade, Pitt St., 02 9223 2953

Robby Ingham Robby Ingham sources the best of international men's and women's brand names like Hugo Boss and Chloe. The MLC building, 19 Martin Pl., 02 9232 6466 and 424-428 Oxford St., Paddington, 02 9332 2124

Zimmermann Wear The mecca of Australian swim and beach wear, it stocks the most coveted bikinis in the country, as well as highly desirable day and evening wear. Level 1, The Strand Arcade, Pitt St., 02 9221 9558

Double Bay

This hamlet of beautiful boutiques caters to the old-money end of town.

Belinda and Belinda Shoe Store This is the hippest women's boutique chain in Sydney—stocking local brands alongside overseas biggies such as Marni and Lanvin. 8 Transvaal Ave., 02 9328 6288

Christensen Copenhagen You'll find cult jeans Paul and Joe and imported designer wear for seriously stylish women. 2 Guilfoyle Ave., 02 9328 9755

Empire Homewares Browse beautiful furniture and luxury housewares sourced from around the globe. 2 Guilfoyle Ave., 02 9328 7556

Louise Mitchell A supplier to one of the poshest linen shops in New York, Mitchell carries velvet quilts and pillowcases. 10 Cross St., 02 9363 1855

Neil Grigg Millinery Spring means one thing on the Sydney high-society calendar—it's race time. Purchase your decadent race-day hat here. 3 Bay St., 02 9328 0079

Queen Street Woollahra

Leave plenty of time to stroll Queen Street, a place to be seen and to spend big.

Akira Isogawa Akira Isogawa is one of a handful of Australian designers to host runway shows in Paris, and its elegant men's and women's clothes are fashion treasures. 12a Queen St., 02 9361 5221

Herringbone No stylish bloke's wardrobe is complete without a Herringbone pink shirt and striped tie. 102 Queen St., 02 9327 6470

Orson and Blake Sydney's first lifestyle store, Orson and Blake merges housewares with apparel and jewelry to make a stylist swoon. 83-85 Queen St., 02 9326 1155

Robert Burton Sydney fashion icon Robert Burton stocks divine Egyptian cotton bed linen, and towels. 10a Queen St., 02 9332 2944

Classic Sydney: The Hotels

Manly Pacific Hotel • Manly • Modern (170 rms)

Why not experience staying by the ocean while you're in the city? The beautiful beachside resort of Manly is just 15 minutes from Circular Quay by jet cat and half an hour away by ferry. You will have to make use of taxis to get home after midnight, though. That aside, what makes this four-star hotel really special is its position right on the famous surf beach. The only thing between you and the ocean waves is a line of tall Norfolk Island pines, which act as a popular roosting spot for thousands of colorful, chattering lorikeets. The rooftop pool and spa is the ideal location to watch the sunrise. The Inspiring Ocean View Rooms are comfortable and have either two double beds or one queen and a sofa bed. The roomside balcony has remarkable ocean views. Rooms on the second floor have larger balconies, but the higher up you go the more impressive the views (so ask for a seventh-floor room). A cocktail lounge, popular with the young set, features a pianist on Friday and Saturday evenings. $$$ 55 North Steyne St. (Raglan St.), 02 9977 7666, accorhotels.com.au

Medina Grand Harbourside • Darling Harbour • Modern (114 rms)

Sometimes it's good to stay in a place where you can walk into an apartment and have everything at your fingertips. This apartment hotel offers bright studios and one-bedrooms with everything you need. Each comes with a full kitchen, and the one-bedrooms come with a laundry and an extra TV. Blue carpets and modern furnishings give the place a simple but fresh look, and balconies, on all rooms above ground level, give you the opportunity to get some fresh air. Premier View rooms are the best option, because they all have views of the water. Premier rooms on the ground floor, however, overlook a courtyard or the Sydney Aquarium. Standard rooms face the city. A good indoor pool, gym, and spa add to the overall convenience. Darling Harbour attractions are nearby. $$$ 55 Shelley St. (King Street Wharf), 02 9249 7000 / 1 300 633 462, medinaapartments.com.au

Observatory Hotel • The Rocks • Timeless (99 rms)

One of Sydney's finest luxury hotels, the Observatory is reminiscent of a grand 19th-century Australian home. Its hushed atmosphere, elegant antiques, and art-filled drawing room and dining rooms lend it the genteel feel of a bygone age of doffed top hats and crinoline. A major attraction is the remarkable indoor swimming pool, easily the most alluring in Australia. It sits beneath a magnificent domed ceiling that resembles a brilliant southern hemisphere sky filled with fiber-optic, twinkling stars. The day spa is one of the most exclusive in the city, and the Galileo restaurant has a wonderful clubby feel and serves exquisite French- and Japanese-influenced delicacies. Deluxe rooms are draped with rich tapestry curtains and come with an antique-style breakfast table, a down-filled armchair, and either a king-size bed, a queen-size bed, or a set of two doubles. Colonial-style sash windows provide charming views of Observatory Hill and the historic timber wharfs of Walsh Bay. It's a ten-minute stroll downhill to the main part of the Rocks. $$$$ 89-113 Kent St. (Argyle St.), 02 9256 2222, observatoryhotel.com.au

Radisson Plaza Hotel • CBD • Modern (362 rms)

Reminiscent in shape to New York's famous Flatiron building, the restored 1920s Italianate sandstone façade of the Radisson Plaza Hotel Sydney is an evocative frontispiece to a contemporary chic interior. This popular business hotel does well with passing tourists and models too, who like its central location and the functionality of its rooms. These favor muted chocolate and gold as their color scheme, and come with data ports and ergonomic workstations, including a movable desk that you can set up in front of the TV if your mind tends to wander. Deluxe rooms are located on the 11th and 12th floors of the hotel and feature full-length glass doors, which open onto a Juliet-style balcony with city views. Here you'll find the famed Bilson's restaurant (see p.115), and the well-regarded Bistro Fax, which serves classic French bistro food with an Australian twist to the traveling salespeople and glamour girls. $$$ 27 O'Connell St. (Pitt St.), 02 8214 0000 / 1 800 333 333, radisson.com/sydneyau_plaza

Shangri-La Hotel Sydney • The Rocks • Modern (556 rms)

Every room at this luxurious five-star hotel has views over the harbor, with many taking in sweeping vistas of the Sydney Opera House and the Sydney Harbour Bridge. Recent guests include Crown Prince Frederick and Princess Mary of Denmark and Princess Victoria of Sweden. Deluxe rooms are large and modern and come with marble bathrooms and either partial views of the Opera House or better ones over Darling Harbour. If you really want a fabulous view toward the Opera House and the near expanse of the Harbour Bridge, then aim for an Executive Grand Harbour Suite, the sixth room up from the bottom of the 19-category room scale. The top five room floors, from level 29 to 34, have use of the Horizon Club lounge, which supplies breakfast and evening canapés. The hotel, as a whole, has an understated grandeur with a touch of Asian flair—many of the guests are Japanese. Banks of artful, colorful bottles lead you into Café Mix on level 1, which serves breakfasts to guests, as well as a lunch and dinner buffet featuring contemporary, Chinese, Indian, and Japanese meals cooked fresh as you watch. The hotel also operates the nearby Harts Pub, where you can have a lunchtime Aussie barbecue in the beer garden Tuesdays to Fridays, and the Rocks Tepenyaki restaurant, which serves good Japanese cuisine. Both Altitude restaurant and the stylish Blue Horizons Bar (see p.126), on the 36th floor, have incredible views across the harbor. The hotel's complimentary health club has a very appealing indoor pool and spa. $$$$ 176 Cumberland St. (Essex St.), 02 9250 6000 / 1 800 222 448, shangri-la.com

Sheraton on the Park • CBD • Timeless (606 rms)

Overlooking Hyde Park and a stone's throw from the city shopping precincts, this elegant modern hotel impresses you as soon as you walk into its three-story lobby with its sweeping grand staircase. A big attraction here is the glorious indoor swimming pool, which seems to flow into the city through huge windows overlooking the park. Another standout is The Conservatory, which has magnificent views you can take in with your afternoon high tea. The chocolate-and-cream rooms are some of the nicest in Sydney, with the pick being the Park View rooms, with leafy outlooks, and the Executive Club Level Rooms, which have access to the Executive Club on the 21st floor. The hotel's Botanica Brasserie offers contemporary dining in a relaxed setting, overlooking leafy Hyde Park. It's known for its seasonal buffet featuring fresh seafood on weekends, and a

Sunday brunch with jazz. The sophisticated Conservatory Bar, which has park views through dramatic two-story windows, is a nice place to sip away the twilight hours. $$$ 161 Elizabeth St. (Market St.), 02 9286 6000, starwoodhotels.com/sheraton

Sir Stamford Double Bay • Double Bay • Timeless (73 rms)
Most hotels are famous for something, even if it's just for the lumpy beds. This hotel's claim to fame is that under a former guise—as the Ritz Carlton Double Bay—it saw the suicide of the famous INXS lead singer Michael Hutchens, who hung himself behind the door of room 524 in November 1997. The hotel was, and still is, a favorite with rock stars and pseudo-royalty, such as Madonna and Bill Clinton. Double Bay, or "double pay," as the rest of Australia knows the place, is Sydney's most exclusive area. The waterfront suburb is packed with upmarket cafes and designer shops, and serviced by a ferry to Circular Quay. The hotel's reception is opulent and grand, with 19th-century china subtly illuminated within antique mahogany sideboards, a Louis XV–style marble fireplace, and artwork by Australian painter Norman Lindsay on the oak-paneled walls. A rooftop pool and an à la carte restaurant provide service to businesspeople using the extensive conference facilities. Rooms are extraordinarily quiet, with plush carpets, marble-floored bathrooms, and replica antiques. The Parlour Rooms are the pick of the bunch below the suites. They feature a large living area with lots of silk and a four-poster bed. $$ 22 Knox St. (New South Head St.), 02 9302 4100, stamford.com.au/ssdb

Sydney Harbour Marriott • Circular Quay • Modern (550 rms)
Three words sum up why this might be the place you choose to stay—location, location, location. The Sydney Harbour Marriott, one of two Marriotts in town, is just a couple of minutes from Circular Quay and the Rocks by foot. Around 30 percent of the rooms have views of the harbor, the best being the Deluxe Bridge View and Deluxe Opera View rooms. Other rooms have elevated views of the city. All rooms are bright and contemporary and were refurbished during a major renovation in 2004, when the hotel changed hands. You can choose between a king-size bed or two doubles. The Marriott's Revival beds are so comfortable that the hotel has had many offers from guests to buy them. The semi-indoor and outdoor pool is fine, but not nearly as nice as some of the others in town. The hotel's Icon Brasseries does a popular seafood buffet for weekend lunches and dinners, and the historic Customs House Bar (renovated in late 2006) has a pleasant courtyard. $$ 30 Pitt St. (Alfred St.), 02 9259 7000 / 1 800 251 251, marriott.com.au

Classic Sydney: The Restaurants

Aria • Circular Quay • Modern Australian

With towering glass windows and front-row views of the Harbour Bridge, the Sydney Opera House, and the ferries puttering around Circular Quay, Aria boasts one of the most enviable spots in the city. The atmosphere is abuzz with business folk and the elegant set making a meal of the 180-degree vista before a show at the Opera House. A leisurely lunch should include the crisp-skin barramundi fish with duck consommé, shaved abalone, and shitake mushrooms, as well as a bottle of white from the first-rate cellar to ease you into the afternoon. The twinkling lights of evening add a sparkle of glamour, and it's best applauded with another signature dish—the twice-cooked sweet pork belly with caramelized apple and balsamic. While all tables have wonderful harbor views, ask for one nearest the glass. *Mon-Fri noon-2:30pm and 5:30-11:30pm, Sat 5-11:30pm, Sun 6-10:30pm.* $$$$ 1 Macquarie St. (Circular Quay East), 02 9252 2555, ariarestaurant.com

The Art Gallery Restaurant • CBD • Modern Australian

Taking in a dose of gallery culture can be hungry work, so it's lucky this bistro-style restaurant is on hand to serve up everything from fine dining to speedier snacks. The best place for a meal is outdoors, shaded from the sun, with a view across the green grass of the Domain and the rooftops of Woolloomooloo, but singles can make friends at the counter bench. There are plenty of wines by the glass and stylish light food. It's ideal either to provide fuel for a pit stop mid-gallery-viewing, or as a destination in itself with a little art on the side. *Mon-Fri noon-3pm, Sat-Sun 10-11:30am and noon-3pm.* $$ The Art Gallery of NSW, Level 5, 1 Art Gallery Rd. (The Domain), 02 9225 1819, trippaswhite.com.au

The Australian Heritage Hotel* • The Rocks • Pub Grub

This classic Aussie spot is a local favorite in the Rocks. *See Classic Nightlife, p.125, for details.* $ 100 Cumberland St. (Glouster St.), 02 9247 2229, australianheritagehotel.com

The Basement Club* • Circular Quay • Continental

Make dinner reservations here to grab a stage-side table for the live music—otherwise it's standing room only. *See Classic Nightlife, p.125, for details.* $$ 29 Reiby Pl. (Bridge St.), 02 9251 2797, basement.com.au

Bathers' Pavilion Restaurant • Balmoral Beach • Modern Australian

Best Beachside Romance Think tranquil beach and bay views and food from a master chef. This beachfront, graciously refurbished former changing shed attracts both the rich and famous and well-heeled locals. But Bathers' genteel, relaxed ambience suits all comers. Chef-owner Serge Dansereau's food features a French foundation with Australian produce—such as his assiette of farmed rabbit in a licorice sauce. If you drop in on a whim and are not dressed appropriately, the cafe beside the restaurant is ideal for a coffee and a quick snack. The best seats are close to the window, and at night the seagulls glow as they roost in rows on the water's shark net. *Daily noon-2:30pm and 6:30-10pm.* $$$$ 4 The Esplanade (Awaba St.), 02 9969 5050, batherspavilion.com.au

Bilson's • CBD • French

Best Fine Dining "Oh-la-la!" you might whisper under your breath in this Francophile hotel foyer eatery. Becalmed by padded damask-clad tables and the gentle swish of efficient waiters, Bilson's caters to serious food lovers and media folk who appreciate French cooking at Michelin levels. The chef, Tony Bilson, is a longstanding identity with some 30 years in the business, which means he can get away with adding flair to a traditional dish. Order some Sydney rock oysters to start with, followed by the slow-cooked veal shank with peppery black kale and an anchovy and garlic purée straight from Provence. *Mon-Fri noon-2:30pm and 6-10pm, Sat 6-10pm.* $$$$ ▭ The Foyer, Radisson Plaza Hotel, 27 O'Connell St. (Hunter St.), 02 8214 0496, bilsons.com.au

The Boathouse on Blackwattle Bay • Glebe • Seafood

As if ready to cast off and sail the harbor, this brasserie-inspired, multiple–award winning seafood restaurant generates raves from all who dine here. From the galley-like kitchen of a historic converted boathouse comes some of the best seafood dishes in the country. Front of house, there are timber floors, crisp linens, and harbor and Anzac bridge views, which only enhances the effect the signature snapper pie has on the regulars. So many people order the snapper pie, in fact, that the last chef quit. He was fed up with spending most of his time rolling out pastry. *Tue-Sun noon-3pm and 6:30-10:30pm.* $$$ ▭ End of Ferry Rd. (Taylor St.), 02 9518 9011, boathouse.net.au

Botanic Gardens Restaurant • CBD • Modern Australian

Set in Sydney's biggest garden, this is a great weekend brunch option after a stroll in the park. Alternatively, you can walk off the consequences of your meal when you're finished. This quintessential city escape is perched a floor above the shrubs and sits in the shade of a rainforest. The best seats in the house are outdoors on the veranda among the dappled greenery. Speed of service and serving sizes respect the fact that many lunch here after a quick dash from their city offices. But it's best enjoyed when you have time to smell the roses. Head Chef Mark Vlcek's food delivers classical touches. Try his signature spatchcock with Madeira jus. *Mon-Fri noon-3pm, Sat-Sun 9:30-11:30am.* $$$ ≡ Royal Botanic Gardens (Mrs. Macquaries Rd.), 02 9241 2419, trippaswhite.com.au

Bungalow 8* • King Street Wharf • Seafood

Fresh seafood is complemented by an indoor-outdoor seating plan and a stylish crowd. *See Classic Nightlife, p.127, for details.* $$ ≡ 8 The Promenade (King Street Wharf), 02 9299 4660, bungalow8.com.au

Buon Ricordo • Paddington • Italian

In the past 17 years, Italian-born chef-owner Armando Percuoco has carved out a clientele of faithful fans devoted to his "la vera cucina," or "true Italian cuisine." There's a fast-paced energy to this restaurant hidden on an inner-city side street. Fettuccine tossed at the table with a truffled egg keeps people returning, as does the house-made fagottini (sausages), whole roasted duck, and, not least, Percuoco's personal charm and passion. Expect to see him bounding out from the kitchen to greet artistic matrons and their younger lovers. Those in the know save themselves for a proper Sicilian cassata or at least leave room for the selection of Italian and Australian cheeses, typifying the blend of traditions Percuoco so masterfully oversees. *Tue-Thu 6:30-10:30pm, Fri noon-2:30pm and 6:30-10:30pm, Sat noon-2:30pm.* $$$$ ≡ 108 Boundary Rd. (Liverpool St.), 02 9360 6729, buonricordo.com.au

Chinta Ria ... The Temple of Love • Cockle Bay Wharf • Malaysian

That huge, smiling, incense-flanked Buddha presiding over the entrance may not look much like Cupid, but given Chinta Ria's subtitle, his powers should count for something. Several years ago, owner Simon Goh brought his Melbourne magic—Malaysian hawker-style food backed by regular jazz sessions—and set it down on the Sydney waterside. This temple to delicious food is crowded with city types during weekday lunchtimes, but evenings are less cluttered with suits and you don't have to book. Jazz accents the menu, with Ella's Wraps (stuffed prawns in fried pastry) and Ayam Blues (battered wok-tossed chicken fillets). The unpretentious kitchen, chairs, and tables make you feel you've escaped to a footpath in Asia, but the sparkling front-row view of Darling Harbour confirms you're still in Sydney. *Mon-Sat noon-2:30pm and 6-11pm, Sun noon-2:30pm and 6-10:30pm.* $$ ≡ Roof Terrace, Level 2, 201 Sussex St. (Market St.), 02 9264 3211, chintaria.com

Claude's • Woollahra • French (G)

Iconic is a word often used to describe this restaurant that has stood out above others in Sydney for decades. After ten years of prominence delivered by chef-owner Tim Pak Poy, the baton was passed in the last couple of years to his Singapore-born former sous chef Chiu Lee Luk. She has run with the challenge, receiving further accolades and even greater prominence for her deft approach to modern French cuisine lightly touched by Asian influences. Claude's petite space in a Federation terrace house—just 40 seats in two elegant dining rooms adorned with Limoges porcelain—is an ideally refined venue for older lawyers and doctors. Choose from either an eight-course degustation menu or a prix-fixe three-course menu for what might turn out to be one of the most sublime meals of your life. *Tue-Sat 7:30-10pm.* $$$$ ⊟ 10 Oxford St. (Queen St.), 02 9331 2325, claudes.com.au

Coast • Cockle Bay Wharf • Italian

The scene from Cockle Bay Wharf is delightful at any time, but many diners can be forgiven for not noticing, especially when classic Italian food from chef Stefano Manfredi is in front of them. Coast's regular menu includes barbecued duck with balsamic vinegar, and roast suckling lamb with rosemary and roast potatoes. But the choice is always so extensive—so a "reduced" menu of three courses for a set price may give you more time to relax and enjoy the waterside ambience. Beloved by dark-suited Central Business District workers for business lunches, Coast restaurant comes alive by night when Darling Harbour's reflection sparkles in the slip of water between the glittering edges of the bay. *Mon-Fri noon-2:30pm and 6-10:30pm, Sat 6-10:30pm, Sun 6-9:30pm.* $$ ≡ Roof Terrace, 201 Sussex St. (King St.), 02 9267 6700, coastrestaurant.com.au

Doyles on the Beach • Watsons Bay • Seafood

Best Beachside Romance Locals almost take this place for granted. Overseas visitors can't believe it: the view, the location, just a step (literally) from the beach. The Doyle family has been serving seafood here since 1885—it's Australia's first seafood restaurant, and has been owned and operated by five generations of the family. Many diners prefer to opt for fish and chips. Others go for a bowl of steamed local mussels or king prawns. Everything tastes better eaten outside with the beach just on the other side of the footpath and a view down the harbor towards the city, where the famous bridge is just a hump on the horizon. For a picnic in the park or a quick fishy fix, Doyles Fishermans Wharf, next door, has identical views and serves takeaway from a mini-menu. Parking in this popular area can be tricky, so go by ferry or water taxi. *Daily noon-3:30pm and 6-9:30pm.* $$$ ≡ 11 Marine Parade (New South Head Rd.), 02 9337 2007

Doyles Palace Hotel* • Watsons Bay • Seafood
Part of the Doyles empire, this charming waterfront spot is great for a meal or a drink. *See Classic Nightlife, p.127, for details.* $ ≡ 10 Marine Parade (Military Rd.), 02 9337 4299, doyles.com.au

Firefly* • Dawes Point • Tapas
Try a great selection of Australian wines with your tapas at this chic wine bar that's popular with a stylish set. *See Classic Nightlife, p.128, for details.* $$ ≡ Pier 7, 17 Hickson Rd. (Sussex St.), 02 9241 2031

Fish at the Rocks • The Rocks • Seafood
This unpretentious eatery, opposite the Lord Nelson Brewery Hotel (see p.129), is a ten-minute stroll through the convict-hewn tunnel called the Argyle Cut. The focus is on fresh seafood, and the whiting fillets in a beer-batter and hand-cut French fries are arguably the best fish and chips in Sydney. The well-crafted food and the friendly service add to the excited buzz of this compact place with its sailing boat pictures on the walls. If you like things a little more mellow, then opt for the small row of tables outside on the sidewalk. If you are ravenous, you might want to start with some freshly shucked oysters. The chocolate mud cake for dessert is a memorable experience. *Daily noon-2:30pm and 6-10:30pm.* $$ ≡ 29 Kent St. (Argyle St.), 02 9252 4614, fishattherocks.com.au

Forty One Restaurant • CBD • French
Best Restaurants with Views The name makes sense when you take the lift to this nest high above Sydney Harbour. Chef Dietmar Sawyere's reputation and his French-influenced haute cuisine are every bit as elevated as the location. Although it was originally accessed from the 41st floor (hence the name), today Forty One's entry is on level 42. With a winning combination of fine food, flawless service, and amazing location, it's little wonder that this restaurant has won many awards and impressed any number of high-flying celebrities, as well as smug locals. It's the ideal big-night restaurant with good views from most tables, though request one at the window so you don't look over other people's heads. *Mon, Sat 6-10pm, Tue-Fri noon-2:30pm and 6-10pm.* $$$$ ≡ Level 42, The Chifley Tower, 2 Chifley Sq. (George St.), 02 9221 2500, forty-one.com.au

Galileo • The Rocks • French/Japanese
Don your best dress and join the Sydney elite and guests of the Observatory Hotel at this grand Orient Express Hotel dining room. With its antique sketches, silk wallpaper and curtains, and walnut furniture and tables, Galileo exudes the cultured feel of a 19th-century club. You'll find only the most sophisticated diners in this spot. The "French with Japanese infusion" menu produces some real standouts, such as the sublime crusted ocean trout. The wine menu is one of the best in Australia, and the sommelier is consistently spot on with his recommendations. It

CLASSIC

all comes together with a precision seen mainly in Michelin-starred restaurants. *Daily 6:30-10:30am and 6:30-10:30pm.* $$$$ – The Observatory Hotel, 89-113 Kent St. (Argyle St.), 02 9256 2215, observatoryhotel.com.au

Golden Century • Haymarket • Cantonese

Best Late-Night Bites This enormous, hall-like Chinese late-night hot spot is just as good for a casual bowl of noodles as a full-blown banquet. The energy is raucous and the service fast and furious, with plenty of local Chinese families. The menu sings with Cantonese classics such as tiny clams in extra-hot sauce, crab three ways, and Peking duck. Come for congee late at night. For an interesting post-binge tipple, try one of the broad range of Chinese liquors, made from barley, sorghum wheat, or even peas. *Daily noon-4am.* $$ ≡ 393-399 Sussex St. (Goulburn St.), 02 9212 3901, goldencentury.com.au

The Golden Sheaf Hotel* • Double Bay • Pub Grub

This classic pub in an upscale neighborhood draws everyone from sports fans to grandmothers. *See Classic Nightlife, p.128, for details.* $$ ▯≡ 429 New South Head Rd. (Knox St.), 02 9327 5877, goldensheaf.com.au

Guillaume at Bennelong • Circular Quay • French (G)

Best Always-Hot Restaurants For sheer prestige value, you have to dine in one of the best eating spots in the world. At night, this eye-catching and sensuous space has the whole twinkling harbor at its feet. A host of glitterati and pre-theater diners edge up to white linen tables and tuck into Guillaume Brahimi's exceptional French-based menu laced with the best Australian produce. At any cost, don't miss the signature basil-infused tuna with mustard-seed vinaigrette. Brahimi's dishes are lovingly matched with local wines by the best floor staff in Sydney. Aim to arrive early to drink in the views with a glass of champagne at the Opera Bar (see p.131). *Mon-Wed and Sat 8-10:30pm, Thu-Fri noon-3pm and 8-10:30pm.* $$$$ B≡ Sydney Opera House (Circular Quay West), 02 9241 1999, guillaumeatbennelong.com.au

Harbour Kitchen and Bar • The Rocks • Modern Australian

The five-star Park Hyatt discreetly wraps itself around a watery point with a stunning view of the Sydney Opera House and lovely harbor. The nearly water-level restaurant, with a dress circle harbor view, is equally unassuming, but dining with the Rolling Stones or royalty can add a real touch of decadence. A New York–style bar with an enviable martini list does its best to tempt you from rushing to the dining area. Executive chef Danny Drinkwater arrived in Sydney via the Dorchester Hotel in London, and his top-notch pedigree is evident in his signature dishes of duck and beetroot tart, and the wood-roasted red snapper fillet, with olive and pine nut crust and caramelized whitlof. The shareable tasting menu is ideal for adventurous couples. *Nightly 6:30-11pm.* $$$ ≡ Park Hyatt Sydney, 7 Hickson Rd. (George St.), 02 9256 1661, harbourkitchen.com.au

Hero of Waterloo* • The Rocks • Pub Grub

This atmospheric pub is one of the oldest and best for live music—it even has a secret tunnel underneath. *See Classic Nightlife, p.128, for details.* $ ≡ 81 Lower Fort St. (Windmill St.), 02 9252 4553, heroofwaterloo.com.au

Imperial Peking Harbourside Restaurant • Circular Quay • Chinese

With the harbor right outside, seafood is the obvious choice at this large restaurant featuring Peking-style cuisine. Specialties include oysters steamed with XO sauce, or seasonal dishes such as lobster Singapore. It's located in Campbell's Storehouse, a piece of Australian colonial history once important for the ships that docked here, but now decorated with wine casks and temple statues. It makes sense, then, that kangaroo is featured in several dishes—Chinese-style, with chili sauce, as a satay, or sizzling, Shanghai-style. Sit outside in the sun rather than inside, where the views are somewhat overpowered by the sandstone walls. *Daily noon-3pm and 6-10:30pm.* $$$ 13 Circular Quay West (George St.), 02 9247 7073, imperialpeking.com.au

Kables • CBD • Modern Australian (G)

This elegant yet cozy restaurant may be tucked inside the Four Seasons Hotel, but who minds entering through that magnificent foyer? Kables has always been a place for special dining. Tourists and locals alike are tempted by quintessential Australian dishes such as Queensland barramundi baked in paperbark, while businesspeople in the city are enamored of the two-course lunch menu, which changes daily. Just a five-minute stroll from the Sydney Opera House, Kables is also the ideal spot for a pre-theater dinner that comes with four hours of parking thrown in, leaving enough time to return for post-performance drinks and dessert. *Daily noon-2:30pm and 6-11pm.* $$$ Four Seasons Hotel, Level 2, 199 George St. (Argyle St.), 02 9250 3226, fourseasons.com/sydney

The Lord Nelson Brewery Hotel* • The Rocks • Pub Grub

Sydney's oldest licensed hotel houses its first boutique brew pub, with decent fare to accompany the many top-notch ales. *See Classic Nightlife, p.129, for details.* $ 19 Kent St. (Argyle St.), 02 9251 4044, lordnelson.com.au

Manly Wharf Hotel* • Manly • Pub Grub

A classic waterfront spot to enjoy a sunset or a meal. *See Classic Nightlife, p.129, for details.* $ East Esplanade, 02 9977 1266, manlywharfhotel.com.au

Manta • Woolloomooloo • Seafood

First there was Manta Ray, dishing out romantic dinners by night, business deals by day, and feeding tourists whenever. Now there's Manta, with the new menu under the direction of chef Stefano Manfredi and his team, casting an Italian accent over seafood offerings selected fresh each morning from the markets. Come here to sit outside in the sun and slurp oysters, or choose a live lobster or crab from the tank and send it away to be grilled or steamed with oil and garlic or chili-herb sauce. *Mon-Sat noon-3pm and 6-10pm, Sun noon-3pm and 6-9pm.* $$$ The Wharf, 6 Cowper Wharf Rd. (Bourke St.), 02 9332 3822, mantarestaurant.com.au

Marque • Surry Hills • French (G)

Best Fine Dining Seriously sophisticated, the Marque offers a small menu of classic French dishes. A *New York Times* food critic recently entered this aubergine-colored room and waxed lyrical about the beet tart, and suggested that the sardine fillet could only have been created by a "culinary wizard." Marque is considered a top dining destination. Chef Mark Best honed his talent for several years in top French and English restaurants, and the edgy flavor combinations of some menu items—roast wood pigeon with parsnip and chocolate tart, or blood sausage with new garlic, sea urchin, and fresh snails—have snagged a devoted clientele, from politicians to actors. *Mon-Sat 6:30-10:30pm.* $$$$ Medina Apartment Building, 355 Crown St. (Foveaux St.), 02 9332 2225, marquerestaurant.com.au

Milsons • Kirribilli • Modern Australian

Business groups for lunch and couples by night is the pattern at this cozy converted cottage restaurant with its view of busy chefs at work in the semi-open kitchen. The earthy colors and clean minimalist lines create a backdrop that sets off the seasonal produce on the contemporary Australian menu. Even though the service is slick, much of the food is "slow-cooked" to maximize flavor. Scoot across in a water taxi and have a special two- or three-course pre-theater dinner before zooming back to the Opera House. *Mon-Fri noon-3pm and 6-10pm, Sat 6-10pm.* $$$ ≡ 17 Willoughby St. (Falcon St.), 02 9955 7075, milsonsrestaurant.com.au

Nick's Seafood Restaurant • Cockle Bay Wharf • Seafood

Be sure to dine outdoors overlooking the sparkling waters of Cockle Bay, the ideal spot to enjoy the fresh seafood for which Nick's has made a name. Celebrate with a seafood platter of crab, prawns, oysters, fish, and lobster, or opt for simply prepared char-grilled fish. It's a busy place—beloved by tourists who soak up the Sydney atmosphere—but it's big enough that you can usually dine on a whim without booking. There's even a marina menu with dishes for boaties to pick up as they sail away. A satellite Nick's fronts the beach at Bondi. *Daily noon-3pm and 6-10pm.* $$$ ≡ The Promenade (Market St.), 02 9264 1212, nicks-seafood.com.au

North Bondi RSL Club* • Bondi Beach • Pub Grub

RSL honor veterans—with simple food and cheap beer. *See Classic Nightlife, p.130, for details.* $$ ≡ 120 Ramsgate Ave. (Campbell Parade), 02 9130 3152, northbondirsl.com.au

The Oaks Hotel* • Neutral Bay • Pub Grub

A local watering hole with all the necessary staples. *See Classic Nightlife, p.130, for details.* $$ ≡ 118 Military Rd. (Ben Boyd St.), 02 9953 5515, oakshotel.com.au

Oh! Calcutta! • Darlinghurst • Indian

Gregarious chef-owner Basil Daniell is omnipresent, not only preparing Indian fare with a difference, but popping out regularly to greet his guests and host each evening's buzzing, busy, and vibrant culinary performance. It's a casual place, so dress down a bit and mix with the locals. It's tiny, too, so you'll be elbow-to-elbow like at a big party. Forget about the usual creamy mush with a couple of nan, come here for the milk-fed goat curry with coconut and ginger, or oxtail curry with celeriac and caramelized onions. If you prefer your kangaroo spicy, then hop down the menu to the roo with sesame seeds, chili, garlic, and lemon. *Mon-Sat 6-10:30pm.* $$ ≡ 251 Victoria St. (Burton St.), 02 9360 3650, ohcalcutta.com.au

Pier • Rose Bay • Seafood (G)

Aptly named, this narrow, glass-walled restaurant juts out over Rose Bay and lures stylish Eastern Suburbs residents as well as food lovers from around the world. Boating types and PR gurus dine inside (every table has a view of the water) or relax with a pre-dinner drink on the balcony, knowing that the best is yet to come. Chef-owner Greg Doyle meticulously sources super-fresh seafood from his team of fishermen, so it's no surprise this place, open over a dozen years, keeps garnering prestigious awards. It's impossible to say what the menu will hold each day as it all depends on the catch, but you can rest assured that it will be almost flapping on your plate. *Daily noon-3pm, Mon-Sat noon-3pm and 6-10pm, Sun noon-3pm noon 6-9pm.* $$$ ≡ 594 New South Head Rd. (Old South Head Rd.), 02 9327 6561, pierrestaurant.com.au

Prime • CBD • Steak House
An appropriately choice position in the stylishly reclaimed General Post Office complex right in the heart of the Central Business District, Prime's hushed and private fine-dining feel suits the "suits" that have already stamped it as their clubby rendezvous for weekday lunches. Its New York–style interior, furnished with leather seats and large tables, is a regular base for businesspeople with clients to impress. The menu of top-quality oysters, Wagyu steaks from the grill, and oxtail and other carnivorous treats is always on mark. There are plenty of carefully chosen high-end reds on the wine list. If you're sealing a big deal, the Chateaubriand would be an extravagant flourish. *Mon-Fri noon-3pm and 6-10pm, Sat 6-10pm.* $$$$ ≡ Lower Ground Floor, GPO, No. 1 Martin Pl. (George St.), 02 9229 7777, gposydney.com.au

Pruniers • Woollahra • Modern Australian
Pretty as a garden party, this could be a quaint French country house, standing back from the road across from a tiny park. The outdoor terrace is ideal for relaxed dining with an upper-crust edge, and there's a conservatory ambience inside where reds, purples, and charcoal play off against linen-clad tables and dishes of lobster and blue swimmer crab souffle. Sunday brunch, accompanied by jazz, is a long and decadent affair, lubricated by "brunchtails" and jugs of mixed drinks. Weekday lunches see inner-city and CBD workers escaping for speedy and cost-effective one- to three-course meal deals. The so-stylish cocktail bar is the place to gather before or after dinner. *Wed-Fri noon-3pm and 6-10pm, Sat 6-10pm, Sun 10am-3pm.* $$$ ≡ 65 Ocean St. (Queen St.), 02 9363 1974, pruniers.com.au

Quay • The Rocks • Modern Australian (G)
Best Always-Hot Restaurants Head chef Peter Gilmore has made quite a name for himself and his food at this restaurant—perched like a ship about to launch into the harbor. By day, the sun sparkles off the Opera House and through the large windows, and by night the North Shore suburbs and Harbour Bridge shimmer above the oil-black water and late-night ferryboats. Book well in advance to ensure a window seat for a front-row view—but ask in advance if there is a cruise ship docked. At times, these boats dock alongside, providing views of portholes rather than the water. Signature dishes include crisped, pressed duck with garlic purée and porcini mushrooms, and seared yellowfin tuna with tomato jelly, roasted eggplant, and basil oil. The two-course express lunch is popular with business diners. *Sat-Mon 6-10pm, Tue-Fri noon-2:30pm and 6-10pm.* $$$$ ≡ Upper Level, Overseas Passenger Terminal, Circular Quay West (George St.), 02 9251 5600, quay.com.au

Redoak Boutique Beer Cafe* • CBD • Pub Grub
Professional types fill the seats here, downing after-work brews before having a bite to eat. *See Classic Nightlife, p.132, for details.* $ ≡ 201 Clarence St. (King St.), 02 9262 3303, redoak.com.au

Renaissance Cafe Patisserie • The Rocks • Cafe
This gem has been serving up fabulous croissants and coffee drinks since the 1970s. With its charming outdoor courtyard seating and tantalizing selection of

authentic French baked goods, it's an ideal place to ease into the day. Conveniently located right by the Rocks, it's also a good place to refuel when you need a break from the urban bustle. *Daily 8:30am-6pm.* $ ≡ 47 Argyle St. (George St.), 02 9241 4878, larenaissance.com.au

Restaurant Balzac • Randwick • French/British

Chunky sandstone walls and huge tables ideal for friendly groups or convivial sharing give a solid feel to this favorite spot, which is proof that suburban restaurants can shine. Pick a table by the sunny windows by day, or cozy up inside at night with chef-owner Matthew Kemp's sublime French/British comfort food. As popular in its new position as it was when it began a few years ago, just streets away, Balzac is a standard of the area now. Be sure to catch the seasonal nine-course degustation with matching wines on the last Sunday of each month. *Tue-Thu 6-10pm, Fri noon-2:30pm and 5:30-10:30pm, Sat 5:30-10:30pm.* $$$ ▯≡ 141 Belmore Rd. (Anzac Parade), 02 9399 9660, restaurantbalzac.com.au

Rockpool • The Rocks • Modern Australian (G)

Best Always-Hot Restaurants Neil Perry, chef-owner of the iconic long-standing Rockpool, has nothing to prove. It's generally accepted as the pinnacle of Sydney dining, and people come to this place with its unpretentious street frontage to enjoy the best Modern Australian daily-changing menu in town. Ask for a downstairs table for the other attraction—the chance to see celebs sashaying along the ramp (as much a catwalk as a gangway) to their tables. Some diners come to be seen too, but most know this dining is as good as it gets, as Perry continues to push culinary boundaries with sparkling local produce and seafood. Rather than serving individual courses, the restaurant favors many smaller offerings in one of its three tasting menus, including one for vegetarians. These range from five to 11 courses. *Tue-Sat 6-11pm.* $$$$ ≡ 107 George St. (Argyle St.), 02 9252 1888, rockpool.com

The Royal Hotel* • Paddington • Pub Grub

Sporty types come here for a relaxing, rowdy good time. *See Classic Nightlife, p.132, for details.* $ ≡ 237 Glenmore Rd. (Heely St.), 02 9331 2604, royalhotel.com.au

Sailors Thai Restaurant and Canteen • The Rocks • Thai

Best Thai Restaurants The upstairs was something of a novelty when it first appeared years ago. Now it's taken for granted, as everyone trusts that the Aussie-influenced, fiery Thai food will be fabulous and fast enough for a snappy lunch. Popular with city workers and close to the the CBD, it's also frequented by plenty of shoppers, tourists, and students. Early birds know to nab balcony tables upstairs with great views. Downstairs in the more formal and serene space, people linger, especially if they've ordered the tasting menu, or if they are seated outside on the terrace of this converted sailors' home in the historic part of the city. *Mon-Fri noon-2:30pm and 6-10pm, Sat 6-10pm.* $$$ ▯≡ 106 George St. (Argyle St.), 02 9251 2466, sailorsthai.citysearch.com.au

Summit Restaurant • CBD • Modern Australian

This revolving restaurant in its landmark position high above the city has been a Big Night Out destination for decades. Now glitteringly refurbished, it still spins slowly above the city skyline, but the menu is slicker under the direction of master chef Michael Moore. Every table has a view, but you're only guaranteed to rub your nose against the glass if you say you're someone famous. In all, it takes 105 minutes for a full rotation. Time enough to concentrate on the fresh local seafood and Australian beef. Enjoy a drink at the adjoining Orbit Bar before dinner. *Sun-Fri noon-3pm and 6-11pm, Sat 6-11pm.* $$$ Level 47, Australia Sq., 264 George St. (Bond St.), 02 9247 9777, summitrestaurant.com.au

Tetsuya's • Haymarket • French/Japanese (G)

Best Fine Dining No other chef has made as much of an impact in Sydney as Japanese-born chef Tetsuya Wakuda. Tetsuya cooks what he chooses each evening, melding French and Japanese flavors and techniques. Everybody who is anybody wants to eat looking over the tranquil Japanese garden—so getting a table is difficult. To have a chance, you need to book at least four weeks in advance.The multitude of awards and accolades he's earned make sense with one taste of his signature confit of ocean trout, which is a fixture of the mega-dish tasting menu that is best experienced with the matching wines option. *Tue-Fri 6-10:30pm and Sat noon-2pm and 6-10:30pm.* $$$$ 529 Kent St. (Bathurst St.), 02 9267 2900, tetsuyas.com

360 Bar and Dining Room* • CBD • Continental

Drink and dine high above the city with a chic set in a sleek space. *See Classic Nightlife, p.133, for details.* $$ Gallery Level, 100 Market St. (Pitt St.), 02 8223 3800, 360dining.com.au

Tilbury Hotel* • Woolloomooloo • Pub Grub

This pub draws a local crowd of mature patrons who like to linger over long, beer-infused lunches. *See Classic Nightlife, p.133, for details.* $ 12-18 Nicholson St. (Cowper Bay Rd.), 02 9368 1955, tilburyhotel.com.au

The Vanguard* • Newtown • Continental

Enjoy dinner and a live music show at this chic see-and-be-seen spot. *See Classic Nightlife, p.133, for details.* $$ 42 King St. (City Rd.), 02 9557 7992, thevanguard.com.au

Victoria Room* • Darlinghurst • Continental

This decadent lounge space draws a hip 20-something clientele for drinking and nibbling. *See Classic Nightlife, p.133, for details.* $$ Level 1, 235 Victoria St. (Liverpool St.), 02 9357 4488, thevictoriaroom.com

The Wharf • Walsh Bay • Modern Australian

It's a trifecta of wonders here—superb dining, plus a "so close you could touch it" harbor view, and the Sydney Theater Company close by for entertainment. This is where to come for a pre-theater quickie or a post-theater drink until midnight. It's at the far end of the historic finger wharf that juts well into the harbor and almost touches the ferryboats. By day, an outdoor table is bliss; by night, sitting indoors looking out at the lights is magic. Delicious food like seared Tasmanian salmon with beetroot relish and horseradish cream stages a performance of its own. The cafe opens two hours before performances, and supper and drinks are available Thursday to Saturday 10pm till late. *Mon-Sat noon-3pm and 6-11pm.* $$$ End of Pier 4, Hickson Rd. (George St.), 02 9250 1761, thewharfrestaurant.com.au

CLASSIC

The White Horse Bar and Brasserie* • Surry Hills • Continental

This is a fashionista favorite with a lovely outdoor terrace. *See Classic Nightlife, p.134, for details.* $ ≡ 381-385 Crown St. (Foveaux St.), 02 8333 9999, thewhitehorse.com.au

Zaaffran • Darling Harbour • Indian

Zaaffran prides itself on presenting traditional Indian fare, but it is the subtle difference to standard Indian menus that has diners coming back for more. Chef Vikrant Kapoor features the restaurant's namesake—saffron in several dishes. Vegetarians do well here, but anyone can dine royally on one of the many banquet menus, or by ordering a thali feast for two. It's served on a silver platter, as eaten by maharajahs in India. Dine on the balcony overlooking Darling Harbour and the city lights to feel even more blessed. *Sun-Thu noon-2:30pm and 6-9:30pm, Fri-Sat noon-2:30pm and 6-10pm.* $$ ≡ Level 2, 345 Harbourside Shopping Centre (Market St.), 02 9211 8900, zaaffran.com.au

Zilver • Haymarket • Chinese

Acclaimed Cantonese Chinese restaurant Silver Spring has a new face—and a new name. Totally refurbished, with timber lattice wall screens and bronze mosaic pillars that create a fitting backdrop for the bustle of yum cha trolleys by day or à la carte service in the evenings, it's energetic and sometimes noisy. Most of the diners are Asian, which confirms the authenticity of the food. Award-winning, Hong Kong–born executive chef Jack Ng describes his cuisine as "thinking outside the wok." Signature dishes include deep-fried or braised mud crab and flaming pork ribs. A Chinese tea menu and a selection of Asian cocktails are interesting, too. *Mon-Fri 10am-3pm and 5:30-11pm, Sat-Sun 9am-3pm and 5:30-11pm.* $$ ≡ Level 1, 477 Pitt St. (Hay St.), 02 9211 2232, zilver.com.au

Classic Sydney: The Nightlife

The Arthouse Hotel* • CBD • Bar/Lounge

Housed in a gorgeous historic Sydney building dating back to the 1830s, the Arthouse Hotel is actually four separate bars and a restaurant. This means there's a space to suit every mood. The main bar, called the Verge, with its soaring ceilings and skylights, successfully blends the historic details of the building with a contemporary and stylish decor. This can get pretty packed most nights. For a more intimate experience, head up to the Attic, a cozier and quieter spot that still has the same stylish look and great cocktails. *Mon-Wed 11am-midnight, Thu 11am-1am, Fri 11am-3am, Sat 5pm-6am.* ≡ 275 Pitt St. (Park St.), 02 9284 1200, thearthousehotel.com.au

The Australian Heritage Hotel* • The Rocks • Pub

Best Historic Drinking Holes For the ultimate Aussie pub experience—drinking, eating, and guffawing with the locals—the Australian Hotel is your first port of call. Whether you're stopping off before a stroll across the Harbour Bridge or quenching a BridgeClimb thirst with a pint of the house specialty (the Bavarian style Scharer's Lager), the Oz is a rocking watering hole suitable for a single drink or a major session. Beer mugs and drinking paraphernalia are littered throughout, with chairs spilling outside onto the sidewalk and long communal benches in the back corner beneath the colonial-era paintings. The gourmet pizzas are delicious, with Australian toppings from BBQ emu to saltwater croc and pepper kangaroo proving popular, although the more simple toppings come highly recommended too. If you're in town for an Aussie public holiday, be it ANZAC day or Australia Day, head to the Australian where the good old-fashioned convict rowdiness overflows. The rounds of two-up and bagpipe "Waltzing Matilda" sing-alongs attract a lively crowd keen to party hard from the minute the pub opens until the last beer is sloshed across the bar. The Australian epitomizes Down Under larrikinism and mischief. *Mon-Sat 11am-midnight, Sun 11am-10pm.* ≡ 100 Cumberland St. (Glouster St.), 02 9247 2229, australianheritagehotel.com

The Basement Club* • Circular Quay • Bar/Live Music

Best Live Music Venues A stalwart of the Oz music scene since the 1970s, the Basement's walls bear witness to the high-quality acts that have wowed audiences in the intimate space. Dizzy Gillespie, Roy Ayers, Eric Bibb, Grace Knight, Janis Ian, and jazz greats of Blue Note Records fame and beyond laid the foundations for the Basement's supreme musical reputation. Prince had an impromptu gig here, and it's not uncommon for visiting musicians to rope off the back Green Room or Blue Note bars and drink into the wee hours. The polished dark wood bar and wooden paneling throughout enhance the underground atmospherics. Add live music, and the venue is transformed into a swaying mass. Reservations for dinner (basic pub grub) and show guarantee a table beneath the stage; otherwise it's standing room only wherever you can find a crevice. These days the musical menu includes funk, reggae, blues, dance, roots, and folk, and when the big festivals hit Australia, the Basement hosts the satellite gigs. Audiences reflect the style of music on offer, but the Basement attracts live music junkies who flock to appreciate the on-stage antics. *Mon-Fri noon-late, Sat-Sun 7pm-late.* C≡ 29 Reiby Pl. (Bridge St.), 02 9251 2797, basement.com.au

Beach Road Hotel • Bondi Beach • Pub

Bondi Beach is a Sydney icon, and the British backpackers can't get enough. Almost as famous as the sandy beach is the suburb's most popular pub, the Beach Road megaplex, and the Brits descend in droves. Summer drinking sessions are synonymous with the Beach Road, and every bar from the beer garden to the front sports bar with television screens and pool tables is heaving with people nightly. Wednesday nights are popular with 20-something singles and the live music from dub to reggae, funk, and acoustica keeps the upstairs bar jumping. Emerging singer-songwriter Lior cut his teeth gigging at the Beach Road, and musician locals and the artsy beach posse can be counted on to support local artists. There's a big dance floor upstairs and a more chilled side bar and colorful couches in the rear dining area. It's a pub where you can be rowdy and uncouth or social and chatty—you can be sure you'll make plenty of mischievous new mates at the Beach Road. *Daily 10am-12:30am.* ≡ 71 Beach Rd. (Glenair Ave.), 02 9130 7247

Blu Horizons Bar • The Rocks • Bar

When the Shangri-La took control of the ANA hotel in 2003, the fate of the hotel's famous top-floor bar with its sweeping Sydney panoramas was uncertain. Thankfully the Blu Horizons bar marks an end to 1980s-style lounging, reinvigorating the space with pale beige and cream armchairs, a spiraling modern chandelier, and "blu"-themed cocktails. The tall windows remain and the unobstructed views of the city are still the centerpiece of the bar, with the most coveted lounge looking straight across the Harbour Bridge from the CBD across to the North Shore. The bar separates the smoking and non-smoking areas, and on weekend evenings there can be a wait of up to two hours for a table. The bar itself overflows with funky 30-something locals. For romantics, the $10,000 Blu Diamond Martini, complete with a real diamond, would make a gorgeous engagement surprise. *Mon-Thu 5pm-1am, Fri noon-2am, Sat 5pm-2am, Sun 5pm-midnight.* Level 36, 176 Cumberland St. (Essex St.), 02 9250 6013, shangri-la.com

The Bourbon • Kings Cross • Bar

Best Late-Night Hangouts Everyone in Sydney knows this iconic hangout as the Bourbon and Beefsteak Bar, which it was from its opening in 1967 until it was rechristened after a major makeover in 2003. Back in the good old days it was an atmospheric unpretentious place with good live music and a cult following, but these days it's a kind of mixture of wine bar, cheap eatery, nightclub, and one-armed–bandit den—all very confusing. Still, it remains a popular late-night hangout for everyone from partying groups of single women to middle-aged men on 40th-birthday party crawls trying to relive their youth. Downstairs is a cavernous and cool-looking bar area and a small dance area guarded by mean-looking bouncers. Upstairs is the Cross Nightclub, which specializes in Funk Fridays. La Fiesta on Saturdays features Latin-inspired house and electro funk groves. Otherwise you can settle for a $10 steak and salad at lunchtime every day, or on Monday and Tuesday evenings. *Daily 10am-6am.* ≡ 24 Darlinghurst Rd. (Kings Cross), 02 9358 1144

Bungalow 8* • King Street Wharf • Restaurant/Bar

For lovers of overflowing seafood platters and steaming pots of mussels, topped off with a refreshing ale, Bungalow 8 is for you. A sprawling bar with multiple outdoor settings, from leather couches on wheels (the place to be) to high stools and tables near the folded-back doors, Bungalow 8 is a waterside beer garden beneath the more upmarket cocktail bar the Loft. Papier-mâché lanterns hang from the bamboo-slatted ceiling, and the long bar houses a diverse selection of tap beers, from West Australian favorite Little Creatures pale ale to Dutch Hoegaarden. Popular with lunching beer colleagues, the tropical beach bungalow vibe seduces boozy lunchers into lingering beyond home time. DJs keep it up-tempo with house tunes and remixed classics, and the good-looking staff bustle about maintaining the fun-loving atmosphere. Tuesdays are all-you-can-eat mussels, and the place is jam-packed with all ages and appetites. Reserve a table and soak up the salty breeze. *Daily noon-late.* ≡ 8 The Promenade (Erskine St.), 02 9299 4660, bungalow8.com.au

Doyles Palace Hotel* • Watsons Bay • Restaurant/Bar

Best Beer Gardens For the seasoned locals who keep the beer garden overflowing during Sunday sessions, the Doyles Palace will never be anything other than the Wato Bay, an affectionate nickname short for its former mantle as the Watsons Bay Hotel. Ignore the lounge bar and sports bar and head straight down Marine Parade and into the waterside beer garden, just meters from the sand. A sprawling expanse of umbrellas, plastic chairs, jugs of beer, and seafood platters, this is one place no visitor to Sydney can afford to miss. The harbor views are spectacular, and sharing your chips with the swooping seagulls is a special Aussie experience. For a stylish entrance, hail a water taxi from Circular Quay and cruise into Watsons Bay, joining the throngs of tourists and locals feasting on the world-famous Doyles seafood and gourmet barbecue. Jazz and funk bands or DJs spinning ambient lounge keep the beer garden grooving on weekends and Sydney's flush Easties, from young families to throngs of mates, maintain a relaxed but vibrant pulse. *Daily 10am-10pm.* ≡ 10 Marine Parade (Military Rd.), 02 9337 4299, doyles.com.au

Epoque Belgian Beer Cafe • Cammeray • Restaurant/Bar

Epoque is a celebration of the exquisite beer traditions of the Belgian monks who brew the many ales on tap or bottled in this beer-lover's mecca. While the monks are not directly involved in the beer cafe, there's an element of beer worship that supplements the religious undertones. Epoque consistently brims with well-heeled 30-somethings, the conservative set from Sydney's lower North Shore. It's the ultimate wintry haven, with dark timber from the floorboards to the bar and tables, and if you can secure a table close to the bar, that's where the action is. In the warmer months, the windows fold back and the balmy night air blends with the whiff of ales and aioli fries, but unfortunately there is no seating on the sidewalk. Epoque attracts an older dining crowd, from 40-plus business types dealing over mussels to families celebrating special occasions. The space is intimate enough not to invite unruly behavior, and Epoque prevails for its Old World authenticity. *Daily noon-late.* ≡ 429 Miller St. (Amherst St.), 02 9954 3811, belgian-beer-cafe.com.au

Firefly* • Dawes Point • Wine Bar

Best Cocktail Lounges Overlooking the newly developed Walsh Bay—the revamped shipping piers rapidly becoming Sydney's hottest address—intimate Firefly is a favorite of the inhabitants of the wharfside luxury apartments and the ultimate spot to drool over the Sydney Harbour lifestyle. The waterfront setting beyond the often overcrowded tourist traps of Circular Quay makes Firefly a must for Sydney newcomers. Sydney's only true wine bar, Firefly has a wine list that includes some of the finest from Australia and the world. The tapas are great, from tuna sashimi to Chinese dumplings. Come at dusk when the bar is dimly lit for a pre-theater tipple and tapas. But tables are limited, and once folks have nabbed one, they're in for the long haul, so get yours early. *Mon-Sat noon-10:30pm.* ▤ Pier 7, 17 Hickson Rd. (Sussex St.), 02 9241 2031

The Golden Sheaf Hotel* • Double Bay • Pub

An old favorite among the well-heeled, well-coiffed Easties, the Golden Sheaf is always brimming with stylish folk. Whether it's sports fans cheering their teams to victory on the big screens in the front bar, ladies in frocks straight from the racetrack scouring for a table in the beer garden, or polo-shirted locals catching up over a few beers and a game of pool, the Sheaf is a friendly and relaxed spot. On a balmy evening, outdoor tables are scarce, but with the new Soda Bar top deck, there are plenty of drinking pit stops to choose from, including communal wooden benches and the high tables and stools overlooking the masses below in the beer garden. On Friday and Saturday nights, DJs spin tunes at Soda Bar, and live bands from reggae to U2 cover bands get the crowds jiving in the back bar on various nights. The suburb's reputation as Double Pay exists for a reason, and the drinks are over-priced. But the Mod Oz bistro food is scrumptious, the gourmet burger a particular winner. *Mon-Wed 10am-1am, Thu-Sat 10am-2am, Sun 11am-midnight.* ▯▤ 429 New South Head Rd. (Knox St.), 02 9327 5877, goldensheaf.com.au

Hero of Waterloo* • The Rocks • Pub

Best Historic Drinking Holes With its sandstone walls and live music, the Hero of Waterloo is the one of the most atmospheric pubs in Australia. Built in 1843 from sandstone quarried out of the nearby Argyle Cut by convicts (the Argyle Cut is that vaulted tunnel on Argyle Street that runs up to another historic pub, the Lord Nelson), its main claim to fame is a tunnel that runs from the cellars to Sydney Harbour. This was used for rum smuggling and for recruiting drunken sailors. This "recruitment" was involuntary, and involved being dropped through a trapdoor, and dragged through the tunnel to a waiting ship. These days the pub is known for its good range of beers, its cozy restaurant, roaring log fires, and its bands. On Wednesday and Thursday evenings it's piano, on Friday it's folk music, and from 2:30pm to 6:30pm on Saturday and Sunday a bunch of old-timers (most are in their 80s!) play jazz. It's a weekend institution. An Irish Jam Session follows. *Mon-Sat 10am-11pm, Sun 10am-10pm.* ▤ 81 Lower Fort St. (Windmill St.), 02 9252 4553, heroofwaterloo.com.au

London Hotel • Balmain • Pub

The London exudes traditional pub charm and is one of the reasons Balmain has a reputation as a prime drinking and dining peninsula. Formerly a working-class suburb populated by dock workers and tattooed ruffians, Balmain has since been given the yuppie overhaul, and young families and conservative nine-to-fivers have infiltrated. But the bohemian buzz remains and the London is a pub worth toasting. The tractor-seat stools along the front balcony offer the best views of Balmain and the Harbour Bridge, while the grand wooden bar is as breathtaking as the selection of tap beers. There's a great pub menu for a quick bite or a full restaurant at the rear. There are also pool tables upstairs. The place to be is on a tractor stool catching the sun's last rays or spilling onto the sidewalk with the locals as they kick along a Sunday session. Mid-20s to 30s dominate and singles abound. *Mon-Sat 11am-midnight, Sun noon-10pm.* 234 Darling St. (Jane St.), 02 9555 1377, thelondonhotel.com.au

The Lord Dudley Hotel • Woollahra • Pub
A classic English-style pub, the Dudley is all leather couches, dark oak, and antique prints. With 15 beers on tap, it's popular with Aussie beer guzzlers both young and old from the Eastern Suburbs' snooty set. With their upturned collars, sports jackets, and well-stuffed wallets, the Dudley regulars are a combination of old money and new who enjoy a few pints from the mother country. Covered in greenery, the Dudley sits on the corner of Jersey Road in Woollahra's leafy back streets, creaking and swaying with gray-haired storytellers, footy fans, and toffee-nosed ladies, making for a colorful array of revelers. There are so many wonderful nooks and crannies to explore, you'll be able to drink at a different lounge, fireplace, or bar every visit, but the leather couches in the Guinness Lounge upstairs are particularly cozy. It's much like a formal drawing room, where a balloon glass of Chivas Regal, a tweed jacket, and pantaloons would not go astray. There are paisley couches by the fireplace and chopped logs ready to blaze the wintry evenings away, and it's not uncommon to find father-and-son pairs immersed in footy banter over a Guinness (or three) by the bar. *Mon-Wed 11am-11pm, Thu-Sat 11am-midnight, Sun noon-10pm.* 236 Jersey Rd. (Trelawney St.), 02 9327 5399, lorddudley.com

The Lord Nelson Brewery Hotel • The Rocks • Pub
Best Historic Drinking Holes Situated at the top of the Rocks, the Lord Nelson brims with convict spirit from Australia's early settlement days. With exposed sandstone brickwork, scuffed wooden floorboards, oak barrels suspended from the roof and lanterns, flags and maritime memorabilia skirting the ceiling's exposed beams, it is Sydney's oldest licensed hotel. The Lord Nelson also houses Sydney's first boutique brewery; you can see the brewer in action through the glass panels or even take part in a brewery tour. The pub brews six specialty beers, including Three Sheets with passionfruit flavors and Nelsons Blood, a rich, creamy porter. Always teeming with beer-guzzling gents of all ages who favor pints and pristine ales, the Lord Nelson attracts discerning drinkers keen for Old World atmosphere and a dash of barfly banter. Huddle around the fireplace during wintry nights. The Lord Nelson also offers accommodation combining colonial comfort with modern facilities. *Mon-Sat 11am-11pm, Sun noon-10pm.* 19 Kent St. (Argyle St.), 02 9251 4044, lordnelson.com.au

Manly Wharf Hotel* • Manly • Pub/Restaurant
Well worth the ferry trip across the harbor from Circular Quay, the Manly Wharf Hotel throbs with surfies and bleached-blond lasses. An upmarket terraced bar where you can pick up or just drink up, Manly's is popular for bachelorette parties with veiled brides-to-be flirting away their last hours of singledom. Funky

young things fill the bar nightly, with weekends a shoulder-to-shoulder squeeze, raising their voices to be heard above the groovy beats. The pebbled walls are reminiscent of Fred Flintstone's furnishings, and the colorful cube stools in the back bar encircle a fireplace. The outdoor deck comes complete with soothing water views and epitomizes Aussie pub culture: laid-back, salty, and jovial. Always heavily booked, the restaurant is also highly recommended. A few beers with the Manly (literally!) locals will not quickly be forgotten. *Mon-Sat 11:30am-midnight, Sun 11:30am-10pm.* East Esplanade, 02 9977 1266, manlywharfhotel.com.au

Midnight Shift • Darling Harbour • Gay Club

Best Gay Scenes Midnight Shift is a legend in the Sydney gay scene. On the lower levels, you'll find a bar with pool tables and a TV. Upstairs it's a club vibe, with dancing and dark corners, complete with DJs and a laser show. In either space, you're certain to meet new friends. *Bar: Mon-Fri noon-late, Sat-Sun 2pm-late; club: Fri-Sun 10am-late.* C ≡ 85 Oxford St. (William St.), 02 9360 4319

North Bondi RSL Club* • Bondi Beach • Pub

While many of Sydney's RSLs enjoy the city's best views, it's rare to include a Returned and Services League behemoth in the list of Sydney's finest bars. Built for the wartime veterans, most RSLs (private clubs like the Elks in the States) are frequented by their old-timer members, and the atmosphere is generally punctuated by squealing poker machines, bright lights, and blue-haired oldies. But there's no better place to toast Australia's most famous beach than from the balcony of the North Bondi RSL with Sydney's glam beachcombers, sexy surfers, and bronzed blondes. This is a local hot spot. In summer the crowd is salty and sandy, coming straight off the beach for a schooner, with Sunday afternoon seafood raffles particularly popular. The folded-back glass doors and large bar area accommodate an afternoon drinking session perfectly—and you're just meters from the beach below if you heat up. The bistro serves a mean meal from simple fish and chips to gourmet seafood salads. Remember to take your hat off at the door and stand for the sunset salute in silence, a special ceremony to commemorate those who lost their lives during the war and for whom the RSL stands. *Mon noon-10pm, Tue-Thu noon-11pm, Fri-Sat 10am-midnight, Sun 10am-11pm.* ≡ 120 Ramsgate Ave. (Campbell Parade), 02 9130 3152, northbondirsl.comau

The Oaks Hotel* • Neutral Bay • Pub

Best Beer Gardens If not for the beer garden and Art Deco function rooms, the Oaks could easily be dismissed as a blokey rugby pub. A popular meeting spot in the center of the North Shore, for university students, families, 50-somethings, and yuppies too, the Oaks' country pub heart comes with an unassuming appeal that will keep the do-it-yourself barbecue smoking. The males choose their own steak and cook it up on the barbecue, while the girls catch up over wine and mussels. Dubbed the "beer factory" for its abundance of bars and eating areas, the Oaks has a lounge bar, beer garden, public bar, gaming room, and function rooms upstairs, not to mention a pizza oven, pub grub, and a Belgian beer cafe. With red tartan carpet, stained glass lamps, and uniformed bar staff sporting ties, the front Garden Palace Bar is adorned with pictures of wigged chief justices and wooden tables and chairs. This is a "G'day, mate" saloon, where tracksuit pants and Ugg boots are worn for comfort, not fashion statements. The Tramway punters' bar is a sleepy public bar scattered with poker machines, while the open lounge above is a gambling oasis dotted with slot machine junkies. But the best is saved for last in the converted publican's quarters, where each room has a pool table and some have a jukebox. Reserve a room for no charge and shoot pool with a few mates and you can forget about the heaving beer factory below. *Daily 10am-1am.* ≡ 118 Military Rd. (Ben Boyd St.), 02 9953 5515, oakshotel.com.au

Opera Bar • Circular Quay • Bar

Best Bars with a View Drinking within Sydney's picture postcard, with the Opera House at your back, the Harbour Bridge before you, and Luna Park's grin beyond, is a memorable experience. It's easy to understand why Opera Bar is packed at every point throughout the day. Happy-snapping tourists share the outside tables with seagulls in the afternoon until the after-five crowd files in for a wind-down drink, followed by the pre-theater crowd for a glass of sparkling wine. Once the curtain goes up on the various shows, it's time for the hip set to take their places at the long bar or on the soft lounges. And when the curtain goes down, keep an eye out for the stars. Opera Bar has got it right. It caters to romantics, with its cozy corners at either end of the long bar—the ultimate spot for canoodling couples. There's room to mingle outside or indoors as you seek out a good looker with whom to admire the harbor view. There are high stools or lounges to cluster around with your mates. There's an outdoor bar with live entertainment from percussion to neo-soul on weekends. *Mon-Thu noon-midnight, Fri-Sat noon-1am, Sun noon-midnight.* ≡ Sydney Opera House, Lower Concourse Level (Circular Quay West), 02 9247 1666, operabar.com.au

Orbit Bar • CBD • Ultra Lounge

Best Bars with a View Stepping into Orbit Bar is like arriving on another planet complete with space-age lamp shades, bright white retro furnishings, and fire engine red carpet. It's a revolving bar, high in the sky, a place where a younger George Jetson might drink cocktails and chat up über–femme-bot babes. As it is, it's a place that attracts a sexy, younger crowd. On level 47 of Australia Square, a skyscraper in the heart of Sydney's financial district, high above George Street and overlooking the harbor, Orbit Bar is a chic spot adjoining the Summit Restaurant. Table service is provided by sexy waitresses dressed in black. It's not uncommon to hear a variety of international accents floating by, from the staff to the cocktail sippers. There is an air of New York cool, a youthful, yuppie crowd and a lingering sense of '80s decadence, whereby sampling the entire cocktail list seems only fair if you have an evening to spend indulging. As you revolve, the view is segmented by mirrored sections, so don't be surprised, when you lift your head from an oyster shot, to be met by your own reflection. *Daily 5pm late.* Level 47, 264 George St. (Bond St.), 02 9247 9777, summitrestaurant.com.au

Paddington Inn • Paddington • Bar/Lounge

While Oxford Street is renowned as Sydney's gay heartland, the top of the street belongs to sophisticates with designer sunglasses, cute terrace houses, and a penchant for the finer things in life. The Paddo Inn is a trendy local pub with polished cement floors, tusk lamps, and a vibrant atmosphere

CLASSIC

throughout the week, catering to the trendoids and wannabes who frequent the area. The windows fold back in summer so the posers can check each other out, but the discreet folk linger in the booths and small rooms off the back bar. Like separate lounge rooms, they are often reserved for functions or overtaken by larger groups of friends keen to party in privacy. Open and spacious, the Paddo is one big room with high ceilings. On weekend nights when it's heaving, you're partying with half of Sydney's hottest pub enthusiasts, and when it's quiet, it's perfect for a refuel before cruising the boutiques or the Saturday Paddington markets. This is a bar where a few quiet drinks can easily become a session of debauchery as the funky jazz and house tunes pulse and the beautiful people shimmy. *Mon-Tue noon-midnight, Wed-Fri noon-1am, Sat 11am-1am, Sun noon-midnight.* ≡ 338 Oxford St. (William St.), 02 9380 5913, paddingtoninn.com.au

Redoak Boutique Beer Cafe* • CBD • Restaurant/Bar

Australians take their beer brewing (and drinking) very seriously. Immaculately presented, with awards for its microbrewery adorning every wall, Redoak Boutique Beer Cafe is a beer mecca, a refined establishment frequented by city suits. The endless selection of beers makes decisions difficult, but most are delicious, so no choice is a bad one. For a sweet-tasting introduction, the Framboise Froment is a raspberry tipple and is very popular, while the sampler foodie plates, matched with beers, provide a good cross-section of Redoak's finest. Often teeming with middle management nine-to-fivers, Redoak is perfect for a boozy lunch or an after-work ale. The high tables and stools fill up quickly, as does the front lounge near the beer vats, the most comfortable space in the bar area. While the bar staff are attentive, they are a little over-eager and would do well to relax, giving the drinkers more space to enjoy themselves. With all the makings of a slick bar, Redoak needs to take the beer game with less pomposity because the ales are superb, the whitewashed walls, polished floorboards, and timber tables are exquisite, and settling into the restaurant after a few brews is a pleasure. *Mon-Sat 11am-late.* ≡ 201 Clarence St. (King St.), 02 9262 3303, redoak.com.au

The Royal Hotel* • Paddington • Pub

At first glance, the Royal is an unassuming Aussie pub complete with sticky carpet, rowdy locals, and blaring TV screens. Frequented by banker types and rugby louts, the front bar doesn't do justice to the three floors above. Head straight upstairs where the second floor opens up to a chic bistro with tables on the balcony and a Modern Australian menu. Follow the dancing elephants on the wall up to the Elephant Bar on level three, where sipping a Flirting Flamingo or Jungle Love cocktail with Paddington's early-30s cool set can be done in the comfort of an armchair or pillowed couch. Much like a homey drawing room, the Elephant Bar is very cozy, with separate rooms encircling the small bar—the best being the bigger room with windows overlooking Paddington below. A rooftop drinking area has recently been added, with sweeping city views from Paddo to the CBD and umbrellas to shade you from the sun's penetrating rays. Jovial and welcoming, the Royal makes you feel like a local. *Mon-Sat 10am-midnight, Sun 10am-10pm.* ≡ 237 Glenmore Rd. (Heely St.), 02 9331 2604, royalhotel.com.au

360 Bar and Dining Room* • CBD • Restaurant/Lounge

Best Bars with a View Ignore the shopping center decor at ground level, brace yourself for the squeaky ascent, and focus on your destination, a well-earned reward after the journey. Watching the sun melt over the rooftops of Sydney's buildings from the top of the Sydney Tower, as you slowly revolve, is a breathtaking experience for tourists and locals alike. The bartenders shake, muddle, and stir a heady list of specialty martinis and daiquiris on the tortoise-shell-like bar, crafted with handmade tiles. The dim lighting creates a magical ambience. Much groovier than in its original incarnation, 360 reopened at the end of 2005. It's one of the highest points in Sydney (there are a few levels above the bar, but you are 305 meters above sea level), and it immerses you in sophisticated furnishings from leather banquettes to white linen–clad tables. Seating in the bar area is limited, but if you sneak in before 5pm and plonk yourself at one of the lounges facing the view at either side of the bar and linger for a cocktail or two, until the sun sets, you won't soon forget Sydney from above. *Sun-Thu 11:30am-1am, Fri-Sat 11:30am-1:30am.* ≡ Gallery Level, 100 Market St. (Pitt St.), 02 8223 3800, 360dining.com.au

Tilbury Hotel* • Woolloomooloo • Pub/Restaurant

Red lanterns, timber decking, and frangipani and olive trees make the Tilbury a beautiful place to spend an afternoon drinking in the sunshine. Just off Woolloomooloo's main drag, It's popular with the upper crust, luring 50-something gents in pressed pants and checked shirts for long lunches, finely coiffed advertising girls and boys flirting over Friday night drinks, and a fresh-faced gay crowd that takes over late on Sunday afternoons. The fine-dining restaurant that looks out onto the terrace is great and the service is friendly. *Mon-Fri 8am-midnight, Sat 9am-midnight, Sun 10am-10pm.* ≡ 12-18 Nicholson St. (Cowper Bay Rd.), 02 9368 1955, tilburyhotel.com.au

The Vanguard* • Newtown • Restaurant/Jazz Bar

Plush velvet curtains frame the Vanguard stage with a baby grand jutting out beneath the mirror ball, sparkling across the 1920s-inspired venue. The Vanguard has built a reputation for featuring the best local and international talent in a cabaret setting, with everyone from Russell Crowe to Missy Higgins and the Finn brothers gracing the stage. Drinkers enjoy the jazz, blues, and roots mix while perched on stools or wooden chairs. Dinner and show packages guarantee a table on the candle-lit main floor with dishes from Italian roast chicken to pork belly, but there's also Cajun Creole tapas for bar snacks. Influenced by New Orleans' sensuous jazz scene, the owners established the Vanguard in the city's little sister suburb, bohemian Newtown, the diverse heart of Sydney's inner west. Be warned: Staff can be rude. *Daily 7pm-midnight.* ≡ 42 King St. (City Rd.), 02 9557 7992, thevanguard.com.au

Victoria Room* • Darlinghurst • Lounge

Best Trendy Hangouts A colonial-style oasis, the Victoria Room is a sophisticated bar where the world slows down and decadence is top of mind. With dimpled leather couches, veiled chandeliers, red wallpaper, cane birdcages, and chaise lounges, Victoria Room possesses an Old World charm. The bartenders mix cocktails in the emerald backlit bar, serving up refreshing seasonal blends and house specialties such as the Sugar Daddy, with sugar cane, and the Miss

Audrey martini, combining apricot and pristine spirits. Controlling the flow of drinkers and diners, the staff never allow the bar to be more than one person deep, and there is often a line onto Victoria Street. Victoria Room is for sophisticates: well-heeled, fashionable 20-somethings who like to be able to hear themselves talk in a bar. Sunday afternoon high tea, complete with cake trolleys and cucumber sandwiches, is very popular. *Tue-Thu 6pm-midnight, Fri-Sat 6pm-2am, Sun 2pm-midnight.* ≡ Level 1, 235 Victoria St. (Liverpool St.), 02 9357 4488, thevictoriaroom.com

The White Horse Bar and Brasserie* • Surry Hills • Restaurant/Bar
Rearing into the Surry Hills sky, the steel-sculpted equine atop the White Horse is a symbol of the bar's sleek design and image-conscious clientele. Formerly a shady haunt where underage drinkers lurked, it has shunned its working-class roots, transforming into a fashionista magnet complete with fashion TV on LCD screens, a Juliet balcony overlooking Crown Street, mood lighting, and brasserie dining. While not strictly a gay bar, the White Horse attracts purse-lipped queens in their 40s as well as well-dressed Eastern Suburbs tarts. The outdoor terrace upstairs is where it's at, and the long wooden tables and stools are populated by inner-city spendthrifts. *Mon noon-10pm, Tue noon-11pm, Wed-Sat noon-midnight, Sun noon-10pm.* ≡ 381-385 Crown St. (Foveaux St.), 02 8333 9999, thewhitehorse.com.au

Classic Sydney: The Attractions

Akira Isogawa • Various • Shop

The fashion creations of Japanese-born Akira Isogawa can easily double as wall art. Sourcing vintage fabrics from overseas or Australia, the designer also exports to premium overseas locations such as Saks Fifth Avenue and top department stores in London and Japan. His work ranges from boho cotton "apron dresses" to exquisite silk organza evening and bridal wear and now includes a new menswear collection. *Mon-Wed and Fri 10am-5:30pm, Thu 10am-8pm, Sat 10am-4pm.* Woollahra: 12a Queen St., 02 9361 5221; CBD: Level 2, The Strand Arcade, Pitt St. (George St.), 02 9232 1078, akira.com.au

Art Gallery of New South Wales (NSW) • CBD • Art Museum

Best Art Spaces Facing the grasslands of the Domain, the Art Gallery of NSW is a mixed-architectural construction with a leaning towards classical Greece. As one of Australia's best art galleries, it prides itself on its permanent collections of colonial art as well as its examples of international art. Temporary exhibits include photography, student creations, and traveling art shows. Aboriginal artworks are exhibited and there's a fine collection of Asian art. *Daily 10am-5pm (Wed until 9pm).* $ Art Gallery Rd. (Mrs. Macquaries Rd.), 02 9225 1744, artgallery.nsw.gov.au

Australian Museum • CBD • Cultural Museum

While not in the same class as some of the world's great natural history museums, very few can boast a collection of Aboriginal artifacts as impressive as the display here. The Albert Chapman Mineral Collection, considered to be one of the top ten private mineral collections in the world, is also a must-see. Elsewhere in the museum you can see some stuffed marsupials, a decent insect display, and a skeleton collection–it includes "Domestic bliss," a man relaxing in his rocking chair, with his skeleton parrot, dog, cat, and a resident rat by his side. *Daily 9:30am-5pm.* $ 6 College St. (William St.), 02 9320 6000, amonline.net.au

Australian National Maritime Museum • Darling Harbour • Cultural Museum

Best Cool Museums Sydney is a maritime city, and this museum dedicated to naval history celebrates its roots. The collection includes paintings, logbooks, scrimshaw work, and all manner of maritime bits and pieces. You have to pay to wander around the ships docked beside it. These include a destroyer, a submarine, a historical racing yacht, and a Vietnamese refugee boat. Taking pride of place is a replica of the *Endeavour*, the ship Captain Cook sailed on when he "discovered" Australia. You can walk into the cabin where he worked and dined, and the mess deck where over 70 sailors, marines, and servants slung their hammocks and ate their meals. *Daily 9:30am-5pm.* $ 2 Murray St. (Pyrmont Bridge Rd.), 02 9298 3777, anmm.gov.au

Dinosaur Designs • CBD • Shop

This is the art you can wear anywhere. The iconic Sydney store now has a shop in New York, taking its colorful vision to the world. No stylish Sydney girl is complete without one or two strings of resin beads from Dinosaur Designs, worn over a dress or a T-shirt, paired with jeans and flip-flops—they are the essential accessories when you are feeling drab. For the home, the resin bowls, spoons, and vases will brighten any corner of the room. *Mon-Fri 9:30am-5:30pm, Sat 10am-4:30pm.* CBD: Level 1, The Strand Arcade, Pitt St. (George St.), 02 9223 2953; Paddington: 339 Oxford St. (William St.), 02 9361 3776; dinosaurdesigns.com.au

Elizabeth Bay House • Elizabeth Bay • Site

Built between 1835 and 1839, Elizabeth Bay House was once described as "the finest house in the colony." It was designed by the most fashionable architect of the time, John Verge, and was the home of a high-ranking civil servant, Alexander Macleay. As with many of Verge's commissions, its construction was curtailed as a result of a sustained drought and overspeculation in land and stock, which resulted in the financial crisis of the early 1840s that devastated early colonial society. Still, this fine colonial house and its furniture offers you an evocative glimpse into the 19th-century lifestyle of a wealthy colonial. *Daily 10am-4:30pm.* $ 7 Onslow Ave. (Elizabeth Bay Rd.), 02 9356 3022

Gavala Aboriginal Art Gallery • Darling Harbour • Art Gallery

Best Art Spaces It might be a commercial enterprise, but this art gallery is one of the finest in Australia and features an extensive collection of Aboriginal paintings by important indigenous artists. Gavala is Aboriginal-owned and it deals directly with the artists and their communities to ensure that they receive payment and recognition. The styles of paintings on offer range from those from the Central Desert in the Northern Territory to contemporary works. The associated shop sells didgeridoos, boomerangs, masks, statues, books, and music. *Daily 10am-9pm.* Shop 131, Harbourside Centre (Darling Rd.), 02 9212 7232, gavala.com.au

Hyde Park Barracks Museum • Hyde Park • Cultural Museum

Best Cool Museums One of Sydney's best museums is housed in an elegant Georgian brick building, designed by the convict architect Francis Greenway and built between 1817 and 1819 by convict labor. It held 600 convict men at any one time, and though transportation to New South Wales ended in 1840, it served as a barracks for another eight years. Later it was home to Irish orphans, "unprotected females," and aged asylum inmates. One room is dedicated to rows of hammocks, and others to pens, pipes, bones, and other materials found under the floorboards or in rats' nests. *Daily 9:30am-5pm.* $ Queens Square, Macquarie St. (Prince Alfred Rd.), 02 8239 2311, hht.nsw.gov.au

Manly • Manly • Neighborhood

"Seven miles from Sydney and a thousand miles from care" was the slogan they once used to tempt visitors to the seaside suburb of Manly. Reached by a half-hour ride on a ferry from Circular Quay, or a 15-minute dash onboard a super-fast jet cat, the main strip of sand is long and golden, and lined with Norfolk Island pines—the roosting place for thousands of lorikeets at dusk. Here, surfers ride the swell and visitors go topless, or wander along the walkway that leads to the tiny, beautiful Shelley Beach, off to your right as you look at the ocean. Dozens of cafes and restaurants line the pedestrian-only Corso and cluster around the oceanfront. The suburb owes its name to Governor Phillips, who noted the "manly" qualities of the local Aborigines. True to their macho nature, they speared him after he disturbed their meal of washed-up whale in 1790.

North Sydney Olympic Swimming Pool • Milsons Point • Sport/Site

This is Sydney's most famous outdoor swimming pool. More world records have been set here than anywhere else—86 since it opened in 1936. Back then it was hailed as the "wonder pool of Australasia" because of the high standard of its facilities and the sophistication of its filtration system. In 2000, the complex underwent major renovation and a new indoor pool and spa were added. Note the strong Art Deco styling and decorative plasterwork of the original part of the complex and, of course, the great views from the cafe. *Mon-Fri 9am-5:30pm, Sat-Sun 9am-9pm.* $ 4 Alfred St. South (Olympic Dr.), 02 9955 2309

Queen Victoria Building • CBD • Shopping

The QVB, as it's known, fills an entire city block. Its dominant feature is a mighty central dome with a copper-sheathed exterior. Inside are four levels of upmarket fashion boutiques, cafes, antique stores, art galleries, and souvenir shops. The building was completed in 1898, and was dedicated to the long-reigning monarch whose statue still sits in a square beside it. Bounded by George, Market, York, and Druitt Streets, 02 9264 9209, qvb.com.au

The Rocks • The Rocks • Neighborhood

Best Historic Sydney Sydney's historic district, located beside Circular Quay, is a fascinating area crammed with alleyways, historic buildings, boutiques, eateries, and colonial pubs. Among the 96 heritage-listed buildings are a former Sailor's Home (which offered cheap board to keep the salty dogs away from kipping the night in a brothel) and the Dawes Point Battery (built in 1791, making it the oldest remaining European structure in Australia). A dirty, dangerous place for much of its history, it was saved from demolition in the 1970s by mass protests and union blockades. One of the best attractions is the Susannah Place Museum (see p.130), which consists of four terrace houses built in 1844.

Royal Botanic Gardens • CBD • Park

Every city needs some green lungs, and this is Sydney's. Wrapped around Farm Cove and stretching from behind the Opera House to the warships docked at Woolloomooloo Bay, the Royal Botanic Gardens offers fabulous harbor views, plenty of picnic lawns, duck ponds, and thousands of plants from around the world. Highlights include the central Palm Grove, which chatters with hundreds of giant fruit bats, a fernery, a giant glasshouse packed with orchids and other tropical species, and a formal rose garden. The gardens, founded by Governor Macquarie, are on the site of the first farm in Australia—which unfortunately failed. For fabulous views of the Opera House and Harbour Bridge, head to Mrs. Macquaries Chair, a stone cutaway where she once sat to admire the scenery. *Daily 7am-5pm.* Macquarie St. (Mrs. Macquaries Rd.) 02 9231 8111, rbgsyd.nsw.gov.au

St. James Church • CBD • Site

Sydney's oldest surviving colonial church was designed by the architect Francis Greenway, a former convict, who was transported to Sydney for 14 years in 1812 after forging a document. It was consecrated as an Anglican church in 1824. Before skyscrapers obscured it, the spire once served as a landmark for ships coming into the harbor. The crypt houses a shop specializing in religious books, jewelry, music, cards, and candles. *Mon-Sat 8:30am-5pm, Sun 7:30am-3pm.* Queens Square, Macquarie St. (King St.), 02 8227 1300, sjks.org.au

St. Mary's Cathedral • CBD • Site

St Mary's Cathedral, a sandstone Gothic Revival structure, stands on the site of an earlier chapel, which was destroyed by fire in 1865. Work on this Catholic place of worship was completed in four stages: the northern section in 1882, the central tower in 1900, the nave in 1928, and the spires in 2000. The north-south orientation of the cathedral means the light penetrates through just three northern end windows for most of the day, making it seem gloomy and dark. But early in the morning, light penetrates the 14 stained-glass windows on the eastern side, and the cathedral becomes brilliant. In the afternoon, the western side windows alight. *Daily 7am-6pm.* College and Cathedral streets (King St.), 02 9220 0400

Strand Arcade • CBD • Shopping

Just off Pitt Street Mall, the city's pedestrian-friendly shopping precinct, the Strand Arcade is an elegant creation, which was previously known as the "City Arcade," and sometimes "Arcade Street." Opened in 1892 and renamed in 1981—after the famous street in London—it aimed to link the promenade with the reputation of Britain's most fashionable shopping street. Also here is the Old Coffee Shop, a tenant since 1892, which serves great coffee from an authentic Bezzera coffee machine. Some of Australia's hottest designers have boutiques upstairs. *Hours vary by store.* Pitt Street Mall (King St.), 02 9232 4199, strandarcade.com.au

Susannah Place Museum • The Rocks • Cultural Museum

Susannah Place Museum ranges over four terrace houses built in 1844. Inside, past a store selling items of days gone by, you'll be able to step back in time to see what life was like in the Rocks during its early days. Up cramped staircases, through tiny kitchens, and into postage-stamp yards, it's a quick but interesting stop. *Mar-Nov daily 10am-5pm. Dec-Feb Sat-Sun 10am-5pm.* $ Susannah Place, 58-64 Gloucester St. (Grosvenor St.), 02 9241 1893, hht.net.au/home

Sydney Aquarium • Darling Harbour • Aquarium

This is one of the world's best aquariums and should be on anyone's itinerary when visiting Sydney. Several smaller tanks show some of the creatures that live in Australia's rivers, but the emphasis is definitely on the oceans. A huge walk-through tank showcases gray nurse sharks and various species of ray, and another concentrates on seals. A large Barrier Reef section ends in a very large display of colorful fish that you can watch to the sounds of classical music. *Daily 9am-10pm.* $$ Aquarium Pier (King St.), 02 8251 7800, sydneyaquarium.com.au

Sydney Jewish Museum • Darlinghurst • Cultural Museum

This two-story museum has two main themes: the Holocaust, which is portrayed in photos and articles upstairs, and Jewish life in early Australia, displayed downstairs. A highlight is a re-creation of Sydney's George Street in the 1840s, with its fanciful combination of mural painting and a 3-D display of shops. *Sun-Thu 10am-4pm, Fri 10am-2pm.* $ 148 Darlinghurst Rd. (Burton St.), 02 9360 7999, sydneyjewishmuseum.com.au

Sydney Observatory • Millers Point • Site

Much of the night sky in the southern Hemisphere is different, of course, to what you see in the north. At night you can look through the telescopes, and during the day there are exhibitions and exciting 3-D space journeys. The observatory began life in 1848, as a simple time-ball tower. Every day at 1pm the time ball would drop, signaling the exact time to the city and harbor below. Soon after, a dome was added to house the telescope, and in 1877 another observation tower was built. *Daily 10am-5pm (night viewings must be booked in advance).* $ Observatory Hill (Argyle St.), 02 9921 3485, sydneyobservatory.com.au

Sydney Opera House • Circular Quay • Site/Venue

Best Only-in-Sydney Experiences The number one Sydney attraction with its iconic white sails sits on an area once known as Cattle Point, where the stock from the First Fleet were landed. Later, the point was named after Bennelong, a local Aborigine who had a hut built for himself on the point in 1791. Over time, the site housed defensive forts and a tram shed before the Opera House was constructed in 1973. Designed by the Danish architect Jørn Utzon, it has five performance spaces. The largest is the Concert Hall, which is used for symphonies, dance, and chamber music. The Opera Theatre, which has acoustics that can only be described as average, hosts opera, ballets, and dance. Three smaller theaters host plays. *One-hour guided tours daily 9am-5pm.* $$ Bennelong Point (Circular Quay West), 02 9250 7111, sydneyoperahouse.com

Sydney Wildlife World • Darling Harbour • Zoo

Sydney Wildlife World shook the tourism world when it announced it would house several thousand animals in its new building down at Darling Harbour. Would this mean the demise of Sydney's Taronga Zoo? Never fear. The animals turned out to be mostly smaller, with the only creatures of notable height being some rare yellow-footed rock wallabies and a solitary cassowary (a flightless bird from far northern Australian rainforests that can slice open your stomach with a single kick from its dagger-like toe.) Apart from these, you'll see snakes and lizards, plenty of insects, a few more birds, koalas (of course), and nocturnal marsupials (like the rare and very cute bilby—chocolate versions of which are gradually replacing the more traditional edible Easter bunny in Australia). *Daily 9am-10pm.* $$ Aquarium Pier (Darling Harbour), 02 9333 9288, sydneywildlifeworld.com.au

Taronga Zoo • Mosman • Zoo

The location here is brilliant: on a hill overlooking the harbor, the Opera House, the bridge, and the city skyline. An aerial cable car takes you from the ferry wharf to the top of the zoo, and from there you walk down the hill past the animals. The best exhibits include the chimpanzee grounds, the lowland gorilla enclosure, and the nocturnal houses—where you can see platypus and Australian marsupials such as the rabbit-eared bilby. Like most zoos, it has its fair share of elephants and zebras, but there are also koalas, kangaroos, and wallabies. *Daily 9am-5pm.* $$ Bradley's Head Rd. (Military Rd.), 02 9969 2777, zoo.nsw.gov.au

Vaucluse House • Vaucluse • Site

This Gothic-style mansion was built in 1803 for William Charles Wentworth, the father of the Australian constitution. The colony's first native-born politician, he once proposed that the NSW government should have its own House of Lords, made up of landholders like himself. But his proposal failed, after the biggest demonstrations ever seen at Circular Quay. Today, the house is Sydney's only remaining 19th-century private estate that still retains its outbuildings, stables, and original gardens. Surrounding the house are 25 acres of formal gardens. *Tue-Sun 10am-4:30pm.* $ Wentworth Rd. (Olola Ave.), 02 9388 7922

Watsons Bay • Watsons Bay • Walk/Site

An afternoon at Watsons Bay on a sunny day is one of the nicest things to do in Sydney. After some barbecued prawns and a jug of beer in the waterside courtyard of the very cool Doyles Palace Hotel, take a stroll past the sailboats and into Sydney Harbour National Park. A short walking track leads you past Camp Cove, Captain Cook's first landing spot in the harbor, and past Lady Jane Beach, the local nudist corner. At the end of South Head you'll find Hornby Lighthouse, which was opened in 1858 after two shipwrecks cost 142 lives. The circular route carries on along the high craggy cliffs of the Gap.

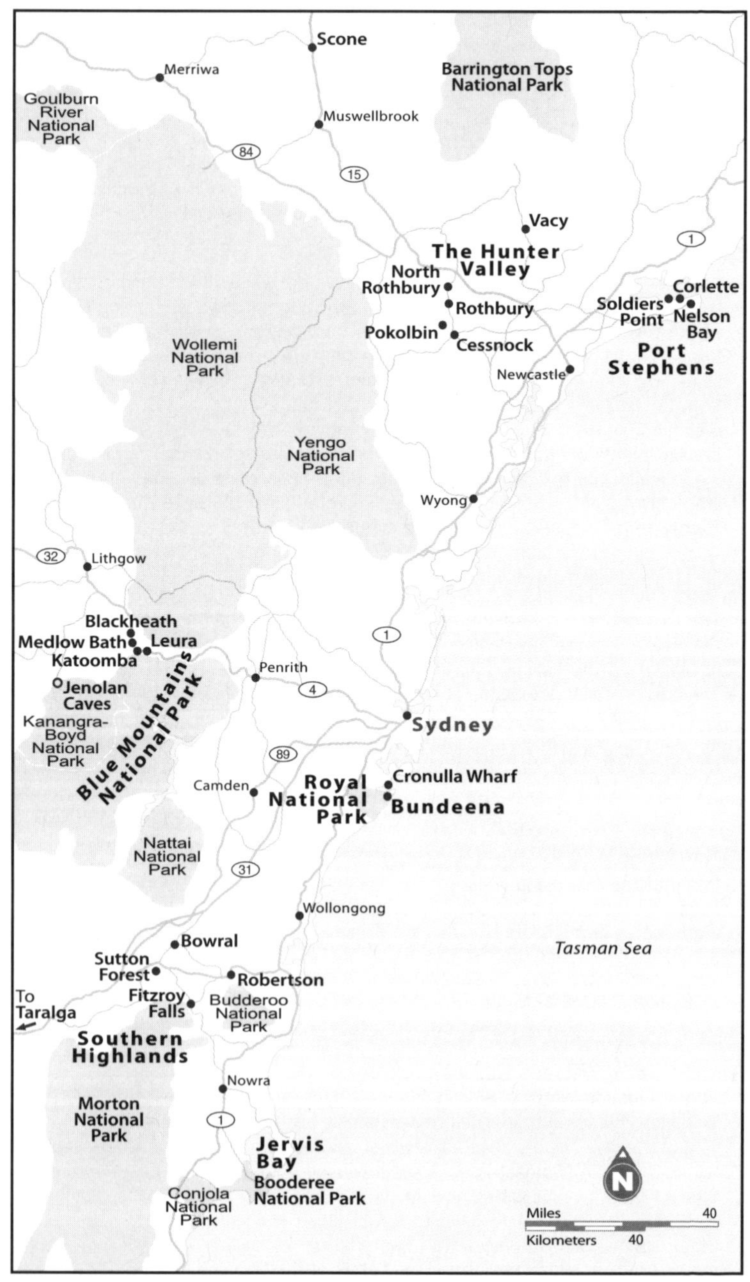
Scone
Merriwa
Barrington Tops National Park
Goulburn River National Park
Muswellbrook
84
15
Vacy
1
The Hunter Valley
North Rothbury
Rothbury
Pokolbin
Cessnock
Corlette
Soldiers Point
Nelson Bay
Port Stephens
Newcastle
Wollemi National Park
Yengo National Park
Wyong
32
Lithgow
Blackheath
Medlow Bath
Leura
Katoomba
Jenolan Caves
Kanangra-Boyd National Park
Blue Mountains National Park
1
Penrith
4
Sydney
89
Camden
Royal National Park
Cronulla Wharf
Bundeena
Nattai National Park
31
Wollongong
Tasman Sea
Bowral
Sutton Forest
Robertson
To Taralga
Fitzroy Falls
Budderoo National Park
Southern Highlands
Nowra
Morton National Park
1
Jervis Bay
Booderee National Park
Conjola National Park
N
Miles 40
Kilometers 40

LEAVING SYDNEY

When you've had your fill of urban fun, it's time to head out of town. From the cooling hills of the Blue Mountains to wine tasting in Hunter Valley, from watching fairy penguins on Phillip Island and exploring the old gold-mining town of Ballarat, to driving along the most scenic road in Australia, drinking wine in the Yarra Valley, and going wild in the Mornington Peninsula, there is something that will please and astonish every visitor. As well as listing the best things to see when you get there, we list the best hotels and places to eat, and fill you in on the most fabulous places to pick up a cool ale or a cocktail.

The Blue Mountains

Hot Tip: July is mid-winter in Australia, and in the Blue Mountains it's time for Yuletide. Log fires, brandy pudding, roast turkey, and tinsel—everyone gets into it, including the hotels and restaurants.

The Lowdown: On a fine day you can see the misty rolls of the Blue Mountains from Sydney Tower, the bluish haze caused by vapors rising from gum trees. Australians tend to exaggerate and, in truth, "the Mountains" are no more than hills. But what hills! These are no sheep-worn hummocks, but jewels of eucalyptus cut with rainforest and chasms that drop away below your feet. There are craggy basalt-rock formations with stories from the Dreamtime—the time of the eternal ancestors in Aboriginal myth—to tell, rugged sandstone tablelands, inaccessible valleys teeming with wildlife, cascading waterfalls, colorful parrots, and the chimes of bell birds. Add stunning walking trails and a line of historic villages bursting with rhododendron flowers and covered by a rime of snow in winter, and you can see how the entire area was named a UNESCO World Heritage site in 2000. Coach tours head up here from the city every day, but to experience the best of it you need to stay for at least three or four days, ensconced in a grand hotel with an open fire. The main township is Katoomba, a rough-and-ready place, with a scattering of good hotels and restaurants. Then there's Leura, famed for its gardens, then Blackheath, the highest village in the mountains and the starting point for some of the best bush walks.

Best Attractions

The Cliff Walk A one-and-a-half-hour tramp from Evans Lookout to Govetts Leap, through banksias, gum, and wattle forests. The cliffs drop away at your feet and the gum trees look like fuzzy matchsticks below.

Jenolan Caves Located 43 miles (70km) west of Katoomba, these fabulous caves are known as some of the world's best. Open for tours since 1866, the caves are a wonderland of stalactites, stalagmites, and underground rivers.

The Scenic Railway and Scenic Skyway Katoomba's most famous man-made attractions are a short and very steep stretch of rail track (once used in coal-mining operations) and a gondola ride above rainforest and fern trees. Scenic World, Katoomba, 02 4782 2699

The Three Sisters The most photographed attraction in the Blue Mountain consists of three tall rock formations sitting proudly above the magnificent Jamison Valley. According to Aboriginal legend, the sisters were turned to rock by a witch doctor to prevent them from being kidnapped by men from a neighboring tribe. Echo Point Rd., Katoomba

Best Restaurants

Chork Dee Local favorite Chork Dee offers some nice Thai dishes with a good lashing of spice. $ 216 Katoomba St., Katoomba, 02 4782 1913

Mes Amis In the cavernous interior of a converted church, diners feast on inspiring French food after a quick prayer. $$ The Old Church, Cnr Waratah and Lurline Sts., Katoomba, 02 4782 1558, mesamis.com.au

Paragon Café The Paragon is an institution you can't miss. Dark-wood paneling and bas relief figures guarding the booths have provided atmosphere since 1916. Great for a quick soup, or cake and coffee. $ 65 Katoomba St., Katoomba, 02 4782 1913

Solitary Warm at night and boasting fabulous cliff views by day, Solitary serves up Modern Australian cuisine that leaps off the plate. $$$ 90 Cliff Dr., Leura Falls, 02 4782 1164, solitary.com.au

Vulcans A simple, comfy restaurant interior downplays the quality of the food at the best restaurant in the Blue Mountains. Wood-fired delicacies are a speciality, and the duck sausage with pickled beetroot is the signature dish. $$$ 33 Govetts Leap Rd., Blackheath, 02 4787 6889

Best Nightlife

Carrington Piano Bar This restored colonial hotel offers live music from Wednesday to Saturday. 15 Katoomba St., Katoomba, 02 4782 1111

Triselies Located near the train station, Triselies has a dance floor and features live music from 9pm to 3am Thursday to Saturday. 287 Bathurst Rd., Katoomba, 02 4782 4026

Best Hotels

The Carrington Hotel If you like British-Raj–style hotels then you'll fall in love with the Carrington. Dating from the 1880s, and restored in 2000, the Carrington oozes charm. $$$ 15-47 Katoomba St., Katoomba, 02 4782 1111, thecarrington.com.au

Echo Point Holiday Villas The closest villas and cottages to the Three Sisters lookout; inexpensive stays with lovely mountain views. $ 36 Echo Point Rd., Katoomba, 02 4782 3275, echopointvillas.com.au

Lilianfels Blue Mountains The most exclusive hotel in the Blue Mountains offers incredible views over Jamison Valley and spacious, antique-filled rooms. $$$$ Lilianfels Ave., Katoomba, 02 4780 1200, lilianfels.com.au

Mercure Grand Hydro Majestic Hotel You can't miss this classical whitewashed former health resort as you drive towards Katoomba. There are fabulous views from the Cloister Rooms, which are either Art Deco or Edwardian. Drop in for coffee. $$$ Medlow Bath, 02 4788 1002, hydromajestic.com.au

Peppers Fairmont Resort This resort has good rooms and a gourmet restaurant. The best things about it are the extensive gardens and large, heated swimming pool. $$$ Sublime Point Rd., Leura, 02 4784 4144, peppers.com.au

Contact

Blue Mountains Tourism Echo Point Rd., Katoomba, 02 4739 6266, visitbluemountains.com.au

National Parks and Wildlife Service Blue Mountains Heritage Centre, Govetts Leap Rd., Blackheath, 02 4787 8877

Getting There: From central Sydney take Parramatta Road, then the M4 Motorway, and next the Great Western Highway from the outskirts of Penrith.

The Hunter Valley

Hot Tip: On weekends, most hotels require a two-night stay.

The Lowdown: Australia's most famous, oldest, and most visited wine region started producing in the 1820s. Centered around the towns of Pokolbin and Cessnock, the Hunter Valley is a picturesque area backed by moody hills. Cheese factories, olive producers, and around 110 vineyards, ranging from boutique to grand in scale, are strung out across the valley, while farther north in the Upper Hunter is rural Australia at its best. Farther north still, you run into Barrington Tops National Park, a mystical world of dense rainforest inhabited by nocturnal marsupials and colorful birds. Most wineries are open for tastings, and many have sumptuous restaurants and cafes that offer al fresco dining among the vines. The best Hunter Valley wines are savory, earthy shirazes that need time to mature, and semillons that are heralded by critics worldwide. There are many good ways to get about—on a tour, by stagecoach, bicycle, or hot air balloon. Pick up a free copy of the *Hunter Valley Wine Country Visitors Guide* at any visitor information center for a full rundown of all the wineries.

Best Attractions

Balloon Aloft Hunter Valley Australia's oldest balloon company takes you on flights across the vineyards with the former World Hot Air Balloon Champion as your guide. Includes a champagne breakfast. 1443 Wine Country Dr., North Rothbury, 02 4938 1955, balloonaloft.com

Barrington Tops National Park This rugged World Heritage–listed park is carved out of an ancient volcano. In the lower valleys you'll find subtropical rainforests full of birds and hanging vines, and up on the plateau there is sub-alpine woodland, which gets snow in winter. National Parks and Wildlife Office, 137 Kelly St., Scone, 02 6540 2300, nationalparks.nsw.gov.au

Hunter Valley Classic Carriages Clip-clop between wineries in a horse-drawn cart while sipping from a bottle of champagne. 02 4991 3655, huntervalleyclassiccarriages.com.au

Hunter Valley Horse Riding and Adventures Ride over 300 acres of rangeland and through gum-tree forests on the lookout for kangaroos and wombats. 288 Talga Rd., Rothbury, 02 4930 7111, hilltopguesthouse.com.au

Best Restaurants

Café Enzo Fusing Sydney style with Italian ambience, this energetic little eatery serves serious coffees, breakfasts, and lunches in a sandstone courtyard framed by a fountain. $ Peppers Creek, Broke Rd., Pokolbin, 02 4998 7233, pepperscreek.com.au

Casuarina Restaurant A warm ochre interior and tableside flambés lit with flair make Casuarina a favorite. An eclectic mix of Thai-style curries, Cajun jambalaya, and Mediterranean seafood dishes add to the exoticism. $$ Hermitage Rd., Pokolbin, 02 4998 7888, casuarinainn.com.au

Chez Pok Restaurant Stylish outdoor settings, an extensive wine cellar, herbs from the garden, and a menu mixing simplicity with fine dining make Chez Pok the most awarded restaurant in the Hunter Valley. $$$ Ekerts Rd., Pokolbin, 02 4993 8999, peppers.com.au

Il Cacciatore Restaurant Il Cacciatore, which in Italian means "the Hunter," specializes in the cuisine of Tuscany. Try the citrus-roasted duck with caramelized figs and sweet potato mash. $$$ 609 McDonald's Rd., Pokolbin, 02 4998 7639, hermitagelodge.com.au

Robert's Restaurant An 1876 barn-sized dining room filled with antiques and flowers, as well as award-winning European-style food, makes this Hunter Valley institution just right for a romantic dinner. $$$ Halls Rd., Pokolbin, 02 4998 7330, robertsrestaurant.com

Best Nightlife

Cessnock Hotel If you still need a drink after all that wine, then head to this classic restored pub, which has a lively bar, a bistro, and an outdoor drinking area. 234 Wollombi Rd., Cessnock, 02 4990 1002

Wentworth Hotel A 1920s drinking hole, featuring live bands towards the end of the week. 32 Vincent St., Cessnock, 02 4990 1364

Best Hotels

Casuarina Country Inn Set around 25 acres of grape vines, these nine amazing split-level suites are done in themes: African, bordello, and others. $$$ Casuarina Estate, Hermitage Rd., Pokolbin, 02 4998 7888, casuarinainn.com.au

Eaglereach Wilderness Resort One moment you're deep in lush rainforest, the next on a breathtaking cliff surrounded by ancient trees and volcanic rock formations. Next to Barrington Tops National Park, Eaglereach offers horse riding, luxurious cabins, and spa treatments. $$$ Summer Hill Rd., Vacy, 02 4938 8233, eaglereach.com.au

Peppers Convent Hunter Valley Once home to the Brigidine Order of Nuns at Coonamble NSW before being carefully transported 400 miles (600km) to the Pepper Tree Estate, this retreat offers elegant rooms with baroque decor. Sip champagne and nibble canapés in the former refectory. $$ Halls Rd., Pokolbin, 02 4993 8999, peppers.com.au

Peppers Guest House A tranquil escape from the rush of the city, Peppers Guest House offers kangaroos at dusk, a veranda to watch the stars from, massages and walking trails, and large rooms with colonial antiques. $$ Ekerts Rd., Pokolbin, 02 4993 8999, peppers.com.au

Contact

Hunter Valley Wine Country Visitors Information Centre *Daily 9am-5pm.* 02 4990 0900, winecountry.com.au

Getting There: Cross the Harbour Bridge to Newcastle. Turn off the highway just before Hornsby and head up the National 1/F3 Freeway. Take the Cessnock exit and follow the signs to the vineyards.

Jervis Bay

Hot Tip: If you have a tent and a sleeping bag, camp at Caves Beach and be woken at dawn by a bird chorus and mobs of kangaroos.

The Lowdown: Jervis Bay, which includes Booderee National Park, is an incredibly beautiful area of coastal cliffs and heaths, white sandy beaches and rock platforms, mangroves and ocean, swamps, lakes, and forests. Booderee is an Aboriginal word from the Dhurga language meaning "plenty of fish." Aborigines still live in the area, and the white-bellied Sea Eagle is their guardian; it's also the National Park logo. The main supply town is Huskisson, where you'll find several restaurants and motels. The park itself is known for its walking trails, deserted beaches, and wildlife—which includes dolphins, kangaroos (you can hand-feed them), and amazing bird life (the colorful lorikeets swoop on you for food). The area exudes sacredness, a reflection of its history as an important Aboriginal meeting place.

Best Attractions

Booderee Botanic Gardens Several walking paths lead off through areas of swamp and coastal heathland filled with wattles, grevilleas, bottlebrushes, and tea trees. Long-necked turtles live in Lake McKenzie. $ Within Booderee National Park, 02 4442 1122

Dolphin Watch Cruises Around 80 bottlenose dolphins live in Jervis Bay, and you're almost guaranteed to see them on a dolphin-watch cruise. You can spot humpback whales close up in May to June and October to November. $$ Owen St., Huskisson, 02 4441 6311, dolphinwatch.com.au

Hyams Beach This secluded beach is purported to have the whitest sand in the world. It squeaks when you walk on it, and the sun's reflection can cause a bad burn, so use plenty of sunblock.

Scuba Diving Scuba-dive in a seal colony, in kelp beds and sponge gardens, and explore wrecks and caves. $$$ Deep 6 Diving, 64 Owen St., Huskisson, 02 4441 5255, deep6divingjervisbay.com

Best Restaurants

The Huskisson Hotel This beachside drinking den, also known as the Husky Pub, offers rooms, live bands, and a bistro serving the usual fish and chips and schnitzels. Outdoor settings are very pleasant on a sunny day. $$ Owen St., Huskisson, 02 4441 5001, thehuskypub.com.au

The Huskisson RSL Club This Returned and Services League club offers cheap drinks and hearty meals. $ Owen St., Huskisson, 02 4441 5282

Best Nightlife

The Huskisson Hotel About the only place in the area to offer anything other than an early sleep, the Husky Pub is a good place to meet the locals, play a game of pool, and listen to an occasional live band. Owen St., Huskisson, 02 4441 5001

Best Hotels

Jervis Bay Guest House Four individual rooms look onto the beach and sea at this cozy guesthouse. The eastern rooms (the Princess Suite and the Sunflower Room) have the best views of the bay from both inside and on their balconies. $$ 1 Beach St., Huskisson, 02 4441 7658, jervisbayguesthouse.com.au

Paperbark Camp Luxurious tents set in the forest come with private bathrooms, comfortable queen or twin beds, locally handcrafted furniture, insect screens, and solar-powered lighting. $$ Woollamia Rd., Jervis Bay, 02 4441 6066, paperbarkcamp.com.au

Contact

Booderee National Park office Village Rd., Jervis Bay, 02 4443 0977, deh.gov.au/parks/booderee

Getting There: Take the Princes Highway south through Wollongong, Kiama, Berry, and Nowra. Eight miles (13km) south of Nowra, turn left into Jervis Bay Road and follow signs to National Park or Huskisson.

Port Stephens

Hot Tip: Port Stephens is a good option to tack onto a tour of the Hunter Valley and Barrington Tops National Park.

The Lowdown: Gorgeous Port Stephens is twice the size of Sydney Harbour. It jumps with pods of dolphins and migratory whales, and is surrounded by Tomaree National Park—a haven for more bird life than you'll see even in Kakadu in the Northern Territory. Two pods of bottlenose dolphins, made up of around 70 individuals, cruise the waters looking for feasts of fish. These inquisitive animals come right up to passing boats, and if you are on a cruise, the chances of seeing them are excellent. The Port Stephens Ferry Service (02 4981 3798) operates daily dolphin-watching cruises at cut rates. Also, if you haven't seen a koala in the wild, then come here to see the region's largest breeding colony. The main township is Nelson Bay, an attractive place with restaurants and fashion boutiques lined up along the waterfront. The small town of Anna Bay is surrounded by excellent surf beaches. The Worimi and Wonarua Aboriginal people formerly inhabited the area, and campfire remains and giant shell middens (shellfish refuge pits) are commonplace, particularly among the sand dunes of Stockton Beach. You can also view a large shell midden (1,240 years old) on Fitzroy Street, in Anna Bay, amid the local urban settlement.

Best Attractions

Dolphin Spotting One of the best operators on the bay runs several cruises on the lookout for dolphins—and whales (in season). $$ Imagine Cruises, 02 4984 9000, imaginecruises.com.au

Koala Bears The Tilligerry Peninsula, which runs along part of the waterfront, supports dozens of wild koalas that feed among the eucalyptus trees.

Stockton Beach The vast sandy expanse of Stockton Beach, which stretches for 20 miles (32 km), is backed by windblown dunes that comprise the largest continuous mobile sand mass in New South Wales.

Best Restaurants

Rock Lobster Restaurant Nelson Bay's premier seafood restaurant is located on a balcony overlooking the bobbing boats. Try the catch-of-the-day seafood platter. $$$ Shop 20, D'Albora Marina 60, Teramby Rd., Nelson Bay, 02 4981 1813, rocklobsterrestaurant.com.au

Sinclair's Inside it's a little noisy, but the seafood and pasta dishes will keep your attention. Buy fresh local oysters from a small booth outside. $ D'Albora Marina, 02 4984 4444

Best Hotels

Pepper's Anchorage Port Stephens This compact resort right on the waterfront and opposite the marina is the best place to stay around here. Rooms are light and luxurious; top-floor options have balconies overlooking the bay. $$ Corlette Point Rd., Corlette, 02 4984 2555, peppers.com.au

Salamander Shores A five-story hotel set in pretty gardens and overlooking the water, Salamander Shores has pleasant rooms, the best of which have a Jacuzzi and a large balcony with a sea view. $$ 147 Soldiers Point Rd., Soldiers Point, 02 4982 7210, salamander-shores.com

Contact

Port Stephens Visitor Information Centre Victoria Parade, Nelson Bay, 02 4980 6900, portstephens.org.au

Getting There: Take the Sydney-Newcastle Freeway to its end, then follow the Pacific Highway signs to Hexham and Port Stephens.

Southern Highlands

Hot Tip: The Robertson Pie Shop, in Robertson, serves the best pies in Australia. It offers 24 varieties.

The Lowdown: The Southern Highlands is part of the Great Dividing Range that separates the coastlands from the drier open plains that lead to the interior of the continent. It's a green oasis, reminiscent of rural England, with fresh country air, quaint historic towns and villages, masses of European trees, and rolling meadows dotted with happy-looking cows. The area was first mapped out by Europeans in 1798 when ex-convict John Wilson and his party were sent south to accumulate information about the area in a bid to discourage convicts from escaping and heading south—many believed that China was only 150 miles away. The most visited town today is Bowral, a yuppified tourist center crammed with boutiques, antique stores, galleries, and cafes. Other towns include Berrima, with its colonial architecture and English village common; Bundanoon, a picturesque town that hosts massed pipe bands and highland games in April; and Robertson, where many of the scenes from the movie *Babe* were shot.

Best Attractions

The Bradman Museum Sir Donald Bradman, who was born in 1908, is considered to be the greatest cricketer of all time. He had an average score of 99.94 runs from 52 test matches for Australia, and spent his boyhood years in Bowral. This interesting museum is dedicated to him—and to all things cricket. St. Jude St., Bowral, 02 4862 1247, bradman.org.au

Morton National Park and Fitzroy Falls Features numerous scenic walks and picnic spots, breathtaking views, and an abundance of native flora and fauna. The waterfall plummets 266 feet (81 meters) into a rainforest valley. Several walks take you around the falls and to its base. You'll encounter up to 48 species of gum tree, lyre birds, and possibly wombats. Morton National Park, Nowra Rd., Fitzroy Falls, 02 4887 7270

Wombeyan Caves About 40 miles (60 km) west of the town of Mittagong (via part-paved and part-dirt road) are some spectacular limestone caverns featuring a number of unique encrustations and deposits. You can take a guided tour of several caves, and there are on-site accommodations and camping. Wombeyan Caves Rd., Taralga, 02 4843 5976

Best Restaurants

Eschalot Servings are generous in this elegant dining room, which makes up part of the boutique Links House hotel. Contemporary cuisine includes crab-stuffed squid with lime and coriander, and duck leg confit with roasted figs. $$ Links House, 17 Links Rd., Bowral, 02 4861 6177, linkshouse.com.au

Fitzroy Inn This historic sandstone inn was once used to house convicts on their way from Sydney and nearby Goulburn (still the site of a major jail). The Modern Italian–style menu is laced with homegrown vegetables and herbs from the garden. $$ 26 Furguson Crescent, Mittagong, 02 4872 3457, fitzroyinn.com.au

Best Nightlife

Robertson Inn This historic hotel in the pretty town of Robertson has some of the best beer in the Southern Highlands. 87 Hoddle St., Robertson, 02 4884 1202

Royal Hotel and Steakhouse Yes, it does steaks, but its country charm is what the locals come for. $$ 255 Bong Bong St., Bowral, 02 4862 5588

Sutton Forest Inn and Bistro Come here for sweeping countryside views by day and live music and crackling fireplaces by night. $$ Illawarra Highway, Sutton Forest, 02 4868 1697

Best Hotels

Berida Manor Spoil yourself in the unrivaled luxury of a bygone era in this sumptuous country manor house with an ambience reminiscent of the 1920s. There's golf, tennis, an indoor pool, sauna, billiards, a cocktail bar, and an elegant restaurant. $$$ 6 David St., Bowral, 02 4861 1177, beridamanor.com.au

Peppers Manor House Southern Highlands The decor is stylish—winter fires burn in the baronial Great Hall and the music room and lounge; in summer, meals are served in a leafy courtyard, with drinks by the pool. Bedrooms are in the main house, in an adjacent garden wing, and in self-contained cottages. $$$ Kater Rd., Sutton Forest, 02 4860 3111, peppers.com.au

Ranelagh House Built in 1924, Ranelagh House is a lovely imitation English manor house set on 13.5 acres of landscaped gardens, complete with statues, swimming pool, fountains, deer and peacocks. Devonshire teas served daily from 10am-5pm. $$ Illawarra Highway, Robertson, 02 4885 1111, ranelagh-house.com.au

Contact

The Southern Highlands Visitor Centre 62-70 Main St., Mittagong, 02 4871 2888, southern-highlands.com.au

Getting There: Join the M5 Motorway/Hume Highway near Sydney Airport and head south toward Goulburn and Canberra. Bowral and other Southern Highlands towns and villages are off to your left.

Bundeena and the Royal National Park

Hot Tip: A short bush track through mangrove swamps leads off from the end of Bonivale beach to a small strip of aqua-green estuary, perfect for a refreshing dip among schools of baby fish.

The Lowdown: This gorgeous area near Sydney was declared a national park in 1879. For tens of thousands of years, the area was occupied by the Dharawal Aboriginal nation, who left their mark with rock carvings that are easily accessible from the little village of Bundeena. In the early days of European settlement, the park was seen as "the lungs of Sydney"—a place for recreation and fresh air. It's a rugged place, with sweeping coastal scenery, isolated beaches, and dense forest and bushland. To get there, take a CityRail train from the center of Sydney to the surfing beachside suburb of Cronulla, then take a ferry to Bundeena village, which is surrounded on three sides by National Park and on the other by Port Hacking. Bundeena boasts four beautiful beaches.

Best Attractions

Aboriginal Rock Carvings To find the rock engravings of whales, fish, and kangaroos created some 5,000 years ago, walk the length of Jibbon Beach to a rock platform. From here a short trek through the bush leads to the site.

Bundeena-Maianbar Art Trail The first Sunday of each month dozens of galleries open to the public in Bundeena and nearby Maianbar. arttrail.com.au

Cronulla National Park Ferries For breathtaking views of the national park, and some of Sydney's finest waterfront houses, jump aboard the *M.V. Tom Thumb 111*, Sydney's oldest operating ferry, for a scenic cruise. Daily in summer, 10:30am. Cronulla Wharf, 02 9523 2990

Sea Kayaking Hire kayaks or join a guided tour to paddle around the fringes of the national park. There is also a night-paddle excursion. Bundeena Sea Kayaks, Bonivale Beach, Bundeena, 02 9544 5294, seakayak.bundeena.com

Best Restaurants

Cafe Manna Located in the grouping of shops visible as you enter Bundeena by ferry, Café Manna has good coffee and a range of sandwiches and light meals. $ 4/22 Brighton St., Bundeena, 02 9523 9555

Passionfruit Café This place serves sandwiches, fish and chips, and light meals. $ 48a Brighton St., Bundeena, 02 9527 6555.

Contacts

visitbundeena.com

Getting There: Bundeena is approximately one hour by car from central Sydney. Follow the signs towards the airport, and then the signs to Wollongong. The turn off to Bundeena and the park is on your left just past the giant roadside murals of dolphins, whales, and cockatoos.

HIT the GROUND RUNNING: SYDNEY

If you've never been here before—or even if you live here—Sydney can seem overwhelming. Which freeway takes you where? Which mountains are those? And by the way, what season is it? If you want to make like a native, you need to know the basics. Here are the facts and figures, including our *Cheat Sheet*, a quick-reference countdown of vital information that'll help you feel like an instant Sydneysider.

City Essentials Sydney

Getting to Sydney: By Air

Sydney International Airport (SYD)

02 9667 9111, sydneyairport.com.au

Sydney Airport is located 7 miles (10km) south of the city center, and the International and Domestic Terminals are 2 1/2 miles (4km) apart. Sydney Airport is a modern facility and it was heavily upgraded prior to the 2000 Sydney Olympics. Also part of the deal back then was a new airport rail line to connect with the city center. Unfortunately, they just tacked it on to a regular route, and you might find trains are full if you arrive at peak commuting times, in the morning and evening as workers come and go. Airport Security is tight and the customs procedures at the International Terminal can be tedious. Make sure you dispose of fruits, vegetables, meats, and plant material at the designated bins before you go through customs, as Australia has very strict quarantine regulations. If in doubt, go through the exit marked by a red sign. Even if you go through the "nothing to declare" exit, your bags will be screened for organic material. Beagle sniffer-dogs look cute in their nice jackets, but they take a keen interest, too. Allow at least two hours to work your way through check-in and immigration if you're leaving the country, and at least an hour if you're flying domestic. The International Arrivals area has a limited duty-free shop where you can buy perfumes and alcohol. You can take two one-liter bottles of standard spirits into Australia. The International

Flying Times to Sydney

Direct From	Airport Code	Time (hr.)
Auckland	AKL	3
Bangkok	BKK	9½
Hong Kong	HKG	9
Kuala Lumpur	KUL	8
London*	LHR	23
Los Angeles	LAX	13½
New York*	JFK	18½
Paris*	CDG	22
Tokyo	NRT	9½
Domestic		
Adelaide	ADL	2
Alice Springs	ASP	3
Brisbane	BNE	1½
Canberra	CBR	¾
Darwin	DRW	5½
Hobart	HBA	1½
Melbourne	MEL	1½
Perth	PER	4½

** Not nonstop flights*

Airlines Serving Sydney and Melbourne Airports

Airlines	Website	Number
Aerolineas Argentinas	aerolineas.com.ar	02 9234 9000
Air Calin	aircalin.nc	02 9244 2211
Air Canada	aircanada.com	1 300 655 767
Air China	airchina.com.cn	02 9232 7277
Air France	airfrance.com	1 300 390 190
Air Mauritius	airmauritius.com	1 300 658 572
Air New Zealand	airnewzealand.com.au	13 24 76
Air Niugini	airniugini.com.au	1 300 361 380
Air Pacific	airpacific.com	1 800 230 150
Air Tahiti Nui	airtahitinui.com	02 9244 2799
Australian Airlines	australianairlines.com.au	1 300 799 798
Austrian Airlines	aua.com/au/eng	1 800 642 438
British Airways	britishairways.com	1 300 767 177
Cathay Pacific	cathaypacific.com	13 17 47
China Airlines	china-airlines.com	02 9231 5588
China Eastern	ce-air.com	02 9290 1148
China Southern	cs-air.cn	02 9233 9788
Egypt Air	egyptair.com	1 300 309 767
Emirates	emirates.com	1 300 303 777
Freedom Air	freedomair.co.nz	1 800 122 000
Garuda Indonesia	garuda-indonesia.com	1 300 365 330
Gulf Air	gulfair.com	1 300 366 337
Hawaiian Airlines	hawaiianairlines.com	02 9244 2377
Japan Airlines	jal.co.jp	02 9272 1111
Korean Air	koreanair.com	02 9262 6000
LanChile	lan.com	1 300 361 400
Malaysia Airlines	malaysiaairlines.com	13 26 27
Pacific Blue	flypacificblue.com	13 16 45
Philippine Airlines	phillipineairlines.com	03 9650 2188
Polynesian Blue	polynesianblue.com	13 16 45
Qantas	qantas.com.au	13 13 13
Royal Brunei Airlines	bruneiair.com	1 300 721 271
Singapore Airlines	singaporeair.com	13 10 11
Thai Airways	thaiair.com	1 300 651 960
United Airlines	united.com	13 17 77
Virgin Atlantic	virgin-atlantic.com	1 300 727 340

Domestic airlines

Airlines	Website	Number
Eastern Australia	qantas.com.au	13 13 13
Jetstar	jetstar.com.au	13 15 38
OzJet	ozjet.com.au	1 300 737 000
REX (Regional Express)	rex.com.au	13 17 13
Qantas	qantas.com.au	13 12 23
Qantas Link	qantas.com.au	13 13 13
Virgin Blue	virginblue.com	13 67 89

Departures area has a range of shops, both inside and outside the immigration hall. Shop duty free after you go through immigration, otherwise you'll have a bit of a wait to pick it up on the other side. You'll find the nicest eateries before you go through immigration, though. One of the best is Café Addio, to your far right, which serves great coffee and Italian snacks. You can store baggage at the International Airport (call 02 9667 9111) for between A$8 and A$11 per 24 hours. The Lost Property number is 02 9667 9583. Shuttle buses operate between the two terminals every few minutes. The Domestic Terminal has a few cafes, a McDonald's, and a Krispy Kreme Doughnuts outlet. Baggage carts are free in the International Terminal arrivals hall, but cost A$4 elsewhere (you need dollar coins for the machine).

Sydney Airport is 15 minutes by train from the city center. The Sydney Visitor Centre (02 9667 6050), outside the Arrivals area, has plenty of maps and other information, and you can also buy Sydney Passes here. It costs around A$30 to get to the city center by taxi.

Rental Cars: All of the following major rental car companies have counters inside Sydney airport.

Agency	Website	Number
Budget	budget.com.au	13 27 27
Delta	deltaeuropecar.com.au	02 9207 9400
Hertz Australia	hertz.com.au	02 9669 2444
Thrifty	thrifty.com.au	1 300 367 227
Limousines:		
DJ Andrews Limousines	djandrewslimos.com.au	02 9317 4188
Liberty limousines	libertylimousines.com.au	0400 816 935

Getting to Sydney: By Land

By Car: From Sydney, the Pacific Highway leads north along the coast to Queensland, and the Princes Highway runs beside the ocean to Melbourne. The Great Western Highway and the M4 motorway lead west to the Blue Mountains, while the boring M5 motorway and Hume Highway travels south to Canberra, and ultimately to Melbourne.

By Train: Australia has a vast and efficient train system that is a great way to see parts of the country most visitors never make it to. The

Austrail Flexi Pass gives you unlimited travel on all lines, making it a great option if you plan on visiting multiple locations. The passes are good for 15 or 22 days within a 6-month period. A 15-day pass is about A$950, and 22 days runs about A$1330. There are also more limited passes, such as the East Coast Discovery Pass, which heads towards Melbourne, that run far less—about A$300. Schedules and information can be found at railsnw.com or by calling 800 717 0108 or 503 292 5055 (in the U.S.).

Driving Distance to Sydney

From	Distance (mi.)	Approx. Time (hr.)
Adelaide	731	20½
Brisbane	456	12
Canberra	156	3
Melbourne (inland)	439	9
Melbourne (coastal)	480	12

By Bus: Greyhound Australia (13 14 99; greyhound.com.au) operates daily coaches between Sydney and Melbourne and vice versa. The trip takes around 10 hours. Coaches leave from beside Central Station in Sydney and from the Transit Centre, 58 Franklin Street (two blocks north of Southern Cross Station).

Getting Around Sydney: Lay of the Land

Sydney is situated around its famous harbor on the east coast of Australia. The city center is compact, with the main thoroughfares of George Street, Pitt Street, and Castlereagh Street running up from the ferry wharfs at Circular Quay to Town Hall and beyond. Cross streets from Town Hall lead to the waterside precinct of Darling Harbour and, in the other direction, from Hyde Park to Kings Cross. The Sydney Harbour Bridge takes you to the northern suburbs, which include Milsons Point, North Sydney, and Manly. Fashionable Oxford Street leads east from Hyde Park towards the eastern suburb beaches, which include Bondi and Bronte.

By Car: You don't need a car to get around Sydney because there are plenty of public transport options, particularly within the city center. Driving anywhere new can be confusing, especially for those not used to driving on the left side of the road. Americans and Europeans are frequently found driving on the right side, especially just after waking up, or trying to go around a roundabout the wrong way. It's funny to see, but dangerous, too. The toll system makes things confusing as well. On toll roads in Sydney, including across the Harbour Bridge and through the Harbour Tunnel, and the Eastern Distributor, which runs northbound from the airport to the North Shore or Wolloomooloo, you can pay cash, but if you find yourself funneled into the Cross City Tunnel (which runs from Darling Harbour to Rushcutters Bay near Kings Cross, and also connects with the Eastern Distributor), then you'll need to call the toll operators (02 90 933 999) and offer to pay them A$3.63 off your credit card. Stupid, huh?

Taxis: You'll find taxis outside most major hotels and at marked taxi ranks. In Sydney you can tell whether a taxi is free by a yellow light on its roof. As well as the fare displayed on the meter, you may find yourself owing extra for tolls. For example, a trip either way on the Sydney Harbour Bridge will add an extra $3, and there's a $2 pick-up fee at Sydney airport.

Agency	Number
Legion Cabs	13 14 51
Premier Cabs	13 10 17
RSL Taxis	02 9581 1111
Taxis Combined	13 33 00

Parking: As in any major city in the world, parking can be a headache, especially if you want to get around the city center. The best bet is not to do it, but use taxis or public transport instead. But if you do want to take the wheel yourself, then you need to obey some simple parking rules. Most city streets come with signs laying these out—it might be as simple as a "P2" sign and an arrow, which means you can park in the direction of the arrow for two hours. Local residents still look for chalk marks on their tires to show a parking inspector has been around and is counting their time down, but don't get caught up in this madness, as it's all done electronically now. There are "loading zones" in the city, which are meant just for that, loading or unloading supply vehicles. If you park there, expect a heavy fine and the ire of a local van driver. On some streets you'll find parking meters, costing up to A$6 an hour or more. You'll need coins, and they don't give change.

Parking Garages

Here are some of the most convenient parking facilities.

- Domain Car Park
  (Sir John Young Crescent, Woolloomooloo Entry via St. Mary's Road).
- Goulburn Street Car Park
  (Corner of Goulburn and Elizabeth Sts. Entry via Goulburn Street)

By Train and Bus: Sydney's publicly owned train system, run by CityRail (13 15 00; cityrail.com.au) is a cheap way to get around the city center. The fact that they are double-decker trains, and thus have more capacity than single-level ones, acts as a good excuse to double the time between services. Oh, and forget about looking at timetables—they are largely ineffective. Even the electronic information boards, which count down the minutes to the next train and are found on most city center underground train platforms, have a mind of their own. A minute on a CityRail information board can equate to five minutes of real time. The system is also limited, and important tourist areas such as Bondi Beach, Manly, and Darling Harbour are not connected to the network. Single tickets within the city center cost A$2.20 to A$2.60. Sydney buses (13 15 00; sydneybuses.info) are an alternative and cost from A$1.70 for a short run. They congregate around Circular Quay, Wynyard, and outside the Queen Victoria Building. To get to Bondi Beach, take a CityRail train to Bondi Junction, and change to a bus.

By Ferry: Delightful green-and-yellow public ferries, based at the deep-water wharfs at Circular Quay, have been puttering across Sydney Harbour for more than 135 years. Also run by Sydney Ferries (13 15 00; sydneyferries.info) are the larger ferry boats to Manly. These are supplemented by the jet cat, a fast catamaran, which costs more to travel on, but cuts the journey time in half, to just 15 minutes. After 7pm, only jet cats run between Circular Quay and Manly, for the same price as the ferry. You buy your ticket, from machines or cashiers at Circular Quay, before travel. Visit the ferry information office opposite Wharf 4 for timetables. Some wharfs outside Circular Quay, such as Darling Harbour, don't have machines or cashiers. Don't be too worried, just buy your ticket at the machines located before the wharf exit at Circular Quay. Single tickets for inner-harbor ferries cost A$5.20, for the Manly ferry A$6.40, and the Manly jet cat A$8.20.

By Tram: If you are based around Central Station in Sydney and wish to get to Chinatown, Darling Harbour, or the Sydney Fish Markets, then one option is to take a tram run by Metro Light Rail (02 8584 5288; metrolightrail.com.au). It's a short journey, since the rail tracks only cover about 2.25 miles (3.6km). Trams leave around every ten minutes. A single ticket costs between A$3 and A$4, depending on distance.

By Monorail: As you walk from Town Hall to Darling Harbour you'll probably notice the monorail trains with their heavy make-up of advertising running briskly along a gray metal rail. The Metro Monorail

(02 8584 5288, metrolightrail.com.au) connects the central business district to Darling Harbour, and is a good option if you have tired feet. A single ticket costs A$4.50.

Sydney Pass: Public transport is a good option to get around Sydney. The popular Sydney Pass includes unlimited travel on Sydney buses, Sydney Ferries, the jet cat to Manly, and CityRail trains, as well as trips on Sydney Explorer coaches, Bondi and Bay Explorer coaches, and three Sydney Harbour cruises. The Sydney Pass costs A$110 for three days of travel over a seven-day period; A$145 for five days over a seven-day period; and A$165 for seven consecutive days. Buy tickets at the information desk at the airport, at the TransitShop at Circular Quay (outside McDonald's), or from the Sydney Ferries ticket offices at Circular Quay.

Other Practical Information

Print Media Sydney's main broadsheet newspaper is the *Sydney Morning Herald* (smh.com.au). An insert each Friday gives details on music gigs, bands, and other events. The competing tabloid, the *Daily Telegraph*, offers a lot more gossip, as does the *Sunday Telegraph* and the *Sun Herald*. On Sunday there's a choice between the upmarket *Sunday Age* and the tabloid *Sunday Herald Sun*. For financial news choose the Australia-wide *Australian Financial Review*, and for general news take a look at the *Australian*. American and British newspapers are often found in the bigger news agencies.

Sydney Radio Stations (a selection)

FM Stations

105.7	Triple J	Latest contemporary
92.9	ABC Classic	Classical
104.9	Triple M	Adult contemporary
96.9	Nova	Classic hits

AM Stations

576	ABC Nat'l	Ideas
702	ABC Local	Local news, chat
630	ABC News	Continuous news
875	2GB	Talk radio
954	2UE	Talk radio

Gay and Lesbian Travel In general, Australia is a very tolerant country when it comes to gay and lesbian people (though, as is true anywhere, the inhabitants of major cities are more so). Sydney has a thriving gay and lesbian presence, concentrated on Oxford Street. The city attracts hundreds of thousands of gay and lesbian people from all over the world who come to Australia to celebrate the Mardi Gras season, which runs through February and March. It culminates in a huge street parade and Mardi Gras Party. For information, pick up the weekly *Sydney Star Observer* (ssonet.com.au).

Numbers to Know (Sydney Hotlines)

Emergency, police, fire department, ambulance, and paramedics	000
Suicide Prevention	13 11 14
Rape Crisis Centre	1 800 424 017
National Roads & Motorists Association (NRMA), breakdowns	13 11 11
Police Stations:	
132 George St., The Rocks	1 800 622 571
570 George St.	13 14 44
Travellers Medical:	
Kings Cross Travellers Clinic 13 Springfield Ave., Kings Cross *Mon-Fri 9am-1pm and 2-6pm, Sat 10am-noon*	02 9358 3066
24-Hour Medical:	
Sydney Hospital 8 Macquarie St.	02 9382 7111
Dental Emergency Service:	
Dr. Ray Khori 793 George St. (opposite Central Station)	02 9211 1011

HIT THE GROUND

Party Conversation—A Few Surprising Facts

- In the archives of the Australian Museum, there's an entry that records that Bondi is an Aboriginal word meaning "a place where a fight with nullas took place." A nulla is an aboriginal hitting club. Countless flint tools have been found under the sand of Bondi Beach. It's believed the area was once an ancient "flint factory."

- When the First Fleet landed at Botany Bay in January 1788, carrying 759 male and female convicts from Britain's overcrowded jails, they found a stowaway on board.

- Sydney staged the world's first "movie" projection in November 1894, a good 12 months before the Lumière Brothers in Paris. Screened in a converted shop on Pitt Street, the 35mm film ran at 40 images per second and was projected through a machine known as a kinetoscope.

- Surfing has always been big in Sydney—in fact, an early settler's journal records two Aboriginal women surfing on strips of bark across the harbor to Bennelong Point, where the Sydney Opera House now stands.

- To finance the building of the Sydney Opera House, tickets in Opera House Lottery went on sale in 1957. Tickets were £5 each (A$10) with a first prize of £100,000 (A$200,000). The lottery lasted, in stages, for 16 years, and eventually 90 percent of the A$102 million construction costs were financed by the proceeds.

- The first known concert on the site of the Sydney Opera House was in March 1791. It was hosted by an Aboriginal man named Bennelong—in the hut Governor Phillip had built for him. It was reported that "24 men, women, and children danced to the accompaniment of beating sticks and hands."

- Thousands of very large gray-headed fruit bats live in the canopies of rainforest trees in Sydney's Royal Botanic Gardens. Park staff tried to deter them by banging a five-gallon drum underneath trees at dawn and dusk to upset their sleeping patterns. The bats took off, only to return when the staff thought they had them beat.

The Cheat Sheet (The Very Least You Ought to Know About Sydney)

If you're going to hang out here, you better know something about the place. Here's a countdown of the 10 most essential facts and factoids you need to keep from looking like a tourist.

10 Local Beaches

Avalon Beach Avalon has a small cafe-culture atmosphere and a long orange-colored beach popular with surfers.

Clovelly Beach Farther up the coast from Bondi and Bronte, this crescent of sand leads off to calm waters and an enclosed saltwater swimming hole.

Coogee Beach Complete with a good sweep of sand and historic sea baths, Coogee is a little sister to Bondi.

Cronulla Beach A huge run of sand in Sydney's south is the only beach in the city reached by train—hence the crowds of surfers.

Curl Curl Beach This quintessential Aussie beach is another surf hangout with a good set of breakers.

Lady Jane Beach A visit to Watson's Bay can be made clothes-optional on this little nudist outpost.

Narrabeen Beach This is real northern beaches surfing turf, with big rollers and bronzed Aussie lifeguards.

Palm Beach Stuck out on a spit, with calm waters on one side and miles of ocean beach on the other, Palm Beach offers astonishing beauty and wealthy homes to envy.

Shelley Beach Come to this tiny curve of sand opposite Manly Beach for crystal-clear water and bathing beauties.

Whale Beach If you want a beach that feels remote and is surrounded by natural cliff-top beauty, then this is the place for you.

9 Major Streets

Argyle Street runs from the base of the Rocks historical district up to the top of Observatory Hill.

Dixon Street Crossing Goulburn Street to the south of Hyde Park is the main thoroughfare in Sydney's "Chinatown."

Elizabeth Street runs from Chifley Square, just south of Circular Quay, and beside Hyde Park and onwards.

George Street runs from the Circular Quay ferries to Town Hall and all the way out to Central Station.

Liverpool Street runs from the beginning of Oxford Street, alongside the southern end of Hyde Park, and into the Spanish quarter.

Macquarie Street runs from the Sydney Opera House, past an edge of the Royal Botanic Gardens, and onward to Hyde Park.

Market Street cuts across the city center from Hyde Park to Darling Harbour.

Oxford Street runs from the far eastern corner of Hyde Park past dozens of boutiques as far as Paddington and beyond.

Pitt Street starts at Circular Quay and runs to Pitt Street shopping mall and on toward Central Station.

Landmarks

Argyle Cut This convict-hewn tunnel leads from the lower reaches of the Rocks toward the 1848 sandstone Garrison Church.

Cadman's Cottage This small sandstone structure on the edge of the Rocks was built in 1815-16 as the "Coxswain's Barracks." It's the oldest building in Sydney.

Fort Denison Visible from the Royal Botanic Gardens, the tiny fort on a tiny island was completed in 1857. Its purpose was to defend Sydney against a possible attack by Russian warships.

Government House An 1845 mock castle in the Royal Botanic Gardens, it has an outstanding collection of 19th- and 20th-century furnishings and decoration.

Macquarie Place Obelisk This 1818 stone statue was built to indicate road distances to various points in the developing colony.

The Mint Museum The Mint Museum and the nearby NSW Parliament House are the two surviving "bookend wings" of the very early triple-wing General Hospital, commenced in 1811, barely 20 years after the first settlement.

Sydney Tower Looking like a marshmallow skewered on a stick, Sydney Tower is more than 984 feet (300m) tall. If you were to walk to the top instead of taking the lifts, you'd have to tackle 1,504 stairs.

Sydney Town Hall Looking like a sandstone wedding cake, Sydney Town Hall is where local government officials and the mayor hang out on working days.

7 Markets

Balmain Markets Squeezed into the grounds of a local church, Balmain Markets reflects a relaxed world of hammocks, cast-stone sculptures, plants, prints, linen, and a variety of homemade snacks. Sat 8:30am-4pm, St. Andrew's Church Darling Street (Curtis Rd.), Balmain.

Bondi Markets The laid-back vibe of these markets is a perfect after-party therapy session. You'll find stalls of chic street T-shirts and secondhand velvet flares, handmade soaps, '80s records, and beautiful people. Sun 10am-5pm, Bondi Beach Public School at the northern end of Campbell Parade.

Manly Markets Just across from the ocean currents are stalls selling everything from jewelry to seascape paintings. The third Saturday 9am-5pm at Manly Village Public School, Darley Road (Wentworth St.).

Paddington Bazaar The crowd at Paddington is cool and colorful and the market is devoted to clothing, paintings, ceramics, wind chimes, and colorful hammocks. Sat 10am-4pm at St. John's Church, Oxford Street (Newcome St.).

Paddy's Markets Sydney's largest city markets feature stalls stocked with discounted clothes, knickknacks, and fruit and vegetables. Thu-Sun 9am-5pm. Hay Street, Hay Market.

The Rocks Market This small but select street market trades in everything from arts and crafts to opals and fossils, vases and bowls, handbags and chocolates. Sat-Sun 10am-5pm, at the northern end of George Street in the CBD.

Sydney Fish Markets The 65 tons of fresh catch that passes through these markets daily ends up in restaurants and households across the city. You can feast on fresh seafood, and watch the pelicans being fed scraps. Daily 7am-sunset, Bank Street (Pyrmont).

6 Parks and Gardens

Bicentennial Olympic Park Near the main stadium that held the Sydney 2000 Olympics, this 247-acre park includes wetlands used by migratory wading birds and pelicans. Daily sunrise-sunset, Australia Avenue (Homebush Bay Dr.).

Centennial Olympic Park Since the park was created in 1888, to commemorate 100 years of British settlement, it has been transformed into a mixture of manicured lawns, rolling open spaces, native and exotic trees, lakes, and sporting fields. Daily sunrise-sunset, along Oxford Street to Paddington Gates.

The Chinese Garden of Friendship Designers from Sydney's sister city, Guangzhou in China, developed the concept for this small but placid garden in Darling Harbour. Daily 9:30am-5pm, at the southern end of Darling Harbour, near Chinatown.

Cook and Phillip Park Just across the road from Hyde Park, this modern public space has water features, grassed terraces, and an Olympic-size pool. Mon-Fri 6am-10pm and Sat-Sun 7am-8pm. 4 College St. (William St.).

The Domain This small area of greenery in front of the Art Gallery of NSW is sometimes a venue for outdoor concerts. The rest of the time, office workers come here to chill and play. Located on the eastern edge Sydney CBD (Art Gallery Rd.).

Hyde Park Today this relatively tranquil setting is popular with office workers seeking time out from the concrete jungle. Located in Sydney CBD (Elizabeth St., College St., St. James Rd., and Liverpool St.).

5 Performing Arts Centers

Belvoir Street Theatre Geoffrey Rush's Company B pumps out powerful plays upstairs here, while a smaller theater downstairs is used for more experimental productions. 25 Belvoir St., 02 9699 3444, belvoir.com.au

Capitol Theatre This is one of Sydney's grandest theaters, completed in 1893. Today it presents major international and local productions, as well as a few rock concerts from time to time. 13 Campbell St., 02 9320 5000, capitoltheatre.com.au

Star City Sydney's casino has two theaters in the complex—the Showroom, which features Las Vegas–style reviews, and the Lyric, Sydney's largest theater, which specializes in musicals, theater, opera, and ballet. 80 Pyrmont St., 02 9777 9000, starcity.com.au

State Theatre Opened in 1929, the impressive State Theatre fuses eclectic elements of Gothic, Italian, and Art Deco design and is often referred to as a "Palace of Dreams." 49 Market St., 02 9373 6852, statetheatre.com.au

Sydney Entertainment Centre The likes of Donny Osmond, Coldplay, and the Dalai Lama come here to sing and talk Buddhism at this enormous indoor arena. 35 Harbour St., 02 9320 4200, sydentcent.com.au

4 Harbour Tours

Captain Cook Cruises Offers several harbor excursions, with commentary, including morning and afternoon coffee cruises, and lunch and dinner options.

The Manly Rocket Express Leaves Darling Harbour and stops off at Circular Quay, Rose Bay, and Manly. You can get off and on again when you want.

Matilda Cruises A range of coffee, lunch, and dinner cruises as well as a one-hour Rocket Harbour Express sightseeing tour eight times daily.

Sydney Ferries Operates public transport ferry cruises from Circular Quay, including an Evening Harbour Lights tour of the harbor.

Typical Aussie Dishes

Hot Chips As opposed to those colder relatives served in a sealed bag, hot chips are the Aussie equivalent of French fries.

Meat Pie What meat? Who knows? But it's a staple, often smothered in tomato sauce (ketchup).

A "sanger" sandwich The typical barbecue dish is a pork sausage slapped between two pieces of white bread and ladled with ketchup.

Scariest Creatures You Are Most Likely to Meet

Stinger Also called a blue bottle, or Portuguese man of war, this floating blue jellyfish can often be found washed up on Sydney's beaches.

Red Back Spider This dangerous little spider can be identified by the red stripe down its back.

Singular Sensation

Sydney Opera House Enjoy a meal, a drink, or a show beneath the gleaming white sails of Sydney's greatest architectural treasure.

Sydney Coffee (quick stops for a java jolt)

Bar Colluzi Italian boxer Luigi Coluzzi introduced Sydneysiders to real coffee in his cafe in the late 1950s. Grab an outdoor stool and watch the street life pass by. 322 Victoria St., Darlinghurst, 02 9380 5420

Café Hernandez The walls of this tiny, atmospheric, 24-hour cafe are crammed with fake masterpieces. You can try coffee from a multitude of countries, including Kenya, New Guinea, Ethiopia, and Guatemala. 60 Kings Cross Rd., Potts Point, 02 9331 2343

The Foyer Coffee with attitude! The staff can seem a bit too cool for their own good from time to time, but the coffee and homemade biscuits keep the regulars coming back. 207 Kent St., 02 9252 9556

The Old Coffee Shop A tenant of the fashionable Strand Arcade since 1892, the Old Coffee Shop oozes respectability. It's the most famous coffee house in Sydney, but only come here if you are nice and polite. Ground Floor, Strand Arcade, 02 9231 3002

Just for Business and Conventions Sydney

Sydney is well geared up for visiting businesspeople, with plenty of hotels in the heart of the city center catering to those who have to work while they travel. Darling Harbour is Sydney's convention central, and it's here that you will find not only the Sydney Convention & Exhibition Centre but also a host of restaurants, bars, and attractions. Those in town for lesser business will probably find themselves in the CBD—Central Business District—the heart of Sydney's downtown, where you'll find skyscrapers, suits, and the everyday bustle of work being done. Of course, this is Sydney, so no one is too interested in an 80-hour work week here. In fact, the number one social custom you need to know about to successfully seal the deal is the Friday lunch. In this town, businesspeople fill the restaurants and bars beginning with the noon meal on Friday, and more often than not never make it back to the office—not with so many beers and cocktails to be enjoyed under the sun.

Addresses to Know

Convention Center

- Sydney CVB
  Level 11, 80 William St.,
  02 9331 4045, scvb.com.au

City Information

- The Sydney VC at the Rocks
  1st Floor, The Rocks Centre, Corner of Argyle and Playfair Sts., The Rocks, 02 9240 8788,
  sydneyvisitorcentre.com

Business and Convention Hotels

A number of hotels that we recommend in our Sydney Black Book cater to business travelers. These include:

Medina Grand Harbourside (p.111) Bright rooms overlooking Darling Harbour with your own private kitchen facilities. $$ 55 Shelley St., King Street Wharf, 02 9249 7000

Radisson Plaza Hotel (p.112) You are right in the heart of the city at this classy hotel with the business traveler in mind. $$ 27 O'Connell St., 02 8214 0000 / 1 800-333 333 in Australia

Shangri-La Hotel Sydney (p.112) Spectacular city views and an understated grandeur with a touch of Asian flair. $$$176 Cumberland St., The Rocks, 02 9250 6000

Sheraton on the Park (p.112) A modern hotel overlooking Hyde Park with excellent business facilities and executive floors. $$$ 161 Elizabeth St., 02 9286 6000

Business Entertaining

Seal the deal over a drink or a fantastic meal at any of these establishments.

Aria (p.114) Amazing views of the harbor and Opera House try to distract you from your gourmet business feast. $$$ 1 Macquarie St., East Circular Quay, 02 9252 2555

Coast (p.116) A walk across the bridge from the Sydney Convention Centre, this seafood eatery has lovely water views. $$ Roof Terrace, Cockle Bay Wharf, Darling Park, 201 Sussex St., 02 9267 6700

Guillaume at Bennelong (p.118) The best place to impress a business client is the Sydney Opera House's famous restaurant. $$$ Sydney Opera House, Bennelong Point, 02 9241 1999

Zaaffran (p.124) You could pop in here for lunch between conferences or lead a posse back afterwards for some modern Indian cuisine. $ Level 2, 345 Harbourside Shopping Centre, Darling Harbour, 02 9211 8900

Also see: **Best Always-Hot Restaurants** (p.18)
Best Fine Dining (p.25)

Ducking Out for a Half-Day

Make time for a quintessential Sydney experience at one of these spots.

Museum of Contemporary Art (p.101) A little bit of culture is always a nice break from the stress of business life. 140 George St., The Rocks, 02 9245 2400

Sydney Opera House (p.138) Take a one-hour tour of the interior or go for a jog around its back flank and head off into the Royal Botanic Gardens afterwards. Bennelong Point, Circular Quay, 02 9250 7111

Also see: **Best Cool Museums** (p.24)
Best Only-in-Sydney Experiences (p.34)
Best Walks (p.39)

Gifts to Bring Home

What fun is unpacking if you can't pull out a treasure or two?

Dinosaur Designs (p.135) This iconic Sydney shop is filled with wearable art from jewelry to clothes. Level 1, The Strand Arcade, Pitt Street Mall (King St.), 02 9223 2953, dinosaurdesigns.com.au

Gavala Aboriginal Art Gallery (p.136) The place to buy didgeridoos and boomerangs. Shop 131, Harbourside Centre, Darling Harbour, 02 9212 7232

Strand Arcade (p.138) This Victorian-era mall is not only a great stop for shopping, but a site worth seeing for the architecture. Pitt Street Mall (King St.), strandarcade.com.au

HIT THE GROUND

Useful Vocabulary

Here are a few basic bits of slang (called "Strine") to help you fit in like a local.

Ant's pants: the most stylish or cool

Arvo: afternoon

Barbie: barbecue

Bail out: depart

The Big Smoke: the big city

Bludger: lazy person

Bonzer: excellent

Bottle-o: liquor store

Mad as a cut snake: angry

Dinki-di: genuine, the real thing

Fair dinkum: true, genuine

G'day: hello

Good onya: good for you, well done

Grog: alcohol

Grub: food

Knickers in a knot: agitated, frustrated

Mate: As in "G'day, mate. How's it goin'?" A popular term of endearment aimed at both strangers and friends.

Pissed: drunk

Plonk: alcohol

Ripper: terrific

She'll be right: Meant to express an assurance that everything will be fine. Australians have an optimism rarely seen elsewhere.

Snog: kiss

Trainers: sneakers

Country Essentials: Sydney and Melbourne

Money Matters: The currency consists of dollars and cents, with the A$5 being the smallest note. By 1996, all Australian banknotes were made of plastic. ATM machines, often referred to as "hole in the wall" machines, are common, so travelers' checks really aren't necessary, unless you feel like you need a backup. There's a Goods and Services Tax (GST) of 10 percent, which applies to almost everything apart from fresh (not processed) food. By law, the GST amount must appear on the bill.

Tipping is common for good service, and to show your disapproval you can choose not to tip. Typically, you only tip taxi drivers, waiters, and sometimes hotel room-service staff. Never tip bar staff in pubs or clubs, it just sets a bad precedent. Some of the world's highest minimum wage guarantees ensure they get paid well anyway. Typically, a standard tip is 10 percent.

Metric Conversion

From	To	Multiply by
Inches	Centimeters	2.54
Yards	Meters	0.91
Miles	Kilometers	1.60
Gallons	Liters	3.79
Ounces	Grams	28.35
Pounds	Kilograms	0.45

Safety: Both Sydney and Melbourne are generally quite safe for tourists, though the usual precautions apply. Lock your valuables in the hotel safe, and carry a hidden money belt around if you are the paranoid type. Be careful around Kings Cross and, to a certain extent, Central Station, in Sydney. Be careful about leaving valuables on Bondi Beach if you go for a swim, there have been reports of things going missing. In Melbourne, be a little wary in the city center late on Friday and Saturday evenings, particularly around the new Southern Cross Station. In an emergency, dial 000. For less serious crimes, ring 13 14 44.

Traveling with Disabilities: The website accessibility.com.au has a rundown of attractions, public toilets, hotels, restaurants, and bars that cater to those with a disability.

Attire: Australia is casual in nature, and suits are only worn if you're doing business. Dress up for most top-class restaurants and cocktail bars, though, and also if you're going to a show at the Opera House. Sophisticated casual is still the rule here, as in most cosmopolitan cities; sleek pants or dresses for women, urban stylish for men. Winters can get quite cool and rain showers can appear at any time. A jumper and light jacket will see you through the worst winter days in Sydney, though a heavier coat is in order in Melbourne. Spring and autumn can bring variable weather, including very warm days. Summers can be hot—so pack a few pairs of shorts, light pants, and T-shirts in your luggage. Don't forget sunscreen and sunglasses, which are a must when the sun comes out. Lobster-red tourists are a common sight after a day on a Sydney beach. Avoid getting burned by covering up with long sleeves and a hat, or reapply high-SPF sunscreen at least every two hours. Bring comfortable shoes because you will probably end up doing a lot of walking. You may see signs on some restaurant and pub doors which state: "No Thongs." They aren't talking about your underwear here! In Australia, thongs mean flip-flops.

Size Conversion

Dress Sizes						
AUS/UK	8	10	12	14	16	18
US	6	8	10	12	14	16
France	36	38	40	42	44	46
Italy	38	40	42	44	46	48
Europe	34	36	38	40	42	44
Women's Shoes						
AUS/US	6	6½	7	7½	8	8½
UK	4½	5	5½	6	6½	7
Europe	38	38	39	39	40	41
Men's Suits						
AUS/UK	36	38	40	42	44	46
US	36	38	40	42	44	46
Europe	46	48	50	52	54	56
Men's Shirts						
AUS/Europe	38	39	40	41	42	43
US	14½	15	15½	16	16½	17
UK	14½	15	15½	16	16½	17
Men's Shoes						
AUS/UK	7	7½	8½	9½	10½	11
US	8	8½	9½	10½	11½	12
Europe	41	42	43	44	45	46

Shopping Hours: Shops are generally open from around 9am to 6pm Monday to Wednesday, and Friday. They stay open until 9pm on Thursday, and close around 5pm on weekends. Melbourne hours are similar, though late-night shopping is on both Thursday and Friday, when shops remain open until either 7pm or 9pm. Most major supermarkets are open 24 hours.

When Drinking Is Legal: The legal drinking age is 18. Closing times for bars and clubs differ with their licenses, but many bars stay open to 3am or 4am and clubs to 5am or 6am. Some bars in Melbourne never seem to shut down. But as in all places, drunk driving laws are strict.

Smoking: If you are a smoker, then you might feel like a leper in both Sydney and Melbourne. It's illegal to light up in any indoor public place, including restaurants and covered public transport stations. You can't smoke on many Sydney beaches either, including Bondi, Bronte, Tamarama, and Manly. Smoking is also banned in all Sydney and Melbourne pubs and bars.

Drugs: All the usual suspects, including marijuana, cocaine, and ecstasy, are illegal in Australia, and you will be up for a heavy fine or a prison sentence if you are caught in possession. As well as patrolling the airports, sniffer dogs and their handlers also roam Sydney streets.

Time Zone: Sydney and Melbourne fall within Australia's Eastern Standard Time Zone—plus 10 hours Greenwich Mean Time (GMT). So, when it's noon in Sydney and Melbourne, it's 10pm the previous day in New York. On the last Saturday night in October clocks are set back one hour, and on the last Saturday night in March they are set forward one hour. This is Eastern Daylight Time, which is commonly called "Daylight Saving."

Additional Resources for Visitors

Visitor Information:

Sydney Visitor Centre at the Rocks *Daily 9am-5pm.* 1st Floor, The Rocks Centre, Argyle and Playfair Sts., The Rocks, 02 9240 8788; sydneyvisitorcentre.com

Sydney Visitors Centre—Darling Harbour *Daily 9:30am-5:30pm.* 33 Wheat Rd., Darling Harbour (near the IMAX Theatre), 02 9240 8788

Melbourne Visitor Information Centre *Daily 9am-6pm.* Federation Square, 03 9658 9658; thatsmelbourne.com.au

Foreign Visitors

Foreign Embassies and Consulates: dfat.gov.au

Passport requirements: http://travel.state.gov/passport/passport_1738.html

Cell phones: Called mobile phones in Australia. Australia's cell phone network is compatible with GSM 900 and 1800, used in Europe, but not with the systems used in the U.S. In Sydney you can hire a mobile at Vodafone Rentals, located on the Arrivals Level of the International Terminal.

Electrical: Electrical current is 240/250V, AC 50Hz, with a plug of three flat-pins. Travelers from most countries will need an adapter. If your appliances are 110V, you will also need a voltage converter. Universal outlets for 240V or 110V shavers are found in leading hotels.

Toll-free numbers in Australia: 1-800-

Telephone directory assistance in Australia: 12455 and 1223

The Latest-Info Websites:

art-almanac.com.au What's on in Australian art galleries

bom.gov.au Weather reports

citysearch.com.au Australian entertainment and restaurant guide

cityrail.info Train service information for Sydney

fasterlouder.com.au Gig guide for music fans

metlinkmelbourne.com.au Tram information for Melbourne

smh.com.au *Sydney Morning Herald* website

ticketek.com.au Events guide with ticket booking service

yellowpages.com.au Business phone directory

whereis.com.au Maps of Sydney, Melbourne, and Australia

whitepages.com.au Residential phone numbers

And, of course, **pulseguides.com**.

SYDNEY BLACK BOOK

You're solo in the city—where's a singles-friendly place to eat? Is there a good lunch spot near the museum? Will the bar be too loud for easy conversation? Get the answers fast in the *Black Book*, a condensed version of every listing in our guide that puts all the essential information at your fingertips.

A quick glance down the page and you'll find the type of food, nightlife, or attractions you are looking for, the phone numbers, and which pages to turn to for more detailed information. How did you ever survive without this?

Sydney Black Book

Hotels

NAME TYPE (ROOMS)	ADDRESS (CROSS STREET) WEBSITE	AREA PRICE	PHONE (02+) 1 800 NUMBER	EXPERIENCE	PAGE
The Blacket Trendy (42)	70 King St. (George St.) theblacket.com	CBD $$$	9279 3030	Hot & Cool	70
Blue, Woolloomooloo Bay Trendy (100)	The Wharf at Woolloomooloo (Cowper Wharf Rd.) tajhotels.com	WO $$$	9331 9000	Hot & Cool	70
Establishment Hotel Trendy (33)	5 Bridge Ln. (Pitt St.) merivale.com.au	CBD $$$	9240 3100	Hot & Cool	*63*, 70
The Kirketon Hotel Trendy (40)	229 Darlinghurst Rd. (Liverpool St.) kirketon.com.au	DH $$	9332 2011 1 800 332 920	Hot & Cool	71
Manly Pacific Hotel Modern (170)	55 North Steyne St. (Raglan St.) accorhotels.com.au	VA $$$	9977 7666	Classic	111
Medina Grand Harbourside Modern (114)	55 Shelley St. (King St. Wharf) medinaapartments.com.au	DH $$$	9249 7000 1 300 633 462	Classic	111
Medusa Hotel Trendy (18)	267 Darlinghurst Rd. (Liverpool St.) medusa.com.au	KC $$$	9331 1000	Hot & Cool	71
Observatory Hotel Timeless (99)	89-113 Kent St. (Argyle St.) observatoryhotel.com.au	TR $$$$	9256 2222	Classic	111
Park Hyatt Sydney Timeless (158)	7 Hickson Rd. (Albion St.) sydney.park.hyatt.com	TR $$$$	9241 1234	Hot & Cool	71
Radisson Plaza Hotel Modern (362)	27 O'Connell St. (Pitt St.) radisson.com/sydneyau_plaza	CBD $$$	8214 0000 1 800 333 333	Classic	112
Sebel Pier One Sydney Trendy (160)	11 Hickson Rd. (George St.) sebelpierone.com.au	TR $$$$	8298 9999 1 800 780 485	Hot & Cool	72
Shangri-La Hotel Sydney Modern (556)	176 Cumberland St. (Essex St.) shangri-la.com	TR $$$$	9250 6000 1 800 222 448	Classic	*105*, 112
Sheraton on the Park Timeless (606)	161 Elizabeth St. (Market St.) starwoodhotels.com/sheraton	CBD $$$	9286 6000	Classic	112
Sir Stamford Double Bay Timeless (73)	22 Knox St. (New South Head St.) stamford.com.au/ssdb	VA $$	9302 4100	Classic	113
Swiss Grand Resort and Spa Trendy (203)	Campbell Parade (Beach Rd.) swissgrand.com.au	BB $$$	9365 5666 1 800 655 252	Hot & Cool	72
Sydney Harbour Marriott Modern (550)	30 Pitt St. (Alfred St.) marriott.com.au	CQ $$	9259 7000 1 800 251 251	Classic	113

Neighborhood (Area) Key

BB = Bondi Beach
CBD= Central Business District
CQ = Circular Quay
DH = Darlinghurst
KC = Kings Cross
KS = Kings Street Wharf
PD = Paddington
PP = Potts Point
SH = Surry Hills
TR = The Rocks
VA = Various
WO = Woolloomooloo

Note regarding page numbers: Italic = itinerary listing; Roman *= description in theme chapter listing.*

Restaurants

NAME TYPE	ADDRESS (CROSS STREET) WEBSITE	AREA PRICE	PHONE (02+) SINGLES/NOISE	EXPERIENCE 99 BEST	PAGE PAGE
Annandale Hotel* Pub Grub	17 Parramatta Rd. (Nelson St.) annandalehotel.com.au	VA $	9550 1078 ≡	Hot & Cool	73
Aqua Dining Modern Australian	North Sydney Olympic Pool crnr Paul &Northcliff aquadining.com.au	VA $$$	9964 9998 =	Hot & Cool	*65*, 73
Aria Modern Australian (G)	1 Macquarie St. (Circular Quay E.) ariarestaurant.com.au	CQ $$$$	9252 2555 B –	Classic	114
The Art Gallery Restaurant Modern Australian	Art Gallery of NSW, 1 Art Gallery Rd. (The Domain) trippaswhite.com.au	CBD $$	9225 1819 B =	Classic	*106*, 114
The Australian Heritage Hotel* Pub Grub	100 Cumberland St. (Glouster St.) australianheritagehotel.com	TR $	9247 2229 ▯ =	Classic	114
Bar Europa* Continental	Basement, 88 Elizabeth St. (King St.)	CBD $$	9232 3377 =	Hot & Cool	73
The Basement Club* Continental	29 Reiby Pl. (Bridge St.) basement.com.au	CQ $$	9251 2797 ≡	Classic	114
Bathers' Pavilion Modern Australian (G)	4 The Esplanade (Awaba St.) batherspavilion.com.au	VA $$$$	9969 5050 –	Classic Beachside Romance	*106*, 114 21
The Bayswater Brasserie Modern Australian	32 Bayswater Rd. (Ward Ave.) bayswaterbrasserie.com.au	KC $$$	9357 2177 =	Hot & Cool	73
Becasse French	204 Clarence St. (Druitt St.) becasse.com.au	CBD $$$	9283 3440 –	Hot & Cool	73
Bentley Restaurant & Bar* Tapas	320 Crown St. (Campbell St.) thebentley.com.au	SH $$	9332 2344 =	Hot & Cool	74
Bill's Continental	433 Liverpool St. (Victoria Ave.) bills.com.au	DH $	9360 9631 =	Hot & Cool	74
Billy Kwong Chinese	3/355 Crown St. (Albion St.)	SH $$	9332 3300 =	Hot & Cool	74
Bilson's French (G)	27 O'Connell St. (Hunter St.) bilsons.com.au	CBD $$$$	8214 0496 –	Classic Fine Dining	*106*, 115 25
Bird Cow Fish Modern Australian	Shops 4 and 5, 50 Crown St. (Rainford St.) birdcowfish.com.au	SH $$$	9380 4090 =	Hot & Cool	75
Bistro Moncur French	116 Queen St. (Moncur St.) bistromoncur.com.au	VA $$$	9363 2519 =	Hot & Cool	75
Bistrode British/French	478 Bourke St. (Devonshire St.)	SH $$	9380 7333 =	Hot & Cool	75
Blue Orange* Fusion	49 Hall St. (Campbell St.)	BB $	9300 9885 =	Hot & Cool	75

Restaurant and Nightlife Symbols

Restaurants	Nightlife	Restaurant + Nightlife
Singles Friendly (eat and/or meet)	Price Warning	Prime time noise levels
▯ = Communal table	C = Cover or ticket charge	– = Quiet
B = Food served at the bar		= = A buzz, but still conversational
(G) = Gourmet Destination		≡ = Loud

Restaurants (cont.)

NAME TYPE	ADDRESS (CROSS STREET) WEBSITE	AREA PRICE	PHONE (02+) SINGLES/NOISE	EXPERIENCE 99 BEST	PAGE PAGE
The Boathouse on Blackwattle Bay Seafood	End of Ferry Rd. (Taylor St.) boathouse.net.au	VA $$$	9518 9011	Classic	115
Botanic Gardens Rest. New Australian	Royal Botanic Grdns. (Mrs. Mac.Rd) trippaswhite.com.au	CBD $$$	9241 2419	Classic	115
Bungalow 8* Seafood	8 The Promenade (King Street Wharf) bungalow8.com.au	KS $$	9299 4660	Classic	*106*, 115
Buon Ricordo Italian	108 Boundary Rd. (Liverpool St.) buonricordo.com.au	PD $$$$	9360 6729	Classic	115
Café Sydney Continental	Level 5,Customs House, 31 Alfred St. (Loftus St.) cafesydney.com	CQ $$$	9251 8683	Hot & Cool	*66*, 76
Cargo Bar* Pub Grub	52-60 The Promenade (Erskine St.) cargobar.com.au	KS $$	9262 1777	Hot & Cool	*66*, 76
Catalina French	1 Sunderland Ave. (New South Head Rd.) catalinarosebay.com.au	VA $$$	9371 0555	Hot & Cool Restaurants w/ Views	76 35
Chinta Ria Malaysian	201 Sussex St. (Market St.) chintaria.com.au	VA $$	9264 3211	Classic	116
Claude's French (G)	10 Oxford St. (Queen St.) claudes.com.au	VA $$$$	9331 2325	Classic	116
Coast Italian	Roof Terr., 201 Sussex St. (King St.) coastrestaurant.com.au	VA $$	9267 6700	Classic	116
Cru* French	Level 3, Overseas Passenger Terminal (Circular Quay W.)	CQ $$$	9251 1188	Hot & Cool	*64*, 76
Danks Street Depot Modern Australian	1/2 Danks St. (Young St.) danksstreetdepot.com.au	VA $$	9698 2201	Hot & Cool Swank Lunch Spots	767 36
Dean's Café Cafe	1/5 Kellett St. (Bayswater Rd.)	KC $	9368 0953	Hot & Cool Late-Night Bites	77 31
Doyles on the Beach Seafood	11 Marine Parade (New South Head Rd.) doyles.com.au	VA $$$	9337 2007	Classic Beachside Romance	*108*, 116 21
Doyles Palace Hotel* Seafood	10 Marine Parade (Military Rd.) doyles.com.au	VA $	9337 4299	Classic	117
Est. Modern Australian	Level 1, 252 George St. (Bridge St.) merivale.com.au	CC $$$$	9240-3010	Hot & Cool Swank Lunch Spots	77 36
Firefly* Tapas	Pier 7, 17 Hickson Rd. (Sussex St.)	VA $$	9241 2031	Classic	117
Fish at the Rocks Seafood	29 Kent St. (Argyle St.) fishattherocks.com.au	TR $$	9252 4614	Classic	*107*, 117
Flying Fish Seafood	19-21 Pirrama Rd. (Harris St.) flyingfish.com.au	VA $$$	9518 6677	Hot & Cool Swank Lunch Spots	*66*, 77 36
Forty One Restaurant French (G)	The Chifley Tower, 2 Chifley Sq. (George St.) forty-one.com.au	CBD $$$$	9221 2500	Classic Restaurants w/ Views	*106*, 117 35
Galileo French/Japanese (G)	89-113 Kent St. (Argyle St.) observatoryhotel.com.au	TR $$$$	9256 2215	Classic	117
Glass Brasserie French	Level 2, 488 George St. (Park St.) glassbrasserie.com.au	CBD $$$	9265 6068	Hot & Cool	*65*, 78

NAME	ADDRESS (CROSS STREET)	AREA	PHONE (02+)	EXPERIENCE	PAGE
TYPE	WEBSITE	PRICE	SINGLES/NOISE	99 BEST	PAGE
Golden Century	393-399 Sussex St. (Goulburn St.)	VA	9212 3901	Classic	*106*, 118
Cantonese	goldencentury.com.au	$$		Late-Night Bites	31
The Golden Sheaf Hotel*	429 New South Head Rd. (Knox St.)	VA	9327 5877	Classic	*106*, 118
Pub Grub	goldensheaf.com.au	$$			
Grand National	161 Underwood St. (Elizabeth St.)	PD	9363 3096	Hot & Cool	78
Pub Grub		$$			
Guillaume at Bennelong	Sydney Opera House (Circ. Quay W.)	CQ	9241 1999	Classic	*107*, 118
French (G)	guillaumeatbennelong.com.au	$$$$		Always-Hot Restaurants	18
Harbour Kitchen & Bar	7 Hickson Rd. (George St.)	TR	9256 1661	Classic	118
Modern Australian	harbourkitchen.com.au	$$$			
Harry's Cafe De Wheels	Cowper Rd. Wharf (Dowling St.)	WO	9357 3074	Hot & Cool	*64*, 78
Australian	harryscafedewheels.com.au	$		Late-Night Bites	31
Hero of Waterloo*	81 Lower Fort St. (Windmill St.)	TR	9252 4553	Classic	118
Pub Grub	heroofwaterloo.com.au	$			
Icebergs Dining Rm. & Bar*	1 Notts Ave. (Campbell Parade)	BB	9365 9000	Hot & Cool	79
Modern Australian/Seafood	idrb.com	$$$		Beachside Romance	21
Il Baretto	496 Bourke St. (Cleveland St.)	SH	9361 6163	Hot & Cool	79
Italian		$			
Imperial Peking Harbourside	13 Circular Quay West	CQ	9247 7073	Classic	*107*, 118
Restaurant Chinese	(George St.) imperialpeking.com.au	$$$			
Industrie Bar*	107 Pitt St. (Hunter St.)	CBD	9221 8001	Hot & Cool	*65*, 79
French	industriebar.com.au	$$$			
Jimmy Liks*	188 Victoria St. (Darlinghurst St.)	PP	8354 1400	Hot & Cool	79
Asian	jimmyliks.com	$$			
Kables	Level 2, 199 George St. (Argyle St.)	CBD	9250 3226	Classic	*108*, 119
Modern Australian (G)	fourseasons.com/sydney/dining	$$$			
Kam Fook	600 Westfield Shopping Centre	VA	9386 9889	Hot & Cool	80
Chinese	kamfook.com.au	$$			
Kobe Jones	29 Lime St. (Erskine St.)	KS	9299 5290	Hot & Cool	80
Japanese		$$			
La Sala*	Ground floor, 23 Foster St.	SH	9281 3352	Hot & Cool	80
Italian	(Campbell St.) lasala.com.au	$$			
Local*	211 Glenmore Rd. (Broughton St.)	PD	9332 1577	Hot & Cool	*65*, 80
Modern Australian	localwinebarandrestaurant.com.au	$$			
Longrain*	85 Commonwealth St. (Hunt St.)	SH	9280 2888	Hot & Cool	*65*, 81
Thai	longrain.com.au	$$		Thai Restaurants	37
The Lord Nelson Brewery	19 Kent St. (Argyle St.)	TR	9251 4044	Classic	119
Hotel* Pub Grub	lordnelson.com.au	$			
Lotus*	22 Challis Ave. (McClay St.)	PP	9326 9000	Hot & Cool	81
Continental		$$			
Lucio's	47 Windsor St. (Elizabeth St.)	PD	9380 5996	Hot & Cool	*65*, 81
Italian	lucios.com.au	$$$			
Manly Wharf Hotel*	East Esplanade	VA	9977 1266	Classic	119
Pub Grub	manlywharfhotel.com.au	$			
Manta	The Wharf, 6 Cowper Wharf Rd.	WO	9332 3822	Classic	119
Seafood	(Bourke St.) mantarestaurant.com.au	$$$			

Restaurants (cont.)

NAME TYPE	ADDRESS (CROSS STREET) WEBSITE	AREA PRICE	PHONE (02+) SINGLES/NOISE	EXPERIENCE 99 BEST	PAGE PAGE
Marque French (G)	355 Crown St. (Foveaux St.) marquerestaurant.com.au	SH $$$$	9332 2225	Classic Fine Dining	*108*, 119 25
Milsons Modern Australian	17 Willoughby St. (Falcon St.) milsonsrestaurant.com.au	VA $$$	9955 7075	Classic	120
Mint* Fusion	62 Bridge St. (Phillip St.) mintbaranddining.com.au	CBD $$$	9240 1210	Hot & Cool	*63*, 81
Nick's Seafood Restaurant Seafood	The Promenade (Market St.) nicks-seafood.com.au	VA $$$	9264 1212	Classic	120
North Bondi RSL Club* Pub Grub	120 Ramsgate Ave. (Campbell Pd.) northbondirsl.com.au	BB $$	9130 3152	Classic	120
The Oaks Hotel* Pub Grub	118 Military Rd. (Ben Boyd St.) oakshotel.com.au	VA $$	9953 5515	Classic Beer Gardens	120 22
Oh! Calcutta! Indian	251 Victoria St. (Burton St.) ohcalcutta.com.au	DH $$	9360 3650	Classic	120
The Old Fitzroy Hotel* Pub Grub	129 Dowling St. (Cathedral St.) oldfitzroy.com.au	WO $	9356 3848	Hot & Cool	82
Otto Italian	Area 8, 6 Cowper Wharf Rd. (Bourke St.) otto.net.au	WO $$$	9368 7488	Hot & Cool	82
Le Petit Creme French	118 Darlinghurst Rd. (Liverpool St.)	DH $	9361 4738	Hot & Cool	82
Phamish Vietnamese	354 Liverpool St. (Boundry St.)	DH $	9357 2688	Hot & Cool	82
Pier Seafood (G)	New South Head Rd. (Old South Head Rd.) pierrestaurant.com.au	VA $$$	9327 6561	Classic	120
Pony Modern Australian	The Rocks Centre (Argyle St.) ponydining.com	TR $$	9252 7797 B	Hot & Cool	83
Prime Steak House	1 Martin Pl. (George St.) gposydney.com.au	CBD $$$$	9229 7777	Classic	121
Pruniers Modern Australian	65 Ocean St. (Queen St.) pruniers.com.au	VA $$$	9363 1974	Classic	121
Quay Modern Australian (G)	Upper level, Overseas Passenger Terminal (George St.) quay.com.au	TR $$$$	9251 5600	Classic Always-Hot Restaurants	*106*, 121 18
Ravesi's* Continental	Campbell Parade (Hall St.) ravesis.com.au	BB $$	9365 4422	Hot & Cool	*65*, 83
Raw Bar Sushi	135 Ramsgate St. (Warners Ave.)	BB $$	9365 7200	Hot & Cool	83
Redoak Boutique Beer Cafe* Pub Grub	201 Clarence St. (King St.) redoak.com.au	CBD $	9262 3303	Classic	122
Renaissance Patisserie Cafe	47 Argyle St. (George St.) larenaissance.com.au	TR $	9241 4878	Classic	*107*, 121
Restaurant Balzac British/French	141 Belmore Rd. (Anzac Parade) restaurantbalzac.com.au	VA $$$	9399 9660	Classic	122
Rockpool Modern Australian (G)	107 George St. (Argyle St.) rockpool.com	TR $$$$	9252 1888	Classic Always-Hot Restaurants	*108*, 122 18

NAME TYPE	ADDRESS (CROSS STREET) WEBSITE	AREA PRICE	PHONE (02+) SINGLES/NOISE	EXPERIENCE 99 BEST	PAGE PAGE
The Royal Hotel* Pub Grub	237 Glenmore Rd. (Heely St.) royalhotel.com.au	PD $	9331 2604	Classic	122
Sailors Thai Restaurant Thai	106 George St. (Argyle St.) sailorsthai.citysearch.com.au	TR $$$	9251 2466	Classic Thai Restaurants	*107*, 122 37
Sean's Panorama British/French	270 Campbell Parade (Ramsgate Ave.) seanspanorama.com.au	BB $$$	9365 4924	Hot & Cool	83
Slip Inn* Thai	111 Sussex St. (King St.) merivale.com.au	CBD $$	8295 9911	Hot & Cool	84
Spice I Am Thai	90 Wentworth Ave. (Elizabeth St.) spiceiam.com	SH $	9280 0928	Hot & Cool Thai Restaurants	*64*, 84 37
Stir Crazy Thai	Shop 5, 1 Broughton St. (Fitzroy St.) stircrazy.com.au	VA $	9922 6620	Hot & Cool	84
Sugaroom* Australian	Shop 2, 1 Harris St. (Elizabeth St.) sugaroom.com.au	VA $$	9571 5055	Hot & Cool	84
Summit Restaurant Modern Australian	Level 47, 264 George St.. (Bond St.) summitrestaurant.com.au	CBD $$$	9247 9777	Classic	*108*, 122
Sushi e Sushi	Level 4, 252 George St. (Bridge St.) merivale.com.au	CBD $$$	9240 3041	Hot & Cool	*63*, 84
Swell* Cafe	Shop 3, 465 Bronte Rd. (Nelson St.) swellrestaurant.com.au	VA $$	9386 5001	Hot & Cool Restaurants w/ Views	*65*, 85 35
Tetsuya's French/Japanese (G)	529 Kent St. (Bathurst St.) tetsuyas.com	VA $$$$	9267 2900	Classic Fine Dining	*107*, 123 25
360 Bar & Dining Room* Continental	Gallery Level, 100 Market St. (Pitt St.) 360dining.com.au	CBD $$	8223 3800	Classic	*108*, 123
Tilbury Hotel* Pub Grub	12-18 Nicholson St. (Cowper Bay Rd.) tilburyhotel.com.au	WO $	9368 1955	Classic	123
The Vanguard* Continental	42 King St. (City Rd.) thevanguard.com.au	VA $$	9557 7992	Classic	123
Victoria Room* Continental	Level 1, 235 Victoria St. (Liverpool St.) thevictoriaroom.com	DH $$	9357 4488	Classic	*107*, 123
The Wharf Modern Australian	End of Pier 4, Hickson Rd. (George St.) thewharfrestaurant.com.au	VA $$$	9250 1761	Classic	123
The White Horse Bar & Brasserie* Continental	381-385 Crown St. (Foveaux St.) thewhitehorse.com.au	SH $	8333 9999	Classic	124
Wildfire Brazilian	Overseas Passenger Terminal (Argyle St.) wildfiresydney.com	TR $$$	8273 1222	Hot & Cool	*64*, 85
Yoshii Sushi	115 Harrington St. (Essex St.) yoshii.com.au	TR $$$$	9247 2566	Hot & Cool	*64*, 85
Young Alfred Italian	31 Alfred St. (Young St.) youngalfred.com.au	CQ $	9251 5192	Hot & Cool	*66*, 86
Zaaffran Indian	Level 2, Harbourside Shopping Ctr. (Market St.) zaaffran.com.au	DH $$	9211 8900	Classic	124
Zilver Chinese	Level 1, 477 Pitt St. (Hay St.) zilver.com.au	VA $$	9211 2232	Classic	124

BLACK BOOK

Nightlife

NAME TYPE	ADDRESS (CROSS STREET) WEBSITE	AREA COVER	PHONE (02+) NOISE	EXPERIENCE 99 BEST	PAGE PAGE
The Annandale Hotel* Live Music	17 Parramatta Rd. (Nelson St.) annandalehotel.com.au	VA C	9550 1078	Hot & Cool Live Music Venues	87 33
Arq Gay Club	16 Flinders St. (Taylor St.) arqsydney.com.au	VA C	9380 8700	Hot & Cool Gay Scenes	87 26
Arthouse Hotel Bar	275 Pitt St. (Park St.) thearthousehotel.com.au	CBD	9284 1200	Classic	*108*, 125
The Australian Heritage Hotel* Pub	100 Cumberland St. (Glouster St.) australianheritagehotel.com	TR	9247 2229	Classic Hist. Drinking Holes	125 28
Bambini Wine Room Wine Bar	185-187 Elizabeth St. (Park St.) bambinitrust.com.au	CBD	9283 7098	Hot & Cool	87
Bar Europa* Lounge	Basement, 88 Elizabeth St. (King St.) bareuropa.com.au	CBD	9232 3377	Hot & Cool	87
The Basement Club* Bar/Live Music	29 Reiby Pl. (Bridge St.) basement.com.au	CQ C	9251 2797	Classic Live Music Venues	*106*, 125 33
Beach Road Hotel Pub	71 Beach Rd. (Glenair Ave.)	BB	9130 7247	Classic	126
Bentley Restaurant & Bar* Restaurant/Bar	320 Crown St. (Campbell St.)	SH	9332 2344	Hot & Cool	88
Blu Horizons Bar Bar	Level 36, 176 Cumberland St. (Essex St.) shangri-la.com	TR	9250 6013	Classic	*106*, 126
Blue Orange* Restaurant/Bar	49 Hall St. (Campbell St.)	BB	9300 9885	Hot & Cool	88
The Bourbon Bar	24 Darlinghurst Rd. (Kings Cross)	KC	9358 1144	Classic Late-Night Hangouts	*108*, 126 32
Bungalow 8* Restaurant/Bar	8 The Promenade (Erskine St.) bungalow8.com.au	KS	9299 4660	Classic	127
Candy's Apartment Nightclub	22 Bayswater Rd. (Ward Ave.)	KC C	9380 5600	Hot & Cool	*64*, 88
Cargo Bar* Bar/Nightclub	52-60 The Promenade (Erskine St.) cargobar.com.au	KS	9262 1777	Hot & Cool	88
The Colombian Hotel Gay bar/Nightclub	117-123 Oxford St. (Crown St.)	DH	9360 2151	Hot & Cool Gay Scenes	*65*, 88 26
Cru* Restaurant/Lounge	Level 3, Overseas Passenger Terminal (Circular Quay West)	CQ	9251 1188	Hot & Cool	89
Darlo Bar Bar	306 Liverpool St. (Darlinghurst Rd.)	DH	9331 3672	Hot & Cool	89
Dolphin Bar Hotel Bar	Crown Hotel, 412 Crown St.	SH	9331 4800.	Hot & Cool	89
Doyles Palace Hotel* Restaurant/Bar	10 Marine Parade (Military Rd.) doyles.com.au	VA	9337 4299	Classic Beer Gardens	127 32
Dragonfly Nightclub	1 Earl St. (Victoria St.)	PP C	9356 2666	Hot & Cool Hot Club Scenes	*64*, 90 30
Epoque Belgian Beer Cafe Restaurant/Bar	429 Miller St. (Amherst St.) belgian-beer-cafe.com.au	VA	9954 3811	Classic	127
Firefly* Wine Bar	17 Hickson Rd. (Sussex St.)	VA	9241 2031	Classic Cocktail Lounges	128 23

NAME TYPE	ADDRESS (CROSS STREET) WEBSITE	AREA COVER	PHONE (02+) NOISE	EXPERIENCE 99 BEST	PAGE PAGE
Fringe Bar Comedy Club/Nightclub	106 Oxford St. (Hopewell St.) thefringe.com.au	PD C	9360 5443	Hot & Cool	90
Gazebo Wine Garden Wine Bar	1/2 Elizabeth Bay Rd. (Greenknowe Ave.) gazebowinegarden.com.au	VA	9357 5333	Hot & Cool	90
The Golden Sheaf Hotel * Pub	429 New South Head Rd.(Knox St.) goldensheaf.com.au	VA	9327 5877	Classic	*106*, 128
Hemmesphere Lounge	Level 4, 252 George St. (Pitt St.) merivale.com.au	CBD	9240 3040	Hot & Cool Cocktail Lounges	*63*, 91 23
Hero of Waterloo* Pub	81 Lower Fort St. (Windmill St.) heroofwaterloo.com.au	TR	9252 4553	Classic Hist. Drinking Holes	128 28
Home Nightclub	The Promenade (Cockle Bay Wharf) homesydney.com	VA C	9266 0600	Hot & Cool	*66*, 91
Hugo's Lounge Lounge	Level 1, 33 Bayswater Rd. (Ward Ave.) hugos.com.au	KC C	9357 4411	Hot & Cool Trendy Hangouts	*64*, 91 38
Icebergs Dining Room and Bar* Restaurant/Lounge	1 Notts Ave. (Campbell Parade) idrb.com	BB	9365 9000	Hot & Cool	*66*, 92
Industrie Bar* Restaurant/Bar	107 Pitt St. (Hunter St.) industriebar.com.au	CBD	9221 8001	Hot & Cool	92
Jimmy Liks* Restaurant/Bar	188 Victoria St. (Darlinghurst St.) jimmyliks.com	PP	8354 1400	Hot & Cool	92
Judgement Bar Bar	189 Oxford St. (Flinders St.) courthousehotel.com.au	DH	9360 4831	Hot & Cool Late-Night Hangouts	92 32
La Sala* Restaurant/Bar	Ground floor, 23 Foster St. (Campbell St.) lasala.com.au	SH	9281 3352	Hot & Cool	92
Lady Lux Nightclub	2 Roslyn St. (Barncleuth Ln.) ladylux.com.au	PP C	9361 5000	Hot & Cool Hot Club Scenes	*64*, 92 30
Local* Restaurant/Bar	211 Glenmore Rd. (Broughton St.) localwinebarandrestaurant.com.au	PD	9332 1577	Hot & Cool	93
The Loft Ultra Lounge	3 Lime St. (Erskine St.) theloftsydney.com	KS	9299 4770	Hot & Cool Cocktail Lounges	*66*, 93 23
London Hotel Pub	234 Darling St. (Jane St.) thelondonhotel.com.au	VA	9555 1377	Classic	128
Longrain* Restaurant/Lounge	85 Commonwealth St. (Hunt St.) longrain.com.au	SH	9280 2888	Hot & Cool	93
The Lord Dudley Hotel Pub	236 Jersey Rd. (Trelawney St.) lorddudley.com	VA	9327 5399	Classic	129
The Lord Nelson Brewery Hotel* Pub	19 Kent St. (Argyle St.) lordnelson.com.au	TR	9251 4044	Classic Hist. Drinking Holes	*107*, 129 28
Lotus* Restaurant/Bar	22 Challis Ave. (McClay St.)	PP	9326 9000	Hot & Cool	93
Manly Wharf Hotel* Pub/Restaurant	East Esplanade manlywharfhotel.com.au	VA	9977 1266	Classic	*107*, 129
Melt Restaurant/Nightclub	12 Kellett St. (King St.) meltbar.com.au	KC C	9380 6060	Hot & Cool	94
Middle Bar Bar	383 Bourke St. (Campbell St.) kinselas.com.au	DH	9331 6200	Hot & Cool	*65*, 94

BLACK BOOK

Nightlife (cont.)

NAME TYPE	ADDRESS (CROSS STREET) WEBSITE	AREA COVER	PHONE (02+) NOISE	EXPERIENCE 99 BEST	PAGE PAGE
Midnight Shift Gay Club	85 Oxford St. (William St.)	DH C	9360 4319	Classic Gay Scenes	130 26
Mint* Restaurant/Lounge	62 Bridge St. (Phillip St.) mintbaranddining.com.au	CBD	9240 1210	Hot & Cool	94
North Bondi RSL Club* Pub	120 Ramsgate Ave. (Campbell Pd.) northbondirsl.com.au	BB	9130 3152	Classic	130
The Oaks Hotel* Pub	118 Military Rd. (Ben Boyd St.) oakshotel.com.au	VA	9953 5515	Classic Beer Gardens	130 22
The Old Fitzroy Hotel* Pub/Theater	129 Dowling St. (Cathedral St.) oldfitzroy.com.au	WO	9356 3848	Hot & Cool	94
Opera Bar Bar	Sydney Opera Hse., Lower Concourse (Circular Quay W.) operabar.com.au	CQ	9247 1666	Classic Bars with a View	*107*, 131 20
Orbit Bar Ultra Lounge	Level 47, 264 George St.(Bond St.) summitrestaurant.com.au	CBD	9247 9777	Classic Bars with a View	*108*, 131 20
Paddington Inn Bar/Lounge	338 Oxford St. (William St.) paddingtoninn.com.au	PD	9380 5913	Classic	*106*, 131
Q Bar Nightclub	34-44 Oxford St. (Pelican St.) qbar.com.au	DH C	9360 1375	Hot & Cool Late-Night Hangouts	95 32
Ravesi's* Restaurant/Bar	118 Campbell Parade (Hall St.) ravesis.com.au	BB	9365 4422	Hot & Cool	95
Redoak Boutique Beer Cafe* Restaurant/Bar	201 Clarence St. (King St.) redoak.com.au	CBD	9262 3303	Classic	132
The Royal Hotel* Pub	237 Glenmore Rd. (Heely St.) royalhotel.com.au	PD	9331 2604	Classic	132
Ruby Rabbit Bar/Nightclub	231 Oxford St. (Riley St.) rubyrabbit.com.au	DH C	9326 0044	Hot & Cool	*65*, 95
Slip Inn* Restaurant/Nightclub	111 Sussex St. (King St.) merivale.com.au	CBD	8295 9911	Hot & Cool Beer Gardens	*66*, 96 22
Spectrum Nightclub	34 Oxford St. (Liverpool St.) pashpresents.com	DH C	9360 1375	Hot & Cool Live Music Venues	96 33
Sugaroom* Restaurant/Bar	Shop 2, 1 Harris St. (Elizabeth St.) sugaroom.com.au	VA	9571 5055	Hot & Cool	96
Swell* Cafe	Shop 3, 465 Bronte Rd. (Nelson St.) swellrestaurant.com.au	VA	9386 5001	Hot & Cool	96
Tank Nightclub	3 Bridge Ln. (George St.) tankclub.com.au	CBD C	9240 3094	Hot & Cool Hot Club Scenes	*65*, 96 30
360 Bar & Dining Room* Restaurant/Lounge	Gallery Level, 100 Market St. (Pitt St.) 360dining.com.au	CBD	8223 3800	Classic Bars with a View	133 20
Tilbury Hotel* Pub/Restaurant	12-18 Nicholson St. (Cowper Bay Rd.) tilburyhotel.com.au	WO	9368 1955	Classic	133
Tonic Lounge/Nightclub	62-64 Kellett St. (Ward Ave.) toniclounge.com.au	KC C	8354 1544	Hot & Cool	97
The Vanguard* Restaurant/Jazz Bar	42 King St. (City Rd.) thevanguard.com.au	VA	9557 7992	Classic	133

NAME TYPE	ADDRESS (CROSS STREET) WEBSITE	AREA COVER	PHONE (02+) NOISE	EXPERIENCE 99 BEST	PAGE PAGE
Victoria Room* Lounge	Level 1, 235 Victoria St. (Liverpool St.) thevictoriaroom.com	DH	9357 4488 ≡	Classic Trendy Hangouts	133 38
The White Horse Bar & Brasserie* Restaurant/Bar	381-385 Crown St. (Foveaux St.) thewhitehorse.com.au	SH	8333 9999 ≡	Classic	134
Zeta Bar Bar/Nightclub	Level 4, 488 George St. (Park St.) zetabar.com.au	CBD	9265 6070 ≡	Hot & Cool Trendy Hangouts	*66*, 97 38

Attractions

NAME TYPE	ADDRESS (CROSS STREET) WEBSITE	AREA PRICE	PHONE	EXPERIENCE 99 BEST	PAGE PAGE
Akira Isogawa Shop	Various akira.com.au	VA	9361 5221	Classic	135
Andrew (Boy) Charlton Swimming Pool Sport	1C Mrs. Macquaries Rd. (Cahill Ex.) cityofsydney.nsw.gov.au	CBD $	9358 6686	Hot & Cool	98
Art Gallery of New South Wales Art Museum	Art Gallery Rd. (Mrs Macquaries Rd.) artgallery.nsw.gov.au	CBD $	9225 1744	Classic Art Spaces	*106*, 135 19
Australian Museum Cultural Museum	6 College St. (William St.) amonline.net..au	CBD $	9320 6000	Classic	135
Australian Nat'l Maritime Museum Cultural Mus.	2 Murray St. (Pyrmont Bridge Rd.) anmm.gov.au	DH $	9298 3777	Classic Cool Museums	*106*, 135 24
Aviation Tours Australia Tour	Sydney Airport sydneyhelitours.com.au	VA $$$$	9317 3402	Hot & Cool	98
The Belinda Stores Shop	Various belinda.com.au	CBD	9328 6288	Hot & Cool	98
Blue Thunder Tour	Various bluethunder.com.au	CBD $$$$	1 800 800 184	Hot & Cool	*63*, 98
BridgeClimb Sydney Sport	5 Cumberland St. (George St.) bridgeclimb.com	TR $$$$	8274 7777	Hot & Cool Only-in-Sydney	*64*, 99 34
Collette Dinnigan Shop	33 William St. (Underwood St.) collettedinnigan.com.au	PD	9360 6691	Hot & Cool	99
Deus Ex Machina Shop/Gallery	98-104 Parramatta Rd. (King Edward St.) deus.com.au	VA	9557 6866	Hot & Cool	99
Dinosaur Designs Shop	Level 1, The Strand Arcade, Pitt St. (George St.) dinosaurdesigns.com.au	CBD	9223 2953	Classic	135
The Diva's Closet Shop	32 William St. (Underwood St.)	PD	9361 6659	Hot & Cool	100
Elizabeth Bay House Site	7 Onslow Ave. (Elizabeth Bay Rd.)	VA $	9356 3022	Classic	136
Gavala Aboriginal Art Gallery Art Gallery	Shop 131, Harbourside Centre (Darling Rd.) gavala.com.au	DH	9212 7232	Classic Art Spaces	136 19

Attractions (cont.)

NAME TYPE	ADDRESS (CROSS STREET) WEBSITE	AREA PRICE	PHONE (02+)	EXPERIENCE 99 BEST	PAGE PAGE
Gleebooks Shop	49 Glebe Point Rd. (Derby Pl.) gleebooks.com.au	VA	9660 2333	Hot & Cool	100
Hyde Park Barracks Museum Cultural Museum	Queens Square, Macquarie St. (Prince Alfred Rd.) hht.nsw.gov.au	CBD $	8239 2311	Classic Cool Museums	*106*, 136 24
Jet Boating on Sydney Harbour Activity	Convention Centre Jetty, Darling Harbour harbourjet.com	CQ $	9698 2110	Hot & Cool Harbor Experiences	*64*, 100 27
Lets Go Surfing Sport	128 Ramsgate Ave. (Campbell Parade) letsgosurfing.com.au	BB	9365 1800	Hot & Cool	*66*, 100
LivingWell Premier Health Club Spa	3/255 Pitt St. (Market St.) livingwell.com.au	CBD $$$$	9273 8800	Hot & Cool	*65*, 100
Luna Park Theme Park	1 Olympic Dr. (Alfred St.) lunaparksydney.com	VA $$	9033 7676	Hot & Cool	*64*, 101
Museum of Contemporary Art Art Museum	140 George St. (Circular Quay) mca.com.au	TR $	9245 2400	Hot & Cool Art Spaces	*64*, 101 19
Museum of Sydney Cultural Museum	37 Philip St. (Bridge St.) hht.net.au	CQ $	9251 5988	Hot & Cool	101
North Sydney Olympic Swimming Pool Sport/Site	4 Alfred St. South (Olympic Dr.)	VA $	9955 2309	Classic	*64*, 136
Oceanworld Sport	West Esplanade (Ferry Terminal) sharkdive.oceanworld.com.au	VA $$	8251 7878	Hot & Cool	*66*, 101
Powerhouse Museum Cultural Museum	500 Harris St. (MacArthur St.) phm.gov.au	VA $	9217 0111	Hot & Cool Cool Museums	*106*, 101 24
Purl Harbour Shop	Unit 4, 16 Hall St. (Jacques Ave.)	BB	9365 1521	Hot & Cool	102
Queen Victoria Building Shopping	George, Market., York, Druitt Sts. qvb.com.au	CBD	9264 9209	Classic	*106*, 137
Royal Botanic Gardens Park	Macquarie St. (Mrs.Macquaries Rd.) rbgsyd.nsw.gov.au	CC	9231 8111	Classic	*105*, 137
Scanlan & Theodore Shop	122 Oxford St. (Palmer St.) scanlantheodore.com.au	PD	9380 9388	Hot & Cool	102
Six Ounce Boardstore Shop	Shop 2, 144-148 Glenayr Ave. (Roscoe St.) sixounceboardstore.com.au	BB	9300 8339	Hot & Cool	102
The Spa at Four Seasons Spa	199 George St. (Essex St.) fourseasons.com/sydney	CBD $$$$	9238 0000	Hot & Cool	102
St. James Church Site	Queens Square, Macquarie St. (King St.) sjks.org.au	CBD	8227 1300	Classic	137
St. Mary's Cathedral Site	College & Cathedral Sts. (King St.)	CBD	9220 0400	Classic	*107*, 137
Strand Arcade Shopping	Pitt Street Mall (King St.) strandarcade.com.au	CBD	9232 4199	Classic	*106*, 138
Susannah Place Museum Cultural Museum	58-64 Gloucester St. (Grosvenor St.) hht.net.au/home	TR $	9241 1893	Classic	*105*, 138
Sydney Aquarium Aquarium	Aquarium Pier (King St.) sydneyaquarium.com.au	DH $$	8251 7800	Classic	*106*, 138

NAME TYPE	ADDRESS (CROSS STREET) WEBSITE	AREA COVER	PHONE (02+)	EXPERIENCE 99 BEST	PAGE PAGE
Sydney by Seaplane Tour	Rose Bay Seaplane Base (New South Head Rd.) seaplanes.com.au	VA $$$$	9974 1455	Hot & Cool	*63*, 102
Sydney Jewish Museum Cultural Museum	148 Darlinghurst Rd. (Burton St.) sydneyjewishmuseum.com.au	DH $	9360 7999	Classic	138
Sydney Observatory Site	Observatory Hill (Argyle St.) sydneyobservatory.com.au	VA $	9921 3485	Classic	138
Sydney Olympic Park Park/Site	1 Showground Rd. (Olympic Park City Rail Station) sydneyolympicpark.nsw.gov.au	VA	9714 7888	Hot & Cool	103
Sydney Opera House Site/Venue	Bennelong Point (Circular Quay) sydneyoperahouse.com	CQ $$	9250 7111	Classic Only-in-Sydney	*63*, *105*, 138 34
Sydney Tower Skywalk Sport	100 Market St. (Pitt St.) skywalk.com.au	CBD $$$$	9333 9222	Hot & Cool Only-in-Sydney	*64*, 103 34
Sydney Wildlife World Zoo	Aquarium Pier (Darling Harbour) sydneywildlifeworld.com.au	DH $$	9333 9288	Classic	139
Taronga Zoo Zoo	Bradley's Head Rd. (Military Rd.) zoo.nsw.gov.au	VA $$	9969 2777	Classic	*106*, 139
Tim Olsen Gallery Art Gallery	76 Paddington St. (Elizabeth St.) timolsengallery.com	PD	9360 9854	Hot & Cool	103
Vaucluse House Site	Wentworth Rd. (Olola Ave.)	VA $	9388 7922	Classic	139

BLACK BOOK

Sydney Black Book
By Neighborhood

Code: H-Hotels; R-Restaurants; N-Nightlife; A-Attractions. Blue page numbers denote listings in 99 Best. Black page numbers denote listings in theme chapters. The Sydney Neighborhoods Map is on p.192.

BLACK BOOK

The Rocks (cont.)

Surry Hills (SH)

Woollomooloo (WO)

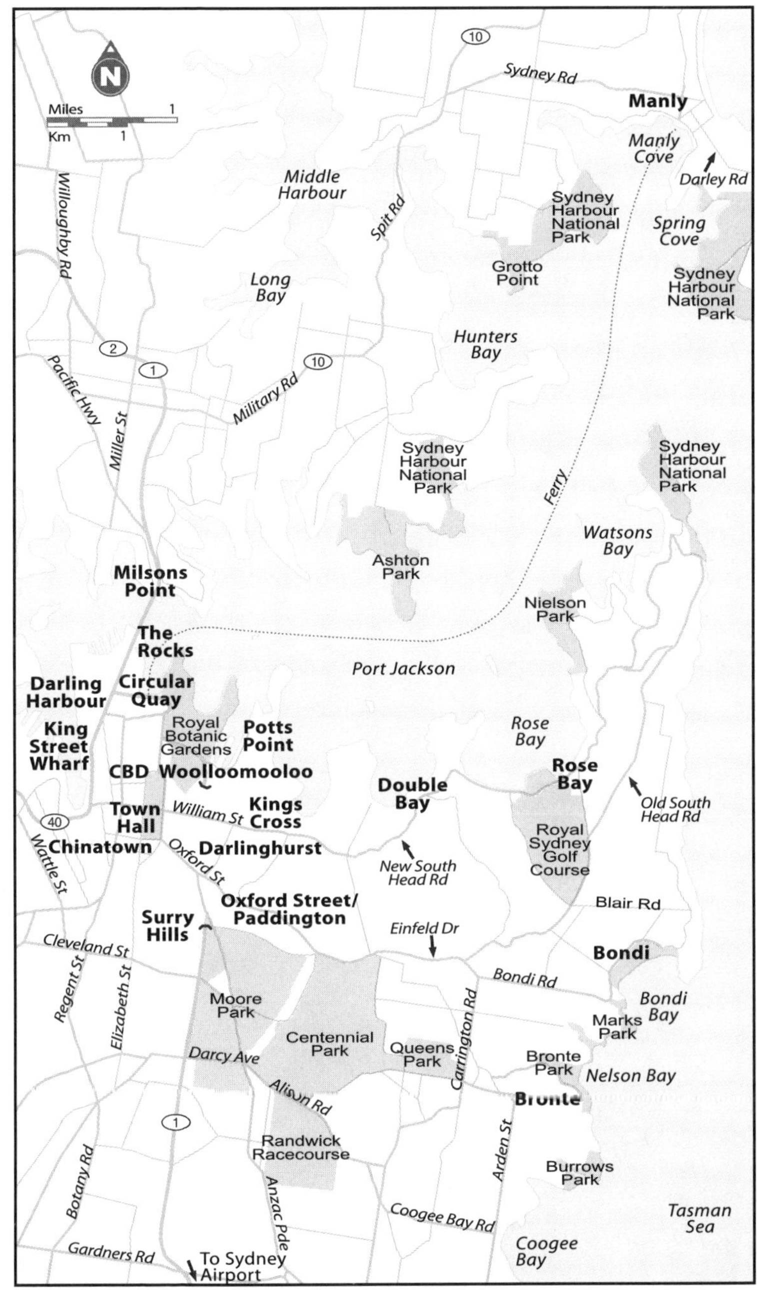

Miles 1
Km 1
10
Sydney Rd
Manly
Manly Cove
Darley Rd
Middle Harbour
Spit Rd
Sydney Harbour National Park
Spring Cove
Grotto Point
Sydney Harbour National Park
Long Bay
Willoughby Rd
Hunters Bay
2
1
10
Pacific Hwy
Military Rd
Miller St
Sydney Harbour National Park
Sydney Harbour National Park
Ferry
Watsons Bay
Ashton Park
Milsons Point
Nielson Park
The Rocks
Port Jackson
Darling Harbour
Circular Quay
Rose Bay
Royal Botanic Gardens
Potts Point
King Street Wharf
CBD
Woolloomooloo
Rose Bay
Double Bay
Town Hall
William St
Kings Cross
Old South Head Rd
40
Royal Sydney Golf Course
Chinatown
Oxford St
Darlinghurst
Wattle St
New South Head Rd
Oxford Street/ Paddington
Blair Rd
Surry Hills
Einfeld Dr
Cleveland St
Bondi
Bondi Rd
Regent St
Elizabeth St
Moore Park
Bondi Bay
Marks Park
Centennial Park
Queens Park
Carrington Rd
Darcy Ave
Bronte Park
Nelson Bay
Alison Rd
1
Randwick Racecourse
Arden St
Burrows Park
Botany Rd
Anzac Pde
Coogee Bay Rd
Tasman Sea
Coogee Bay
Gardners Rd
To Sydney Airport

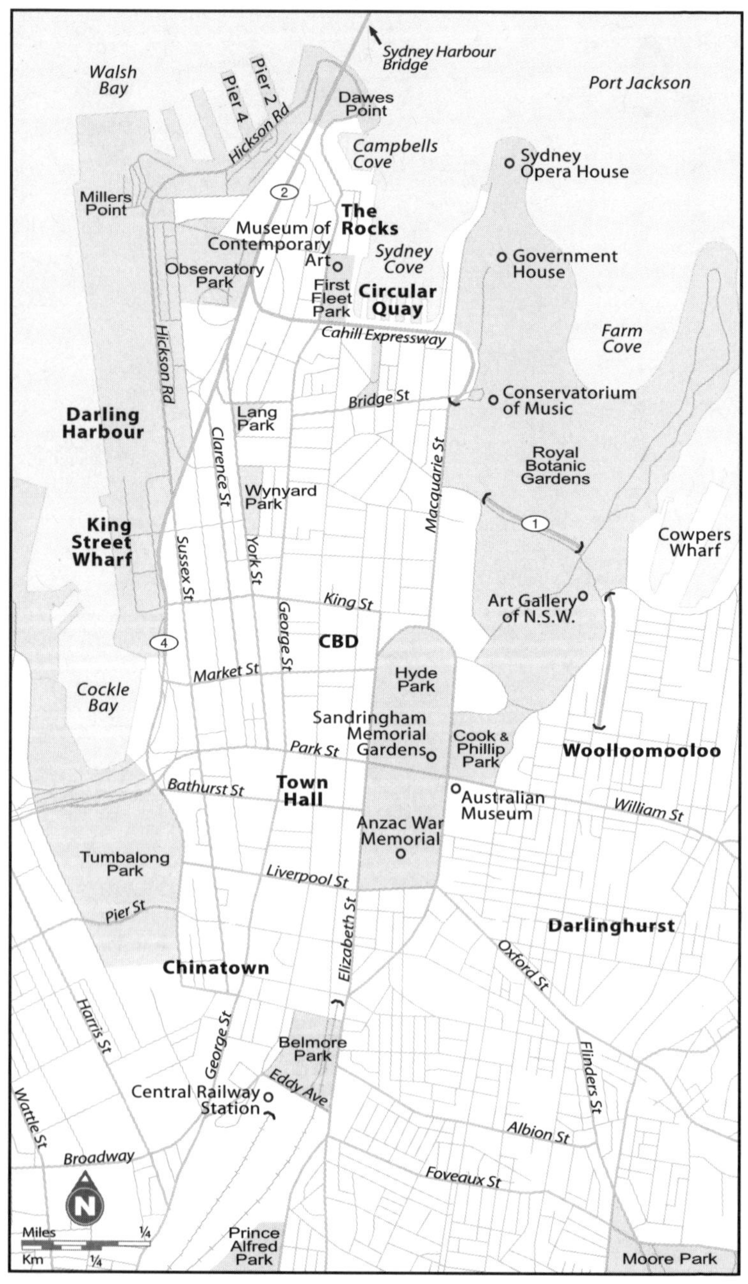

Sydney Harbour Bridge
Walsh Bay
Pier 2
Pier 4
Hickson Rd
Dawes Point
Port Jackson
Campbells Cove
Sydney Opera House
Millers Point
The Rocks
Museum of Contemporary Art
Sydney Cove
Government House
Observatory Park
First Fleet Park
Circular Quay
Cahill Expressway
Farm Cove
Hickson Rd
Bridge St
Conservatorium of Music
Darling Harbour
Lang Park
Clarence St
Royal Botanic Gardens
Macquarie St
Wynyard Park
King Street Wharf
Sussex St
York St
Cowpers Wharf
King St
George St
Art Gallery of N.S.W.
CBD
Market St
Hyde Park
Cockle Bay
Sandringham Memorial Gardens
Cook & Phillip Park
Woolloomooloo
Park St
Bathurst St
Town Hall
Australian Museum
William St
Anzac War Memorial
Tumbalong Park
Liverpool St
Pier St
Elizabeth St
Darlinghurst
Oxford St
Chinatown
Harris St
George St
Belmore Park
Flinders St
Eddy Ave
Central Railway Station
Wattle St
Albion St
Broadway
Foveaux St
N
Miles
¼
Km
¼
Prince Alfred Park
Moore Park

"Sydney" by Mary Lou Dauray, 2007, commissioned by Pulse Guides

Original oil painting on clayboard, 14"h x 11"w

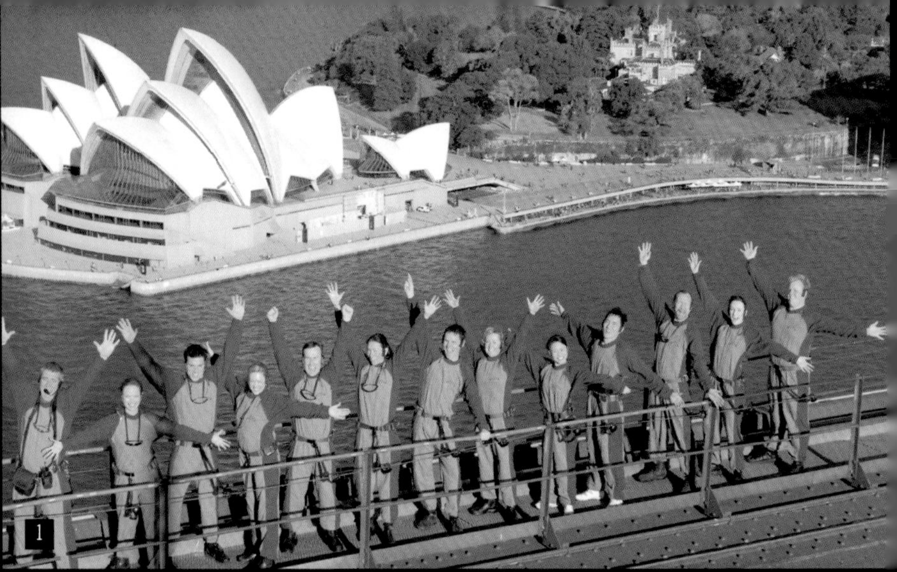

1

2

3

4

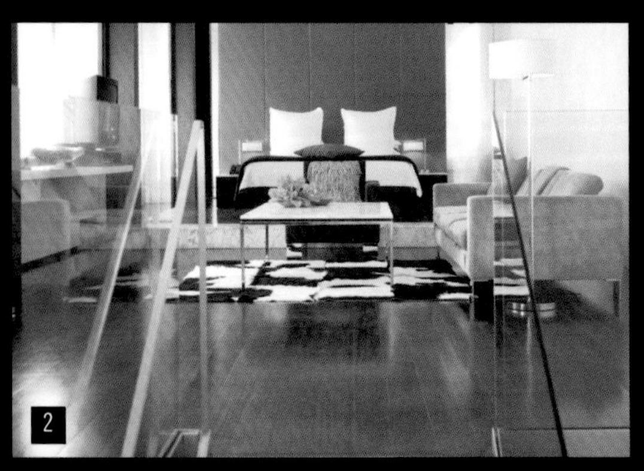

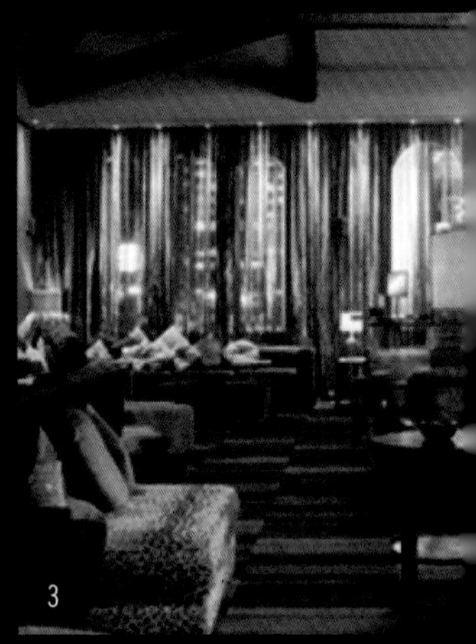

1. BridgeClimb Sydney (p.99)
2. Establishment Hotel (p.70)
3. Hemmesphere (p.91)
4. Icebergs Dining Room & Bar (p.79)

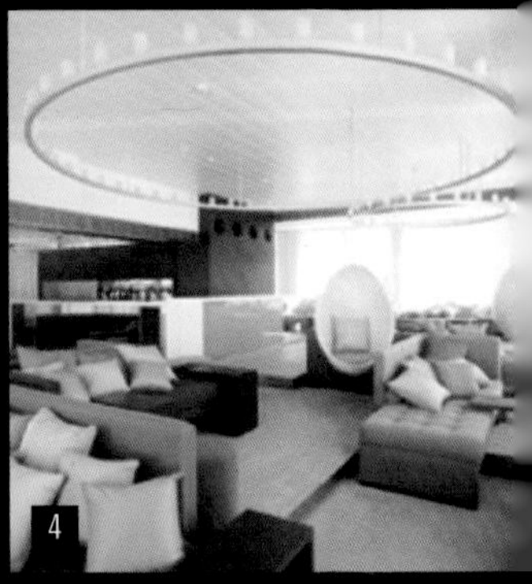

HOT & COOL

5. Lady Lux (p.92)
6. Aqua Dining (p.73)
7. Luna Park (p.101)
8. Slip Inn (p.96)

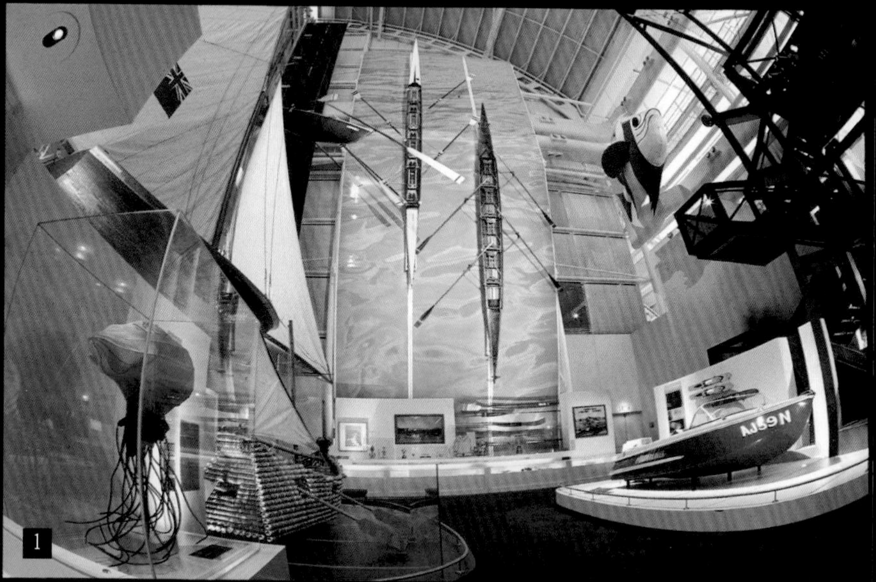

1

2

3

4

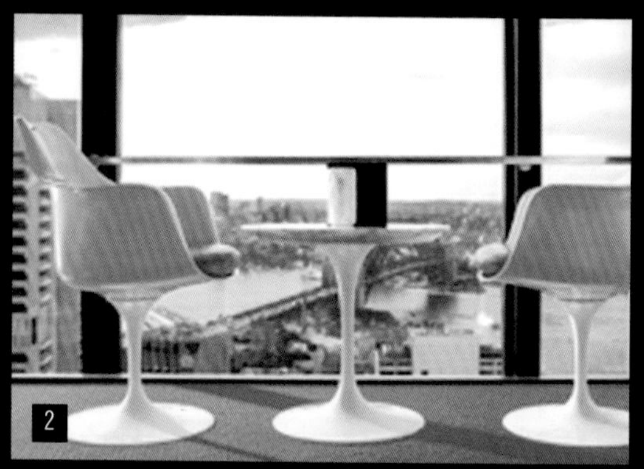

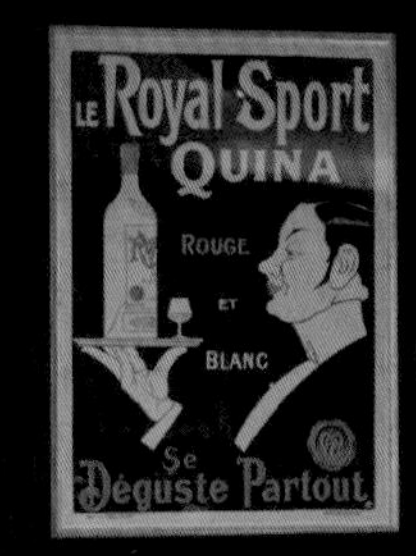

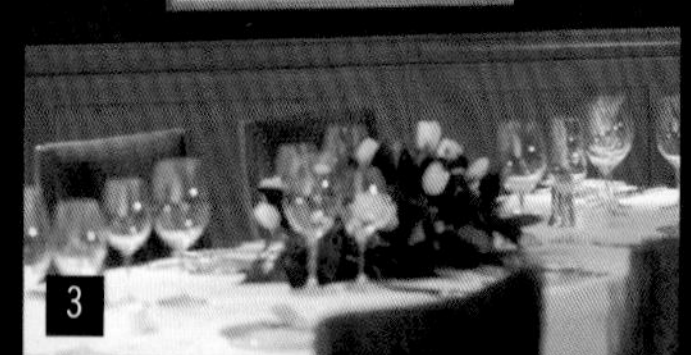

1. Australian National Maritime Museum (p.135)
2. Orbit Bar (p.131)
3. Forty One Restaurant (p.117)
4. Rockpool (p.122)

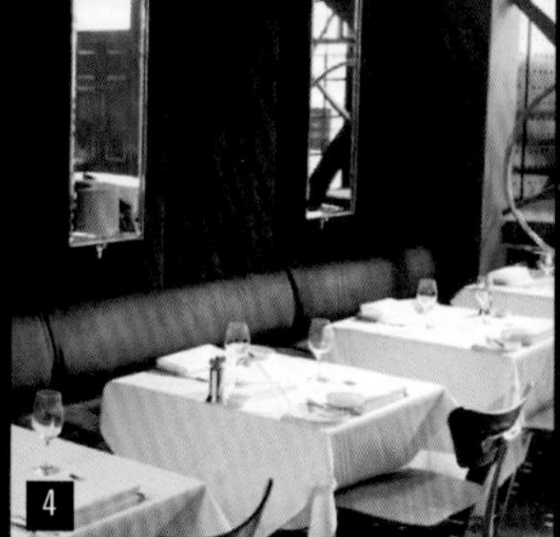

CLASSIC

5. Marque (p.119)
6. Sydney skyline
7. Guillaume at Bennelong (p.118)
8. 360 Bar & Dining Room (p.133)

CLASSIC

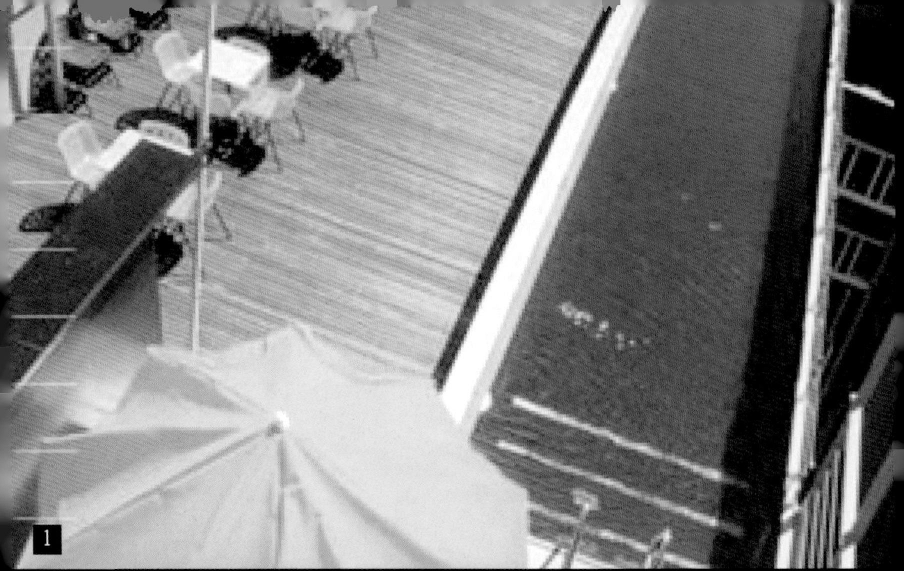

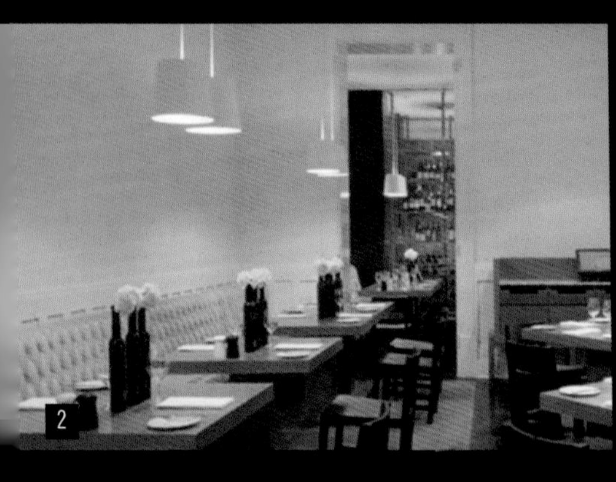

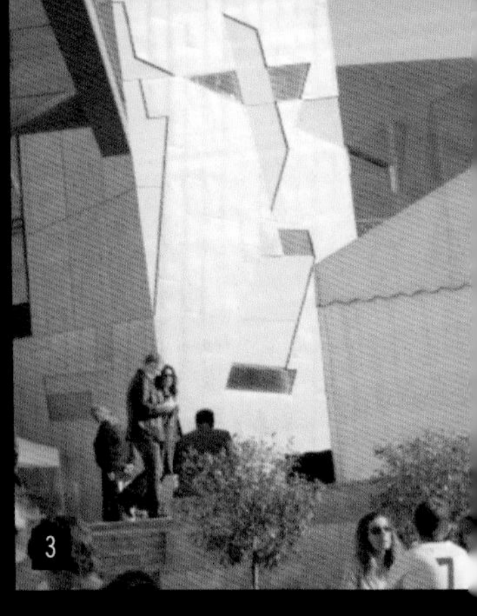

1. Adelphi Hotel (p.206)
2. Comme (p.212)
3. Federation Square (p.230)
4. Langham Hotel (p.208)

MELBOURNE

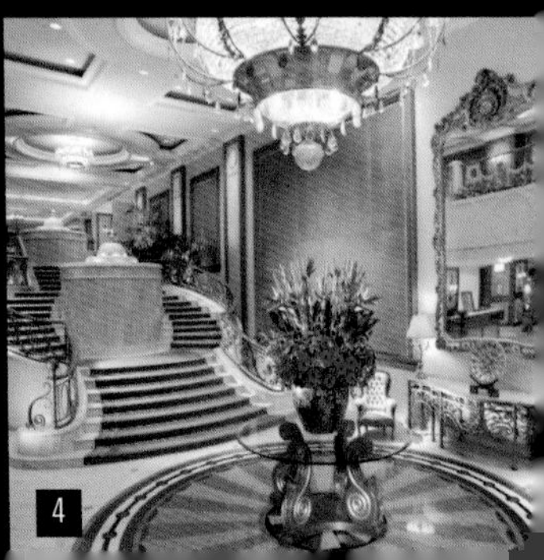

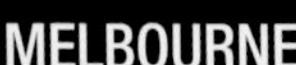

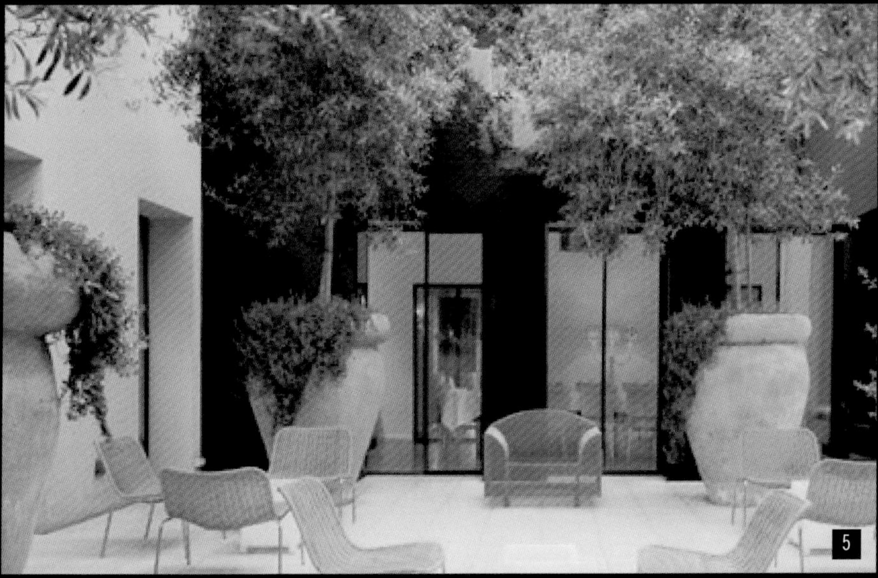
5

6

7

8

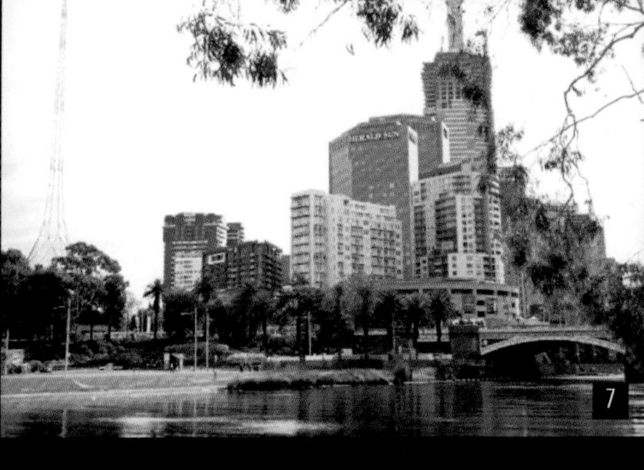

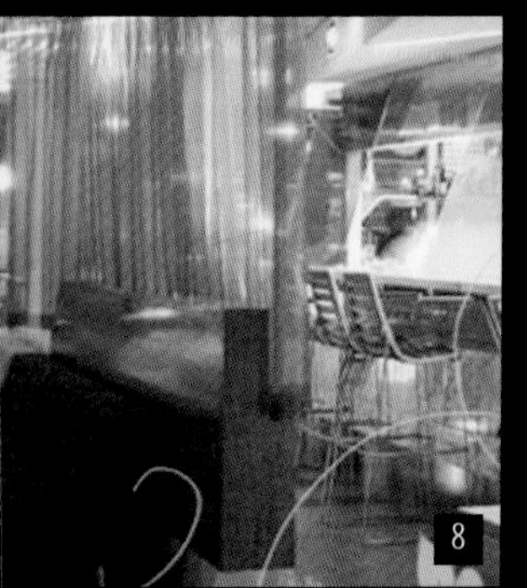

5. Circa (p.212)

6. The Prince Hotel (p.208)

7. Prince's Bridge, Southbank

8. Taxi Dining Room (p.218)

1

2

3

Photo Credits courtesy of:

HOT & COOL

1. BridgeClimb Sydney
2. Merivale Group
3. Merivale Group
4. Icebergs Dining Room and Bar
5. Lady Lux
6. Treacle/Ripples Cafe Group
7. Mary Lou Dauray
8. Merivale Group

CLASSIC

1. Australian National Maritime Museum
2. Steven McArthur/The Summit Pty Ltd
3. Robert Billington
4. Rockpool Bar & Grill
5. Rendezvous Hotels
6. Mary Lou Dauray
7. Matthew Penfield
8. Epic Media Inc.

MELBOURNE

1. Adelphi Hotel
2. Tim Bott
3. Mary Lou Dauray
4. Leonardo Media
5. Circa
6. Luxe Hotels
7. Andrew Dunn
8. Transport Hotel Group

PRIME TIME

1. Mary Lou Dauray
2. Gloria Hassan
3. Ann-Marie Calihanna

1. Prime Time: Melbourne Cup (p.59)

2. Prime Time: Melbourne Cup (p.59)

3. Prime Time: Gay & Lesbian Mardi Gras, Sydney (p.56)

Introduction to Melbourne

At first glance, the state capital of Victoria—with its well-ordered downtown grid, stately historic buildings, and vast parklands—looks like a model British colonial city. But despite the veneer of church spires and European trees, Melbourne (pronounced Mel-bun) is quick to reveal its split personality. On the one hand there are top-class restaurants, hip cocktail spots, and glitzy clubs that attract the fashion-conscious crowd who shop in the city's famed boutiques. On the other, the city beats a path to the underground, with eccentric theme bars favored by the arty set, and down-at-the-heels pubs that pump out live music until the early hours. But there's one thing that always brings the diverse city dwellers together—sport, of course. The Melbourne Grand Prix might have its supporters, but Aussie Rules football is the name of the game here, while cricket at the Melbourne Cricket Ground has a fanatical following, too. And then there's the Melbourne Cup, the race of the nation, when the whole city grinds to a halt to see the horses gallop. It's such an institution that it has led to the creation of a state-wide holiday.

Melbourne: What It Was

All these things are merely the latest blips in the history line, though. For at least 40,000 years, much of modern-day Melbourne was occupied by the Wurundjeri tribe, part of a loose confederation of five groups who shared a similar language and identified themselves as the "Kulin" nation. Since the period they call the Dreamtime, they had fished the Yarra River for fish and eels, hunted kangaroos and other animals along its banks, and traded furs and food, axes, and medicines. The Kulin were defined by their social moiety, or totem—either the eagle or the raven. They inherited their totem from their father, and it dictated their social relationships, down to whom they would marry. Regular tribal meetings reinforced alliances, as well as being the focus for trade, initiations, and celebrations. One important meeting place lies buried beneath the Melbourne Cricket Ground.

For at least 40,000 years, much of modern-day Melbourne was occupied by the Wurundjeri tribe, part of a loose confederation of five groups who shared a similar language and identified themselves as the "Kulin" nation.

Then, in 1835, the 30-ton schooner *Rebecca*, captained by John Batman, sailed up from Tasmania and appeared in Port Phillip. On May 29, Batman anchored his ship a short distance from the heads and made several excursions inland. On one of these trips, Batman attempted to sign a treaty with eight Aboriginal elders. He presented them with mirrors, knives, and scissors and promised them more in the years ahead. In return they handed over a possum-skin cloak—and, in Batman's mind, a huge tract of land. No doubt there was some confusion. As the Aborigines saw it, land could never be owned, so how could anyone buy it or sell it?

Key Dates

1835	Melbourne founded.
1836	Settlers form a government.
1837	Plans for city grid laid out.
1847	Melbourne proclaimed a city.
1851	Gold Rush begins.
1861	First Melbourne Cup horse race takes place.
1863	State funeral for explorers Burke and Wills.
1880	Ned Kelly hanged at the Melbourne Gaol.
1956	Melbourne Olympics held.
2006	Melbourne Commonwealth Games.

Before returning to Tasmania, Batman instructed three white men, and five Aborigines from New South Wales, to stay behind to build a hut and start a garden. That same year, the schooner *Enterprize* sailed up the Yarra River and anchored beside Batman's small colony to land stores and livestock. It was a new beginning and the end of Aboriginal inheritance.

The Governor of New South Wales, Sir Richard Bourke, promptly stamped out any notion of a valid treaty with the local tribes. He issued a proclamation stating that all treaties with Aborigines would be dealt with as if the Aborigines were trespassers. With this in mind, the Secretary of State, Baron Glenelg, authorized Bourke to mark out a township and sell allotments of land to any settler that could afford one.

It was left up to the Assistant Surveyor-General, Robert Hoddle, to lay out the town. It would be called Melbourne, as a compliment to the Prime Minister of Great Britain.

Ten years later, Melbourne was declared a city, but it only really took off with the discovery of gold. In 1851, a prospector who had returned to the colony after trying his luck in the California Gold Rush found a speck of gold in a water hole near Bathurst in New South Wales. Four months later, gold fever struck as big finds turned up. The Victorian authorities, eager to prevent the city's population from joining the gold frenzy in NSW, offered a reward of £200 for any gold found within 200 miles of Melbourne. Just six months after, gold was discovered at

Ballarat, and a short time later at Bendigo Creek. The finds were so huge that Victoria was soon producing more than a third of the world's gold, and in just two years the state's population had boomed from 77,000 to more than half a million.

Melbourne's most notable heirs to the mantle of legend were the explorers Burke and Wills, and the famous outlaw Ned Kelly. The former presented a tale of inland exploration, the latter an example of frontier lawlessness.

Of course, gold meant money, and in Melbourne the buildings went up, each grander and more impressive than the last. Just as in San Francisco, Chinese gold prospectors congregated in what would become known as Chinatown, and settlers from almost every European nation brought their earnings, and their families from back home, and settled down in the bustling state capital. All that was needed now were some heroic stories to go with it.

Melbourne's most notable heirs to the mantle of legend were the explorers Burke and Wills, and the famous outlaw Ned Kelly. The former presented a tale of inland exploration, the latter an example of frontier lawlessness.

On the 20th of August, 1860, Robert O'Hara Burke, with Wills acting as his surveyor, led an expedition of 16 men out of Melbourne. They were aiming to be the first people to cross the continent from south to north. After spending two months waiting around for fresh supplies at Coopers Creek in central Australia, Burke and Wills, with two others, set off north. They reached the Gulf of Carpentaria on February 1861. Battling through some of the harshest territory on earth, they returned to Coopers Creek, only to miss a carved sign on a gum tree, which instructed them to dig for buried supplies. The rest of the group had left to return south, two days earlier. Burke and Wills survived for two months before they died. Of the other two men, one perished on his way back from the Gulf, and the other was rescued by Aborigines. Burke and Wills lie buried in Melbourne General Cemetery.

As for Ned Kelly, a descendant of Irish immigrants, he's now perceived as a working-class hero who fell victim to powerful interests keen on evicting his family from their land in northeastern Victoria. After the murder of three policeman and a couple of bank robberies, the Kelly Gang faced armed police in one last standoff, dressed in their suits of homemade armor. Kelly was finally captured and hung in the Old Melbourne Gaol in 1880.

History marched on, and the city solidified itself as a conservative bastion, which was finally softened by mass immigration, particularly from Greece—even today there are more Greeks in Melbourne than in Athens. Ancient Greece, of course, was the birthplace of the Olympics, and in 1956, against all odds, Melbourne was host to the world's greatest sporting festival. There were many problems before the Games took place, not least because of Australia's stringent quarantine laws, which forced the equestrian events to be held in the capital of Sweden. But, finally, the Olympics burst forth, gracing the Melbourne Cricket Ground, the site of the 2006 Commonwealth Games. Melbourne was on the map at last.

Melbourne: What It Is

Today's Melbourne is a cultural melting pot, and the influx of thousands of immigrants each year—from Italians and Lebanese, to Vietnamese and Chinese—continues to make its mark on this relaxed metropolis. Central Melbourne's streets rumble with trams passing beside graceful marble-clad shopping arcades. In Chinatown, the smell of fresh-cooked noodles and seafood floats through the air. On Lonsdale and Russell Streets, bustling Italian restaurants and cafes spill onto the sidewalk, while in Melbourne's Greek Precinct, baklava and late-night souvlaki lure visitors. From the buzzing riverside promenade of Southbank, which stretches along the cultured banks of the Yarra River, to the bayside suburb of St. Kilda, with its bohemian cafes and its youthful, raw, and funky feel, Melbourne is consistently voted one of the most livable cities in the world.

Of course, talk to a resident of Sydney and you'll get a different story. These two cities have a long-lasting rivalry over which is Australia's truest gem. But those loyal to Melbourne make a good argument. It might rain more than Sydney and the winters might be colder, but that only means that the strengths of its culture don't end with the sand and surf. Melbourne is known for its festivals and theaters, its wonderful shopping, and its dazzling restaurant scene. There are more bars in Melbourne than in almost any city of its size, and a strong artistic leaning means that many of them are unique—the better to cater to all those splintered facets of this fun-loving society. Art is in the lifeblood of Melbourne, with two major galleries gracing the town center, and works of wacky art

Today's Melbourne is a cultural melting pot, and the influx of thousands of immigrants each year—from Italians and Lebanese, to Vietnamese and Chinese—continues to make its mark on this relaxed metropolis.

scattered across the city's streets. And if that's not enough, there's always Federation Square, with its wonky piazza and futuristic façade, to stimulate your mind as you sip a cocktail or enjoy a meal in one of its prime-spot eateries and bars.

When it comes to the crunch, Melbourne's where it's at in Australia. No wonder everyone loves it, and so many people keep flocking south to this elegant enclave of sophistication and fun.

Welcome to fabulous Melbourne ...

Melbourne

How does Melbourne compare to Sydney? If you ask the residents of this small and sophisticated spot, they'll quickly tell you a dozen reasons why their home is vastly superior. Like Los Angeles and San Francisco, these sister cities have very different identities and competitive natures. Melbourne sniffs at Sydney's flash and dash, preferring a more stately elegance and an appreciation of the finer things in life. It's a melting pot of cultures and cuisines, a vibrant, artistic place crammed with classic restaurants, cozy bars tucked down lanes, glamorous cocktail lounges, colonial and modernist hotels, and superb shopping. It's a cultured place, but not a stuffy one. Get ready, because Melbourne is here to show you how a grown-up has fun.

Note: Venues in bold are described in detail in the listings that follow the itinerary. Venues followed by an asterisk (*) are recommended as both a restaurant and a destination bar.

Melbourne: The Perfect Plan (3 Nights and Days)

Perfect Plan Highlights

Thursday

Afternoon	**Ian Potter, ACMI, NGV, Melbourne Zoo**
Cocktails	**Transport, Meyers Place, Gin Palace**
Dinner	**Taxi, Comme's*, Ezard's**
Nighttime	**Pony, Cookie***
Late-Night	**Canary Club, Cherry Bar, Boutique**

Friday

Breakfast	**European***
Morning	**Botanic Gardens, Mel. Museum, Gaol**
Lunch	**Vue de Monde, Syracuse***
Afternoon	**Spa, shopping**
Cocktails	**Mdm. Brus.*, Longrain***
Dinner	**MoVida*, Longrain*, Mini**
Nighttime	**Polly**
Late-Night	**Supper Club***

Saturday

Morning	**Station Pier, shopping**
Lunch	**Cicciolina*, Café di Stasio**
Afternoon	**Aurora Spa**
Cocktails	**Pelican*, Vineyard**
Dinner	**Circa, Donovan's*, Stokehouse***
Nighttime	**Prince, Esplanade**
Late-Night	**Revolver Upstairs**

Morning After

Brunch	**Pearl**

Hotels: **Langham Hotel** and **The Prince Hotel**

Thursday

2pm Head for Federation Square, Melbourne's most distinctive site, and a bustling area for people-watching—and art. Here you'll find the strange geometric conglomeration of buildings that house **the Ian Potter Centre: NGV Australia**, with its illustrious collection of Australian art. Spend an hour or two browsing its galleries, but save your energy—you've got more art stops coming. Next door is the **Australian Centre for the Moving Image (ACMI)**, dedicated to the magic of the silver screen. For a broader view of the world, check out the international offerings at the nearby **National Gallery of Victoria**. If art is too tame, take a train from Flinders Street Station to Royal Park and **Melbourne Zoo**, Australia's best and oldest animal house. Don't miss the butterfly house, the gorilla enclosure, or the Great Flight Aviary. You can recaffeinate in the mock village in the recently completed elephant enclosure.

6pm Art is thirsty work, so stroll across Fed Square's cobblestone piazza to **Transport**, the enormously popular zinc-clad pub where you can sample a huge range of international beer inside or outside, facing the river or even a piazza. In summer, **Meyers Place** is a great spot for a drink, and in bad weather, **Gin Palace** is one of the town's favorite bolt-hole bars.

8pm Dinner **Taxi**, a mix of Japanese and European flavors, is on the floor above Transport, so your dinner is just seconds away. It comes with brilliant views of the city through glass and steel mesh walls. Didn't book? **Comme's*** French/Spanish food is just a short stroll away, as is **Ezard's** exciting modern Australian flavors, in the Adelphi Hotel.

10pm Melbourne is jammed with little bars, but if you want to shake your booty, head to the seedy, grungy **Pony Club** where you may find live bands or DJs and an unpretentiously good way to dance off dinner. **Cookie*** on Swanston Street is another stylish place to groove.

Midnight Decisions, decisions. Will it be the leather daybeds, cocktails, tapas, and lounge-house DJs at **Canary Club**, or the raucous rock sounds at **Cherry Bar** in AC/DC Lane?

2am Hop a cab and check out the chic **Boutique**. Another great option is **Double Happiness and New Gold Mountain**—two local favorites by one owner, stacked on top of each other.

9am Mingle with politicians lining up for some of the best coffee in town at the dark wood and marble **European***. Try the corn cakes.

10am Walk off breakfast with a turn around the 'Tan—the favorite walk-jog track of Melbournites, which runs around the **Royal Botanic Gardens**. Then wander into the gardens themselves. It's a glorious adventure, from the ornamental lake, to the native species section, and a waterlily garden that would make Monet moan. Take some time to visit the Shrine of Remembrance, built to honor veterans of WWI. Its rooftop gives a stellar view over the city. Or walk to the Exhibition Gardens, home to both the World Heritage–listed Exhibition Building and the sleek modernist **Melbourne Museum**. Don't miss the museum's living Forest Gallery or the Bunjilaka Aboriginal cultural center—one of the largest collections of Aboriginal artifacts anywhere. Make sure to save a half-hour to visit the creepy **Old Melbourne Gaol** where Australia's most infamous outlaw was hung.

1pm Lunch **Vue de Monde**'s modern French food and industrial chic dining room is spectacular—and spectacularly expensive—at night, which is why the lunch deal packs the place out, so book ahead. If you can't get in, then **Syracuse***—romantically

Mediterranean and wine-focused is nearby.

3pm **The Chuan Spa** at the Langham is a great place to relax. It's an intimate space with a lovely indoor pool and a roof deck. Don't miss the natural rock-lined steam shower. For a bit of retail therapy instead, **Flinders Lane** is waiting. It's home to a profusion of small commercial galleries, edgy furniture and lighting showrooms, designer clothing and accessories stores, bars, cafes, and restaurants. You'll find local favorites like **Akira Isogawa** and **Alice Euphemia**. Check the side alleys, too.

6pm **Madame Brussels***, a quirky astro-turf and 1960s garden-furniture-decorated bar on the third level of a nondescript office block, is a Friday night tradition for many. Not only does it make great cocktails, but there is a large balcony that is popular even in winter, thanks to blankets handed out by the handsome staff. Not into heights? Have your drinks in **Longrain**'s* bustling lounge while you wait for a table.

8pm Dinner **MoVida*** will make you happy, particularly if you are fond of authentic tapas, Spanish wine, and flatteringly lit spaces full of good-looking people. **Longrain***, a Melbourne legend, has excellent modern Thai food and a lively scene. Or check out **Mini** for a fresh spin on Greek in casually chic surrounds.

10:30pm Hop in a cab to the nearby neighborhood of Fitzroy to enjoy a few fab drinks at the sexy *Moulin Rouge*-esque cocktail bar **Polly**.

1am You haven't experienced late-night Melbourne if you've never been to the **Melbourne Supper Club***. Be prepared to stand in line on the weekends unless you're a visiting rock star, in which case you'll be whisked up the stairs and given a comfortable seat on one of the many leather couches.

10am It's time for a hotel switch to visit the other Melbourne—the relaxed beach town just a few miles away by cab, but light-years away in vibe. Check into **the Prince**, a small, beautifully designed hotel right in the middle of all the St. Kilda action and a short stroll from St. Kilda Beach.

11am Walk down to the palm-lined shore for a bayside stroll to Port Melbourne. Check out dogwalkers, rollerbladers, and exercise fanatics before reaching Station Pier, the perfect spot for a drink or a coffee at one of the many cafes and restaurants. You might even see a wild penguin or two at the end of the pier. If more shopping is in order, a 5-minute stroll up Acland Street from the Prince will find you among colorful shops hawking everything from pastries to cute dresses.

1pm Lunch All that fresh sea air should have made you hungry, so lunch at **Cicciolina*** is next, a casual French-style joint with delicious Mediterranean food and a short, smart wine list. Also close by is **Café di Stasio**, a smart, classic Italian joint with great food.

3pm If the spa didn't make your list in the city center, you get another chance to relax, unwind, and detox at the Prince's own spa, **Aurora**, a tranquil, leafy place with an extensive range of skin and body treatments.

6pm Time to retox. At **Pelican***, a nicely designed tapas-style bar with a nifty indoor-outdoor seating arrangement, there's perfect people-watching—while sipping great wine. Or head for the **Vineyard** on Acland Street, which caters to an always excitable young and fashionable crowd.

8pm Dinner It's back to the Prince for dinner at its flagship restaurant, **Circa**, a beautiful, romantic space with superb contemporary Australian food. The wine list—and the help you get deciphering it—is awesome. If you want to stray a little further afield, **Donovan's*** restaurant on St. Kilda Beach is like a luxurious beach house complete with a great chef cooking elegant, simple, contemporary meals. You could also do your drinking and dining at **Stokehouse*** on the beach—opt for an upstairs seat and linger over the sunset.

10pm Check out who's playing at the **Prince Bandroom**—it constantly plays host to local and overseas acts—or come later for One Love, featuring some of the best DJs around. Or find a happening local scene at **the Esplanade Hotel**.

1am Best bet by far at this time of night and on this side of town is **Revolver Upstairs**. Great drinks, decor, and DJs and—even better—it doesn't close until noon on Sunday.

The Morning After

Pearl in Richmond has one of the best brunches in town. The streetside terrace is a lovely place to eat coddled egg toasties with caviar, especially with a glass of champagne—bring your sunglasses.

Melbourne: The Key Neighborhoods

Lygon Street in **Carlton** is Melbourne's Little Italy. Immigrants installed the first Gaggia espresso machines in the 1950s, bringing that essence of the old country to roost here. The street is brimming with cafes, pizzerias, trattorias, and gelati bars.

The **Central Business District (CBD)**, starting at Collins and Spring Streets, is affectionately known as the "Paris end of town." Skyscrapers tower above luxury stores. Running parallel to the south is Flinders Lane, where commercial galleries sit cheek-by-jowl with lunch spots. Exhibition Street, between Collins and Flinders, is fast becoming design central.

You'll find all sorts in **Fitzroy**. Brunswick Street groans under the weight of down-beat bars, cocktail lounges, upbeat cafes, and restaurants. Peppered among these joints are hip stores. The west side of Smith Street is officially Fitzroy, but Collingwood has greater claims to it. This once seedy-as-hell strip is slowly evolving into a cool alternative to Brunswick Street for eats, treats, and threads.

South Yarra is home to the Royal Botanic Gardens. As you venture further into South Yarra, you'll find a thoroughly gentrified suburb full of impressive terrace houses and manicured cottage gardens. Chapel Street is its spine, and the end closest to Toorak Road boasts luxe shopping and cafe society. The grittier end of Chapel Street between Commercial Road and Dandenong Road is home to hip bars and clubs.

If New York never sleeps, bayside **St. Kilda**—filled with hip beach types—only shuts its eyes from 7am to 9am. Shop on Barkly Street for local designer fashion and streetwear.

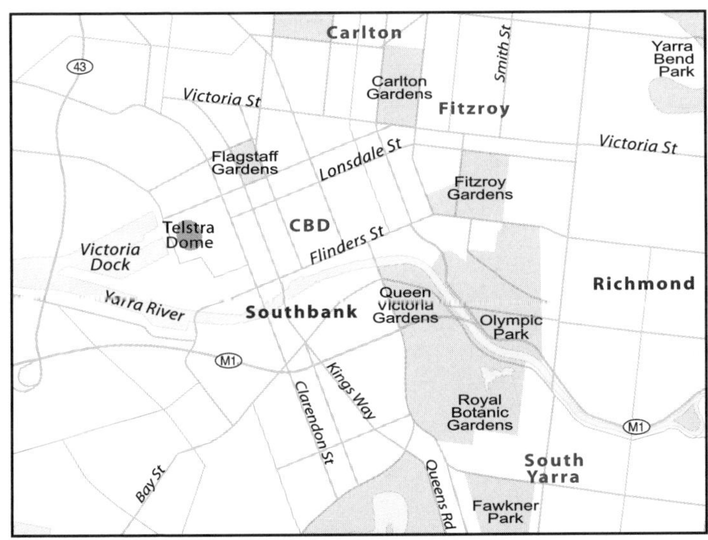

Melbourne: The Shopping Blocks

Collins Street (in the CBD)

Collins Street at the "Paris end" from Spring Street to Swanston Walk is the brand queen's dreamland. Gucci, Ferragamo, Chanel, Vuitton, Bally, Hermès, and Georg Jensen vie for space with the best of the local boutiques.

Le Louvre An old-fashioned salon where the clothes are brought to you from the back. Fashionistas love it. 74 Collins St., 03 9650 1300

Miss Louise Shoes galore—from stilettos to cute little flats. Grand Hyatt, 123 Collins St., 03 9654 7730

General Post Office (in the CBD)

The gracious halls of the General Post Office or GPO have been architecturally refitted to suit a bevy of boutiques. Wandering this elegant enclave of shops can take up an afternoon. 350 Bourke St. (Elizabeth St.)

Akira Isogawa One of Melbourne's most loved high-fashion gods combines Japanese touches with modern sensibilities. 03 9663 5003

Belinda Hip clothes and accessories for fashionable women. 03 9663 7845

Spacecraft Avant-garde textile shop. 03 9662 2012

QV (in the CBD)

QV is GPO's rival, another new-style mall for sophisticated shoppers. Located at the corner of **Lonsdale and Swanston Streets**, its layout mimics traditional labyrinthine old-world alleys. Lonsdale St. (Swanston St.), qv.com.au/fashion.html

Cactus Jam Two stores under the same name offer hip fashions for men and women. 03 9654 0798

Christensen Copenhagen Sleek purveyor of European and U.S. lines, from Paul & Joe to Tocca. 350 Bourke St., 03 9663 7845

Nicola Finetti Fluid, flowing women's wear from an architect turned designer. 03 9663 7886

Flinders Lane and Little Collins Street (in the CBD)

Flinders Lane and **Little Collins Street** bristle with fabulous finds. Here's where the boutique hide-and-seek begins in earnest.

Chiodo Unusual and stylish menswear. Basement, 114 Russell St., 03 9663 0044

Cose Ipanema One-stop shop for cutting-edge designer labels. 113 Little Collins St., 03 9650 3457

e.g. etal Jewelry from the best local designers. Basement, 167 Flinders Ln., 03 9639 5111

Husk Chic women's clothes from across the globe. 176 Little Collins St., 03 9663 0655

St. Kilda

Shopping is a secondary pleasure to pursue in **St. Kilda** where the good life reigns. All along Acland Street and its surrounds you'll find great boutiques, tons of pastry shops, and lots of fashionistas.

Chronicles Books A lovely bookshop to browse for local authors and major best-sellers alike. 91 Fitzroy St., 03 9537 2677

Scheherazade This Jewish deli and pastry shop is a great place to try the decadent cakes this area is known for. 99 Acland St., 03 9534 2722

Milla Trendy women's designer fashions fill the racks at this boutique. 208 Barkly St., 03 9537 1750

Zimmerman This line from sisters Nicky and Simone was launched in 1990 and has quickly gained an international following—especially for the swimsuits. 188b Barkly St., 03 9357 1900

Melbourne: The Hotels

Adelphi Hotel • City Center • Modern (34 rms)

Acclaimed worldwide as an icon in design, the Adelphi fuses art and straight lines with bright color and simplicity. It was created out of a former warehouse, and true to that history, it's edgy, sharp, and burnished with plenty of metal. Rooms are decked out in a simple, angular style, each with a leaning leather couch, stainless steel coffee table and desk, and either a king-size bed or twin doubles. Premier king rooms are large and have a generous bathroom. Deluxe rooms have two oversized single beds, and are smaller in scale than the premier rooms. The lap pool on the roof is an outstanding example of contemporary design. One end is suspended over the footpath below and has a glass bottom. It's quite a thrill to swim out over the pedestrians nine floors below. $$$ 187 Flinders Ln. (St. Kilda Rd.), 03 9650 7555, adelphi.com.au

The Como Melbourne • South Yarra • Timeless (107 rms)

Right in the heart of the upmarket shopping and restaurant strip of South Yarra, The Como is an exceptional five-star hotel with impeccable service, wonderful attention to detail, and a very high rate of return guests. This even includes a little yellow duck in the bathtub. All rooms are larger than most you'll find in other deluxe hotels, and some come with spas, balconies, and kitchens. With 25 different floor plans, you should be able to find a room with what you want. The best choice would be one of the six with their own private Japanese courtyards, perfect for sitting next to the trickling fountain with a glass of wine. These rooms come in studios, open plans with living area, and one-bedrooms. The Hotel Como is one of the few in the world to offer video-conference capability from every room. Simply connect your computer to the television and you can have a person-to-person video talk. Hotel chauffeurs can pick you up from the airport, and the hotel offers free limousine service three times each weekday morning to the Central Business District. Apart from the Brasserie, where you can eat breakfast, there is no restaurant on site. However, the hotel operates a "charge-back" plan where you can get room service delivered from several of the great eateries on vibrant Chapel Street. $$$ 630 Chapel St. (Toorak Rd.), 03 9825 2222 / 1 800 033 400 in Australia, mirvachotels.com.au

Crown Towers • Southbank • Modern (482 rms)

Melbourne's only casino hotel is a focal point for all those who wish to try their luck on the gaming tables. The complex includes more than 40 restaurants, so you won't be short of a place to eat. Hotel rooms are spacious and modern and finished with richly toned fabrics, warm timber, and original artworks. Floor-to-ceiling windows in the deluxe rooms offer sweeping views of the city skyline, the Yarra River, or picturesque Port Phillip Bay. The better views, of course, come from the higher floors—15 to 29—so be a bit insistent when you book. All rooms come with spacious marble bathrooms complete with a spa and television, more than 40 in-room entertainment channels, and separate dressing rooms. $$$ 8 Whiteman St. (Clarendon St.), 03 9292 6666 / 1 800 811 653 in Australia, crowntowers.com.au

Grand Hotel • City Center • Grand (115 rms)

If you're a fan of the magnificent hotels of yesteryear, then you'll adore staying in one of the most imposing and impressive Victorian buildings in Melbourne. The structure dates from 1886, when it served as the headquarters of the Victorian Railways Commission. Its huge scale is epitomized in the sheer expanse of the long, high-ceilinged corridors with rich red Pullman-type carpets and mirrored walls, and some of the palatial two-story apartments, many of which span two levels. You have a choice of studio, one- to three-bedroom apartments, and executive suites to choose from. All of them have full kitchens, thick carpets, and comfortable beds. The large indoor pool and spa with retractable roof are excellent, as are the Mediterranean courtyard gardens, gym, sauna, and cozy Library Lounge Bar. The Café Grand Restaurant delivers local, organic, and seasonal produce to the table, while the adjacent Café Grand Piano Bar offers a relaxed ambience, with live blues and jazz to accompany your aperitif or nightcap.$$$ 33 Spencer St. (Flinders St.), 03 9611 4567 / 1 300 361 455 in Australia, grandhotelsofitel.com.au

Grand Hyatt Melbourne • City Center • Timeless (547 rms)

One of Melbourne's glitziest hotel towers is known for its huge, decadent lobby area, which features columns of rare tropical wood, and its fabulous views of the city and the Yarra River, visible even from the corridors as you await your elevator. Famous actors, royalty, tennis stars, and Grand Prix drivers regularly stay here, and even the most wealthy of them are surprised when they find out that the exterior windows look gold because they are sprayed with 26.4 pounds (12kg) of 24-karat gold dust. Among the room classifications, the best are the very large Grand Club rooms, which have a lounge area, Art Deco–inspired decor, amazing views, and a wonderful Italian marble bathroom. Stay in these and you also get access to the Grand Club room, which serves breakfast, light snacks, and evening canapés and cocktails. Also consider the Grand View King rooms, which are smaller but also offer fabulous views. Bar Deco, on Level 6, has one of the world's most expensive cocktails, based on a very nice bottle of French Champagne. It costs A$1,200, and you get to finish the bottle. To work it off, you have Australia's largest hotel gym on the premises, which offers spinning classes as well as yoga and Pilates. $$$$ 123 Collins St. (Russell St.), 03 9657 1234, melbourne.grand.hyatt.com

The Hatton • South Yarra • Timeless (20 rms)

Making functional and artistic use of a historic Italianate mansion, the Hatton blends plump balustrades, smooth waxed floorboards, stained-glass windows, generous verandas, and high ceilings with industrial-style stainless steel and sparkling glass. The hotel is decorated with antique tables, cupboards, chests, and decorative artwork. The predominantly neutral color scheme, interspersed with walls of orange and aubergine, allows the original architectural features to shine through. Lighting effects using colored gels create an almost theatrical atmosphere throughout the lobby area. The best rooms are the Superior rooms, which have a king-size bed, a plasma TV, antique furniture, and an enamel bathtub. Rooms at the front of the hotel overlook pretty Victorian terrace houses, and those at the back have views across the trees in the Botanic Gardens. Three superior rooms downstairs have their own private courtyards. $$ 65 Park St. (St. Kilda Rd.), 03 9868 4800, hatton.com.au

Hotel Lindrum • City Center • Modern (59 rms)

Reminiscent of New York's SoHo area, Flinders Lane is home to glamorous boutiques and some of the country's most respected labels, drawing fashion lovers and design students from across Australia. The boutique Hotel Lindrum, with its sleek interior design and a natural color scheme of muted browns and creams, is right at home here. Classic wood floors are combined with rich furnishings and muted lighting to create a chic sense of style. Deluxe rooms have panoramic views over the Botanic Gardens and the Melbourne Cricket Ground. A rich wool carpet is bordered by recycled timber, which carries through into the bathroom. There's even a pillow menu. $$ 26 Flinders St. (Spring St.), 03 9668 1111, hotellindrum.com.au

Langham Hotel Melbourne • Southbank • Timeless (387 rms)

Ask any taxi driver and he'll tell you that the Langham is the best hotel in Melbourne. A member of the Leading Hotels of the World, the Langham causes a stir in any refined soul. As soon as you enter through its expansive marble foyer and see the magnificent Waterford crystal chandelier hanging above a gracious water feature, you start to feel it. And it just gets better from here. Take the elevator or the classic central staircase up to the rooms and you'll find that many have panoramic views over the Yarra River. The best are the deluxe corner rooms, which look out across the river and the city skyline. Sumptuous gold fabrics and textiles create a warm and welcoming atmosphere and Italian marble bathrooms add to the exceptionally luxurious experience. The hotel's Chaun Spa is one of the best in the southern hemisphere. $$$$ 1 Southgate Ave. (City Rd.), 03 8696 8888, langhamhotels.com

Marque Hotel • St. Kilda • Trendy (80 rms)

It's well worth leaving the city center behind for a while and experiencing the trendy inner-city vibe and nightlife of St. Kilda. A hotel of choice is this boutique option, which defines itself by its simplicity rather than its attitude. The minimalist style is evident as soon as you enter the lobby and approach the compact, slanted marble reception desk, backlit with aqua-green wall panels. Deluxe rooms are a bit too simple to be really comfortable (though you probably won't spend much time there). They contain a bed, a few bits of modern furniture, and a TV in the corner—so go for the Executive Spa Suite, which is better furnished and looks out onto a small Zen garden. Play Rooms, which are circular, are more fun, and have a large spa bath right at the foot of the bed. The small Hub Bar downstairs has stools rather than chairs, and funky flamingo-pink lighting. Try the "seriously pinky" vodka. $$ 35-37 Fitzroy St. (Acland St.), 03 8530 8888 / 1 800 621 621 in Australia, rendezvoushotels.com

The Prince Hotel • St. Kilda • Trendy (39 rms)

Funky St. Kilda is blessed with one great designer hotel—the Prince. As soon as you enter the bright pink-lit lobby with its sweeping staircase, you know you're in for a groovy experience. The dark-paneled corridors lead to four room categories. The best of these, if you don't go for the suite, are the superior rooms. These come with a balcony overlooking busy Fitzroy Street, and are decorated in earthy hues and lit by tube lamps. Square bathtubs and sinks are designer additions to most bathrooms, and the rooms come with queen-size beds, Bose radios, and Loewe TVs. The Prince is home to Minc, a Berlin-style underground cocktail bar complete with muraled cabaret-style walls, half hidden behind heavy purple drapes. You'll find Circa here too. With its broad floorboards, white leather banquettes, and low wicker lamps, it's one of Melbourne's sexiest and most romantic restaurants. And for a relaxing massage treatment, step upstairs to the Aurora Spa Retreat. $$$ 2 Acland St. (Fitzroy St.), 03 9536 1111, theprince.com.au

Rialto Hotel • City Center • Grand (224 rms)

The intricate red and yellow brick Rialto Hotel is one of Melbourne's finest examples of fin de siècle architecture. For those unfamiliar with the term, it's french for "end of the century"—the 19th century in this case. Roughly, it refers to a type of design that expresses opulence and decadence, and in the Rialto Hotel's case this is evident in its façade of towers, arches, and exquisite brickwork. Needless to say, the opulence carries on inside its European-style interior, with its elegant, intimate, and comfortable common areas. French style and gold-flushed carpets and decor flow through the standard rooms, but deluxe rooms are bigger and you can ask for one with a Juliet balcony. All deluxe rooms overlook a magnificent nine-story atrium. Executive king rooms are bigger still, and have a lounge area too. The hotel is home to one of the city's chicest eateries, Café Rialto, which serves up European-inspired dishes. $$$ 495 Collins St. (Elizabeth St.), 03 9620 9111 / 1 800 331 330 in Australia, rialtohotel.com.au

Sofitel Melbourne • City Center • Timeless (363 rms)

This beautiful luxury five-star hotel is located at the so-called "Paris end" of Collins Street, which is a reference to the area's European architecture and upmarket boutiques. The guest rooms start on level 36 of the tower, with the lower levels filled with offices. The height ensures that every room has spectacular views of the city. Recently refurbished corner king rooms, located between floors 36 and 49 offer magnificent 180-degree views over Melbourne from two walls of floor-to-ceiling windows. A plasma-screen television comes standard. Superior king bayview rooms also have superb views over Melbourne and beyond, to Port Phillip Bay. The glass-topped 35th floor Atrium bar offers twinkling city lights, moody music, and intimate nests of lounges beneath soaring swathes of silver fabric. $$$ 25 Collins St. (Spring St.), 03 9653 0000 / 1 800 656 565 in Australia, sofitelmelbourne.com.au

Melbourne: The Restaurants

Ay Oriental Tea House • South Yarra • Yum Cha

David Zhou has a superb Chinese restaurant called David's just around the corner from the Oriental Tea House, but it's this unique business on one of Melbourne's main fashion drags that's getting all the attention. The Oriental Tea House serves yum cha—the Aussie equivalent of dim sum—all day (from traditional trolleys at peak times), matched with amazing tea and beautiful wine in a former pub, decorated with a strangely compelling mix of 1920s Shanghai chic and 1960s pop art. Tea-based cocktails and bamboo steamers full of prawn dumplings provide the perfect pick-me-up after a hard day's shopping, and if you like the tea, the shop at the front will happily sell you some. *Sun-Wed 10am-10pm, Thu 10am-11pm, Fri-Sat 10am-11:30pm.* $ 455 Chapel St. (Cliff St.), 03 9824 0128, orientalteahouse.com.au

Bar Lourinha • City Center • Spanish

Best Tapas Hip, sparse decor—patterned wallpaper, concrete floors, wooden bar—and seating that is limited to stools (at the bar and around two communal tables) focus the attention on the brilliantly tasty food and the edgy city crowd washing it down with manzanilla and tempranillo. The list of 20-plus small dishes runs from grilled lambs' tongues to lime-cured yellowfin tuna to sticky pork and coriander salad. Smart service, good tunes, and interesting art ensure a full house most nights. *Mon-Wed noon-11pm, Thu-Fri noon-1am, Sat 4pm-1am.* $$ 37 Little Collins St. (Meyers Pl.), 03 9663 7890, barlourinha.com.au

Becco* • City Center • Italian

Whether you choose to spend the night in Becco's terrazzo-floored, flatteringly lit bar working your way through the 20-plus wines by the glass and great range of bar snacks (chicken and veal-stuffed olives are a must), or decide on a full Italian feast in the split-level dining room, it will be a night well spent. Tucked down a lane in a beautifully preserved 1950s building, Becco's combination of well-groomed staff, attractive interior, and expertly cooked Italian food ensure a constantly buzzing space, full of businesspeople on the make, lovers on the smooch, and Italo-philes soaking up the Old Country vibe. *Mon-Sat noon-late.* $$$ 11-25 Crossley St. (Bourke St.), 03 9663 3000, becco.com.au

Belgian Beer Café Bluestone* • South Yarra • Pub Grub

A great outdoor area complete with barbecues makes this spot a favorite on sunny days. *See Melbourne Nightlife, p.220, for details.* $ 557 St. Kilda Rd. (Moubray St.), 03 9529 2899

The Botanical* • South Yarra • Australian

Best Brunches The Botanical can often seem like a club for the dyed, the enhanced, and the nipped-and-tucked, but there is nothing fake about its flavorful, expertly cooked food and its knee-weakening wine list. The sleek beige and blond wood dining room is designed so that everybody can watch everybody else, including the legions of chefs toiling in the open kitchen. The food—particularly the sublime poached egg with truffled polenta—is good enough to keep your attention firmly on your plate, even though the botanical garden is just across the street. After dinner, cocktail lovers head for the glam 1970s-themed Bubble Bar out back. *Mon-Fri 7-11:30am, noon-3pm, and 6-11pm, Sat-Sun 8-11:30am, 12:30-3pm, and 6-11pm.* $$ B ≡ 169 Domain Rd. (Millswyn St.), 03 9820 7888, thebotanical.com.au

Brunetti • Carlton • Cafe/Pasticceria

Spread over several storefronts in Melbourne's Italian heartland, Brunetti is a heaving Roman-style machine of a place, incorporating a cafe, restaurant, gelateria, and stunning pasticceria with gleaming glass cases full of traditional Italian cakes and pastries. Outside, the cluster of tables is jammed with beautiful Italian parents decked out in Prada, with their cute, Armani-clad offspring in tow. They down espresso and bomboloni while academics from nearby Melbourne University ponder philosophy and cappuccino froth. *Sun-Fri 6am-11pm, Sat 6am-midnight.* $ B ≡ 194-204 Faraday St. (Lygon St.), 03 9347 2801, brunetti.com.au

Café Di Stasio • St. Kilda • Italian

If you want to make like a Melbournite, a meal at Café Di Stasio is a must. The moodily lit, cozy cave atmosphere with its closely spaced, heavily draped tables, attended to by veteran waiters, is a favorite of locals great and small. Tales of hedonistic behavior from industry heavyweights and soap starlets abound. The solid Italian food is often great and almost always good, and there is a suitably impressive wine list to match. You may feel a bit neglected if there are well-loved regulars in the house, but the bonhomie is generally democratic and the experience never less than memorable—one way or another. *Daily noon-3pm and 6-11pm.* $$ ≡ 31 Fitzroy St. (Acland St.), 03 9525 3999

Canary Club* • City Center • Spanish

Best Tapas This split-level restaurant and lounge is one of the city center's hottest spots. Upstairs you'll find leather daybeds for lounging in a sleek mezzanine space, while downstairs there are tables and chairs in the bar area. In both spaces, there are accents of dark wood and lots of fashionable 20- and 30-somethings munching on the excellent tapas and drinking cocktails and Spanish beers. *Mon-Tue 4pm-1am, Wed-Sat 4pm-3am.* $$ ≡ 6 Melbourne Pl. (Little Collins St.), 03 9663 1983

Carlisle Wine Bar* • Balaclava • Italian

You could come to this long, dark wine bar just for a meal. The rustic Italian dishes (roasted rabbit, duck ragout, pan-fried gnocchi) are excellent and totally simpatico with the dimly lit, wood-paneled, continental cool of the place. But hang around after dinner and watch the Carlisle transform. The lights get lower, the music (from two turntables behind the bar) gets louder, and the room takes on a sexier vibe as it turns into a bar for grown-ups. There's a fantastic wine list. *Mon-Fri 3pm-1am, Sat-Sun 11am-1am.* $ ≡ 137 Carlisle St. (Camden St.), 03 9531 3222

Cicciolina* • St. Kilda • Italian

The tables are always full at this St. Kilda institution and there are no reservations, so be prepared to wait. Fortunately there's a glamorously scruffy bar in back with a jovial atmosphere that eases the pain of hanging out. When you're finally ushered into the dim bistro, with its scribbled specials boards, dark wood, and closely packed tables, the attentive staff and simple, inventive cooking (linguine with salmon and capers) begin to unravel the mystery of Cicciolina's popularity. An after-dinner nightcap back in the bar may make the attraction clearer. *Mon-Sat noon-11pm, Sun noon-10pm.* $ ≡ 130 Acland St. (Belford St.), 03 9525 3333

Circa • St. Kilda • Continental (G)

Best Fine Dining Housing a certifiably hip hotel, an edgy vodka bar, a live music venue, a day spa, and a rowdy, beer-swilling pub-style bar, the Prince is also home to one of Melbourne's finest restaurants. The dining room at Circa is a glamorously romantic space, popular with well-heeled hipsters, with white leather seating, wooden floors, wafting black and pink curtains, and dramatic spotlights. The food blends Old World technique with New World daring to create stunning dishes like smoked eel carpaccio with baby lettuce and gewürztraminer jelly. Desserts are particularly fine with the Circa "Snickers" being a standout. *Mon-Fri, Sun 7-11am, noon-3pm, and 6:30-10:30pm, Sat 7-11am and 6:30-10:30pm.* $$$ B ≡ The Prince, 2 Acland St. (Fitzroy St.), 03 9536 1122, circa.com.au

Comme* • City Center • Fusion

Best Always-Hot Restaurants One of the most stylish bars and restaurants in the city, Comme effortlessly combines beautiful ornate heritage features with clean modern architectural lines, vast spaces, and handsomely designed furniture. Comme Bar is to the right of the grand entrance stairway, across an expanse of white marble. It has excellent cocktails, clever bar snacks, and good-looking people lolling about on giant leather ottomans. Comme Kitchen is tucked behind the staircase, just a short stagger from the bar. It's a cozy and chic little room with a menu of Spanish and French dishes with a modern twist. *Mon-Fri noon-2:30pm and 6-10pm, Sat 6-10pm.* $ ≡ 7 Alfred Pl. (Collins St.), 03 9631 4000, comme.com.au

Cookie* • City Center • Thai

Cookie is a hot nightspot, but those in the know also flock here for great Thai food. *See Melbourne Nightlife, p.221, for details.* $ ≡ 252 Swanston St. (Lonsdale St.), 03 9663 7660

The Deanery • City Center • Modern Australian

Along with the fantastic, international wine list, the hulking cellar here shows that this is a place that's serious about wine, though in an ironic, young-and-hip kind of way that suits the designer surroundings of deconstructed wine barrels as wall decoration. The food is rustic and wine-friendly, and might include stuffed zucchini flowers or savory beef and duck dishes. On Fridays the place is packed and roaring, but other nights are calmer and more romantic. *Mon-Fri noon-late, Sat 6pm-late.* $$ B ≡ 13 Bligh Pl. (Flinders Pl.), 03 9629 5599, thedeanery.com.au

Donovan's* • St. Kilda • Mediterranean

Right on the beach, with superb views of Port Phillip Bay, Donovan's conjures the expensive, well-appointed, but wonderfully casual beach house that should be yours. Everything about this former bathers' pavilion is comfortable—from the upholstered chairs to the friendly service and menu of skillfully cooked food that offers both the simple (splendid fish and chips) and the intricate (stuffed baby squid with anchovy fritters). There is an amiable bar and lovely lounge area with an open fireplace for pre-dinner drinks, and, of course, there's St. Kilda beach for a post-dinner stroll. It's the perfect venue for make-believe millionaires. *Daily noon-late.* $$ ≡ 40 Jacka Blvd. (Cavell St.), 03 9534 8221, donovanshouse.com.au

European* • City Center • Continental

Best Brunches It has been said that three things sum up Melbourne: dark wood, red wine, and espresso, which perhaps makes European the quintessential Melbourne restaurant. It's a place that hums from breakfast through a nightcap, with often excellent food that takes its cues from rural France, Italy, and Spain. There's also an all-European wine list (a good excuse for keeping the well-informed, good-looking staff at your table). Inside, there's a black-and-white tiled floor and seating tucked into romantic nooks. The streetside cluster of tables is frequented by the stylish and beautiful of all ages, checking each other out over consistently excellent coffee and Campari-based cocktails. *Sun-Thu 7:30am-11pm, Fri-Sat 7:30am-midnight.* $$ ≡ 161 Spring St. (Bourke St.), 03 9654 0811

Ezard • City Center • Modern Australian (G)

The sleek, modern space in the basement of the hip Adelphi Hotel is a great place to check out Modern Australian cuisine. Owner-chef Teague Ezard loves big flavors, creative presentations, and specialty ingredients. His mainly Asian-influenced dishes give your tastebuds a workout with their salty-sweet-hot-sour-fishy combinations. The clean-lined room offers great visibility, so you can see what your well-heeled fellow diners are eating—and wearing. Spot-on service will not only help you with the difficult task of choosing the right wine for such genre-bending food, but can also guide you towards the perfect nearby bar for an after-dinner nightcap. *Mon-Fri noon-2:30pm and 6pm-late, Sat 6pm-late.* $$ ⊟ The Adelphi, 187 Flinders Ln. (Swanston St.), 03 9639 6811, ezard.com.au

Fifteen Melbourne • City Center • Continental

Like the original Fifteen in London, Fifteen Melbourne was conceived by Jamie Oliver and is part restaurant and part charity, taking in disadvantaged youth and training them to be chefs. It is a good idea and one that can make you feel virtuous just by ordering another course. The basement location with its open kitchen is a comfortably modern space, divided so you can do dark and moody or light and bright. The food is straightforward, Italian-style fare making the most of great ingredients—prosciutto, clams, octopus, lentils—and combining them with a minimum of fuss. Some of the execution can be a little clumsy, but any bumps with the food are smoothed over with an excellent wine list and knowledgeable, enthusiastic service. *Mon-Sat noon-3pm and 6-10pm.* $$ ⊟ 115 Little Collins St. (enter from George Parade), 1 300 799 415, fifteenmelbourne.com.au

Fog* • South Yarra • Modern Australian

Fog may look more like a nightclub than a restaurant, but once the food starts hitting the table you soon understand that there's substance behind the style. The cavernous, split-level dining room is decked out with dark walls and glossy black pillars, and has a central, catwalk-like strip of electric blue carpet down which you make your fabulous entrance. The food, from U.S. chef Jeremy Sutphin, is a pleasing mix of flavors that straddle continents (America, Europe, Asia) in clever, tasty combinations. A great little bar out back has a terrace with an open firepit for chilly nights and is a good pre- or post-dinner spot for mingling with skimpily clad young locals. *Tue-Fri noon-1am, Sat 10am-2am.* $$ ≡ 142 Greville St. (Grattan St.), 03 9521 3155, fog.com.au

Gertrude Street Enoteca* • Fitzroy • Italian

Small Italian plates complement a fine wine selection in this cosy and very stylish spot that's popular with a hip set. *See Melbourne Nightlife, p.223, for details.* $$ ⊟ 229 Gertrude St. (Smith St.), 03 9415 8262, gertrudestreetenoteca.com

Grossi Florentino* • City Center • Italian (G)

The three distinct parts of Grossi Florentino all add something to Melbourne's reputation as one of the best Italian food destinations outside of Italy. Upstairs is the big occasion restaurant, complete with gorgeous murals, chandeliers, heavy linen, and a lengthy, expensive menu dripping with beautifully handled lobster and truffles. Downstairs, there's the Grill, a stylish, Rat Pack–style joint with snappy energy and simply excellent food, or the more casual Cellar Bar, with moody lighting, Roman styling, and well-dressed city folk downing simple pasta, pastries, and good wine and coffee after a gallery opening or a theater premiere. *Restaurant: Mon-Fri noon-3pm, Mon-Sat 6-11pm; Grill: Mon-Sat noon-3pm and 6-11pm. Cellar Bar: Mon-Sat 7:30am-midnight.* $$ ≡ 80 Bourke St. (Exhibition St.), 03 9662 1811, grossiflorentino.com.au

I Carusi 2 • St. Kilda • Pizza

I Carusi 2 is the dictionary definition of the Modern Melbourne Pizza Joint (MMPJ). There is the pared-down back dining room—all wooden floors, big windows, and whitewashed walls with the only splash of color coming from a giant vintage poster advertising mopeds. There is the succinct Italian-dominated wine list and the studiously casual Italian-dominated staff. There is the hand-scribbled menu detailing ingredients on thin but chewy crusts. And there is the crowd of well-dressed young professionals, a few with their restaurant-savvy kids in tow, grabbing a good, quick bite. Simple, stylish, and tasty, I Carusi is everything an MMPJ should be. *Nightly 5-11pm.* $$ ≡ 231 Barkly St. (Blessington St.), 03 9593 6033

Interlude • Fitzroy • Continental

Tucked among Brunswick Street's retro-bohemian mix of cafes and bars, Interlude's carpeted floors, linen-swathed tables, and plushly upholstered banquettes appear strangely conservative—but the food is anything but. The menu is degustation-only, with 8, 11, or 25 tiny, elaborate, and often quite mad courses, many of them pilfered from U.S. groundbreakers like New York's WD-50. It all works, even when artichoke ice cream is teamed with balsamic vinegar and macadamia nuts, or Beluga caviar shares a bowl with chervil juice, oyster jelly, and lychees. Sit back and let the charming, enthusiastic staff guide you. Your experience will be enjoyable, crazy, and sometimes unbelievable. *Tue, Sat 6:30-10:30pm, Wed-Fri noon-3pm and 6:30-10:30pm.* $$$ – 211 Brunswick St. (Gertrude St.), 03 9415 7300, interlude.com.au

Journal* • City Center • Cafe

Who would think that the dusty, dark wooden shelves of a library could inspire one of the city's most popular and stylish cafes? At the crossroads of the Flinders Lane and Degraves Street cafe hub, where the young and stylish hunt for lunch, Journal's eclectic mix of wood and tiles, communal tables overhung with book shelves, and '70s retro armchairs somehow comes together to make this a great place for a simple lunch (rolls made to order, superb salads) or, later in the day, when the pace slows, a civilized and sexy venue for a glass of wine or two. *Mon-Fri 7am-late, Sat 7am-6pm.* $ ▯≡ Shop 1, 253 Flinders Ln. (Degrave St.), 03 9650 4399

Ladro • Fitzroy • Italian

You'll have to book ahead if you want to get your hands on what is arguably Melbourne's best pizza. This white-walled, concrete-floored restaurant is noisily packed to the rafters every night, its marble-topped tables heaving with a food-savvy urban crowd digging into gloriously thin and crispy pizzas topped with everything from olive paste to pork sausage to buffalo mozzarella. There are also rustically cooked roasts, homemade pasta, and heavenly risotto served by a flirt-worthy staff. An Italian-heavy wine list completes the smart and very popular scene. *Wed-Sun 6-11pm.* $$ 224 Gertrude St. (Smith St.), 03 9415 7575

Longrain* • City Center • Thai (G)

Best Always-Hot Restaurants Longrain has plugged a glaring hole in the Melbourne dining scene, offering bright and bouncy Thai flavors in a groovy warehouse setting to a grateful, quality-Thai-deprived public. An offshoot of the Sydney restaurant of the same name, Longrain has an eccentric seating policy built around communal tables and enforced waiting in the bar area at the back of the cavernous space. Fortunately the bar snacks and superb cocktails make the wait bearable, and the food, when you're finally seated, lives up to expectations. Superb green mango salad topped with crabmeat, or a mouth-watering caramelized pork hock, make Longrain a triumph of flavor over attitude. *Mon-Fri noon-2:30pm and 6-11pm, Sat 6-11pm.* $$ 44 Little Bourke St. (Spring St.), 03 9671 3151, longrain.com.au

Mario's • Fitzroy • Cafe

It has been 20 years since Mario's revolutionized the Melbourne cafe scene with all-day breakfasts, good service (courtesy of smart-mouthed waiters in vests and ties), and consistently good coffee. The retro-groovy formula has been so extensively copied that Mario's can seem like part of the norm. But it maintains its edge with excellent lasagna, hangover-busting spaghetti carbonara, and a nonchalantly cool vibe that attracts homegrown and international celebrities, who are left unmolested in the crowded space. Observed individually, nothing at Mario's—wine list, menu, decor—is particularly remarkable, but the sum of its parts adds up to something unique. *Sun-Wed 7am-midnight, Thu-Sat 7am-1am.* $$ 303 Brunswick St. (Johnson St.), 03 9417 3343

Melbourne Supper Club* • City Center • Continental

The entrance is an unmarked wooden door, and inside you'll find Melbourne's scenesters sipping swank drinks and munching on delicious snacks. *See Melbourne Nightlife, p.224, for details.* *Sun-Mon 8pm-4am, Tue-Thu 5pm-4am, Fri 5pm-6am, Sat 8pm-6am.* $ Level 1, 161 Spring St. (Bourke St.), 03 9654 6300

Mini • City Center • Greek

Mini is a modern Greek restaurant that channels the spirit of the taverna while managing to remain chic and exciting. Tucked down a dumpster-strewn lane, this split-level semi-basement joint with its terrazzo floor, groovy wooden furniture, and hanging chrome light fixtures has a buzzing energy most nights of the week that turns into a roar as the weekend hits. The food takes Greek staples—eggplant, feta, octopus—and turns them into wonderfully tasty dishes of various sizes, making this a good place for a snack or a fun night out. *Mon-Fri 8am-late, Sat 6pm-late.* $ 141 Flinders Ln. (enter from Oliver Ln.), 03 9650 8830, minirestaurant.com.au

Mirka at Tolarno Hotel • St. Kilda • Continental

Named for Mirka Mora, the artist responsible for the vibrant murals in the main dining room, Mirka at Tolarno is a revamped and revitalized version of a St. Kilda landmark that had lost its luster. A bucket of cash has been thrown at the place, which has not only restored and expanded the murals and replaced the kitchen, but added an art gallery at the back that doubles as a dining room and a very popular bar that is full to overflowing most nights with a crowd savvy about food and fashion. Classic Euro-inspired dishes are the order of the day—steak tartare, game bird terrine, paella, roast duck—matched with a wine list that is fond of European labels. The bar serves an excellent breakfast every morning. *Daily noon-midnight.* $ B≡ Hotel Tolarno, 42 Fitzroy St. (Canterbury Rd.), 03 9525 3088, mirkatolarno.com

MoVida* • City Center • Spanish

Best Tapas Like any self-respecting Spanish tapas bar, MoVida is tucked down a cobblestone lane with only an illuminated sign to mark its presence. It could ditch the sign and still attract the same crowd of young scenesters and seasoned city dwellers jostling for attention and space at the bar. For dining, tables should be booked at least a week in advance. The crowd is drawn in by the terra-cotta-hued rustic good looks, fantastic Spanish wine list, superbly tasty tapas, and undeniable buzz. Service can verge on the abrupt, but don't take it personally, and they won't either. *Sun-Mon noon-10pm, Tue-Sat noon-10:30pm.* $$ ≡ 1 Hosier Ln. (Flinders Ln.), 03 9663 3038, movida.com.au

Observatory Cafe • South Yarra • Cafe

Nestled among the historic observatory buildings at the main entrance to the Royal Botanic Gardens, Observatory Cafe is the perfect pit stop during, or starting point before, a stroll through the gorgeous gardens. There's a fantastic mix of indoor and outdoor seating, all of which make the most of the view—whether you are in one of the glasshouse-like interiors, under an umbrella in the vast forecourt, or tucked among herbs and tomatoes in the kitchen garden out back. You have to line up to order, but the wait is worth it and the coffee is surprisingly consistent given the inevitable crush on sunny days. *Daily 7am-5pm.* $ B▯≡ Royal Botanic Gardens, Birdwood Ave. (Dallas Brooks Dr.), 03 9650 5600

The Panama* • Fitzroy • Continental

Best Always-Hot Restaurants The Panama is hidden up two flights of rickety stairs, but your adventurousness is rewarded with entrance to a huge loft space possessing floor-to-ceiling arched windows (with fabulous urban views) and a gaggle of sophisticated bohemians. There is good European-style bistro food to be had in the "Dining Room"—think classic coq au vin and charcuterie—while the rest of the wooden-floored acreage is given over to a retro-loungey bar, complete with a short, smart Euro-centric wine list, laid-back DJs, and a pool table. *Wed-Sat 6:30-10:30pm.* $$ ≡ Level 3, 231 Smith St. (Moor St.), 03 9417 7663

Pearl • Richmond • Modern Australian (G)

Best Brunches Pearl is one of Australia's best restaurants, providing a superb snapshot of modern haute-Australian cooking. The stark white room, softened by shimmering opalescent lights and an acoustically correct black rubber floor, is constantly filled with a fashion-conscious crowd enjoying the spectacle of some of Melbourne's best waiters serving some of its best cuisine. Owner-chef Geoff Lindsay appropriates flavors from Asia, the Middle East, and beyond, shaping superb ingredients into works of art—flecked with gold, surrounded by rose petals, or tufted with Iranian fairy floss. *Daily 9am-3pm and 6-11pm.* $$ B≡ 631-633 Church St. (Howard St.), 03 9421 4599, pearlrestaurant.com.au

Pelican* • St. Kilda • Tapas Bar

Pelican has transformed this once-overlooked street corner into a vibrant hub. The visionaries behind the Melbourne Supper Club teamed up with the famed designers of Meyer's Place and Public to create this architectural innovation. A wraparound terrace makes it an indoor-outdoor spot, drawing in St. Kilda's brightest young things. Giant portholes cut into slatted timber walls give peeks into other areas, while gas heaters and cozy nooks mean that nippy nights are as pleasurable on the deck as they are inside. The use of recycled wood and stained-glass paneling gives the bar and dining area charm. Communal tables and benches are perfect for easy socializing. Top dishes include delectable Spanish mussels, spicy meatballs, char-grilled sardines and octopus, and roast vegetables. *Daily 7:30am-1am.* $ 16 Fitzroy St. (Park St.), 03 9525 5847

Punch Lane • City Center • Continental

With its wooden floors, red leather armchairs, and rowdy, convivial atmosphere, Punch Lane feels like a bar where everybody knows your name, even on your first visit. It's a flexible place, where you feel as comfortable popping in for a glass of wine accompanied by some tapas or charcuterie as you do settling in for a long, three-course meal. Tables are tightly packed—but relax and you may find yourself in conversation with the friendly folks next to you and end up ordering another bottle of wine just because it feels like you're in the right place at the right time. *Mon-Fri noon-11pm, Sat-Sun 5:30-11pm.* $$$ 43 Little Bourke St. (Punch Ln.), 03 9639 4944, punchlane.com.au

Rockpool • Southbank • Modern Australian

The southern branch of the internationally acclaimed Rockpool in Sydney, this outpost may be a more straightforward kind of place, but, in sticking to cooking brilliant ingredients simply and with great skill, it has quickly become one of the hottest tickets in town. The huge restaurant with its high ceilings, wood and stone features, and open kitchen certainly makes a sizeable impression and has suitably big prices to match. Steak plays a big part on the menu here—all dry aged—but the seafood is also among the best in the city and, similarly, the wine list and service keep standards up. River and city views and the flash and dazzle of the casino add to Rockpool's distinctive buzz. *Sun-Fri noon-3pm and 6-11pm, Sat 6-11pm.* $$ Crown Complex, Southgate, 03 8648 1900, rockpoolmelbourne.com

Shoya* • City Center • Japanese (G)

Shoya is like a high-quality department store for Japanese food, a big, heaving, multi-level joint that does a lot of things surprisingly well. There's a barbecue area where you can grill your own morsels, a sushi bar, an à la carte restaurant, private karaoke rooms, and a sleek lounge on the top floor. You wouldn't come here for crack service—all those different areas seem to confuse things—but the quality and artistry of the sashimi, the great range of sake, and the sense of fun and excitement make it well worth a visit. *Mon-Thu noon-2:30pm and 6-10:30pm, Fri 6-11pm, Sat noon-2:30pm and 6-11pm, Sun 6-10:30pm.* $ 25 Market Ln. (Bourke St.), 03 9650 0848, shoyamelbourne.com

Stokehouse* • St. Kilda • Mediterranean

The Stokehouse gets checks in all the right boxes—interesting, tasty food, wonderful wine list, attentive service, elegantly casual room, great views—but such a list does not do justice to just how marvelous lunch upstairs on the wide outside terrace overlooking Port Phillip Bay on a sunny day can make you feel. At night, the wood-floored dining room turns romantic as lights sparkle on the water outside and the full, buzzy room hums like a well-oiled, hedonistic machine. Downstairs, the cafe bar churns out pizza and pasta to young funsters but it's upstairs that remains the definitive Melbourne experience. *Daily noon-3pm and 6-10pm.* $$ ≡ 30 Jacka Blvd. (Cavell St.), 03 9525 5555, stokehouse.com.au

Supper Inn • City Center • Chinese

Supper Inn has been packing them in for 25 years. At first glance, you may wonder why. Tucked up a dingy flight of stairs in a lane off the main Chinatown drag, the dining room is all wood-veneer paneling, pink vertical blinds, and bare tables with plastic chopsticks and thimble-sized wine glasses. But it's the wonderfully tasty, mostly Cantonese food, coupled with a late closing time, that lures famished hospitality workers and post-gig revelers to happily line up on the stairs for their chance to get their lips around superb congee, suckling pig, spicy quail, and hot-and-sour soup. Abrupt service and glaring lighting add to the no-frills experience. *Nightly 5:30pm-2:30am.* $$ ≡ 15 Celestial Ave. (Little Bourke St.), 03 9663 4759

Syracuse* • City Center • Mediterranean

Is this Melbourne's most romantic room? With high ceilings, ornate arches, marble tabletops, and tangled labyrinth of mismatched wooden furniture, Syracuse is the sort of place that whispers sweet nothings, even if you're here with your grandmother. But granny might find the young besuited business crowd a little noisy, the lengthy wine list too confusing, and the light a little too dim for her liking. At lunchtime, there is a more structured approach to food, while at night tapas and snacks are on order as ties get loosened and wine flows. *Mon-Fri 7:30am-11pm, Sat 6pm-late.* $$ B≡ 23 Bank Pl. (Little Collins St.), 03 9670 1777

Taxi Dining Room • City Center • Fusion (G)

Best Fine Dining Not only does Taxi have the best river and city views in town—through soaring expanses of glass—but it offers equally exciting food. It's a combination of traditional Japanese flavors and classic European cooking influenced by Asia, completing a culinary circle. The sleek dining room with its lofty ceiling conjures a chic 1960s airport lounge aesthetic, and the buzz of the crowd of bright young things and seasoned diners certainly helps the room take flight. Spunky wait staff lift the experience, as does a lengthy wine list featuring a remarkable selection of sake. After dinner, head upstairs to Transit bar for cocktails and caviar into the wee hours. *Daily noon-3pm and 6-10:30pm.* $$$ B≡ Transport Hotel, Level 1, 2 Swanston St. (Flinders Ln.), 03 9654 8808, transporthotel.com.au

Three, One, Two • Carlton • Modern Australian (G)

Some would argue that Andrew McConnell is Melbourne's best chef, and a visit to his chic restaurant may have you agreeing. McConnell's food is not only fabulously tasty but is also beautiful to look at, and the composition of each artful dish can have you gasping before you've taken a bite. Relaxed and assured staff deliver each plate with the fervor of the converted, explaining, for example, how an intricate plate of cured, smoked, and pickled fish has been created. The crowd is as serious and arty as the food, but the atmosphere is relaxed and the overall experience quite blissful. *Tue-Sat 9am-3pm and 6:30-10:30pm, Sun 9am-3pm.* $$$ – 312 Drummond St. (Faraday St.), 03 9347 3312, 312.com.au

Tutto Bene • Southbank • Italian

There are many reasons to love Tutto Bene—from the excellent balcony views of the city across the Yarra River to the house-made gelati—but the best reason is the risotto. Owner-chef Simon Humble is a regular (and successful) invitee to risotto cooking competitions in Italy. The lengthy list of stirred-to-order arborio rice dishes here will have you joining the cheer squad. Add some classic Italian dishes that do veal and duck just right and you have an excellent venue for a long lunch on a sunny day, or a fortifying feast before your bar crawl. *Daily 10am-late.* $$$ Mid Level, Southgate Promenade (Southgate Ave.), 03 9696 3334, tuttobene.com.au

Vlado's • Richmond • Steak House

Vlado's is a Melbourne institution that has been packing 'em in for more than 40 years. The reason? The meat. There's nothing special about the decor or the desserts, but in this male-dominated crowd, who cares? Especially when you can watch the man himself—Vlado Gregurek—working the grill like a maestro, churning out perfectly cooked, excellent cuts of steak that reveal the reason for the restaurant's longevity at first chew. *Mon-Fri noon-3:30pm and 6-11pm, Sat 6-11pm.* $$$ 61 Bridge Rd. (Normanby Pl.), 03 9428 5833

Vue de Monde • City Center • French (G)

Best Fine Dining Vue de monde is one of the few Melbourne restaurants that can aspire to "gastro-temple" status. All the details are in place—superb French cutlery and glassware, heavy linen, staggeringly expensive wine list, impeccable service—but the spare room, with its bare wooden floors and unadorned walls, make this a modern, unstuffy version of a fine diner. Owner-chef Shannon Bennett looks like a rock star, and his witty, cheeky take on classic French food—offered as degustation-only at night—has a certain rock sensibility itself. There are nightly offerings of foie gras, waygu beef, and white truffles. A not-to-be-missed experience for the food explorer. *Tue-Fri noon-2:30pm and 6:30-9:30pm, Sat 6:30-9:30pm.* $$$$ 430 Little Collins St. (Bank Pl.), 03 9691 3888, vuedemonde.com.au

Wall Two 80 • St. Kilda • Cafe

Known to its fans as the Wall, this tiny, crowded, hipster cafe delivers some of the best coffee in town from its pulpit-like counter. There is a communal laid-back vibe to the place that comes partly from its admirably calm staff and diminutive size, and partly from its mixture of shared tables and bench seating. Prime position on nice days is on an outside bench against a sun-warmed wall, the perfect spot to read the paper while watching bohemians and business types happily while away the time. There are plenty of soup-and-sandwich cafe staples to choose from. *Daily 6:30am-6pm.* $ Rear 280 Carlisle St. (Nelson St.), 03 9593 8280, wallcoffee.com.au

Yu-u • City Center • Japanese

Don't waste your time trying to find Yu u if you don't have a reservation. This ultra-cool Tokyo-esque basement joint, with its graffiti-strewn entrance, is full most nights and it turns the unbooked away. Secure a table and you'll be in for a fine time, particularly if you score one of the armchairs at the low-slung concrete bar. There's no sushi, but the sashimi is excellent, as is the yakitori, cooked to order by traditionally dressed staff on a smoky grill behind the bar. The atmosphere is industrial and dimly lit. It's a perfect starting-point for a night on the town. *Mon-Fri noon-2:15pm and 6-9:30pm.* $$ 137 Flinders Ln. (Russell St.), 03 9639 7073

Melbourne: The Nightlife

Becco* • City Center • Restaurant/Bar

A stylish place to dine on excellent Italian, or while away the hours in the bar. *See Melbourne Restaurants, p.210, for details.* 11-25 Crossley St. (Bourke St.), 03 9663 3000, becco.com.au

Belgian Beer Café Bluestone* • South Yarra • Beer Garden

Best Outdoor Drinking Spots Lazy afternoons in spring and summer bring beer drinkers out in droves. If you're one, there's no better place to congregate than on the lawns of Belgian Beer Cafe. Conversations buzz along with live jazz, blues, soul, or Latin tunes. The outdoor bar and bratwurst-laden barbecue save you from trekking indoors. With a large selection of Belgian brews on tap and 23 bottled varieties, there's bound to be more than one that suits your tastes. In the wintry months, retreat into the hallowed halls. The bluestone walls are timber-paneled and the perimeter is sectioned into welcoming booths. Hungry? Do as the Belgians do, enjoy a pot of "moules et frites" (mussels and fries). Other authentic satisfiers include Flemish beef stew, or veal and pork sausages on "stoemp" mash with vegetables and bacon. *Mon-Fri 8am-1am, Sat 11am-1am, Sun 11am-11pm.* 557 St. Kilda Rd. (Moubray St.), 03 9529 2899

The Botanical* • South Yarra • Restaurant/Bar

Looking across to the glorious Royal Botanic Gardens, the Botanical has an enviable position in the heart of blue-blood Melbourne. Its Bubble Bar is a study in sophistication, and Champagne cocktails are a specialty here. The Raspberry and Vanilla Bellini is a sparkling little number whose fresh berries are liquor-laced with vanilla, while the Sin Fizz hides her effervescent slap of French brut behind a kiss of lychee. *See Melbourne Restaurants, p.210, for details.* *Mon-Fri 7-11:30am, noon-3pm, and 6-11pm, Sat-Sun 8-11:30am, 12:30-3pm, and 6-11pm.* 169 Domain Rd. (Millswyn St.), 03 9820 7888, thebotanical.com.au

Boutique • Prahran • Nightclub

Best Hot Club Scenes If a clothes boutique is small, exclusive, and reassuringly expensive by definition, apply that description to this tiny but opulent club to get a sense of its vibe. It is appropriately named given that it sits above the upscale fashion and retro-cool stores that line Greville Street. The sleek, sumptuous interior is geared to seduction and excess. Thursdays you'll run amok with lush university students. Chic chicks and laughing lads make Boutique their own on Fridays. And on Saturdays, you might find that a mature conversation bubbles over another glass of the finest French. *Thu-Sat 9pm-4am.* C 134 Greville St. (Graten St.), 03 9525 2322, boutique.net.au

Canary Club* • City Center • Restaurant/Lounge

This split level restaurant and lounge is one of the city center's hottest spots, with a tapas menu to make your mouth water. *See Melbourne Restaurants, p.211, for details.* *Mon-Tue 4pm-1am, Wed-Sat 4pm-3am.* 6 Melbourne Pl. (Little Collins St.), 03 9663 1983

Carlisle Wine Bar* • Balaclava • Restaurant/Bar

The rustic Italian food here is just as good as the wine—stop by for dinner or just a bottle and a snack. *See Melbourne Restaurants, p.211, for details. Mon-Fri 3pm-1am, Sat-Sun 11am-1am.* ≡ 137 Carlisle St. (Camden St.), 03 9531 3222

Cicciolina* • St. Kilda • Cocktail Bar

Another study in sumptuous interiors, Cicciolina's cozy back bar welcomes those waiting for a table in the always-hot bistro. Locals are keen to keep this bolt-hole a secret, with good reason. Horseshoe-shaped booths are perfect for groups of friends, or you might dare to share one with people you don't yet know. *See Melbourne Restaurants, p.211, for details.* ≡ 130 Acland St. (Belford St.), 03 9525 3333

Comme* • City Center • Restaurant/Lounge

This sleek spot draws local style-setters in droves for cocktails and dinner. *See Melbourne Restaurants, p.212, for details.* ≡ 7 Alfred Pl. (Collins St.), 03 9631 4000, comme.com.au

Cookie* • City Center • Restaurant/Bar

Cookie's winning recipe is the fusion of beer barn and busy bistro serving authentic Thai food at affordable prices. Head up a couple of flights of marble stairs and you'll be greeted by a bouncer ready to usher you into the rising din. Since opening, this large Euro-style space has won many devotees among design students from the neighboring universities as well as slick suits from the corporate sphere. The vibe positively buzzes as the week wears on, becoming electric by the weekend. If you need a slightly quieter nook to converse in, there's an almost-secret annex behind the bar. Others may prefer to gravitate to the slim balconies that look over Swanston Street for a dose of fresh air. *Daily noon-11pm.* ≡ 252 Swanston St. (Lonsdale St.), 03 9663 7660

The Corner Hotel Rooftop Bar • Richmond • Bar

Best Summer View Bars Rock gods, pop icons, folk heroes, and rappers unite with their devotees at The Corner. This landmark vies with the Prince for the title of epicenter of Melbourne's live-music scene. The Corner's bandroom has played host to Australia's best acts as well as the gamut of indie international acts from as far afield as Iceland and Sweden. Head to the website for gig listings and sign up for the newsletter for the latest lowdowns. Next door, the public bar is an unpretentious locale with its fair share of resident barflies and smart young things who are happy to chill out or play pool all evening. But what you're really here for is the roof: Upstairs, the beer garden is becoming a summer magnet. While it has just been renovated, the rooftop retains its downbeat feel with recycled timbers, sandblasted brickwork, and exposed steel girders. Grab a jug of lager, sit back, and watch the sky darken as trains roll into and out of Richmond Station. *Mon-Sat noon-3am, Sun noon-1am.* ≡ 57 Swan St. (Stewart St.), 03 9427 7300, cornerhotel.com

Donovan's* • St. Kilda • Restaurant/Bar

Donovan's is a beachfront favorite, perfect for a cocktail and a sunset, or a lingering meal. *See Melbourne Restaurants, p.212, for details.* ≡ 40 Jacka Blvd. (Cavell St.), 03 9534 8221, donovanshouse.com.au

Double Happiness and New Gold Mountain • City Center • Bar

Best Winter Bolt-hole Bars At the top end of Chinatown, Double Happiness is creating its own cultural revolution. The tunes are hip and the cocktails are Far East of ordinary. On any given night, a cool frat of design, art, and media types chats over several elixirs. Espresso Martinis and Miss Chao's Suicide—an apple-ginger vodka martini—are a great way to kick-start any evening here. Settle in with Mr. Fu—a long drink made with chili-infused vodka, ginger ale, fresh coriander, and lime—or a Dictatorship of the Proletariat for a punchy variation on the Bloody Mary theme. Like the names of the drinks, Double's decor has a China-under-Mao flavor with communist propaganda posters lining the walls and good luck charms tucked into any available nook behind the bar. The gas fire does an admirable job of banishing the winter chill, and bottle-lockers keep regulars coming back for more. True to form, the bar snacks veer toward Asian influences, with steamed dumplings or a delivery of super-fresh Japanese dishes from the neighboring restaurant Kappo Okita to sate your hunger. Upstairs is the lush lounge New Gold Mountain, a contemporary twist on Shanghai's opium dens. *Double Happiness: Mon-Wed 5pm-1am, Thu 5pm-3am, Fri 4:30pm-3am, Sat 6pm-3am, Sun 6pm-1am. New Gold Mountain: Nightly 5pm-5am.* 21 Liverpool Ln. (Bourke St.), 03 9650 4488, double-happiness.org

The Esplanade Hotel • St. Kilda • Nightclub

Best Hot Club Scenes "The Espy" is an institution. It's a self-proclaimed "great white magnet" that attracts punters from all walks of life. Music fuels their souls and the kitchen feeds starving students, struggling artists, and under-nourished rockers. Hailing from the 1930s when it took the dress-circle position overlooking the bay from the palm-lined Upper Esplanade, this grand old lady has witnessed all aspects of St. Kilda's bohemian revelry. Though it's sprawling, there's no room for pretense here. Super-sized Maori bouncers give posers a suspiciously long glance and are truly equipped to ensure there's no trouble inside. The front bar boasts a once-gracious staircase and ubiquitous sticky carpet. Bands and comedians keep everyone entertained. Venture further and you find the poolroom and Gershwin Room, which play host to a wealth of local and international music acts. *Sun-Thu noon-1am, Fri-Sat noon-3am.* 11 Upper Esplanade (Victoria St.), 03 9534 0211, espy.com.au

European* • City Center • Restaurant/Bar

It's all dark wood and sophistication at this classic spot, making it perfect for a nightcap or an afternoon glass of wine. *See Melbourne Restaurants, p.212, for details.* 161 Spring St. (Bourke St.), 03 9654 0811

Fog* • South Yarra • Restaurant/Lounge

This buzzing continental spot feels more like a club than a restaurant, making it a perfect spot for a night on the town. *See Melbourne Restaurants, p.213, for details.* 142 Greville St. (Grattan St.), 03 9521 3155, fog.com.au

The George Hotel • St. Kilda • Bar/Nightclub

The operators behind the George smartly realized that one of the keys to success in St. Kilda is diversification. Under one umbrella you'll find five distinct bars, each with its own personality. Patrons gravitate to the spot that best suits their clothes. The Melbourne Wine Room is a tiled echo chamber that gets loud, brash, and ultra-busy on Friday and Saturday nights when burly blokes scope out the ladies ordering more and more bubbles. The Birdcage sushi spot is an annex for pre-drinking diners who lap up sake and plum wines, while the White Room attracts dress-up dolls and fancy guys out to posh it up. The Georges Lane Back Bar and Gallery is a haven for those wanting to avoid the scene-stealers in the other bars. If none of those strike your fancy, there's always the grunge-fueled Snake Pit that hints at the seedier side of St. Kilda's colorful history. Join the rail-thin smokers in tight jeans at the bar, play pool, or amuse yourself by guessing travelers' accents. *Wine Room Bar: Mon-Thu 3pm-1am, Fri-Sun 12:30pm-2am. Georges Lane Bar: Mon-Thu 6pm-1am, Fri-Sun 7pm-2am.* C ≡ 125-129 Fitzroy St. (Grey St.), 03 9525 5599

Gertrude Street Enoteca* • Fitzroy • Wine Bar

Since it opened a few years ago, this wine bar has quickly charmed its way into the hearts of the food- and vino-loving folks north of the city. Step inside and you'll be greeted with that rare form of friendly, knowledgeable hospitality that will have you tasting your way through an astounding array of wines from Australia, New Zealand, and Europe. The walls of the inner sanctum are sectioned with floor-to-ceiling nooks displaying hundreds of wines. Small tables and booth seating make the bar a lively place where locals stop in for a glass or two. Outside there's an olive-grove courtyard perfect for hiding out on warmer evenings. One co-owner's Italian origins are reflected in the antipasto platters laden with aged air-dried wagyu beef, melt-in-your-mouth prosciutto, pork terrine, and taleggio and pecorino cheeses. Enoteca also operates as a wine shop, which is ultra-convenient if you're here waiting for a designer pizza from Ladro opposite. *Mon-Tue 8am-9:30pm, Wed 8am-11pm, Thu–Sat 8am-midnight.* – 229 Gertrude St. (Smith St.), 03 9415 8262, gertrudestreetenoteca.com

Gin Palace • City Center • Cocktail Bar

Best Winter Bolt-hole Bars With its tucked-away location and discreetly signed entry ("GP"), Gin Palace feels like a secret. It doesn't matter that the secret has been out for close to a decade. Secluded alcoves, antique couches, and petite table settings give Gin Palace its baroque elegance. Subtle lighting and extraordinary service by the uniformed bar staff contribute to the unmistakably seductive ambience. You can stop in for a drink with the after-work crew, but the ideal way to enjoy this bar is to come for a sterling martini, settle into the rich velvet upholstery, and stay late. It's worth taking time to sample the array of spirits that glint behind the bar. Gin Palace lives up to its name with some 18 varieties on offer. Try the '51 for an award-winning twist on the classic martini—dry gin swirled into a Cointreau-glazed glass and garnished with anchovy-stuffed olives. *Nightly 4pm-3am.* – 190 Little Collins St. (Russell Pl.), 03 9654 0533

Grossi Florentino* • City Center • Restaurant/Lounge

This multi-level spot offers up excellent Italian to an artsy set that frequents the nearby galleries. *See Melbourne Restaurants, p.214, for details.* ≡ 80 Bourke St. (Exhibition St.), 03 9662 1811, grossiflorentino.com.au

Journal* • City Center • Restaurant/Bar

Local professionals of the creative and hip type love Journal for a bite to eat or a cocktail after work. *See Melbourne Restaurants, p.214, for details.* ≡ Shop 1, 253 Flinders Ln. (Degrave St.), 03 9650 4399

Longrain* • City Center • Restaurant/Lounge

Melbourne's hottest Thai restaurant has an equally hot lounge scene of a fashionable set waiting for tables and munching bar food. *See Melbourne Restaurants, p.215, for details.* *Mon-Fri noon-2:30pm and 6-11pm, Sat 6-11pm.* ≡ 44 Little Bourke St. (Spring St.), 03 9671 3151, longrain.com.au

Madame Brussels • City Center • Cocktail Bar

Best Summer View Bars When you feel like moving up in the world, head to Madame Brussels'. Her generous north-facing terrace is dressed with Old World white wrought-iron garden settings. The well-versed staff hints at the possibility of trolleys laden with oysters shucked to order for guests to sup with French champagne, or pitchers of Pimms garnished with lashings of mint, orange, and cucumber certain to quench your thirst on warm afternoons. Follow the winding path inside and you'll find yourself in a faux lawn–lined haven. This is a bar where you can converse and cavort in fine company. Ms. Brussels herself would approve—this notorious madam was romantically linked to the Duke of Edinburgh when he visited Melbourne in 1867, and her aristocratic inclinations inform the decor and ambience of this elevated bar. *Mon-Sat 4-11pm, Sun noon-11pm.* – Level 3, 59 Bourke St. (Spring St.), 03 9662 2775, madamebrussels.com

Melbourne Supper Club* • City Center • Wine Bar

Best After-Hours Scenes Upstairs from the European is a bar that's a world apart. Well-worn Chesterfield lounge suites, timber paneling, Cuban cigars, and a veritable tome of a wine list—that extends from $8 sauvignon blancs to $2,000 magnums of Krug—make the Supper Club perfect for intimate conversation or massive celebrations. It's become the favored haunt of Melbourne's night owls, who love the laid-back tunes, gentleman's club atmosphere, and quick-draw service. The best seats in the house are beneath an enormous arch window that has a privileged view over Parliament House and St. Patrick's Cathedral. As the name suggests, Supper Club offers a selection of small plates at all hours. Lamb meatballs, duck terrines, smoked salmon blinis, and a cheese plate can add up to a substantial meal. Even the ham and cheese toasties are anything but ordinary. *Mon-Thu 5pm-4am, Fri-Sun 7pm-5am.* C≡ Level 1, 161 Spring St. (Bourke St.), 03 9654 6300

Meyers Place • City Center • Bar

Best Winter Bolt-hole Bars If Melbourne is famous for its tucked-away bars, this is the one that started it all. Meyers Place is an unsigned bolt-hole with a downbeat charm. It gets busy on Thursdays and Fridays as the after-work thirst kicks in. Luckily, spillover into the lane is allowed. The architects who made their mark with this bar definitely made the most of a tight space. Timber finishes, a cut-concrete bar, and shag-pile wall panels create a comfort zone in which you immediately feel at ease. *Mon 5pm-2am, Tue-Thu 5pm-3am, Fri 4pm-4am, Sat 5pm-4am, Sun 5pm-1am.* ≡ 20 Meyers Pl. (Bourke St.), 03 9650 8609

MoVida* • City Center • Restaurant/Bar

Spanish wines and tapas draw in a sophisticated, stylish crowd at this city center hot spot. *See Melbourne Restaurants, p.216, for details.* ≡ 1 Hosier Ln. (Flinders Ln.), 03 9663 3038, movida.com.au

The Panama* • Fitzroy • Restaurant/Bar

This retro lounge is a favorite for locals to relax with a drink and a bite to eat. *See Melbourne Restaurants, p.216, for details.* ≡ Level 3, 231 Smith St. (Moor St.), 03 9417 7663

Pelican* • St. Kilda • Restaurant/Lounge

Cocktails, wine, beer, and tapas are the order of the evening in this cozy spot with a wrap-around patio—a favorite of St. Kilda hipsters. *See Melbourne Restaurants, p.217, for details. Daily 7:30am-1am.* ≡ 16 Fitzroy St. (Park St.), 03 9525 5847

Polly • Fitzroy • Cocktail Bar

If you have an aversion to grunge, bypass all the cafes, bars, and souvlaki joints on Brunswick Street and head straight for Polly. This opulent space is swathed in Moulin Rouge sex appeal. Crimson velvet drapes and antique chaises lounges seem to hail from French parlors, while the oversize tropical aquarium adds a mesmerizing glow to the low boudoir lighting. There's a monumental cocktail list, and just making your first selection could take all night. Take a risk by hinting at your favorite flavors and letting the bartender invent an original for you. On weekends, Polly positively roars with enthusiastic chatter from the jostling crowd of chic and savvy 20- and 30-somethings. Weeknights, there's more of a conversational hum with locals getting cozy and sipping their elaborate cocktails. *Tue-Sat 5pm-1am, Sun 4-11pm.* ≡ 401 Brunswick St. (Westgarth St.), 03 9417 0880, pollybar.com.au

Pony Club • City Center • Lounge/Live Music

Best After-Hours Scenes Pony Club is not for the faint-hearted. Not that it's all whips and spurs, but this is a punchy joint that serves up lashings of post-rock and post-punk noise along with basic spirits and brews. Inside, red walls are lined with pony portraits and hunt scenes. Downstairs, retro lamps provide just enough light so you can find a spot on Nanna's old couches, and the tunes are old-school familiar. Upstairs, live acts with big amps and guitars bring black-clad kids onto the dance floor for an addled take on the spinning and wheeling that's usually reserved for whirling dervishes. Hop on, it'll be quite a ride. And the rocking horse won't stop until 7am. *Tue-Thu 6pm-late, Fri-Sun 5pm-7am.* ≡ 68 Little Collins St. (Westwood Pl.), 03 9662 1026, pony.net.au

The Prince Bandroom • St. Kilda • Live Music

Best Hot Club Scenes The Prince is an icon. The hit list of international and local acts that play the Prince Bandroom is legendary and about as diverse as it gets. Brit-pop, post-rock, death metal, electronica, hip-hop, iconic rap, and everything in between gets a shot at lifting the roof here. On the musical menu you'll find the likes of Franz Ferdinand, De La Soul, Scissor Sisters, Radio Birdman, Wolfmother, Resin Dogs, Bright Eyes, RJD2, DJ Krush, Grandmaster Flash, Blackalicious and even Hate Breed. It's also one of the best acoustically tuned venues, which means you'll enjoy the sonic excursions even more. Beyond bands, Saturday nights are devoted to club-hounds (and puppies) who wag their tails to the DJ's mix of happy house and bop-laden beats. For an ounce of respite, head to the balcony or back room where lounge-lovers enjoy everything at their own pace. *Pub and lounge bars daily noon-1am; Band Room select weeknights 8pm-1am, weekends 8pm-3am, Sat 9pm-6am.* C≡ The Prince, 29 Fitzroy St. (Acland St.), 03 9536 1168, princebandroom.com.au

Revolver Upstairs • Prahran • Lounge

Best After-Hours Scenes Revolver Upstairs has a seedy allure. This warehouse space was reclaimed from post-industrial extinction and has been the surrogate lounge-room of die-hard party people for over ten years. It's an institution, and one that is completely anti-establishment. Glamour doesn't live here, so only visit if you're looking for a dose of cheeky, twisted fun. The smaller front bar is where you'll find live performances. In the cavernous back bar, poster art lines the walls. The space is low-lit by upside-down lamps and the pinpoints of smoldering cigarettes. Banks of couches are life support for the never-go-home crowd. There's no dance floor but everyone's happy to shimmy in the aisles near the DJs who are busy spinning the latest underground grooves. *Mon-Thu noon-3am, Fri noon-Sat noon, Sat 5pm-Sun noon, Sun 5pm-6am.* ≡ Level 1, 229 Chapel St. (Anchor Pl.), 03 9521 5985, revolverupstairs.com.au

Riverland • City Center • Lounge

Sitting riverside below Federation Square, Riverland cleverly mixes indoor and outdoor space with a myriad of seating options (picnic benches overlooking the water, plywood-clad nooks inside the historic bluestone vaults, tables for two under trees) and great views of the city framed by the gracefully curved undersides of bridges. Gas heaters keep the outside spaces viable even on chilly nights, and a great variety of bar snacks (including barbecued organic sausages with sauerkraut served on a bun) helps soak up the quantities of alcohol that a session by the river seems to require. Riverland attracts a crowd that morphs from city workers during the day to post-cinema, pre-gig hipsters at night. *Daily 7am-midnight.* ≡ Vaults 1-9, Federation Wharf (under Princes Bridge), 03 9662 1771, riverlandbar.com

Shoya* • City Center • Restaurant/Lounge (G)

Karaoke and sake. Really, what more do you need to know? *See Melbourne Restaurants, p.217, for details.* ≡ 25 Market Ln. (Bourke St.), 03 9650 0848, shoyamelbourne.com

Stokehouse* • St. Kilda • Restaurant/Bar

Right on the water in St. Kilda, this multi-level spot has a perfect patio for watching the sun set with a cocktail in hand. *See Melbourne Restaurants, p.217, for details.* ≡ 30 Jacka Blvd. (Cavell St.), 03 9525 5555, stokehouse.com.au

Syracuse* • City Center • Restaurant/Bar

A long (and complex) wine list and Mediterranean nibbles makes this a great, central spot for a night out or a cocktail. *See Melbourne Restaurants, p.218, for details.* ≡ 23 Bank Pl. (Little Collins St.), 03 9670 1777

Transit Lounge Garden • City Center • Lounge

Best Summer View Bars At last, Melbourne's bars are embracing the high-life. Transit Lounge Garden gets it right with a third-story space above the Taxi Dining Room. The interior is filled with modern Chesterfields and the generous terrace enjoys expansive views across the Yarra, Southbank, the city skyline, and the gardens. On warm nights this is the place to be. The service is slick and knowledgeable, which helps when navigating the extensive wine and spirits list. Cocktails are inspired by premium drops and the restaurant's fresh ingredients. Instrumental acts strike up on weekends, giving Transit the air of a '40s or '50s jazz club and attracting a discerning set of connoisseurs and sophisticates. *Nightly 6pm-4am.* Transport Hotel, Level 3, Federation Square (Princes Bridge), 03 9654 8808, transporthotel.com.au

Transport • City Center • Beer Garden

Best Outdoor Drinking Spots Transport reinvents the concept of the traditional corner pub by creating an open, airy space with splash-down surfaces and seating installations that take their cue from hard-wearing street furniture. There's no sticky carpet here. And it's big, bold, and noisy to boot. At full tilt, 650 bodies can drink together here, so bring your mates or get ready to make some new ones. The architects have put everything on display, including the mezzanine-level keg room and the beer lines that run down Deco-style sculptural loops of stainless steel. *Mon-Thu noon-1am, Fri-Sun noon-3am.* Federation Square (Princes Bridge), 03 9654 8808, transporthotel.com.au

Tusk Back Bar • Windsor • Bar

You'd be forgiven for thinking you've stepped into a French courtesan's boudoir when you find the petite Back Bar. Tucked just behind the main drag of Chapel Street, it cultivates its own society of luxe-loving 20- and 30-somethings who make themselves at home in the opulent interior of antique furnishings, velvet drapery, gilded mirrors, embossed wallpaper, and pressed-metal ceilings. Mood lighting and seductive tunes set the conversational vibe. On chilly nights, there's a glowing open fire. *Sun-Wed 7pm-1am, Thu-Sat 7pm-3am.* 67 Green St. (Chapel St.), 03 9529 7899, backbar.com.au

The Vineyard • St. Kilda • Beer Garden

Best Outdoor Drinking Spots Smart operators have transformed this once-forlorn steak restaurant into the pumping heart of St. Kilda. And like that vital organ, the Vineyard never seems to stop. Cute kids, cool cats and late-loving locals are attracted to the pulse of this place. A large al fresco seating area makes the most of the prime position beside Luna Park's rickety roller-coaster and the palm-filled O'Donnell Gardens. You can camp at this hot spot morning, noon, and night. Bands play on Thursday nights. The door dudes get strict as the floor space fills, so it's best to arrive earlier if you're looking to stay late. *Daily 9am-3am.* 71a Acland St. (Shakespeare Grove), 03 9534 1942

Melbourne: The Attractions

Alice Euphemia • City Center • Shop

With its off-street location in the Nicholas Building arcade, Alice Euphemia is a fashion find devoted to the best of Australian and New Zealand designers. The range of labels is always evolving and the lines are forward-thinking and original. Each tends to have a personality that attracts a following. Gwendolynne's antique lace dresses, Gorman's boating style, Jain's eclecticism, Obus's schoolgirl tailoring—all found favor here. Now there's a new crop of top talent in store. *Mon-Fri 10am-6pm, Sat 10-5pm.* Shop 6, 37 Swanston St. (Flinders Ln.), 03 9650 4300, aliceeuphemia.com

Assin • City Center • Shop

The name might mean "like so," but it could just as easily be short for fashion assassin—signaling death to slavish loyalty to trends. Long live style with substance! By stocking eminent labels exclusively in Melbourne, Assin has created devoted fans for nouveau-cool brands Marni, Viktor & Rolf, Project Alabama, and Hussein Chalayan. The shoes and accessories are a step ahead, too. The window displays don't give much away, but it's worth descending into the chasm of this basement boutique. *Mon-Thu 10am-6pm, Fri 10am-7pm, Sat 10am-5pm, Sun noon-5pm.* 138 Little Collins St. (Exhibition St.), 03 9654 0158, assin.com.au

Aurora Spa Retreat • St. Kilda • Spa

If you're staying at the Prince Hotel in St. Kilda, or even if you're not, then take the spiral staircase that curves through the intimate foyer of this premier spa retreat and head up to a lounge area warmed by dappled light filtered through external patterned screens. Among the treatments on offer is the Aurora's signature "Kitya Karnu." While you lie in the steam room you get smothered in a blend of essential oils. This is followed by a desert salt exfoliation, the placement of cool river stones over the meridian lines of your body, and a facial cleanse. Then it's on to a hair treatment and a scalp massage. The actor Geoffrey Rush loves this place, and so do Melbourne's ladies of leisure, so make sure you book a place well in advance. The hotel offers stay and spa packages. *Tue-Thu 10am-9pm, Mon and Fri 10am-8pm, Sat 9am-6pm, and Sun 10am-5pm.* $$$$ The Prince Hotel, 2 Acland St. (Fitzroy St.), 03 9536 1130, aurorasparetreat.com

Australian Centre for Contemporary Art (ACCA) • Southbank • Art Museum

Best Culture The first thing you notice about this building is that it seems to be a rusting hulk, which it is. The exterior looks like a shipping container, and the lack of a paint surface plus the abundant scratched graffiti, courtesy of the local youth, could make it seem like an eyesore. But this is art, so bring it on. The gallery is relatively small and split into several spaces, and usually there's a theme to what's showing. Exhibits change regularly, but you can always expect things to tease your mind, in a post-modernist sort of way. In all, it acts as Melbourne's fun park of strange aesthetics and fantasy. *Mon 10am-5pm (by appointment only), Tue-Fri 10am-5pm, Sat and Sun 11am-6pm.* $ 111 Sturt St. (Grant St.), 03 9697 9999, accaonline.org.au

Chapel Street Bazaar • Prahran • Market

This maze of stalls is brimful of retro wares big and small that can help you recapture whatever era you remember most fondly. Step back in time to admire everything from 1940s to 1970s furniture to cut glassware, Bakelite bits and bobs, veiled hats, silk gloves, old school threads, monster sunglasses, toy car collections, and racks of vinyl LPs. It's a treasure trove extraordinaire. *Mon-Fri 10am-5:30pm.* 217-223 Chapel St. (High St.), 03 9529 1727

Chiodo • City Center • Shop

This cavernous space boasts a post-industrial aesthetic where cut concrete, exposed steel, and gloss finishes collide. Inside, labels include Comme des Garçons, Fred Perry, and Adidas Y-3. The eponymous menswear label includes limited-edition printed T-shirts, dress shirts embellished with unusual details, knits and pants to give the modern man a distinctively urbane style. *Mon-Thu 10am-6pm, Fri 10am-7pm, Sat 10am-5pm.* 114 Russell St. (Little Collins St.), 03 9663 0044, chiodo.net.au

Christensen Copenhagen • City Center • Shop

Danes and design are synonymous. With its gloss-white interior, this boutique brings a touch of Scandinavian cool to Melbourne. Inside, fine accessories complement the mainstay of stylish day wear and party frocks. Seasonal selections are carefully curated to step ahead of the current looks. Its range extends to cult Euro labels such as Missoni, Paul & Joe, Petit Bateau, Matthew Williamson, and Burberry. *Mon-Fri 10am-6pm, Sat 10am-5pm.* QV2, 17-19 Albert Coates Ln. (Swanston St.), 03 9650 7130, christensencopenhagen.com.au

Christine • City Center • Shop

Christine Barro puts accessories on a pedestal, and her shop is revered for her attention to such fashionable details. At the entrance, a slim-lined vitrine displaying three exquisite pieces is enough to pique the interest of any sophisticate. Head down the tartan-carpeted stairs and into the red-walled chamber. The space is reminiscent of Chinese lacquer cabinets, a fitting treasure trove for Sonia Rykiel accessories, Anya Hindmarsh totes, Luella handbags, Etro tops, and many more fancy finds. *Mon 10am-5pm, Tue-Fri 10am-6pm, Sat 10-5pm.* 181 Flinders Ln. (Lush Ln.), 03 9654 2011

Chuan Spa • Southgate • Spa

Transport yourself to a dreamy state of relaxation at the best spa in Melbourne, named for the Chinese word for water. Treatments here center around Chinese medicine and the five elements. The space is not large, but it's well laid out and very serene. Often you'll find yourself sharing space with only a few other patrons, especially in off hours. If you love spending money on your body, then try the three-hour Serenity Shen treatment, which begins with a signature stone therapy massage, followed by a long soak in a private geisha tub. Next, the ultimate facial indulgence awaits, with essential oils and a revitalizing cool marine algae mask, followed by herbal tea in your private suite. As well as a range of treatments, massages, and facials for both men and women, the spa has a wonderful half-moon hot pool overlooking the city and Federation Square, and a tranquil lap pool below a glass dome. There's a well-equipped gym here, and the spa runs yoga, Pilates, and tai chi classes. *Mon-Sat 10am-8pm, Sun 10am-6pm.* $$$$ Langham Hotel, 1 Southgate Ave. (City Rd.), 03 8696 8111, chuanspa.com

Collette Dinnigan • South Yarra • Shop

Our Collette. As one of Australia's most celebrated fashion designers, Dinnigan shines in the international spotlight with catwalk shows in Paris and a Chelsea boutique in London. Her designs are quintessentially feminine. Floaty, sensuous silks shimmer with intricate hand beading and embroidery. The use of exquisite vintage lace and antique fabrics gives the evening gowns an Old World glamour that stars like Cate Blanchett and Nicole Kidman epitomize on the red carpet. *Mon-Fri 10am-6pm, Sat 10am-5pm.* 553 Chapel St. (Toorak Rd.), 03 9827 2111, collettedinnigan.com

e.g. etal • City Center • Shop

This shop is home to the work of the cream of the crop of local contemporary jewelers. Window exhibitions put the focus on a particular designer, but inside more than 50 makers are represented. Some concentrate on finding innovative ways to interpret gold, silver, and platinum. Others experiment with form and texture through nontraditional materials such as resins, spun recycled plastic bags, and found fragments. You'll find pieces that are challenging, thought-provoking, individual, exquisite, and whimsical. If you're taken by a designer's style but can't find the perfect piece, have a chat about commissioning your heart's desire. *Mon-Thu 10am-6pm, Fri 10am-7pm, Sat 10am-5pm.* 185 Little Collins St. (Russell St.), 03 9663 4334, egetal.com.au

Fat 272 • City Center • Shop

Like Alice Euphemia, Fat is a hub for local design talent. The labels and accessories here often inspire cult followings, like the bracelets and necklaces fashioned from budgie tags. The emphasis lies mostly in unusual offbeat street wear, but you'll also find dress-up pieces and smart jackets that take casual up a notch to cool. *Mon-Thu 10am-6pm, Fri 10am-7pm, Sat 10am-6pm, Sun 10am-5pm.* 272 Chapel St. (Chatham St.), 03 9510 2311, fat4.com

Federation Square • City Center • Site

Best Culture Fans of inventive and funky architecture will be impressed by Melbourne's relatively new city square, located on the edge of the Yarra River and across the road from Flinders Street Station. The place was made possible by reducing the number of railway lines running parallel to the Yarra River from 53 to 12, and by demolishing a couple of ugly gas and fuel towers in the mid-1990s. The resulting civic space is a large, irregular, open piazza cobbled with misshapen paving stones and bordered by a conglomerate of buildings encased in strangely reflective, industrial-style geometric designs. You'll find the Ian Potter Centre: NGV Australia; the Australian Centre for the Moving Image (ACMI), Champions Australian Racing Museum and Hall of Fame (about racehorses), the National Design Centre, and several restaurants and bars. Flinders St. (Swanston St.), federationsquare.com.au

Gallery Gabrielle Pizzi • City Center • Art Gallery

The late Gabrielle Pizzi was perhaps Australia's most passionate collector and exhibitor of Aboriginal artwork. This was a woman who championed contemporary indigenous artists and promoted their work here and abroad, heralding an international appreciation and market force that continues today. The gallery still carries her name and philosophy, representing artists from the communities of Balgo Hills, Papunya, Utopia, Maningrida, Haasts Bluff, and the Tiwi Islands, as well as work by the most innovative city-based painters, photographers, video artists, and installation artists. *Tue-Fri 10am-5pm, Sat 11am-4pm.* Level 3, 75-77 Flinders Ln. (Exhibition St.), 03 9654 2944, gabriellepizzi.com.au

Geisha • City Center • Spa

Experience the calm and delicate ways of the Geisha spa, set in a unique Japanese environment perfect for soothing the senses. A team of hair stylists, masseurs, and treatment specialists has set up base in this calming, tatami-matted, paper-walled haven. Slip into a Japanese robe, sip tea in the traditional tearoom, and let your mind and body bathe in sound, aroma, and sensuality. Take some time out to enjoy the most indulgent and complete treatment, Tengoku, a five-hour therapy that includes a relaxation massage, a hair and scalp massage, and a sushi lunch. If you're feeling a little sore after your journey to the Land Down Under, then opt for a shiatsu massage, the traditional Japanese deep-tissue technique. *Tue-Wed 11am-7pm, Thu 11am-8pm, Fri 11am-9pm, Sat 9am-6pm.* $$$$ 1st Floor, 285 Little Collins St. (Elizabeth St.), 03 9663 5544, geishaonline.com

Gorman • Fitzroy • Shop

It's a relief to find Gorman among the retro stores and street wear that crowds Brunswick Street's sidewalks. The corner shop has an inviting atmosphere with a Scandinavian twist. Lisa Gorman has been doing it her way since 1999, and her casual styles range from golf-inspired to reminiscent of a school sports-day social to winter warmers that you could wear mushroom-picking in Siberia. This young designer always favors natural fibers—cotton, wool, cashmere—as well as leather and sheepskin, and finds intriguing ways to add details that make her designs stand out from the crowd. *Mon-Thu 10am-6pm, Fri 10am-7pm, Sat 10am-6pm, Sun 11am-5pm.* 235 Brunswick St. (Bell St.), 03 9419 5999, gorman.ws

Harrolds • City Center • Shop

Harrolds aims a cut above when it comes to menswear. The upstairs area in this newly revamped emporium is appointed like a gentleman's club, complete with marble bar and wait staff. In the late afternoon, consider the cut, cloth, and color of a new suit over a single-malt scotch or a gin and tonic. Bespoke tailoring is a specialty. Downstairs you'll find an impressive array of shirting, casual attire, accessories, perfumes, and toiletries. *Mon-Thu 9:30am-6:30pm, Fri 9:30am-7:30pm, Sat 10am-5pm, Sun 11:30am-5pm.* 101 Collins St. (Exhibition St.), 03 8660 7888, harrolds.com.au

Husk • City Center • Shop

It's a small world after all—inside the jewel-box of a shop called Husk. Bohemian treasures from the four corners of the globe fill the niches, vitrines, and racks. Moroccan leather wares, trinkets and glass, accessories for home and body, scented and spiced parfums and toiletries sit alongside men's and women's wear sourced from Australia to Scandinavia. Go on! Try something on, if only to find your way to the changing rooms via the forest of faceted mirrors. *Mon-Fri 10am-6pm, Sat-Sun 11am-5pm.* 176 Collins St. (Swanston St.), 03 9663 0655, husk.com.au

Le Louvre • City Center • Shop

Le Louvre may well be the reason that the top of Collins Street is still known as "the Paris end" of town. Fabulously dressed windows hint at the opulent delights within, but there are no clothes on display inside. Established in 1922 as Melbourne's first French salon–style boutique, Le Louvre stays true to form with appointment-only showings. Once you arrive for a private viewing, you'll be invited to take a seat on a gilded chaise and designs will be brought down for your consideration. The collections include the latest from European couturiers—designs you'll find nowhere else in Australia. *Mon-Sat by appointment.* 74 Collins St. (Exhibition St.), 03 9650 1300

Little Salon • Fitzroy • Shop

Little Salon is just that, a small store that is a cross between a shop and gallery. In its arched window you'll spy the wares of mostly local creatives and designers. There are ceramics as fine as a lace doily and acrylic jewelry in appealing motifs such as baby fawns, prancing ponies, swallows, and doves. Handbags and purses sit above two racks of one-off clothing. This is the perfect place to find unique gifts for your favorite people. *Mon-Thu 10am-6pm, Fri 10am-7pm, Sat 10am-6pm, Sun 11am-5pm.* 71 Gertrude St. (Fitzroy St.), 03 9419 7123

The Melbourne Cricket Ground • Richmond • Site/Sport

The Melbourne Cricket Ground, or the MCG, as it's more commonly known, was the main site for the 1956 Melbourne Olympics and the 2006 Commonwealth Games. A cultural icon, the MCG rivals Lords in England as one of the two most important cricket grounds in the world. It also hosts Australian Rules football (AFL) games and major rock concerts. The stadium, which can seat around 100,000, has been a sporting mecca since the first buildings went up in 1854. Soon after, the first games of Australian Rules football were played here, after the cricketer T.W. Wills, a former captain of the famous Rugby school's cricket and rugby teams in the UK, invented the game. He saw it as a way to keep cricketers fit during winter. As well as regular AFL matches, the stadium hosts the Grand Final in late September each year. The Boxing Day Test is the one you should try to get tickets for if you are interested in seeing some international cricket. *Tours of the MCG take place several times a day on non-match days.* $$ Brunton Ave. (Jolimont St.), 03 9657 8888, mcg.org.au

Melbourne Aquarium • Queen's Wharf • Tour

If you missed out on diving with the sharks in Sydney, then you can do it here. Even novice divers get to climb into the enormous shark tank and scuba-dive among gray nurse sharks, seven gill sharks, giant rays, and thousands of fish. An added attraction is a glass-bottom boat ride on the surface, where you can get up close to the monsters of the deep. You can also explore under the surface of Victoria's bays, estuaries, and rivers in the habitats area. A highlight is the floor-to-ceiling coral atoll, housing hundreds of fish straight from the Great Barrier Reef—but beware, there are lots of kids and chaos here. *Mon-Sun 9:30am-5pm.* $$ Queens Wharf, Flinders St. (Kings St.), 03 9620 0999, melbourneaquarium.com.au

Melbourne by Balloon • City Center • Tour

Up, up, and away! The sight of a bright yellow hot-air balloon riding the currents over the city center is an odd vision from the ground, but imagine the views you get from the basket. The hour-long flight takes off around dawn, when the wind is usually the most gentle, and the balloon floats right over the city center and out into the suburbs. The only noise is the occasional burst of flame from the burners, and the surprised cry of a solitary seagull or two. One of the great things about ballooning is that even people who are scared of heights can do it, because the lack of connection with the ground convinces the mind that all is well. The experience starts and ends at the Grand Hyatt Melbourne, and the hotel puts on a gourmet champagne breakfast to celebrate your return. *Daily hours vary.* $$ Grand Hyatt, 41 Dover St. (Russell St.), 03 9427 7596, hotairballooning.com.au

Melbourne Museum • Carlton • Cultural Museum

The modernist, interactive Melbourne Museum is the largest museum complex in the southern hemisphere. Spread over six huge levels, half of which are below ground, the museum draws on the latest technology to give an insight into Australia's flora, fauna, and culture. Highlights include Bunjilaka, an award-winning Aboriginal and Torres Strait Islander cultural center, which houses the most comprehensive collections of local indigenous artifacts in the world. Another striking exhibit is the Forest Gallery, a living interpretation of Victoria's tall temperate forests. It features around 80,000 plants, as well as snakes, birds, fish, and frogs. Other great attractions include a real blue whale skeleton and a fabulous insect and butterfly collection. There are lots of real-life exhibits, too. *Daily 10am-5pm.* 11 Nicholson St. (Gertrude St.), 03 8341 7777, melbourne.museum.vic.gov.au

Melbourne Zoo • Parkville • Zoo

The best, and oldest, zoo in Australia contains more than 350 animal species from around the world. Although Melbournites consistently claim that it is the oldest zoo in the world, that honor belongs to London Zoo, which opened to the public in 1847—Melbourne is actually the 11th oldest, having opened in 1862. Among the best exhibits are the butterfly house, a free-flight aviary of Australian native birds, and a lowland gorilla exhibition. An Australian section houses kangaroos, wallabies, emus, platypus, and koalas. Worth checking out are the Twilight series of summer concerts, which take place here on Friday, Saturday, and Sunday evenings from roughly January 5 to February 26. Bring some champagne and a picnic. *Daily 9am-5pm.* $ Elliot Ave. (Flemington Rd.), 03 9285 9300, melbournezoo.com.au

National Gallery of Victoria: Ian Potter Centre • City Center • Art Museum

This gallery features more Australian art on permanent display than any other in the world. Spanning from the colonial period to the present, the collection has more than 20,000 works, with 800 on display at any time. The most famous piece of artwork is *The Shearing of the Rams*, by Tom Roberts, which was painted between 1888 and 1890. Other important works are by Sidney Nolan and Russell Drysdale, and a large collection of Aboriginal art also takes pride of place. Exhibitions are changed frequently to show the full breadth and diversity of the collection. *Tue-Sun 10am-5pm.* Federation Square (Flinders St.), 03 8662 1555, ngv.vic.gov.au

National Gallery of Victoria International (NGV) • Southbank • Art Museum

Best Culture Mario Bellini, a leading Italian architect and designer, is responsible for the masterpiece redesign of this gallery. The lighting is perfect, and the high ceilings and open spaces show off the works in all their glory. The gallery has one the most comprehensive collections of international artworks in Australia. Among the regulars are four works each by Constable and Gainsborough, three each by Turner and Rubens, and two by Rembrandt. Traveling exhibitions include such recent showcases as Rembrandt and Pissarro masterpieces. A nice cafe and the high-quality Garden Restaurant are also on the premises. *Wed-Mon 10am-5pm.* 180 St. Kilda Rd. (Southbank Blvd.), 03 8620 2222, ngv.vic.gov.au

Nicola Finetti • City Center • Shop

Like Akira, Nicola Finetti is an Australian designer par excellence. Sensual and modern, he swapped architecture for fashion to enjoy more immediacy of creative expression, and it shows in every one of his signature styles. His evening collections are red-carpet favorites, featuring dresses worked in delicate fabrics, layers, and detail. The diffusion line is anchored in harder contrast fabrics—denims, tweeds, wool—with bold, textural details. *Mon-Fri 10am-6pm, Sat 10am-5pm.* QV2 17-19 Albert Coates Ln. (Swanston St.), 03 9663 7886, nicolafinetti.com

Old Melbourne Gaol • City Center • Site/Tour

Built between 1841 and 1864, the cramped Old Melbourne Gaol was used to accommodate short-term prisoners, lunatics, and some of the colony's most notorious criminals, including the famous bush ranger Ned Kelly, who was hung here on November 11, 1880. The scaffold where Ned Kelly was strung up is on display, as is his gun and a suit of armor worn by one of his gang. In all, 135 people swung from the gallows here. One of the spookiest displays is a set of chilling death masks. During World War II, the gaol was briefly reopened as a military detention barracks for Australian, German, Italian, and American military prisoners. You can lock yourself in a tiny cell if you want, or take part in a hair-raising night tour—it's reported to be haunted. *Daily 9:30am-5pm. Night tours at various times, check schedule.* $ Russell St. (Victoria St.), 03 9663 7228

Rippon Lea House Museum and Historic Garden • Elstenwick • Site

Just 5 miles (8km) from the city center is one of the most impressive grand old Victorian houses in the country. It was built in 1868 by socialite Sir Frederick Thomas Sargood and dedicated to his mother, Emma Rippon. Lea is an old English word for meadow. The house has dozens of rooms decked out in original furniture and artworks, and out in the grounds there are stables and outhouses. The 13 acres of landscaped gardens are a special highlight, and include a conservatory, a lake, a lookout tower, extensive flower beds and shrubbery, and an orchard. *Daily 10am-5pm.* $ 192 Hotham St. (Gleneira Rd.), 03 9523 6095

Royal Botanic Gardens • South Yarra • Site

Melbourne's cool winters and hot summers resemble the climate of much of California, which results in perfect growing conditions for a vast range of plants. These gardens are by far the largest in Australia. Large grassy expanses give way to intimate plantings of everything from succulents to rainforest. Enter the mysterious world of the Fern Gully, where you can follow a stream through displays of lush tree ferns, visit an enchanting herb garden, and see a range of eucalyptus and thousands of deciduous trees that burst into color in the fall. Around 28,000 gray-headed flying foxes (very large bats) live here, and you can see them roosting overhead at several points in the park. *Daily 7:30am-6pm (hours change by season).* Birdwood Ave. (Domain Rd.), 03 9252 2300, rbg.vic.gov.au

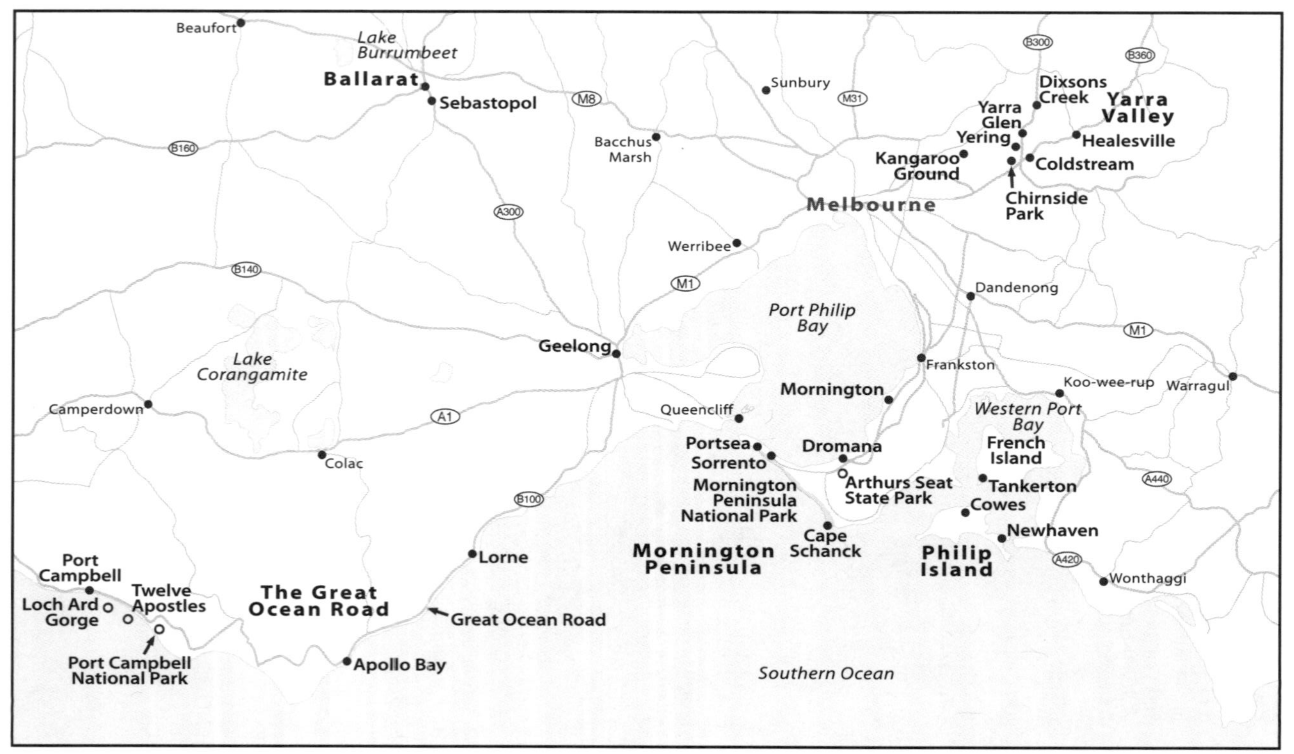
Beaufort
Lake Burrumbeet
Ballarat
Sebastopol
Sunbury
Dixsons Creek
Yarra Valley
Yarra Glen
Yering
Healesville
Kangaroo Ground
Coldstream
Chirnside Park
Bacchus Marsh
Melbourne
Werribee
Dandenong
Port Philip Bay
Geelong
Lake Corangamite
Frankston
Camperdown
Mornington
Koo-wee-rup
Warragul
Queencliff
Western Port Bay
French Island
Portsea
Sorrento
Dromana
Colac
Arthurs Seat State Park
Tankerton
Mornington Peninsula National Park
Cowes
Newhaven
Cape Schanck
Mornington Peninsula
Philip Island
Lorne
Wonthaggi
Port Campbell
Twelve Apostles
The Great Ocean Road
Loch Ard Gorge
Great Ocean Road
Port Campbell National Park
Apollo Bay
Southern Ocean
B300
B360
M8
M31
B160
A300
B140
M1
A1
B100
A440
A420

LEAVING MELBOURNE

When you've had your fill of urban fun, it's time to head out of town. From the cooling hills of the Blue Mountains to wine tasting in Hunter Valley, from watching fairy penguins on Phillip Island and exploring the old gold-mining town of Ballarat, to driving along the most scenic road in Australia, drinking wine in the Yarra Valley and going wild in the Mornington Peninsula, there is something that will please and astonish every visitor. As well as listing the best things to see when you get there, we list the best hotels and places to eat, and fill you in on the most fabulous places to pick up a cool ale or a cocktail.

Ballarat

Hot Tip: The Eureka Ballarat Pass includes unlimited entry to most of the area's attractions.

The Lowdown: Victoria's largest inland city, with a population of around 90,000, was the site of the Victorian gold rush, which kicked off in 1851 after prospectors found gold nuggets strewn across the ground. Within a year 20,000 people, including many from China, had flocked to the area to try to strike it rich. The rush lasted until the 1860s, with some larger operators staying on site until the end of the First World War. The wealth created here is evident in the fine historic buildings that line Ballarat's streets. Of more importance than gold, though, are the political events that unfolded here. Soon after the gold rush started, the government arrived with a plan to issue month-long licenses, which had to be paid even if no gold was found. Each month you needed a new, and costly license, and the government enforcers used brutal methods to extract the money from you. Resentment peaked in 1854, when prospectors began demanding political reforms, including the right to vote, secret ballots, and parliamentary elections. When the owner of the Eureka Hotel murdered a miner, the place exploded. Some 20,000 miners joined forces, burning down the hotel, and erected their own revolutionary flag above a stockade. The stockade was attacked at dawn and 24 miners were killed. Still, the revolt resulted in cheaper fees—and the vote.

Best Attractions

Ballarat Fine Art Gallery Come here to see the original Eureka Flag as well as a good collection of Australian art from artists such as Sydney Nolan, Russell Drysdale, and Fred Williams. 40 Lydiard St., 03 5320 5858

Blood on the Southern Cross A breathtaking sound and light show takes you through one of the most important events in Australia's history. Sovereign Hill, Bradshaw St., 03 5337 1199

Eureka Stockade Centre Multimedia displays take you through the Eureka Rebellion above the site of the original miners' stockade. Eureka St., 03 5333 1854

The Gold Museum Like gold? Then come and see some of the largest nuggets found at Ballarat, as well as displays on the history of gold mining in the area. Bradshaw St., 03 5337 1107

Sovereign Hill Australia's best outdoor museum features a whole reconstructed gold-rush town complete with actors dressed in period costumes, a Victorian school, horse-drawn carriages, and blacksmiths. Bradshaw St., 03 5337 1100, sovereignhill.com.au

Best Restaurants

Agostinos Come here for fine Italian food including seafood, chicken dishes, pizza, and pastas dished up inside a pleasant woody interior. $ 8 Victoria St., 03 5333 3655

The Boatshed Restaurant Perched on the edge of a lake, the Boatshed offers European cuisine with an Italian bent, and watery views from an outdoor terrace. $ 27a Lake Wendouree Foreshaw, 03 5333 5533

The Bonshaw Restaurant You'll find this farm-based eatery just a five-minute drive from the center of Ballarat. Refined food, including kangaroo fillet and rack of lamb, is served up in a tranquil rural environment. $$ Corner of Tait and Smythesdale Sts., Sebastopol, 03 5335 8346

Best Nightlife

Irish Murphy's Typical Irish pub with Guinness on tap and live bands most nights. 36 Sturt St., 03 5331 4091

Lake View Hotel Pleasant historic pub with good food and panoramic lake views. 22 Wendouree Parade, 03 5331 4592

Sturt Street Blues Blues fans will love this atmospheric music venue. It hosts local acts every night. Corner of Sturt and Dove Sts., 03 5332 3676

Best Hotels

Ballarat Miners Cottages For something different, stay at one of two small, renovated cottages. The best is Carrigg House, a three-bedroom gem with a spa. $$ 36 Glazebrook St., 0418 131 545 (mobile), ballarat.com/minerscottages

Ballarat Heritage Homestay Five individual Victorian and Edwardian cottages lend a feeling of the gold rush to your stay. Expect open fires, clawfoot tubs, and an overall historic feel. $$ 185 Victoria St., 03 5332 8296, heritagehomestay.com

The Sovereign Hill Lodge Built to resemble the 1850s government camp that was used to control and tax the gold mines, these colonial-style buildings house nice heritage rooms with mid-Victorian decor and four-poster beds. $$ Magpie St., 03 5333 3409, sovereignhill.com.au

Sovereign Hill Motor Inn This four-star motel is right next to the main attractions and features a pool, spa, private courtyards, and several self-contained apartments to complement the comfy standard rooms. $$$ 223 Main Rd., 03 5331 3955, sovpark.com

Contact

Ballarat Visitor Information Centre 39 Sturt St., 03 5320 5800 / 1 800 446 633 in Australia, visitballarat.com.au

Getting There: Drive out of Melbourne on the Western Freeway, which runs directly to Ballarat.

Phillip Island

Hot Tip: Come here to see koalas in the wild.

The Lowdown: Phillip Island is famed for Australia's most popular wildlife event—the parade of fairy penguins that make their way up the beach to their burrows each day at dusk. It's quite a lucrative business for the island, and they've even built a small amphitheatre so you can sit and watch them in comfort, without disturbing the tired-out creatures. The island is also home to plenty of koalas and more than 16,000 fur seals, which rest up on Seal Rocks. The best way to get close to them is on a boat cruise. Dramatic coastal scenery, unusual rock formations, koalas, great white sharks, and world-class motorcycle races add to the charm and the excitement of this island linked to the mainland by a causeway.

Best Attractions

Fast Bikes Over three days in mid-September, the world's fastest motorcycle riders come to Phillip Island to compete in the Australian Motorcycle Grand Prix. Phillip Island Circuit, bikes.grandprix.com.au

Helicopter Flights Zip over the island's interior and along the coastline, taking in fur seal colonies and the Grand Prix circuit. $$$ Phillip Island Helicopters, 03 5956 7316

Penguin Parade Watch hundreds of tiny fairy penguins cross Summerland Beach to return to their sand burrows after a day out fishing for food. 03 5951 2800, penguins.org.au

Shark Fishing Jump on board for some serious fishing for mako, blue and thresher sharks as well as other large edible fish. $$$ T-Cat Charters, 0409 504 974 (mobile)

Best Restaurants

Chicory Restaurant Serving contemporary cuisine with an Asian twist, Chicory has tables outdoors in spring and summer and romantic candlelight all year around. $$ 115 Thompson St., Cowes, 03 5952 2655

Taylors Waterside Restaurant Come here for oceanfront dining at the island's premier seafood restaurant. It specializes in lobster and seafood platters. $$$ 1215 Phillip Island Tourist Rd., Cowes, 03 5956 7371

Best Nightlife

Isle of White Hotel A large, rambling pub with a sunny beer garden and a late-night cocktail bar. The Esplanade, Cowes, 03 5952 2560

Salamander Shores Sports Bar Don't expect much from the nightlife in sleepy Port Stephens. One of the only options is this hotel bar, which has walls decked out in sporting memorabilia and live entertainment on Friday and Saturday evenings. 147 Soldiers Point Rd., Soldiers Point, 03 4982 7210

Best Hotels

The Continental Phillip Island Choose a spa room and lap up the waves outside at this four-star classic right on the waterfront. $$$ The Esplanade, Cowes, 03 5952 2316

Glen Isla House A beautiful, historic place set on huge grounds across from the sea with heritage-style rooms. This is arguably the best place to stay on the island. $$$$ 230-232 Church St., Cowes, 03 5952 1882

Contact

Phillip Island Information Centre Phillip Island Tourist Road, Newhaven, 03 5956 7447, phillipisland.net.au

Getting There: Take the Monash Freeway (M1) out of Melbourne and turn south onto the South Gippsland Highway (M420). Turn onto the Bass Highway (A420), then take the Phillip Island turnoff to San Remo. Cross the bridge onto Phillip Island.

The Great Ocean Road

Hot Tip: Try your luck at surfing on Bells Beach, which has some of the world's most perfect waves—oh, and sightings of great white sharks.

The Lowdown: Australia's most scenic coastal driving route hugs the dramatic coastline for 66 miles (106km) between Torquay and Warrnambool. As well as soaring cliffs and expansive ocean views, it offers long stretches of beach and rainforest, and some very impressive rock formations.Some of the best are found on a 17-mile (27km) stretch between Princeton—the start of Port Campbell National Park—and Peterborough, where you'll find the Twelve Apostles, a series of incredible rock pillars that have their feet in the sea. Other natural features along this truly remarkable stretch of coastline include Pudding Basin Rock, Island Arch, the Razorback, Muttonbird Island, Thunder Cave, the Blowhole, Bakers Oven, London Bridge, and the Grotto. Extensive boardwalks and viewing platforms ensure that visitors get the best views of these sweeping, awe-inspiring vistas. Small settlements along the route include Torquay, a township dedicated to surfing (check out the Surfworld Museum); Lorne, which has a good beach and some nice eateries; and Apollo Bay, a quiet coastal town and a former whaling station.

Best Attractions

Loch Ard Gorge With towering cliffs above a small, sandy beach, this is a moving place when you consider it was the site of one of Victoria's most tragic shipwrecks. Fifty-two people died after a sailing ship, the iron clipper Loch Ard, rammed into the sheer cliffs of nearby Muttonbird Island in stormy weather in June 1878, just days from completing a three-month voyage from England to Melbourne. There were only two survivors, who washed up here.
Port Campbell National Park

The Twelve Apostles When they say "twelve apostles" they really mean eight. Actually, until July 2005 there were nine, but then one collapsed. The tallest of these sea-battered limestone columns is 148 feet (45m) high.
Port Campbell National Park

Best Restaurants

Ba ba lu This unpretentious place serves up organic food including great tapas and inspirational Mod Oz cooking. $ Lorne, 03 5289 1808

Chris's at Beacon Point Restaurant Situated on a hilltop with commanding views of the bay, this sandstone restaurant is a fine-dining stopover not to be missed. $$$ Apollo Bay, 03 5237 6411

Waves The best eatery in town has a good seafood dinner menu. $$
Port Campbell, 03 5598 6111

Best Nightlife

Grand Pacific Hotel Overlooking the beach is a stylish bar offering jazz on Saturday evenings. 268 Mountjoy Parade, Lorne, 03 5289 1609

Lorne Hotel A shade terrace overlooking the town is the place to be on warm summer evenings. Bands play downstairs most weekends. Corner of Mountjoy Parade and Bay Sts., Lorne, 03 5289 1409

Best Hotels

Bayside Gardens The front rooms in this pleasant complex have good views, and you can hear the roar of the ocean. All rooms have a separate bedroom and lounge area. $$ 219 Great Ocean Rd., Apollo Bay, 03 5237 6248, baysidegardens.com.au

Cumberland Lorne Resort Apartments in this sporty resort are spacious, and more than half have panoramic ocean views. $$ 150-178 Mountjoy Parade, Lorne, 03 5289 2400

Contact

Geelong and Great Ocean Road Visitors Centre Stead Park, Princes Highway, Geelong, 03 5275 5797, greatoceanrd.org.au

Getting There: From Melbourne take the Princes Highway to Geelong, then follow the signs to Torquay, 58 miles (94km) South-west of Melbourne; Port Campbell National Park 177 miles (285km) South-west of Melbourne.

Yarra Valley

Hot Tip: The 2005 vintage was the best in the Yarra Valley since 1997.

The Lowdown: The Yarra Valley is just a one-hour drive from downtown Melbourne. The area, crisscrossed with cycling and walking trails, is home to several national parks and is studded with wineries and gourmet restaurants. The main town in the area is Healesville, an attractive place set on the confluence of two rivers with a backdrop of hills and vineyards. There are plenty of galleries and antique stores, and there's even a day spa. The town is also home to the Healesville Sanctuary, one of the best places in Australia to see native animals and birds. Some 44 wineries dot the local area, and most offer free tastings at the cellar door.

Best Attractions

Coldstream Hills One of Australia's most prestigious wineries was founded by renowned Australian wine writer James Halliday. An exquisite range of premium wines represents the pinnacle of cool-climate winemaking in Australia. 31 Maddens Ln., Coldstream, 03 5964 9410, coldstreamhills.com.au

Erring Farm This rustic Australian cellar has a door displaying antique copper tools. Incredible views and premium estate wines helped this winery win 76 awards including a trophy for Best Pinot Noir. St. Huberts Rd., Yering, 03 9739 0461, yeringfarm.com.au

Healesville Sanctuary Featuring more than 200 species of native mammals, reptiles, and birds all in a natural bushland setting, the sanctuary's fauna includes Tasmanian devils, kangaroos, emus, wallabies, wombats, koalas, echidnas, and dingoes. Badger Creek Rd., Healesville, 03 5957 2800, zoo.org.au

Healesville Skin and Spa Day Centre On offer are facials, massages, seaweed wraps, manicures and everything else you need to relax. 103 Maroondah Hwy., Healesville, 03 5962 1912, healesvilledayspa.melbourneaustralia.com.au

St. Huberts One of the pioneering wineries of the Yarra Valley in the 1800s, the estate vineyard, replanted in the 1960s, is now considered one of the finest vineyard sites in the valley. Corner of St. Huberts Rd. and Maroondah Hwy., Coldstream, 03 9739 1118, sthuberts.com.au

Tarrawarra Estate Boasting one of the most beautiful properties in the Valley, excellent wines, and an elegant cafe, Tarrawarra also houses an important, acclaimed collection of Australian art in a gorgeous rammed-earth gallery. 311 Healesville-Yarra Glen Rd., Yarra Glen, 03 5957 3510, tarrawarra.com.au

Best Restaurants

Banq Café and Wine Bar Good coffee and main dishes including steaks, veal, yabby (crayfish) risotto, as well as burgers and gourmet sandwiches. $ 255 Bell St., Yarra Glen, 03 9730 2122, banq.com.au

Bella Vedere A beautifully located restaurant that is fanatical about local, seasonal produce and has its own bakery and garden. $$ Badger's Brook Winery, 874 Maroondah Hwy., Coldstream, 03 5962 6161, badgersbrook.com.au

Cru Restaurant A relaxed restaurant with breathtaking views and European-inspired food that takes its cues from the freshest and tastiest local ingredients. $$ Outlook Hill Estate, 97 School Ln., Tarrawarra, 03 5962 6966 outlookhill.com.au

De Bortoli Winery and Restaurant Interesting wines made from some of the oldest vines in the valley, delicious Italian food, and a new cheese shop and maturation room make De Bortoli a memorable place to visit. $$ Pinnacle Ln., Dixons Creek, 03 5965 2271, debortoli.com.au

Fergusson Winery and Restaurant Fergusson's combines great regional cuisine, fine wine, and history for an unforgettable experience. $$ 82 Wills Rd., Yarra Glen, 03 5965 2237, fergussonwinery.com.au

3777 Perched high on a hillside with views of the Valley, 3777 does city chic in a beautifully natural setting. Modern Australian food makes the most of the local produce and is matched with a local-leaning wine list. $$ Mount Rael Retreat, 140 Healesville-Yarra Glen Rd., Healesville, 03 5962 1977, mtrael.com.au

Wattleseed Restaurant This family-owned restaurant has a good menu with plenty of steaks, pastas, kangaroo, and oysters. $$ 117 Maroondah Hwy., Healesville, 03 5962 3327, wattleseed.com.au

Best Nightlife

Healesville Hotel Try this place for its large beer garden and great food. 256 Moondah Hwy., Healesville, 03 5962 4002, healesvillehotel.com.au

Best Hotels

Grovedale Olives These two Tuscan-inspired, self-contained studios have spectacular views across olive groves and the mountains beyond. Each has a spa, a self-contained kitchen, air conditioning, and a wood fire. $$ 123 Garden Hill Ct., Kangaroo Ground, 03 9712 0089, grovedaleolives.com

Melba Lodge A boutique bed and breakfast with eight well-appointed rooms, some with spas. Features a six-person spa room, a billiard room and bar, and three guest lounges. $$ 939 Melba Hwy., Yarra Glen, 03 9730 1511, melbalodge.com.au

Myers Creek Cascades A top-class hideaway; rooms have spas and panoramic rainforest views. Perfect for a romantic stay. $$$ 269 Myers Creek Rd., Healesville, 03 5962 3351, myerscreekcascades.com.au

The Sebel Lodge Yarra Valley This boutique hotel features one of the area's best day spas and golf courses. Golf is included with your room. $$$ Heritage Ave., Chirnside Park, 03 9760 3333, hgcc.com.au

Contacts

Yarra Valley Visitor Centre Old Court Rd., Haker St., Healesville, 03 5962 2600, visityarravalley.com.au

Getting There: From Melbourne, take the Eastern Freeway to the Springvale Road exit; turn right onto Springvale Road and then left onto the Maroondah Highway. Follow the road through Ringwood to Healesville.

Mornington Peninsula

Hot Tip: Avoid summer weekends when the crowds from Melbourne come looking for a bit of fresh air.

The Lowdown: The Mornington Peninsula is only an hour's drive from Melbourne, but with its vineyards, olive groves, historic house retreats, seaside villages, and magnificent coastline, it seems like a world away. More than 50 wineries allow tastings and the area has a reputation for its pinot noir and chardonnay. The coast is lined with good beaches, while Cape Schanck Coastal Park is home to gray kangaroos, echidnas, and many other animals. The two main Peninsula towns are Sorrento and Portsea. Sorrento is a sleepy town in winter but heaves with tourists in summer. It was declared Victoria's first official settlement in 1803. Portsea is popular with wealthy Melbournites, who have holiday mansions alongside the beach.

Best Attractions

Arthur's Seat State Park Arthur's Seat is the most familiar of all Port Phillip Bay landscape features. Reach the 314-meter summit by chairlift for spectacular views of the bay and Port Phillip Heads. Chairlift: 03 5987 2565

Cape Schanck Lightstation This spot, built in 1859, is still operational. It offers a museum, coastal views, and guided tours. Cape Schanck, 03 5988 6184

French Island A ferry from Stoney Point takes you to this wild and windswept island. It's mostly National Park and has the largest colony of koalas in Victoria. French Island Visitor Information Centre, Bayview Rd., Tankerton, 03 5980 1209

Mornington Peninsula National Park This park hugs the coastline and offers superb views of rugged beaches and wild stretches of forest. Point Nepean Rd., Portsea, 13-19-63, parkweb.vic.gov.au

Morning Peninsula Regional Gallery The gallery features works by Australian artists. 4 Vancouver St., Mornington, 03 5975 4395

Best Restaurants

Stringer's A Mornington Peninsula institution, Stringer's is good for breakfast and tasty lunches; it's a great place to try local wines. $ 2 Ocean Beach Rd., Sorrento, 03 5984 2010

Montalto Housed in a simple but beautiful glass and timber building on a vineyard and olive grove, Montalto is the perfect place for a long lunch on a sunny day. $$ 33 Shoreham Rd., Red Hill South, 03 5989 8412, montalto.com.au

Contacts

The Peninsula Visitor Information Centre Point Nepean Rd., Dromana, 03 5987 3078, visitmorningtonpeninsula.org

Getting There: Take the Nepean Highway south out of Melbourne and take it along the gorgeous coast all the way to the Peninsula.

HIT the GROUND RUNNING: MELBOURNE

If you've never been here before—or even if you live here—Melbourne can seem overwhelming. Which freeway takes you where? Which mountains are those? And by the way, what season is it? If you want to make like a native, you need to know the basics. Here are the facts and figures, including our *Cheat Sheet*, a quick-reference countdown of vital information that'll help you feel like an instant Aussie.

City Essentials Melbourne

Getting to Melbourne: By Air

Melbourne Airport (MEL)

03 9297 1600, melair.com.au

Melbourne Airport, also known as Melbourne Tullamarine Airport, is located 14 miles (22km) northwest of the city center. It serves 23 international airlines and six domestic ones and, while small in comparison to Sydney Airport, you'll find all the usual facilities. There are a range of restaurants and cafes here, but the pick of the bunch is P.J. O'Briens, which looks like a typical Irish pub. It serves nice—though pricey—beers and has a good menu offering traditional pub grub. Travelers Information Service booth is located in the International Arrivals area; luggage carts cost $4.

Taxis cost around $40 for the 25-minute trip to the city. Alternatively, the Skybus shuttle (03 9335 2811, skybus.com.au) leaves every 15 minutes from outside the terminal, 7am-7pm, stopping at Southern Cross Station. Plan to catch a taxi or tram from here. It costs $15.

Please see p.155 for a list of airlines that serve Melbourne Airport.

Rental Cars: The following companies have counters inside Melbourne airport.

Agency	Website	Number
Avis Australia	avis.com.au	03 9338 1800
Budget	budget.com.au	13 27 27
Delta	deltaeuropecar.com.au	03 9241 6100
Hertz Australia	hertz.com.au	03 9338 4044
Thrifty	thrifty.com.au	1 300 367 227
Limousines:		
Academy Waterford Limousines	stretchlimos.com.au	1 300 304 808
Caddy Limousines	caddylimos.com.au	1 800 639 878

Getting to Melbourne: By Land

By Car: The trip to Melbourne along the coastal Princes Highway is a nicer but longer option than the inland Hume Highway. Along the route you travel through plenty of seaside towns and pass lots of national parks. It takes around 12 hours of nonstop driving to get to Melbourne from Sydney by the Princes Highway, though a journey of at least three or four days is preferable. It's a nine-hour straight drive from Sydney to Melbourne via the Hume Highway.

Driving Distance to Melbourne

From	Distance (mi.)	Approx. Time (hr.)
Adelaide	425	9
Canberra	283	6
Sydney (inland)	439	9
Sydney (coastal)	480	12

By Train: Countrylink (13-22-32; countrylink.com.au) runs trains from Central Station throughout New South Wales and south to Canberra and Melbourne. Trains to Melbourne from Sydney leave twice daily at 7:45am (arriving in Melbourne at 6:55pm) and at 8:40pm (arriving in Melbourne at 7:35am). Trains from Melbourne's Southern Cross Station to Sydney depart daily at 8:30am (arriving at 7:55pm) and 7:55pm (arriving at 6:56am). V/Line (13-61-96; vlinepassenger.com.au) operates trains throughout regional Victoria, from Southern Cross Station. The Overland train (13-61-96; gsr.com.au) runs daily between Melbourne and Adelaide, taking 12 hours. Schedules can be found at railsnw.com or by calling 800 717 0108 or 503 292 5055 (in the US).

By Bus: Greyhound Australia (13-14-99, greyhound.com.au) operates daily between Sydney and Melbourne. The trip takes around ten hours. Coaches leave from beside Central Station in Sydney and from the Transit Center at Swanston and Franklin Streets in Melbourne.

Getting Around Melbourne

Lay of the Land: Central Melbourne is laid out in a grid, with the town center concentrated around Russell and Elizabeth Streets running north, and Collins Street and Lonsdale Street running south. The Yarra River runs along the city's southern fringe, and beyond in the bayside suburb of St. Kilda. City suburbs surround the center, with Carlton to the north, Fitzroy to the east, and South Yarra to the southeast.

By Car: The good news about driving in Melbourne is that the city is laid out as a grid, so navigating is fairly easy—as long as you remember to drive on the left side. A U.S. driver's license will do the trick as long as you don't plan on staying more than three months, and you're required to have it with you at all times behind the wheel. Seatbelts are also required.

"Hook turns" are a tricky part of Melbourne that you need to be aware of.

Because of the trams, some places require that cars turning right actually do it from the left lane. To do it, drive forward in the left lane and wait on the far left side of the road. When the light turns orange—and you've checked that oncoming traffic has stopped—go ahead and make your turn to the right. As with school buses in the U.S., cars are required to stop behind a tram when it is stopped.

Taxis: You'll find taxis outside most major hotels and at marked taxi ranks. In Melbourne two yellow lights mean a taxi is vacant, and just one means it's occupied. As well as the fare displayed on the meter, you may find yourself owing extra for tolls. For example, there's a $2 pickup fee at Melbourne Airport.

Agency	Number
Arrow	13 22 11
Embassy Taxis	13 17 55
Silver Top Taxis	13 10 08
13 CABS	13 22 27

Parking: Parking is by meter in downtown areas, but it can be hard to find a spot during peak hours. Don't let the meter run out—fines are hefty. Parking garages are plentiful and run $5 an hour, and up to $20 a day.

Parking Garages: Here are some of the most convenient parking facilities.

- City Square Car Park (202 Flinders Ln.)
- Council House Car Park (200 Little Collins St.)

By Train: Flinders Street Station is the hub of train activity in Melbourne. From here, you can catch metro trains to local and suburban destinations.

By Tram and Bus: Melbourne has one of the oldest tram networks in the world, run by Metlink Melbourne (13-16-38,metlinkmelbourne.com.au). These days several hundred trams run over 202 miles (325km) of track. Taxi drivers might hate them, but Melbournites love their favorite form of non-smoggy transport. Trams run to all suburbs, including to the bayside suburb of St. Kilda, and are an efficient and heart-warming way to get around. Tickets are good for either two hours or the whole day. Buy tickets at ticket machines on trams (coins only) or at vending machines at many shops and information booths that sport the blue Metcard sign. The City Circle Tram is the best way to get around the center of Melbourne—and best of all, it's free. The burgundy-and-cream trams travel a circular route in either direction around the city grid, leaving roughly every ten minutes. There's even limited commentary. Burgundy signs mark City Circle Tram stops. Buses are part of the same system, and your ticket will work on them as well.

Other Practical Information

Gay and Lesbian Travel Melbourne's gay and lesbian scene is concentrated in the inner-city suburb of Prahan, particularly along Commercial Road. There are more venues in Collingwood and Abbotsford. Midsumma (midsumma.org.au) is Melbourne's main gay party, show, and arts festival. It takes place between mid-January and mid-February.

Print Media The newspaper of choice in Melbourne is *The Age* (theage.com.au), which also has an events guide every Friday. *The Herald Sun*, Australia's largest-selling daily, is also here (news.com.au/heraldsun).

Melbourne Radio Stations (a selection)

FM Stations

107.5	Triple J	Latest Contemporary
105.9	ABC Classic	Classical

AM Stations

621	ABC Nat'l	Ideas
774	ABC Local	local news, chat
1026	ABC News	continuous news

Country Essentials

See p.171-74 regarding: Money Matters, Metric Conversion, Safety, Traveling with Disabilities, Attire, Size Conversion, Shopping Hours, Drinking, Smoking, Drugs, Time Zone, and Additional Resources for Visitors.

Numbers to Know (Melbourne Hotlines)

Emergency, police, fire department, ambulance, and paramedics	000
Rape Crisis Centre	1 800 424 017
National Roads & Motorists Association	13 11 11
Police Stations:	
228-232 Flinders Ln.	03 9247 6666
24-Hour Medical:	
Royal Melbourne Hospital Grattan St., Parkville	03 9342 7000
Dental Emergency Service:	
Royal Dental Hospital of Melbourne	03 9341 1040

Party Conversation—A Few Surprising Facts

- In 1838, an Aboriginal called Tullymarine was caught stealing potatoes from a settler's farm. He was captured and put in Melbourne gaol, which was made of wood and bark. He burnt it down and escaped. After being recaptured, he was transported to Sydney and jailed there. After his release he walked south, 560 miles (900km) back to Melbourne. Today, the suburb that's home to Melbourne Airport—Tullamarine—is named after him.

- *The Story of the Kelly Gang* was the first ever narrative full-length feature film in Australia. When it came out in 1910, the Victorian government banned the film because it believed it incited people to crime.

- ACDC Lane (off Flinders Lane, a block and a half from Swanston Street) celebrates the heavy metal rock group AC/DC. Because of street signage rules, the lane's name is without the band's trademark lightning slash. However, a Melbourne artist has fixed a metal lightning flash above and below the official sign.

- Two American brothers, William and Ralph Foster, who sailed from New York in 1887, invented Australia's most famous beer, Foster's lager. They set up the Foster's Brewing Company on Rokeby Street in Collingwood, Melbourne, and brewed their first beer in 1888.

- Melbourne was briefly named "Batmania" after one of its founders, John Batman. Other proposed names included Bareheep, Bearbrass, Bareport, Barehurp, and Bareberp.

- The scenic railway at Luna Park in the Melbourne suburb of St. Kilda is the world's oldest operating roller-coaster. It started operation in 1912.

- Australia's most famous opera singer, Dame Nellie Melba, who was born in Melbourne in 1861, had a dessert created for her by a chef at the Savoy Hotel in London. It's called Peach Melba—and old Aussie ladies just love it.

- Vegemite was invented in Melbourne—and it's still made at a local factory in Fisherman Bend.

The Cheat Sheet (The Very Least You Ought to Know About Melbourne)

They may be in the same country, but Sydney and Melbourne are very different places. Here's the scoop on a few things you need to know to pass as a local in this sophisticated little city.

Important Streets

Acland Street is part of casual bohemian St. Kilda. It's best known for its thriving café culture and enticing eateries that draw locals from all over town, and tourists from around the globe, especially on weekends.

Bourke Street is one of the main thoroughfares in the Central Business District. Lined with financial institutions and home to countless retailers, including the Bourke Street Mall and a couple of major department stores, it's a popular destination for locals and tourists alike.

Brunswick Street in Fitzroy is the hipster heartland, with shops galore and countless restaurants, cafes, bars, and lounges where locals of all stripes gather to socialize and mingle.

Chapel Street has many charms, including a good number of trendy restaurants and cafes, and plenty of boutiques, ranging from funky local designers to glitzy international chains.

Melbourne's best-known thoroughfare, **Collins Street** is the city's financial center. Lined with some gorgeous examples of Victorian-era architecture, it's also home to the city's top international designer boutiques. If you need a new pair of Ferragamos, or the latest from Vuitton, you'll find it here.

Fitzroy Street is the main drag of funky, beachy St. Kilda and is best known for its thriving party life.

Flinders Lane and **Little Collins Street**, both located in the Central Business District, are a treasure trove of boutiques carrying edgy and unusual finds, often made by local designers.

Lonsdale Street is a major commercial thoroughfare that runs through the Central Business District.

Lygon Street is Melbourne's Little Italy. Sprinkled with cafes and enticing Italian trattorias, it's lined with outdoor terraces, making it a perfect place to enjoy a leisurely meal on a warm evening.

9 Public Street Art

A Chunk of Library Part of a column and the top of a small corner of a building is wedged into the ground on the corner of Latrobe and Swanston streets.

Blowhole You get to jump through a few hoops at this Docklands sculpture.

Brunswick Street Street Signs Humorous and philosophical street signs mark the buildings here.

Bunjil the Eagle A new sculpture in Docklands shows a representation of the supreme creator, an eagle, important to the Aboriginal people of southeast Australia. Located in the Village Docklands, Wurundjeri Way (Collins St.).

Cow up a Tree A Docklands favorite, the carcass of an enormous black-and-white cow stands upside-down at the top of a tree. Located in the Village Docklands.

Larry La Trobe A bronze dog that sits in the Melbourne City Square near the corner of Swanston and Collins Street. Passersby rub his nose and sit on him.

The Public Purse A giant brown and silver purse, looking like a closed clam, is the highlight of the corner of Bourke and Elizabeth Streets.

Three Businessmen Who Brought Their Own Lunch Three rather thin metal men with briefcases stand looking bemused on the corner of Bourke and Swanston Streets.

The Vault The most controversial Australian sculpture ever is a three-winged metal "yellow peril" construction on the banks of the Yarra River.

8 Major Tram Routes

Tram 1 This line travels from East Coburg to South Melbourne Beach and then to the Arts Centre via the city center.

Tram 8 Goes from Bourke Street Mall to South Yarra via Flinders Street in the city center. Perfect for Flinders shopping.

Tram 30 Tram 30 travels from the Docklands to St. Vincent's Plaza via Latrobe Street in the city center (weekends only).

Tram 35 Known as the City Circle Tram, this is a free service that runs around the Central Business District, or CBD.

Tram 70 Take tram 70 to get to the Docklands; travels via Swanston Street from the city center.

Tram 79 Heads from North Richmond all the way out to St. Kilda beach, via Chapel Street in South Yarra.

Tram 96 Take tram 96 from St. Kilda Beach to get to East Brunswick; travels via the Bourke Street Mall.

Tram 112 Leaving St. Kilda beach, catch tram 112 heading to West Prahan via Collins Street in the city center.

7 Famous Aussies

Nicole Kidman Although she was born in Hawaii, her family moved Down Under shortly after.

Mel Gibson The Gibson clan moved to Australia when young Mel was only 12—his father didn't want his boys drafted into the Vietnam War, so they left the States behind.

Phar Lap The states had Seabiscuit, Aussies had Phar Lap. This horse was the hero of Depression-era Australia, and rumors of foul play by gangsters surrounded his death.

Thomas Keneally This prolific Booker Prize–winning author penned *Schindler's List.*

Steve Irwin The famed Crocodile Hunter died from a stingray whipping its tail into his heart.

Neville Bonner Born in an era of segregation, Bonner grew up to become Australia's first Aboriginal Senator in 1971.

Edward "Ned" Kelly Melbourne's most infamous outlaw and part of the "Kelly Gang," he was first arrested at age 15.

6 Theaters

Comedy Theatre This building, a replica of a Renaissance palace in Florence, has a distinctly Spanish interior—typical New World mishmash. Nonetheless, it hosts a diverse range of theater and comedy that is some of the best in the city. Corner of Exhibition and Lonsdale Streets.

Forum Theatre Adding glamour to cabaret and rock concerts are lavish molded plaster, reproduction casts of Greek and Italian sculptures, and a soaring blue ceiling punched with stars. 150 Flinders St., CBD.

Her Majesty's Theatre Dame Nellie Melba sang her first opera at the Art Deco Her Majesty's Theatre. Ballerinas Anna Pavlova and Dame Margot Fonteyn also performed here. It has an illustrious history combined with a fine contemporary program. 219 Exhibition St., CBD.

Princess Theatre One of the world's grandest Victorian theaters features domed mansard roofs, cast-iron filigree, and a marble staircase and foyer. The seasonal program isn't too shabby either. 163 Spring St., CBD.

Regent Theatre Built in 1929 as a "picture palace," the Regent Theatre is an extravagant, large Spanish Gothic hall, which hosts major shows. 191 Collins St., CBD.

Victorian Arts Centre Melbourne's main performing arts complex includes a concert hall, theaters, and a huge outdoor music area. This is where you'll catch top visiting shows and cultural events. 100 St. Kilda Rd., CBD.

Parks and Gardens

The Alexandra Gardens These historic gardens on the edge of the Yarra River include a star-shaped garden bed designed to represent the Federation of Australia. Located off St. Kilda Road, at the feet of Princes Bridge between the Yarra River and Alexandra Avenue.

Carlton Gardens The World Heritage–listed Royal Exhibition Building and surrounding gardens make up one of the few surviving 19th-century exhibition precincts in the world. Located at Victoria Parade, between Carlton and Nicholson streets.

Fitzroy Gardens An English cottage built by Captain Cook's parents. Located at Wellington Parade, between Clarendon and Lansdowne Streets.

Kings Domain Best known for Latrobe's Cottage, Victoria's first Government House. It was transported brick by brick from England in 1836. Located on the eastern edge of CBD (Art Gallery Road).

The Treasury Gardens These small and peaceful gardens are inhabited by scores of brushtail possums. Look out for the memorial to John F. Kennedy near the lake. Located between Fitzroy Gardens and Spring Street on the eastern edge of the CBD.

Markets

Friday Produce Market This "Farmers Market" in Federation Square offers high-quality Victorian produce, including seasonal fruit, preserves, smoked trout, and cheeses.

Lygon Court Art and Craft Market Come to the famous Italian strip for this Sunday art and craft market. Sun noon–5pm, Lygon Court Piazza, Carlton.

Queen Victoria Market This almost-daily Melbourne institution houses several hundred stalls selling everything from live animals to bargain-basement clothes. An easy walk from Melbourne Central Station (Elizabeth Street exit). Walk north along Elizabeth or William Street to reach the market.

St. Kilda Esplanade Art and Craft Market A Sunday market with 200 stalls of bric-a-brac, arts, crafts, and jewelry. Upper Esplanade, St. Kilda, between Cavell and Fitzroy Streets.

City Fixtures

State Houses of Parliament You can view political proceedings from the public gallery inside this imposing building. It was the home of the Australian government before it moved to Canberra.

St Paul's Cathedral Inside this Gothic Revival Anglican cathedral are gold mosaics, while outside stands a statue of Matthew Flinders, the captain of the first vessel to circumnavigate the Australian mainland.

St Patrick's Cathedral Best known for its beautiful stained-glass windows, St. Pat's is a Roman Catholic worship place associated with the Irish immigrants who fled the potato famine in the mid-19th century.

Men's Night Out

Goldfinger's Get up close to pole dancers. 584 Lonsdale St., City Center, 03 9670 9457, goldfingers.com.au

The Men's Gallery Exotic nude shows, Miss Australia competitions, and a midnight mass strip all make for an erotic evening of fun for the boys. 601 Lonsdale St., City Center, 03 9670 0331

Singular Sensation

Enjoying a drink at a cafe on **Federation Square,** whose quirky design and top-rate eateries have made it an iconic and popular meeting place.

Melbourne Coffee (quick stops for a java jolt)

Baristas 101 Its wooden floorboards, bistro chairs, and gilded mirrors lend this place a Parisian elegance. Coffee is a major focus, but the pizzas, sandwiches, and pastries are worth trying too. 100 Flinders St., 03 9654 4377

Café Duomo The hip come to sip in this elegant but somehow laid-back alleyway cafe. The Block Arcade, 282 Collins St., 03 9650 5041

Hopetoun Tea Rooms This venerable spot traces its heritage back to a tearoom run by the Victorian Ladies Work Association between 1893 and 1907. The Block Arcade, 282 Collins St., 03 9650 2777

Pellegrini's Espresso Bar Pellegrini's poured its first espresso in 1954, back when it was one of the first cafes in Australia to serve real Italian-style coffee and pasta. 66 Bourke St., 03 9662 1885

Just for Business and Conventions Melbourne

With its compact downtown area and well-laid-out streets, Melbourne is an easy city to do business in, especially if your business is in the Central Business District (CBD). From upscale boutique hotels to hidden bolt-hole bars and world-class restaurants, there are plenty of options within walking distance of the office towers that fill the downtown city streets. Nearby is Southbank, the home of both the Convention Center and the Crown Casino, a large complex with plenty of gaming and fun. And only a short tram ride away are suburbs like the waterfront St. Kilda, where a weary worker can escape for a half-day of relaxation.

Addresses to Know

Convention Center

- Melbourne CVB
  Level 12, IBM Centre, 60 City Rd., Southbank, 03 9693 3333, mcvb.com.au

City Information

- Melbourne VC
  Federation Sq., Cnr Swanston and Flinders Sts., 03 9658 9658, thatsmelbourne.com.au

Melbourne proved it's a city that can handle major happenings when it hosted the Commonwealth Games in 2006, and more than 90,000 visitors flooded the city. Determined to continue to grow in the area of conventions, the city recently commissioned a new 5,000-seat convention center that is slated to open in 2009.

Business and Convention Hotels

A number of hotels that we recommend in our Melbourne Black Book cater to business travelers. These, along with some additional choices, include:

Crown Towers This casino hotel is right in the heart of convention territory and close to the city center. $$$ 6 Whiteman St., Southbank, 03 9292 6666 or 1 800 811 653 in Australia, crowntowers.com.au

Langham Hotel Melbourne A short walk to the convention center, the Langham is the best address in Melbourne. $$$ 1 Southgate Ave., Southgate, 03 8696 8888, langhamhotels.com

Grand Hyatt Melbourne With a huge, luxurious lobby and a central location, this hotel is always a good bet. $$$ 124 Collins St., City Center, 03 9657 1234, melbourne.grand.hyatt.com

Business Entertaining

Melbourne is known for sophisticated dining. Seal the deal over a drink or a fantastic meal at any of these establishments.

Becco (p.210) Below a cocktail bar is this business favorite, serving up modern Italian. $$ 11-25 Crossley St., 03 9663 3000, becco.com.au

Ezard (p.213) Dark wood, red wine, and fine espresso make this a fine dining classic. $$$ The Adelphi Hotel, 187 Flinders Ln., 03 9639 6811, ezard.com.au

Grossi Florentino (p.214) This excellent Italian joint has a fine dining space upstairs and a more casual room below. $$$ 229 Gertrude St., 03 9662 1811, grossiflorentino.com.au

Syracuse (p.218) An eclectic mix of furnishings, a fabulous wine list, and modern Mediterranean food, slap bang in the business district. $$ 22 Bank Pl., 03 9670 1777, syracuserestaurant.com.au

Also see: **Best Always-Hot Restaurants** (p.41)
Best Fine Dining (p.44)
Best Tapas (p.48)

Ducking Out for a Half-Day

Make time for a quintessential Melbourne experience at one of these spots.

Federation Square (p.230) Fans of funky architecture will be impressed by Melbourne's city square, located opposite the Melbourne Convention Centre at Southbank. Corner of Flinders and Swanston Sts., 03 9655 1900

National Gallery of Victoria International (NGV) (p.234) This modernist landmark is filled with an international collection that makes an excellent way to spend a few hours. 180 St. Kilda Rd., 03 8620 2222, ngv.vic.gov.au

Royal Botanic Gardens (p.235) Whether you take a turn around the outside fitness track or wander into these lush gardens, you're sure to forget all about meetings and agendas. Birdwood Ave., 03 9252 2300, rbg.vic.gov.au

Also see: **Best Culture** (p.43)
Best Outdoor Drinking Spots (p.46)
Best Walks (p.49)

Gifts to Bring Home

What fun is unpacking if you can't pull out a treasure or two?

Colette Dinnigan (p.230) This Aussie designer is a legend in women's wear. 553 Chapel St. (Toorak Rd.), 03 9827 2111

Little Salon (p.232) Chock-full of finds by local designers and artists, this place is somewhere between a shop and a gallery. 71 Gertrude St. (Fitzroy St.), 03 9419 7123

Myer The grande dame of Melbourne's department stores has 12 floors of potential gifts. 314 Bourke Street Mall, City Center, 03 9661 1111

Alexandra Pde
N
Miles
½
Kilometers
½
University of Melbourne
Elgin St
Nicholson St
Johnston St
Royal Pde
Barkly St
Grattan St
Carlton
University Square
Lincoln Square
Argyle Square
Melbourne Museum
Smith St
Elizabeth St
Swanston St
Rathdowne St
Royal Exhibition Buildings
Carlton Gardens
Fitzroy
Victoria St
Queen Victoria Market
Victoria Pde
Latrobe St
Albert St
Flagstaff Gardens
Lonsdale St
Russell St
Exhibition St
Parliament House of Victoria
Lansdowne St
Fitzroy Gardens
CBD
Treasury Gardens
William St
Wllington Pde
Elizabeth St
Federation Square
Yarra Park
Flinders St
Flinders Street Station
King St
Brunton Ave
Melbourne Cricket Ground
Alexandra Gardens
Garden Square
Alexandra Ave
Yarra River
Crown Entertainment Complex
Queen Victoria Gardens
Crown Casino
Swan St
Southbank
Sidney Meyer Music Bowl
Melbourne Exhibition Centre
Olympic Park
Sturt St
Kings Domain
M1
City Rd
Government House
M1
Kings Way
St Kilda Rd
Clarendon St
Shrine of Remembrance
Moray St
Royal Botanic Gardens
Park St

MELBOURNE BLACK BOOK

You're solo in the city—where's a singles-friendly place to eat? Is there a good lunch spot near the museum? Will the bar be too loud for easy conversation? Get the answers fast in the *Black Book*, a condensed version of every listing in our guide that puts all the essential information at your fingertips.

A quick glance down the page and you'll find the type of food, nightlife, or attractions you are looking for, the phone numbers, and which pages to turn to for more detailed information. How did you ever survive without this?

Melbourne Black Book

Hotels

NAME TYPE (ROOMS)	ADDRESS (CROSS STREET) WEBSITE	AREA PRICE	PHONE (03+) 800 NUMBER	PAGE
Adelphi Hotel Modern (34)	187 Flinders Ln. (St. Kilda Rd.) adelphi.com.au	CC $$$	9650 7555	206
The Como Melbourne Timeless (107)	630 Chapel St. (Toorak Rd.) mirvachotels.com.au	SY $$$	9825 2222 1 800 033 400	206
Crown Towers Modern (482)	8 Whiteman St. (Clarendon St.) crowntowers.com.au	SB $$$	9292 6666 1 800 811 653	206
Grand Hotel Grand (115)	33 Spencer St. (Flinders St.) grandhotelsofitel.com.au	CC $$$	9611 4567 1 300 361 455	207
Grand Hyatt Melbourne Timeless (547)	123 Collins St. (Russell St.) melbourne.grand.hyatt.com	CC $$$$	9657 1234	207
The Hatton Timeless (20)	65 Park St. (St. Kilda Rd.) hatton.com.au	SY $$	9868 4800	207
Hotel Lindrum Modern (59)	26 Flinders St. (Spring St.) hotellindrum.com.au	CC $$	9668 1111	208
Langham Hotel Melbourne Timeless (387)	1 Southgate Ave. (St. Kilda Rd.) langhamhotels.com	SB $$$$	8696 8888	208
Marque Hotel Trendy (80)	35-37 Fitzroy St. (Acland St.) rendezvoushotels.com	SK $$	8530 8888 1 800 621 621	208
The Prince Hotel Trendy (40)	2 Acland St. (Fitzroy St.) theprince.com.au	SK $$$	9536 1111	208
Rialto Hotel Grand (244)	495 Collins St. (Elizabeth St.) rialtohotel.com.au	CC $$$	9620 9111 1 800 331 330	209
Sofitel Melbourne Timeless (363)	25 Collins St. (Spring St.) sofitelmelbourne.com.au	CC $$$	9653 0000 1 800 656 565	209

Restaurants

NAME TYPE	ADDRESS (CROSS STREET) WEBSITE	AREA PRICE	PHONE (03+) SINGLES/NOISE	99 BEST	PAGE PAGE
Ay Oriental Tea House Yum Cha	455 Chapel St. (Cliff St.) orientalteahouse.com.au	SY $	9824 0128 B =		210

Neighborhood (Area) Key

CC = City Center	**SB** = Southbank
CL = Carlton	**SK** = St. Kilda
FZ = Fitzroy	**SY** = South Yarra
PR = Prahran	**VA** = Various
RM = Richmond	

Note regarding page numbers: Italic = itinerary listing; Roman *= description in theme chapter listing.*

NAME TYPE	ADDRESS (CROSS STREET) WEBSITE	AREA PRICE	PHONE (03+) SINGLES/NOISE	99 BEST	PAGE PAGE
Bar Lourinha Spanish	37 Little Collins St. (Meyers Pl.) barlourinha.com.au	CC $$	9663 7890 [B] ▯ ≡	 Tapas	210 48
Becco* Italian	11-25 Crossley St. (Bourke St.) becco.com.au	CC $$$	9663 3000 =		210
Belgian Beer Café Bluestone* Pub Grub	557 St. Kilda Rd. (Moubray St.)	SY $	9529 2899 ≡		210
The Botanical* Australian	169 Domain Rd. (Millswyn St.) thebotanical.com.au	SY $$	9820 7888 [B] =	 Brunches	210 42
Brunetti Cafe/Pasticceria	194-204 Faraday St. (Lygon St.) brunetti.com.au	CL $	9347 2801 [B] =		211
Cafe Di Stasio Italian	31 Fitzroy St. (Acland St.)	SK $$	9525 3999 =		*202*, 211
Canary Club* Spanish	6 Melbourne Pl. (Little Collins St.)	CC $$	9663 1983 =	 Tapas	211 48
Carlisle Wine Bar* Italian	137 Carlisle St. (Camden St.)	VA $	9531 3222 =		211
Cicciolina* Italian	130 Acland St. (Belford St.)	SK $	9525 3333 =		*202*, 211
Circa Continental (G)	2 Acland St. (Fitzroy St.) circa.com.au	SK $$$	9536 1122 [B] –	 Fine Dining	*202*, 212 44
Comme* Fusion	7 Alfred Pl. (Collins St.) comme.com.au	CC $	9631 4000 ≡	 Always-Hot Rest.	*200*, 212 41
Cookie* Thai	252 Swanston St. (Lonsdale St.)	CC $	9663 7660 ≡		212
The Deanery Modern Australian	13 Bligh Pl. (Flinders St.) thedeanery.com.au	CC $$	9629 5599 [B] =		*202*, 212
Donovan's* Mediterranean	40 Jacka Blvd. (Cavell St.) donovanshouse.com.au	SK $$	9534 8221 =		212
European* Continental	161 Spring St. (Bourke St.)	CC $$	9654 0811 =	 Brunches	*200*, 212 42
Ezard Modern Australian (G)	187 Flinders Ln. (Swanston St.) ezard.com.au	CC $$	9639 6811 –		*200*, 213
Fifteen Melbourne Continental	115 Little Collins St. (George Parade) fifteenmelbourne.com.au	CC $$	1300 799 415 –		213

Restaurant and Nightlife Symbols

Restaurants
Singles Friendly (eat and/or meet)
▯ = Communal table
[B] = Food served at the bar
(G) = Gourmet Destination

Nightlife
Price Warning
[C] = Cover or ticket charge

Restaurant + Nightlife
Prime time noise levels
– = Quiet
= = A buzz, but still conversational
≡ = Loud

Restaurants (cont.)

NAME TYPE	ADDRESS (CROSS STREET) WEBSITE	AREA PRICE	PHONE (03+) SINGLES/NOISE	99 BEST	PAGE PAGE
Fog* Modern Australian	142 Greville St. (Grattan St.) fog.com.au	SY $$	9521 3155		213
Gertrude Street Enoteca* Italian	229 Gertrude St. (Smith St.) gertrudestreetenoteca.com	FZ $$	9415 8262		213
Grossi Florentino* Italian (G)	80 Bourke St. (Exhibition St.) grossiflorentino.com.au	CC $$	9662 1811		214
I Carusi 2 Pizza	231 Barkly St. (Blessington St.)	SK $$	9593 6033		214
Interlude Continental	211 Brunswick St. (Gertrude St.) interlude.com.au	FZ $$$	9415 7300		214
Journal* Cafe	Shop 1, 253 Flinders Ln. (Degrave St.)	CC $	9650 4399		214
Ladro Italian	224 Gertrude St. (Smith St.)	FZ $$	9415 7575 B		214
Longrain* Thai	44 Little Bourke St. (Spring St.) longrain.com.au	CC $$	9671 3151	 Always-Hot Rest.	*201*, 215 41
Mario's Cafe	303 Brunswick St. (Johnston St.)	FZ $$	9417 3343		215
Melbourne Supper Club* Continental	Level 1, 161 Spring St. (Bourke St.)	CC $	9654 6300		215
Mini Greek	141 Flinders Ln. (enter from Oliver Ln.) minirestaurant.com.au	CC $	9650 8830 B		*201*, 215
Mirka at Tolarno Hotel Continental	42 Fitzroy St. (Canterbury Rd.) mirkatolarno.com	SK $	9525 3088 B		215
MoVida* Spanish	1 Hosier Ln. (Flinders Ln.) movida.com.au	CC $$	9663 3038	 Tapas	*201*, 216 48
Observatory Cafe Cafe	Royal Botanic Grdns., Birdwood Ave. (Dallas Brooks Dr.)	SY $	9650 5600 B		216
The Panama* Continental	Level 3, 231 Smith St. (Moor St.)	FZ $$	9417 7663	 Always-Hot Rest.	216 41
Pearl Modern Australian (G)	631-633 Church St. (Howard St.) pearlrestaurant.com.au	RM $$	9421 4599 B	 Brunches	216 42
Pelican* Tapas Bar	16 Fitzroy St. (Park St.)	SK $	9525 5847 B		*202*, 217
Punch Lane Continental	43 Little Bourke St. (Punch Ln.) punchlane.com.au	CC $$$	9639 4944 B		217
Rockpool Modern Australian	Crown Complex, Southgate rockpoolmelbourne.com	SB $$	8648 1900 B		217
Shoya* Japanese (G)	25 Market Ln. (Bourke St.) shoyamelbourne.com	CC $	9650 0848		217
Stokehouse* Mediterranean	30 Jacka Blvd. (Cavell St.) stokehouse.com.au	SK $$	9525 5555		*202*, 217
Supper Inn Chinese	15 Celestial Ave. (Little Bourke St.)	CC $$	9663 4759		218

NAME TYPE	ADDRESS (CROSS STREET) WEBSITE	AREA PRICE	PHONE (03+) SINGLES/NOISE	99 BEST	PAGE PAGE
Syracuse* Mediterranean	23 Bank Pl. (Little Collins St.)	CC $$	9670 1777 B		*200*, 218
Taxi Dining Room Fusion (G)	2 Swanston St. (Flinders Ln.) transporthotel.com.au	CC $$$	9654 8808 B	Fine Dining	*200*, 218 44
Three, One, Two Modern Australian	312 Drummond St. (Faraday St.) 312.com.au	CL $$$	9347 3312		218
Tutto Bene Italian	Mid Level, Southgate Prom. (Southgate Ave.) tuttobene.com.au	SB $$$	9696 3334		219
Vlado's Steak House	61 Bridge Rd. (Normanby Pl.)	RM $$$	9428 5833 B		219
Vue de Monde French (G)	430 Little Collins St. (Bank Pl.) vuedemonde.com.au	CC $$$$	9691 3888 B	Fine Dining	*200*, 219 44
Wall Two 80 Cafe	Rear 280 Carlisle St. (Nelson St.) wallcoffee.com.au	SK $	9593 8280		219
Yu-u Japanese	137 Flinders Ln. (Russell St.)	CC $$	9639 7073		219

Nightlife

NAME TYPE	ADDRESS (CROSS STREET) WEBSITE	AREA COVER	PHONE (03+) NOISE	99 BEST	PAGE PAGE
Becco* Restaurant/Bar	11-25 Crossley St. (Bourke St.) becco.com.au	CC	9663 3000		220
Belgian Beer Café Bluestone* Beer Garden	557 St. Kilda Rd. (Moubray St.)	SY	9529 2899	Outdoor Drinking Spots	220 46
The Botanical* Restaurant/Bar	169 Domain Rd. (Millswyn St.) thebotanical.com.au	SY	9820 7888		220
Boutique Nightclub	134 Greville St. (Graten St.) boutique.net.au	PR C	9525 2322	Hot Club Scenes	*200*, 220 45
Canary Club* Restaurant/Lounge	6 Melbourne Pl. (Little Collins St.)	CC	9663 1983		*200*, 220
Carlisle Wine Bar* Restaurant/Bar	137 Carlisle St. (Camden St.)	VA	9531 3222		221
Cicciolina* Cocktail Bar	130 Acland St. (Belford St.)	SK	9525 3333		221
Comme* Restaurant/Lounge	7 Alfred Pl. (Collins St.) comme.com.au	CC	9631 4000		221
Cookie* Restaurant/Bar	252 Swanston St. (Lonsdale St.)	CC	9663 7660		*200*, 221
The Corner Hotel Rooftop Bar	57 Swan St. (Stewart St.) cornerhotel.com	RM	9427 7300	Summer View Bars	221 47
Donovan's* Restaurant/Bar	40 Jacka Blvd. (Cavell St.) donovanshouse.com.au	SK	9534 8221		221

Nightlife (cont.)

NAME TYPE	ADDRESS (CROSS STREET) WEBSITE	AREA COVER	PHONE (03+) NOISE	99 BEST	PAGE PAGE
Double Happiness & New Gold Mountain Bar	21 Liverpool Ln. (Bourke St.) double-happiness.org	CC	9650 4488 ≡	Winter Bolt-hole Bars	*200*, 222 50
The Esplanade Hotel Nightclub	11 Upper Esplanade (Victoria St.) espy.com.au	SK	9534 0211 =	Hot Club Scenes	*202*, 222 45
European* Restaurant/Bar	161 Spring St. (Bourke St.)	CC	9654 0811 =		222
Fog* Restaurant/Lounge	142 Greville St. (Grattan St.) fog.com.au	SY	9521 3155 =		222
The George Hotel Bar/Nightclub	125-129 Fitzroy St. (Grey St.)	SK C	9525 5599 ≡		222
Gertrude Street Enoteca* Wine Bar	229 Gertrude St. (Smith St.) gertrudestreetenoteca.com	FZ	9415 8262 –		223
Gin Palace Cocktail Bar	190 Little Collins St. (Russell Pl.)	CC	9654 0533 –	Winter Bolt-hole Bars	*200*, 223 50
Grossi Florentino* Restaurant/Lounge	80 Bourke St. (Exhibition St.) grossiflorentino.com.au	CC	9662 1811 =		223
Journal* Restaurant/Bar	Shop 1, 253 Flinders Ln. (Degrave St.)	CC	9650 4399 =		223
Longrain* Restaurant/Lounge	44 Little Bourke St. (Spring St.) longrain.com.au	CC	9671 3151 ≡		*201*, 224
Madame Brussels Cocktail Bar	Level 3, 59 Bourke St. (Spring St.) madamebrussels.com	CC	9662 2775 –	Summer View Bars	*201*, 224 47
Melbourne Supper Club* Wine Bar	Level 1, 161 Spring St. (Bourke St.)	CC C	9654 6300 =	After-Hours Scenes	224 40
Meyers Place Bar	20 Meyers Pl. (Bourke St.)	CC	9650 8609 ≡	Winter Bolt-hole Bars	*200*, 224 50
MoVida* Restaurant/Bar	1 Hosier Ln. (Flinders Ln.) movida.com.au	CC	9663 3038 ≡		224
The Panama* Restaurant/Bar	Level 3, 231 Smith St. (Moor St.)	FZ	9417 7663 =		225
Pelican* Restaurant/Lounge	16 Fitzroy St. (Park St.)	SK	9525 5847 =		*202*, 225
Polly Cocktail Bar	401 Brunswick St. (Westgarth St.) pollybar.com.au	FZ	9417 0880 ≡		*201*, 225
Pony Club Lounge/Live Music	68 Little Collins St. (Westwood Pl.) pony.net.au	CC	9662 1026 ≡	After-Hours Scenes	*200*, 225 40
The Prince Bandroom Live Music	29 Fitzroy St. (Acland St.) princebandroom.com.au	SK C	9536 1168 ≡	Hot Club Scenes	*201, 202*, 225 45
Revolver Upstairs Lounge	Level 1, 229 Chapel St. (Anchor Pl.) revolverupstairs.com.au	PR	9521 5985 ≡	After-Hours Scenes	*202*, 226 40
Riverland Lounge	Vaults 1-9, Federation Wharf (Princes Bridge) riverlandbar.com	CC	9662 1771 ≡		226
Shoya* Restaurant/Lounge	25 Market Ln. (Bourke St.) shoyamelbourne.com	CC	9650 0848 =		226

NAME TYPE	ADDRESS (CROSS STREET) WEBSITE	AREA COVER	PHONE (03+) NOISE	99 BEST	PAGE PAGE
Stokehouse* Restaurant/Bar	30 Jacka Blvd. (Cavell St.) stokehouse.com.au	SK	9525 5555		226
Syracuse* Restaurant/Bar	23 Bank Pl. (Little Collins St.)	CC	9670 1777		226
Transit Lounge Garden Lounge	Federation Square (Princess Bridge) transporthotel.com.au	CC	9654 8808	 Summer View Bars	226 47
Transport Beer Garden	Federation Square (Princes Bridge) transporthotel.com.au	CC	9654 8808	 Outdoor Drinking Spots	*199*, 227 46
Tusk Back Bar Bar	67 Green St. (Chapel St.) backbar.com.au	VA	9529 7899		227
The Vineyard* Beer Garden	71a Acland St. (Shakespeare Grove)	SK	9534 1942	 Outdoor Drinking Spots	*202*, 227 46

Attractions

NAME TYPE	ADDRESS (CROSS STREET) WEBSITE	AREA PRICE	PHONE (03+)	99 BEST	PAGE PAGE
Alice Euphemia Shop	Shop 6, 37 Swanston St. (Flinders Ln.) aliceeuphemia.com	CC	9650 4300		*201*, 228
Assin Shop	138 Little Collins St. (Exhibition St.) assin.com.au	CC	9654 0158		228
Aurora Spa Retreat Spa	2 Acland St. (Fitzroy St.) aurorasparetreat.com	SK $$$$	9536 1130		*202*, 228
Australian Centre for Contemporary Art (ACCA)	111 Sturt St. (Grant St.) Art Museum accaonline.org.au	SB $	9697 9999	 Culture	228 43
Chapel Street Bazaar Market	217-223 Chapel St. (High St.)	PR	9529 1727		229
Chiodo Shop	114 Russell St. (Little Collins St.) chiodo.net.au	CC	9663 0044		229
Christensen Copenhagen Shop	QV2, 17-19 Albert Coates Ln. (Swanston St.) christensencopenhagen.com.au	CC	9650 7130		229
Christine Shop	181 Flinders Ln. (Lush Ln.)	CC	9654 2011		229
Chuan Spa Spa	1 Southgate Ave. (City Rd.) chuanspa.com	SB $$$$	8696 8111		*201*, 229
Collette Dinnigan Shop	553 Chapel St. (Toorak Rd.) collettedinnigan.com.au	SY	9827 2111		230
e.g. etal Shop	185 Little Collins St. (Russell St.) egetal.com.au	CC	9663 4334		230
Fat 272 Shop	272 Chapel St. (Chatham St.) fat4.com	CC	9510 2311		230

Attractions (cont.)

NAME TYPE	ADDRESS (CROSS STREET) WEBSITE	AREA PRICE	PHONE (03+)	99 BEST	PAGE PAGE
Federation Square Site	Flinders St. (Swanston St.) federationsquare.com.au	CC	(no phone)	Culture	230 43
Gallery Gabrielle Pizzi Art Gallery	Level 3, 75-77 Flinders Ln. (Exhibition St.) gabriellepizzi.com.au	CC	9654 2944		230
Geisha Spa	1st Fl., 285 Little Collins St. (Elizabeth St.) geishaonline.com	CC $$$$	9663 5544		231
Gorman Shop	235 Brunswick St. (Bell St.) gorman.ws	FZ	9419 5999		231
Harrolds Shop	101 Collins St. (Exhibition St.) harrolds.com.au	CC	8660 7888		231
Husk Shop	176 Collins St. (Swanston St.) husk.com.au	CC	9663 0655		232
Le Louvre Shop	74 Collins St. (Exhibition St.)	CC	9650 1300		232
Little Salon Shop	71 Gertrude St. (Fitzroy St.)	FZ	9419 7123		232
The Melbourne Cricket Ground Site/Sport	Brunton Ave. (Jolimont St.) mcg.org.au	RM $$	9657 8888		232
Melbourne Aquarium Tour	Queens Wharf, Flinders St. (Kings St.) melbourneaquarium.com.au	VA $$	9620 0999		232
Melbourne by Balloon Tour	41 Dover St. (Russell St.) hotairballooning.com.au	CC $$	9427 7596		233
Melbourne Museum Cultural Museum	11 Nicholson St. (Gertrude St.) melbourne.museum.vic.gov.au	CL	8341 7777		*200*, 233
Melbourne Zoo Zoo	Elliot Ave. (Flemington Rd.) melbournezoo.com.au	VA $	9285 9300		*199*, 233
National Gallery of Victoria: Ian Potter Centre Art Museum	Federation Square (Flinders St.) ngv.vic.gov.au	CC	8662 1555		*199*, 234
National Gallery of Victoria International (NGV) Art Museum	180 St. Kilda Rd. (Southbank Blvd.) ngv.vic.gov.au	SB	8620 2222	Culture	234 43
Nicola Finetti Shop	QV2 17-19 Albert Coates Ln. (Swanston St.) nicolafinetti.com	CC	9663 7886		234
Old Melbourne Gaol Site/Tour	Russell St. (Victoria St.)	CC $	9663 7228		*200*, 234
Rippon Lea House Museum & Historic Garden Site	192 Hotham St. (Gleneira Rd.)	VA $	9523 6095		235
Royal Botanic Gardens Park	Birdwood Ave. (Domain Rd.) rbg.vic.gov.au	SY	9252 2300		*200*, 235

Melbourne Black Book
By Neighborhood

Code: H-Hotels; R-Restaurants; N-Nightlife; A-Attractions. Blue page numbers denote listings in 99 Best. Black page numbers denote listings in theme chapters. The Melbourne Neighborhood Map is on p.271.

BLACK BOOK

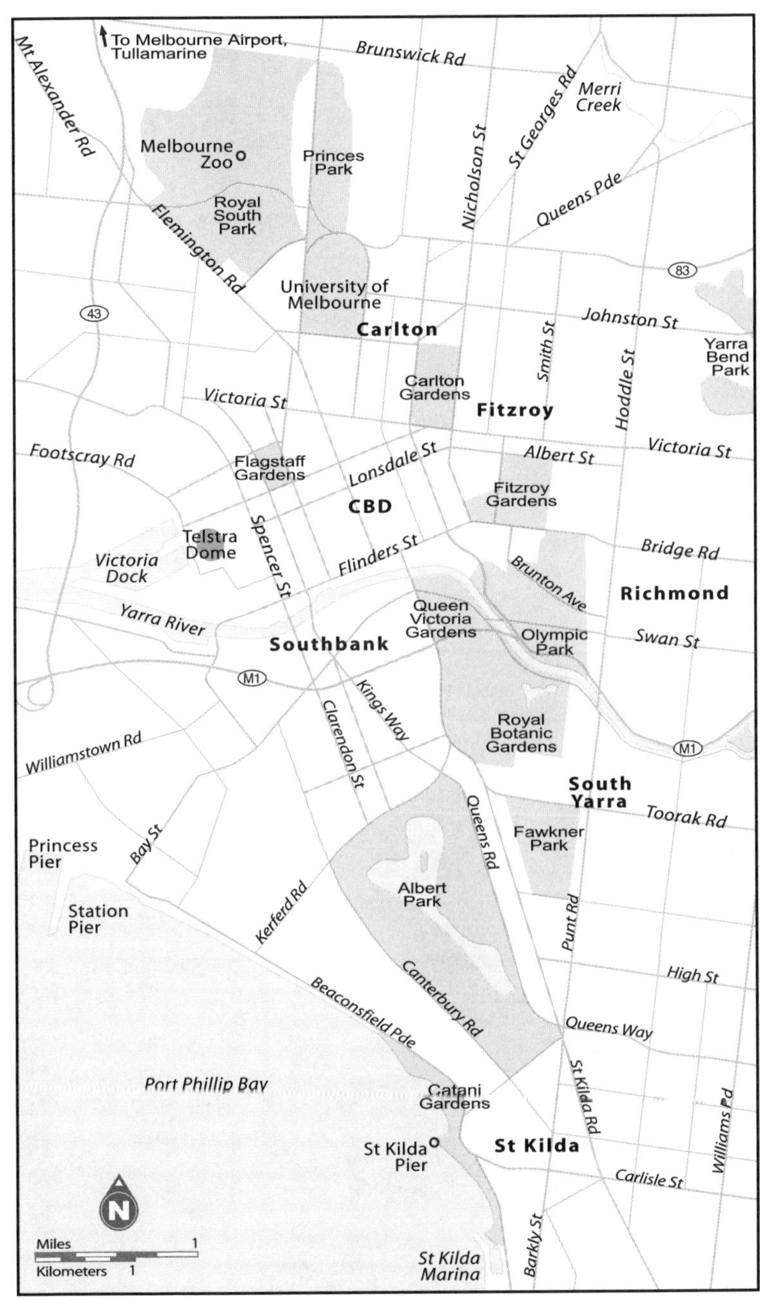
To Melbourne Airport, Tullamarine
Brunswick Rd
Mt Alexander Rd
Merri Creek
St Georges Rd
Nicholson St
Melbourne Zoo
Princes Park
Royal South Park
Queens Pde
Flemington Rd
University of Melbourne
83
43
Carlton
Johnston St
Smith St
Yarra Bend Park
Hoddle St
Carlton Gardens
Victoria St
Fitzroy
Footscray Rd
Flagstaff Gardens
Lonsdale St
Albert St
Victoria St
CBD
Fitzroy Gardens
Telstra Dome
Spencer St
Victoria Dock
Flinders St
Bridge Rd
Brunton Ave
Richmond
Yarra River
Queen Victoria Gardens
Southbank
Olympic Park
Swan St
M1
Kings Way
Clarendon St
Royal Botanic Gardens
Williamstown Rd
M1
South Yarra
Toorak Rd
Queens Rd
Fawkner Park
Princess Pier
Bay St
Station Pier
Albert Park
Kerferd Rd
Punt Rd
High St
Canterbury Rd
Beaconsfield Pde
Queens Way
Port Phillip Bay
Catani Gardens
St Kilda Rd
St Kilda Pier
St Kilda
Williams Rd
Carlisle St
N
Miles 1
Kilometers 1
Barkly St
St Kilda Marina

BLACK BOOK

All You Need To Know